Trübner's Oriental Series

THE SHÁHNÁMA OF
FIRDAUSÍ

Trübner's Oriental Series

PERSIA
In 13 Volumes

I	The Gulistān	
	Edward B Eastwick	
II	Yúsuf and Zulaikha	
	Ralph T H Griffith	
III	Essays on the Sacred Language, Writings, and Religion of the Parsis	
	Martin Haug	
IV	The Sháhnáma of Firdausí Vol I	
	Arthur George Warner and Edmond Warner	
V	The Sháhnáma of Firdausí Vol II	
	Arthur George Warner and Edmond Warner	
VI	The Sháhnáma of Firdausí Vol III	
	Arthur George Warner and Edmond Warner	
VII	The Sháhnáma of Firdausí Vol IV	
	Arthur George Warner and Edmond Warner	
VIII	The Sháhnáma of Firdausí Vol V	
	Arthur George Warner and Edmond Warner	
IX	The Sháhnáma of Firdausí Vol VI	
	Arthur George Warner and Edmond Warner	
X	The Sháhnáma of Firdausí Vol VII	
	Arthur George Warner and Edmond Warner	
XI	The Sháhnáma of Firdausí Vol VIII	
	Arthur George Warner and Edmond Warner	
XII	The Sháhnáma of Firdausí Vol IX	
	Arthur George Warner and Edmond Warner	
XIII	The Quatrains of Omar Khayyám	
	E H Whinfield	

THE SHÁHNÁMA OF FIRDAUSÍ

VOL VI

ARTHUR GEORGE WARNER AND
EDMOND WARNER

R Routledge
Taylor & Francis Group

LONDON AND NEW YORK

First published in 1912 by
Routledge, Trench, Trübner & Co Ltd

Reprinted in 2000, 2002 by
Routledge
2 Park Square, Milton Park, Abingdon, Oxon, OX14 4RN

Simultaneously published in the USA and Canada by Routledge

711 Third Avenue, New York, NY 10017

Transferred to Digital Printing 2008

Routledge is an imprint of the Taylor & Francis Group

First issued in paperback 2013

The publishers have made every effort to contact authors/copyright holders
of the works reprinted in *Trübner's Oriental Series*.
This has not been possible in every case, however, and we would
welcome correspondence from those individuals/companies
we have been unable to trace.

These reprints are taken from original copies of each book. In many cases
the condition of these originals is not perfect. The publisher has gone to
great lengths to ensure the quality of these reprints, but wishes to point
out that certain characteristics of the original copies will, of necessity, be
apparent in reprints thereof.

British Library Cataloguing in Publication Data
A CIP catalogue record for this book
is available from the British Library

The Sháhnáma of Firdausí

ISBN 978-0-415-24543-2 (hbk)
ISBN 978-0-415-86589-0 (pbk)

THE

SHÁHNÁMA OF FIRDAUSÍ

DONE INTO ENGLISH BY

ARTHUR GEORGE WARNER, M.A.

AND

EDMOND WARNER, B.A.

"The homes that are the dwellings of to-day
Will sink 'neath shower and sunshine to decay,
But storm and rain shall never mar what I
Have built—the palace of my poetry."

FIRDAUSÍ

VOL. VI

LONDON

KEGAN PAUL, TRENCH, TRÜBNER & CO. LTD

BROADWAY HOUSE, CARTER LANE, E.C.

1912

CONTENTS

		PAGE
GENEALOGICAL TABLE OF THE SÁSÁNIANS	. . . .	3
ABBREVIATIONS	. . . .	5
NOTE ON PRONUNCIATION	. . . .	8

THE KAIÁNIAN DYNASTY (concluded)

DÁRÁB—

SECT.

1. How Dáráb built the City of Dárábgird 20
2. How Dáráb defeated the Host of Shu'íb . . 21
3. How Dáráb fought with Failakús and took to Wife his Daughter 22
4. How Dáráb sent back the Daughter of Failakús to Rúm, and how Sikandar was born . . . 25

DÁRÁ, SON OF DÁRÁB—

1. How Dárá harangued the Chiefs and took Order for the Realm 34
2. The Death of Failakús and Sikandar's Accession to the Throne 35
3. How Sikandar went as his own Ambassador to Dárá 38
4. How Dárá fought with Sikandar and was worsted . 42
5. How Dárá fought with Sikandar the second Time . 43
6. How Sikandar fought with Dárá the third Time, and how Dárá fled to Kirmán 46
7. How Dárá wrote to Sikandar to propose Peace . 49
8. How Dárá was slain by his Ministers . . . 50
9. How Dárá told his last Wishes to Sikandar and died 52
10. How Sikandar wrote to the Nobles of Írán . . 57

SIKANDAR—

1. How Sikandar sat upon the Throne of Írán . . 85
2. How Sikandar wrote to Dilárái and Rúshanak, the Wife and Daughter of Dárá, touching the Nuptials of Rúshanak 85
3. How Dilárái answered the Letter of Sikandar . 87

SIKANDAR (*continued*)—

SECT.   PAGE

4. How Sikandar sent his Mother, Náhíd, to fetch Rúshanak, and how he Married her . . . 89

5. How Kaid of Hind had a Dream, and how Mihrán interpreted it 91

6. How Sikandar marched against Kaid of Hind and wrote a Letter to him 98

7. How Kaid of Hind answered Sikandar's Letter and announced the Sending of the Four Wonders . 99

8. How Sikandar sent back the Messenger to receive the Four Wonders 100

9. How Sikandar sent Ten Sages with a Letter to inspect the Four Wonders of Kaid of Hind . 101

10. How the Ten Sages brought the Daughter, the Cup, the Leech, and the Sage, from Kaid of Hind to Sikandar 103

11. How Sikandar tested the Sage, the Leech, and the Cup sent by Kaid of Hind 104

12. How Sikandar led a Host against Fúr of Hind and wrote a Letter to him 110

13. How Fúr answered the Letter of Sikandar . . 111

14. How Sikandar arrayed his Host to fight with Fúr of Hind and made iron Steeds and Riders filled with Naphtha 112

15. How the Host of Sikandar fought with the Host of Fúr, how Fúr was slain by Sikandar, and how Sikandar seated Sawurg upon the Throne of Fúr 116

16. How Sikandar went on a Pilgrimage to the House of the Kaaba 119

17. How Sikandar led his troops from Judda toward Misr 121

18. Sikandar's Letter to Kaidáfa, Queen of Andalús, and her Answer 123

19. How Sikandar led his Troops to Andalús and took the Hold of King Faryán 124

20. How Sikandar went as an Ambassador to Kaidáfa and was recognised by her 127

21. How Kaidáfa counselled Sikandar 132

22. How Tainúsh, the Son of Kaidáfa, was wroth with Sikandar, and how Sikandar took Precaution against him 134

SIKANDAR (*continued*)—

SECT. PAGE

23. How Sikandar made a Compact with Kaidáfa and returned to his Troops 138

24. How Sikandar went to the Country of the Brahmans, inquired into their Mysteries, and received an Answer 143

25. How Sikandar came to the Western Sea and saw Wonders 147

26. How Sikandar reached the Land of Habash, fought, and was victorious 149

27. How Sikandar reached the Land of the Narmpái, how he fought and was victorious, how he slew a Dragon, ascended a Mountain, and was forewarned of his own Death 150

28. How Sikandar reached the City of Women, named Harúm, and saw Wonders there . . . 153

29. How Sikandar went into the Gloom to seek the Water of Life and spake with Birds and Isráfíl 159

30. How Sikandar went to the East, saw Wonders, and built a Barrier against Yájúj and Májúj . . 163

31. How Sikandar saw a Corpse in a Palace of Jewels on the Top of a Mountain, and the Speaking Tree, and how he was warned of his Death . 166

32. How Sikandar marched his Army to Chín, carried his own Letter to Faghfúr, and returned to his Army with the Answer 169

33. How Sikandar returned from Chín, made war against the Sindians, and went to Yaman . 174

34. How Sikandar marched toward Bábil and found the Treasure of Kai Khusrau in a City . . 176

35. How Sikandar went to the City of Bábil, wrote a Letter to Arastálís, and received his Answer . 178

36. Sikandar's Letter to his Mother 181

37. How Sikandar's Life ended and how they carried his Coffin to Iskandaríya 183

38. How the Sages and other Folk lamented Sikandar 185

39. How the Mother and Wife of Sikandar lamented him 187

40. Firdausí's Complaint of the Sky and Appeal to God 189

THE ASHKÁNIAN DYNASTY

SECT.   PAGE

1. The Praise of Mahmúd 207
2. The Tribal Kings 210
3. How Pápak saw Sásán in a Dream and gave him a Daughter in Marriage 211
4. How Ardshír Pápakán was born, and of his Case with Ardawán 213
5. How Ardawán's Slave-girl fell in Love with Ardshír and how he fled with her to Púrs . . . 217
6. How Ardawán heard of the Flight of Ardshír with the Damsel and pursued them 220
7. How Ardawán wrote to Bahman, his Son, to take Ardshír 223
8. How Tabák helped Ardshír, fought with Bahman, and conquered him 225
9. How Ardawán led forth his Host for Battle with Ardshír and was slain 227
10. How Ardshír fought with the Kurds and was defeated 230
11. How Ardshír attacked the Kurds by Night and overthrew them 232
12. The Story of Haftwád and the Case of the Worm . 232
13. How Ardshír fought with Haftwád and was worsted 236
14. How Mihrak of Jahram sacked the Palace of Ardshír 237
15. How Ardshír heard about the Worm and made Shift to slay it 239
16. How Ardshír slew Haftwád 244

THE SÁSÁNIAN DYNASTY

ARDSHÍR PÁPAKÁN—

1. How Ardshír Pápakán sat upon the Throne in Baghdád 258
2. The Case of Ardshír and the Daughter of Ardawán 259
3. How Shápúr was born to Ardshír by the Daughter of Ardawán, and how after seven Years Ardshír heard of his Son and acknowledged him . . 261
4. How Ardshír, to find out the Future of his Reign, sent to Kaid of Hind, and Kaid's Reply . . 266
5. The Adventure of Shápúr with the Daughter of Mihrak, and his taking her to Wife . . . 268

ARDSHÍR PÁPAKÁN (*continued*)—
SECT.   PAGE
   6. How Urmuzd was born to Shápúr by the Daughter
        of Mihrak 271
   7. Of the Wisdom of Ardshír and his Method of
        administering the Realm 273
   8. How Kharrád praised Ardshír 284
   9. On the Faithlessness of Fortune 285
  10. How Ardshír charged Shápúr and died . . . 286
  11. Thanksgiving to the Maker and Praise of Mahmúd,
        the great King 291

SHÁPÚR, SON OF ARDSHÍR—
   1. How Shápúr sat upon the Throne and delivered a
        Charge to the Chieftains 295
   2. How Shápúr fought with the Rúmáns, how Bazá-
        núsh, their General, was taken Prisoner, and
        how Cæsar made Peace with Shápúr . . 296
   3. How Shápúr seated Urmuzd upon the Throne and
        died 299

URMUZD, SON OF SHÁPÚR—
   1. How Urmuzd addressed the Assembly . . . 302
   2. How Urmuzd gave up the Throne to Bahrám,
        charged him, and died 303

BAHRÁM, SON OF URMUZD—
   1. How Bahrám succeeded to the Throne, charged
        the Nobles, and died 307

BAHRÁM, SON OF BAHRÁM—
   1. How Bahrám, Son of Bahrám, ascended the Throne,
        charged the Nobles, and died 311

BAHRÁM BAHRÁMIYÁN—
   1. How Bahrám Bahrámiyán succeeded to the Throne
        and died four Months after 313

NARSÍ, SON OF BAHRÁM—
   1. How Narsí succeeded to the Throne, counselled
        his Son, and died 315

URMUZD, SON OF NARSÍ—
   1. How Urmuzd, Son of Narsí, ascended the Throne,
        and how his Life ended 318

SHÁPÚR, SON OF URMUZD, SURNAMED ZÚ'L AKTÁF—

SECT.   PAGE

1. How Shápúr, Son of Urmuzd, was born forty Days after his Father's Death, and how he was crowned 328

2. How Táír, the Arab, carried off the Daughter of Narsí and married her, how Shápúr went to Yaman to fight him, and how his Daughter fell in Love with Shápúr 330

3. How Táír was bemused by his Daughter and how she came to Shápúr, who took the Hold and slew Táír 333

4. How Shápúr went disguised as a Merchant to Rúm, how he was taken by Cæsar, and how Cæsar ravaged the Land of Írán 335

5. How the Damsel took Measures to free Shápúr, and how he fled with her from Rúm . . 339

6. How the High Priest and the Captain of the Host, hearing of Shápúr's Arrival, went to him with the Troops 345

7. How Shápúr made a Night-attack, and how Cæsar was taken 346

8. How Shápúr went to Rúm and fought with Yánus, Cæsar's Brother 351

9. How the Rúmans placed Bazánúsh upon the Throne of Cæsar; his Letter to Shápúr and the Answer 353

10. How Bazánúsh went to Shápúr and made a Treaty of Peace 355

11. How Mání, the Painter, came to Shápúr with Pretence of being a Prophet, and was slain . 358

12. How Shápúr made his Brother Ardshír Regent till his own Son should grow up, and how his Days ended 360

ARDSHÍR, BROTHER OF SHÁPÚR—

1. How Ardshír sat upon the Throne and gave a Charge to the Officers 363

SHÁPÚR, SON OF SHÁPÚR—

1. How Shápúr, Son of Shápúr, sat upon the Throne and gave a Charge to the Officers . . . 365

BAHRÁM, SON OF SHÁPÚR—

SECT. PAGE

1. How Bahrám sat upon the Throne and gave a
Charge to the Officers 368

YAZDAGIRD, SON OF SHÁPÚR—

1. How Yazdagird sat upon the Throne and gave a
Charge to the Officers 374
2. How Bahrám Gúr, Son of Yazdagird, was born and
sent to be brought up by Munzir, the Arab . 375
3. How Bahrám went to the Chase with a Damsel
and how he displayed his Accomplishment . 382
4. How Bahrám showed his Accomplishment in the
Chase before Munzir 384
5. How Bahrám came with Nu'mán to Yazdagird . 386
6. How Yazdagird put Bahrám in Bonds, how he
escaped by the good Offices of Tainúsh, and
how he returned to Munzir 389
7. How Yazdagird, by the Advice of an Archmage,
went to the Spring of Sav and was killed by a
Water-horse 391
8. How the Íránians took Counsel and placed Khusrau
upon the Throne 394
9. How Bahrám Gúr heard of the Death of his Father
and invaded Írán 395
10. How the Íránians heard of Bahrám's Pillaging and
wrote to Munzir, and how he replied . . 397
11. How Bahrám Gúr arrived at Jahram with the Host
of Munzir, and how the Íránians went out to
him 400
12. How Bahrám Gúr harangued the Íránians as to his
Fitness to rule, how they rejected him but promised him the Kingship if he would take the
Crown from between the Lions . . . 402
13. How Bahrám and Khusrau went to the Waste, and
how Bahrám slew the Lions and took his Seat
upon the Throne 409

INDEX 413

THE SHÁHNÁM·A

GENEALOGICAL TABLE OF THE SÂSÂNIANS

(According to the Shâhnáma [1])

Sásán = *d.* of Pápak

Ardshír Pápakán (22) = *d.* of Ardawán

Shápúr (23) = *d.* of Mihrak

Urmuzd (24)

Bahrám (25)

Bahrám (26)

Bahrám (27)

Narsí (28)

Núsha = Táír   Urmuzd (29)

Málika = Shápúr (30) = Diláfrúz-i-Farrukhpái   Ardshír (31)

Shápúr (32)

Bahrám (33)   Yazdagird (34)

a daughter   Sapinúd *d.* of Shangul = Bahrám Gúr (35)   Narsí
and many other
wives

Yazdagird (36)

Pírúz (38)   Hurmuz (37)

Persian lady = Kubád (40)   Balásh (39)   Jámásp

d. of the Khán = Núshírwán (41) = a Christian lady

Hurmuzd (42)   five   Núshzád
other
sons

Rustam   Maryam = Khusrau (43) = Shírín and Gurdya *s.* of Bahrám
d. of   Parwíz   Chubína
Cæsar

Kubád (44)
(Shirwí)   Nastúr   Sháhryár   Farúd   Mardánsháh

Ardshír (45)   Yazdagird (50)

Guníz (46)   Farrukhzád (49)   many   Púrúndukht (47)   Ázarmdukht (48)
(usurper)   other sons

---

[1] From Khusrau Parwíz onward some of the relationships, left vague in
the poem, are given from other sources.

ABBREVIATIONS

C.—Macan's edition of the Sháhnáma.
L.—Lumsden's   do.
P.—Mohl's   do.
T.—Tihrán   do.
V.—Vullers'   do.

AM. The Voiage and Travayle of Sir John Maundeville, Knight. . . . Edited . . . by John Ashton.

AS. The Sháh Námeh of . . . Firdausí. Translated and abridged . . . By James Atkinson, Esq.

BAG. A History of Ancient Geography. By E. H. Bunbury, F.R.G.S.

BAN. A Plain and Literal Translation of the Arabian Nights' Entertainments . . . By Richard F. Burton.

BBR. Buddhist Records of the Western World. Translated from the Chinese of Hiuen Tsiang (A.D. 629). By Samuel Beal.

BHA. The History of Alexander the Great, being the Syriac Version of the Pseudo-Callisthenes. Edited . . . with an English Translation and Notes, by Ernest A. Wallis Budge, M.A.

BLEA. The Life and Exploits of Alexander the Great, being a Series of Translations of the Ethiopic Histories of Alexander. . . . By E. A. Wallis Budge, Litt.D., F.S.A.

DAA. Arriani Anabasis. . . . F. Dübner.

DAI. Arriani Indica. . . . F. Dübner.

DEI. J. Darmesteter, Études Iraniennes.

DHA. The History of Antiquity. From the German of Professor Max Duncker. By the late Evelyn Abbott, M.A.

EHI.   The History of India as told by its own Historians. By Sir H. M. Elliot, K.C.B.

GDF.   The History of the Decline and Fall of the Roman Empire. By Edward Gibbon, Esq. With Notes by Dean Milman and M. Guizot. Edited, with additional Notes, by William Smith, LL.D.

GH.   The Land of the Hittites. . . . . By John Garstang, D.Sc.

GKS.   Kleine Schriften von Alfred von Gutschmid.

HB.   The Country of Balochistan. . . . By A. W. Hughes, F.R.G.S.

HQC.   Q. Curtius Rufus. . . . ed. Edmundus Hedicke.

JRGS. The Journal of the Royal Geographical Society.

LAN.   The Arabian Nights' Entertainments. A New Translation from the Arabic. . . . By Edward William Lane.

MA.   Alexandre le Grand. . . . Par Paul Meyer.

MCAI. Ancient India as described by Megasthenês and Arrian. . . . By J. W. M'Crindle, M.A.

MCI.   The Invasion of India by Alexander the Great. . . . By J. W. M'Crindle, M.A. . . . New Edition.

MF.   Reliqua Arriani et Scriptorum de rebus Alexandri M. Fragmenta collegit. . . . Carolus Muller.

MM.   Maçoudi : Les Prairies d'Or. Texte et Traduction, par C. Barbier de Meynard et Pavet de Courteille.

MPC.   Pseudo-Callisthenes, primum edidit Carolus Mullerus.

NAR.   Beiträge zur Geschichte des Alexanderromans, von Prof. Dr. Th. Nöldeke in Denkschriften der . . . Akademie der Wissenschaften. . . . . Wien, 1890.

NIN.   Das Iranische Nationalepos von Theodor Nöldeke.

NK.   Geschichte des Artachšír i Pâpakân aus dem Pehlewi übersetzt . . . von Th. Nöldeke.

NT.   Geschichte der Perser und Araber zur Zeit der Sasaniden . . . von Th. Nöldeke.

RK.   The Koran : Translated . . . by the Rev. J. M. Rodwell, M.A.

RM.   The Rauzat-us-safa; or, Garden of Purity. . . By . . .
Mirkhond. . . . Translated . . . by E. Rehatsek.

RSM.   The Seventh Great Oriental Monarchy. By George
Rawlinson, M.A.

SK.   The Koran. . . . Translated . . . . by George Sale, Gent.

SM.   History of the Early Kings of Persia. . . . Translated
from the original . . . Persian of Mirkhond . . . by
David Shea.

SP.   The Periplus of the Erythraean Sea. . . . Translated
from the Greek and annotated by Wilfred H. Schoff,
A.M.

WPT.   Dr. E. W. West's Translation of the Pahlaví Texts in the
Sacred Books of the East. Reference to Parts and
pages.

YMP.   The Book of Ser Marco Polo . . . newly translated. . . .
By Colonel Henry Yule, C.B.

ZT.   Chronique de Abou-Djafar-Mo'hammed-Ben-Djarir-Ben-
Yezid Tabari, traduite. . . . Par M. Hermann Zotenburg.

NOTE ON PRONUNCIATION

â as in " water."

î as in " pique."

û as in " rude."

a as in " servant."

i as in " sin."

u as in " foot."

ai as in " time."

au as *ou* in " cloud."

g is always hard as in " give."

kh as *ch* in the German " buch."

zh as *z* in " azure."

II

THE KAIÁNIAN DYNASTY
(Concluded)

XVIII

DÁRÁB

HE REIGNED TWELVE YEARS

ARGUMENT

Dáráb establishes himself upon the throne, defeats the Arabs and the Rúmans, and marries the daughter of Failakús, the Cæsar. Conceiving, however, a dislike for his spouse, he sends her back to her father, at whose court her child is born, named Sikandar, for the reason given in the story, and brought up by Failakús as his own son and heir. Dáráb meanwhile marries again, has another son—Dárá—falls into ill-health, appoints Dárá his successor, and dies.

NOTE

At this point in the Sháhnáma, in as much as this and the two following reigns deal almost entirely with the subject of Alexander the Great, who is known to Orientals under the name of Iskandar or Sikandar, there is an important change in the provenance and character of the subject-matter. We have had an instance already in which it seemed probable that recourse was being had indirectly to Greek writers,[1] but in the present case the debt to them is indisputable. The basis of the whole account is Greek, and so in a great measure is the superstructure, but the latter to some extent has been pulled down and rebuilt, modified in detail, and added to, by Egyptian, Arabic, and Persian hands. As a general introduction to the three following reigns, therefore, it will be well to set before the reader in outline such facts as are necessary for the proper understanding of the accounts given in the reigns in question.

Alexander the Great, in his expedition to the East, was accompanied by a literary and scientific staff, in order that the results

[1] See Vol. v. p. 281.

11

achieved might be handed down to posterity in a way worthy of
so great an occasion. Thus Eumenes kept the royal diary,[1] Bæton
and Diognetus recorded the distances traversed,[2] Aristobulus was
interested in matters geographical, ethnological, and botanical,[3]
while Callisthenes and others drew up general histories. Some
of Alexander's commanders too, such as Ptolemy, son of Lagus,
who became King of Egypt, Nearchus, the admiral, and Onesicritus, the pilot, of Alexander's fleet, also left accounts, as did
others who were contemporaries but took no part in the expedition. The result was a large assortment of kindred works, not
one of which is extant in its original form, though later writers
have preserved a good deal of the substance, and in some cases
fragments, of the originals. Thus Arrian, our best authority on
the whole subject, based his *Anabasis* on Ptolemy and Aristobulus,[4] and in his *Indica* made much use of Nearchus.[5] Arrian,
however, tells us that even Ptolemy and Aristobulus were not
always in agreement,[6] and further, that though Alexander's expedition served to explode many fables, it at the same time led
to the fabrication of fresh ones.[7] Onesicritus, for instance, who,
though only the pilot, claimed in his account to have been the
admiral,[8] of Alexander's fleet, heard tell of two dragons, or
serpents, measuring 80 and 140 cubits in length respectively,[9]
and speaks of whales off the coast of Balúchistán as being half a
stade, *i.e.* over 100 yards, long, and broad in proportion.[10]
Bæton relieved the prosaic details of mensuration with the
account of a sylvan folk—natives of Mount Imaus—who had
backward-pointing feet.[11] Again, the question as to whether or
no the Amazons visited Alexander split the early authorities into
two separate camps.[12] We may conclude, therefore, that the
seeds of the Romance that grew up in later times round the
personality of Alexander the Great were sown in his lifetime.
The growth thus started not merely increased in bulk by a
natural process of evolution in succeeding centuries, but also
absorbed materials that originally had no connexion at all with
him and his undertakings. Thus, for example, when the historic
facts of his career had grown somewhat dim in the popular mind,
the expedition in B.C. 332 of his uncle Alexander I. of Epirus to

[1] MF, p. 121.   [2] *Id.* 134.   [3] *Id.* 94.
[4] DAA, Pref., Bk. v. c. 7.   [5] DAI, c. 18 *seq.*   [6] DAA, iii. 4 ; iv. 14.
[7] *Id.* v. 4.   [8] *Id.* vi. 2.   [9] MF, p. 50, fr. 7.
[10] *Id.* p. 57, fr. 30. This, however, was quite a moderate estimate.
Pliny, in his *Nat. Hist.*, lib. ix. sect. 2, ed. Ludovicus Janus, speaks of
" Balænæ quaternum jugerum."
[11] *Id.* 135, fr. 3.   [12] Plutarch, *Life of Alexander*, c. 46.

Italy became part of his legend,[1] and he was credited later on with having visited Candace, the Ethiopian queen, at Meroe. We may assume, too, that the experiences of the rank and file of his time-expired veterans, military and naval, lost nothing in the telling. Speaking generally too, the travellers' tales, often based on misunderstood metaphor or misinterpreted natural phenomena —tales such as in after-times were told by the friar Odorico and Sir John Maundeville—would add their quota to the romance of the subject. The reader will find examples of such fables in the reign of Sikandar. Long before his time, however, they had made their way from India to Greece. Homer knew something of them, so did Herodotus, so did Hecatæus probably, and so beyond doubt did Ctesias. Moreover, no form was too monstrous or abnormal for the Indian imagination to conceive with respect to god or demon or beings, like the Rákshasas, who were a blend of demon and of man. The companions of Alexander merely heard over again what earlier adventurers had heard, but their association with Alexander brought about a special association of such tales with him.

It should be noted further that the Greeks, like ourselves, had two Indies—an Eastern and a Western—and consequently the fables derived from and respecting the Indians or, as they were called, Ethiopians, were held to apply to the West as well as to the East.[2]

It was in Egypt—the land which he had delivered from the hated Persians and where Ptolemy and his successors had maintained the Alexandrian tradition and had ruled with so much glory—and it was at Alexandria, which the great conqueror had founded and where he was buried, that the Greek Romance of Alexander, so far as we are aware, first received literary form and expression. The author is unknown, but appears to have written about the third century of the Christian era. The authorship is attributed in one of the extant MSS. of the work to the historian Callisthenes, the relative of Aristotle through whose influence it came about that he accompanied Alexander to the East. His rough comments, however, on Alexander's adoption of Persian customs were not well received by the conqueror ; he was imprisoned and died in captivity. The title of "The Pseudo-Callisthenes," by which the Romance now is known, is said to have been bestowed upon it in the first instance by Isaac Casaubon.[3]

The work no longer is extant in what we may call its primitive form, but this, branching in three directions, gave rise to a numerous progeny of MSS., of which some twenty still survive.

---

[1] NAR, p. 4; MPC, Bk. i. c. 29.   [2] See p. 68.   [3] MA. ii. 4.

Three of them, known as A, B, and C respectively, are preserved in the National Library in Paris, and to one or other of these three the rest of the MSS. are said to conform in character.[1] The MS. known as A, a very early Latin version of the Romance supposed to have been made by one Julius Valerius early in the fifth century A.D., and an Armenian version of about the same date,[2] are looked upon as representing collectively the nearest approximation that we possess to the original work. The MS. known as B is the only one of the three that attributes the authorship to Callisthenes.[3]

During the seventh century A.D. some Greek text of the Romance, conforming generally to the A type, was translated into middle Persian, or Pahlaví, as it is called, and this Pahlaví version was retranslated shortly afterwards into Syriac. No trace of the Pahlaví version remains, and there is no scrap of historical evidence to indicate that such a work ever existed, but the Syriac version is still extant, and has been edited with an English translation by Budge. We call it BHA, and shall have occasion frequently to refer to it in the ensuing pages.

It was the publication of this Syriac version that led Professor Nöldeke to infer, and satisfactorily to prove, that a Pahlaví version of the Pseudo-Callisthenes once must have existed. Such proofs naturally are very technical, but one example may be given by way of illustration. It concerns the transliteration of proper names unknown to the Syriac translator. Nöldeke found that in the Syriac version the letter *l* was substituted for the letter *r* in such words as Osiris, Abdera, Kraterus, Parmenion, and others, while, on the other hand, *r* was substituted for *l* in Platæa, Eumelus, Candaules, &c. Now, there is nothing in the form of these two letters, as they are written in Greek, Arabic, or in Syriac itself to account for such substitutions and interchanges, but it so happens that in Pahlaví the same sign stands for both *l* and *r*, and the conclusion follows that the Syriac version was made not from the Greek or Arabic, but from the Pahlaví.[4]

Appended to all the MSS. of the Syriac version, distinct from it, but, like it, based upon the Pseudo-Callisthenes, there is

---

[1] *Id.*   [2] MPC, p. xxvi.   [3] *Id.* viii. and I.
[4] The proofs referred to above will be found set out at large in NAR, p. 11 *seq.* The present writer desires to take this opportunity to acknowledge generally and once for all his indebtedness not only to this work, but also to Professor Nöldeke's edition of the Kárnámak-i-Ardshír-i-Pápakán (NK) and of Tabarí's History of the Sásánians (NT). The first two concern the present volume of this translation only, but the last will be in constant requisition till the end. All three, and to them we must add the Íránian National Epos (NIN), are invaluable.

extant a Syriac Christian Legend of Alexander which claims to be taken from the manuscripts in the house of the archives of the kings of Alexandria.[1] This Legend was composed about the years A.D. 514 or 515, and seems to have been suggested by an incursion of the Huns through the Caucasus, which took place at that time. The author writes as one horror-stricken at the uncouth aspect and savagery of the invaders, and at the ruin caused by them. Shortly after its composition, it was turned into verse, with some additions by the Syriac poet, Jacob of Sarúg, who died in A.D. 521. The legend, and the additions thus made to it, derive respectively from branches B and C of the Pseudo-Callisthenes, and their subject-matter became known to Muhammad, who made use of it in the Kurán, where Alexander is referred to under the title of "Zú-'l-karnain," or "The Two-horned," that name having been suggested by the Legend, where we read: "The Lord said to him (Alexander), 'Behold I have magnified thee above all kingdoms, and I have made horns of iron to grow on thy head, that thou mayest thrust down the kingdoms of the earth with them."[2] Naturally, Zú-'l-karnain became an interesting personality to the followers of Muhammad. The passage in the Kurán referring to him was much commented on, and the Syriac accounts of him were translated into Arabic. Now it was to the interest of learned Persians, living under Arab rule in the centuries succeeding the Muhammadan conquest of Írán, to impress their masters with the sense of the past greatness of the empire that they had subdued, and for this purpose the legends of the vanquished race were translated into Arabic. It obviously was desirable that so great a hero as Alexander, and one so interesting to the followers of the Prophet, should be utilised, and in order to effect this the whole Persian traditional view of Alexander was altered. As we have seen already,[3] he was held in hate and horror in Sásánian times as the arch-persecutor and would-be exterminator of Zoroastrianism; he was one of a trinity of ill, of which the other two were Zahhák and Afrásiyáb. Persians, however, that had been converted to, or had been brought up in, the Muhammadan Faith soon came to regard Alexander from another standpoint. To them he was no longer an evil being who had striven to uproot the true religion, but the hero commissioned by God to overthrow a false one, in fact another Asfandiyár with other and better aims, for had not his credentials been countersigned by the

[1] BHA, p. 144.
[2] *Id.* 156. There is a similar passage, p. 146. For the Syriac Legend generally see NAR, 27 *seq.* For the passage in the Kurán see pp. 77–78.
[3] See Vol. i. pp. 59, 61, 63, and *cf.* pp. 224, 240.

Prophet himself ? This change of view robbed such memories as
still survived of Alexander's triumph over Darius Codomanus of
much of their bitterness, and it only remained to abate it altogether by legitimating the conqueror's position. This was
easily managed, for the author of the Pseudo-Callisthenes had
suggested a way. Concerned for the honour of his country by
birth or adoption, he had made Alexander out to be the son of
the last native king of Egypt—Nectanebus II.—who had succeeded, it was said, in passing himself off to Olympias, the wife of
Philip II. of Macedon, during the latter's absence at the wars, as
no less a person than Amen-Ra, the two-horned god of Egypt.
The Egyptians were old hands at this sort of falsification. Herodotus tells us [1] that Cambyses, after his conquest of Egypt, was
made out by the Egyptians to be the son of Nitetis, a daughter
of Apries. What Egyptians had done the Persians could do, the
necessary story was substituted for that of Nectanebus, as we
shall read in this reign, Sikandar became the eldest son of Sháh
Dáráb, and the oppressor of Írán one of its national heroes.

At what precise period Alexander assumed his station in the
long line of the Sháhs is not known, and probably never will be.
In the Pahlaví version, made, it would seem, by some one who
was neither an orthodox Zoroastrian nor an orthodox Muhammadan, he was still, as we see from its Syriac representative. the son
of Nectanebus ;-in Firdausí he is the son of Dáráb. Between the
two accounts there is a space of some three centuries or more.
We may reduce the interval somewhat by assuming, as we may,
that the metamorphosis had been completed in the days when
Firdausí was growing up, and a new edition of the Bástán-náma
in modern Persian was being compiled in the middle of the tenth
century by order of Abú Mansúr. [2] This, we may assume, contained a version of the Pseudo-Callisthenes as it existed after
centuries of adaptation by Persian and Arabic hands. The ascription of a Persian paternity to Alexander can be traced further
back. It was known to Tabarí who died in A.D. 922, and to
Dínawarí who died in A.D. 896. [3] Neither of them endorses the
story, but merely gives it a place among the other accounts that,
in accord to the method of Arabic historians, they give of the
same event. As these accounts consist of the statements of older
authorities, we may consider that the story was current early in
the ninth century A.D. Most unfortunately the work that, more
than all others, would have thrown light upon that and many
another point, and taken us back to the middle of the eighth century, is no longer extant. This was the Arabic translation of the

---

[1] Bk. iii. c. 2.   [2] See Vol. i. p. 67 *seq.*   [3] See NAR, pp. 35, 44.

Bástán-náma made by Ibn Mukaffa. He was a Zoroastrian who became a Muhammadan late in life, thereby, as was said of him, merely exchanging one corner of hell for another, as his orthodoxy was more than suspect. He was learned both in the Pahlaví and in the Arabic, and was put to death about A.D. 760. It is not unlikely that he was responsible for the inclusion of Alexander among the legitimate Sháhs. By all accounts he was just the right man in the right place for such an undertaking.

It is hoped that the above sketch may be sufficient to indicate the provenance of the Romance of Alexander the Great and how it came about that it was incorporated into Íránian national legend. It will be seen that it reached Firdausí in a. mingled stream. The basis is Greek, and the Pseudo-Callisthenes itself is based on history. The broad facts are there. It tells us that Alexander was a Grecian king, that he conquered Egypt, invaded and subdued Írán, penetrated into India, defeated Porus, returned, died at Babylon, and was buried at Alexandria. Its author introduced Egyptian elements and additions, and it underwent further adaptations at Persian and Arab hands. These will be noted and dealt with as they occur in this and the two following reigns. The vogue of the Pseudo-Callisthenes, however, is not to be circumscribed within such limits as these. For many centuries it superseded the more historic accounts of Alexander that still are extant ; and versions, in addition to those already mentioned, have appeared in Latin, Hebrew, Turkish, Ethiopic,[1] Coptic, English, French, German, Italian, Spanish, Norwegian, Swedish, Dutch, Slavonic, Malay, and Siamese.[2]

Dáráb, the last of the mythical Sháhs, does not appear in the Zandavasta, with which at this point we part company. In order to connect him with the Kaiánian dynasty he was made the hero of a foundling legend, as we saw in the previous volume.[3] His name was suggested by that of his successor Dárá—the historical Darius Codomanus—who was remembered in connexion with the invasion of Persia by Alexander the Great, and his inclusion among the Sháhs was due to the necessity of providing his successor with a father. Later on he was called upon again to act in that capacity to his successor's conqueror.

§ 1. Dárábgird, now Dáráb, is in Párs, some fifty miles south of the salt lake Niris, which also is referred to.

§ 2. Border wars between the Íránians and the northern Arabs were of frequent occurrence.[4] For Shu'íb *cf.* NT, p. 57, *note.*

[1] Also edited and translated by Budge, and referred to in this work as BLEA.

[2] See BHA, p. lxxxviii. *seq.*   [3] Vol. v. p. 294 *seq.*

[4] *Cf.* pp. 322, 330, Vol. i. p. 11, ii. p. 81.

§§ 3–4. The account here given of the incidents that led up to the birth of Sikandar is a Persian substitution for the Egyptian story told in the Pseudo-Callisthenes,[1] and in the Syriac version.[2] The oft-told tale is briefly as follows. Nectanebus[3] was king of Egypt and a great magician. By his magic arts he had triumphed on all occasions over his enemies. At length the time came when he perceived that his spells no longer would avail to protect his country from invaders, so, disguising himself, he fled to Macedonia, where he set up as a soothsayer. His fame soon reached the ears of Olympias, the wife of Philip of Macedon, who then was absent on a campaign. She had heard a rumour that he intended to divorce her and take another spouse. Accordingly she made up her mind to consult Nectanebus, and summoned him. He came, and at once was smitten with her beauty. She sought his advice on the matter of the divorce, and he told her that the rumour was not false, but that he could help her. He then went on to inform her that she would have a son by the two-horned god of Egypt—Amen. With the aid of dreams sent by his magic arts he reconciled first her and then Philip to the situation, personated the god himself, and thus became the father of Alexander the Great, taking good care that the birth of the child should occur at the most auspicious astrological moment.

The foal, stated in the text to have been born at the same time as Alexander, is of course the famous steed Bucephalus, which accompanied him in his campaigns as far as the river Hydaspes, the modern Jhílam, and either was killed by the son of Porus when Alexander was forcing the passage of that river or died shortly afterwards of toil and decrepitude at the age of thirty years. Alexander founded two cities by the river in memory of his charger and of his victory over Porus, and named them respectively Bucephala (Jalálpúr?) and Nicæa (Mong?).[4] It is only in the Persian and Ethiopic versions of the Pseudo-Callisthenes that the births of Alexander and Bucephalus are made to synchronise, which shows that both accounts come from an Arabic source, for as the Syriac version represents a no longer extant Pahlaví version, so the Ethiopic derives from a lost Arabic one. In the Ethiopic version Bucephalus is a mare.[5]

---

[1] MPC, Bk. i. c. 1–12.   [2] BHA, Bk. i. c. 1–12.

[3] Historically, Nectanebus II., or more properly Nekht-neb-f, of the thirtieth dynasty, was the last native king to rule in Egypt. The Persian Sháh, Artaxerxes Ochus, after having been repulsed by him in several campaigns, succeeded in conquering the country in B.C. 343. Nectanebus escaped to Ethiopia.

[4] DAA, Bk. v., c. 14, 19; MCI, p. 110, *note*.

[5] BLEA, pp. 19, 37.

§ 3. We have here a reference to Russia if the reading is correct. P reads " Sús." The word " Rús " (Byzantine 'Pῶs) dates from the ninth century A.D.,when Northmen (Scandinavians) founded the Russian Empire. It may be a corruption of *rothsmen,* " rowers." [1] The Russians were in evidence in Firdausí's days. [2]

§ 4. In the Pseudo-Callisthenes, Bk. i. c. 13, and in the Syriac version *loc. cit.*, Philip is said to have chosen the name Alexander in memory of a dead son, so called, whom he had had by a former wife. According to one of the accounts in Tabarí, the mother of Alexander was the daughter of the king of the Rúmans and named Halái (Olympias ?). The Sháh, her husband, finding that she was troubled by an unpleasant odour, gave orders that means should be found to remedy this. The doctors agreed to exhibit the wood of a tree called in Persian *sandar.* They boiled it and washed her with the extract. This, to a great extent, did away with the smell, but not entirely, and, as the cure was not complete, the Sháh sent her back to her father. She was already with child, however, and when her son was born she composed his name by putting her own and that of the tree together, and called him Halái-Sandarús, that is the primitive form of Al Iskandarús. [3] Sandar appears to be a shortened form of *sandarús,* the Arar tree, *Callitris quadrivalvis,* a native of north-west Africa, which produces the resin known as " gum juniper " or " sandarach," the latter a word often used in the Sháhnáma. [4] Firdausí takes a different view of the meaning of Iskandar. He makes that word equivalent to Iskandarús, but he attributes to it apparently its proper meaning. It is derived either from the Greek σκόροδον, garlic; or the Latin *ascalonium,* shallot. In any case the treatment that the lady underwent appears to have been more or less homœopathic in character.

[1] See GDF, vii. 80, and *note. Encyclopœdia Britannica,* 11th ed., *s.v.* Russia.
[2] *Cf.* Vol. iv. p. 316.   [3] NAR, p. 44.   [4] *Cf.* Vol. i. p. 74.

§ I

How Dáráb built the City of Dárábgird

V. 1775 Now from the Maker on earth's king call we
A benediction down. That Sháh sun-faced,
Who, O Abú'l Kásim! the world hath graced
With lovingkindness and with equity,
Doth make of right and justice all his quest,
And in his justice suffereth naught amiss.
Oh! be the world bright with that crown of his—
Mahmúd's—and may his whole career be blest.
May he be young till youth itself be o'er,
And live till life itself shall be no more!

What said the ancient, rustic bard who told
About Gushtásp, renowned Bahman,[1] and chiefs
Whose counsels prospered, told about Dáráb,
And of the rede and usance of Humái?
Now when Dáráb[2] sat on the Kaian throne
He girded up his loins, oped wide his hand,
And thus harangued the archmages and the chiefs,
The magnates and the prudent-hearted sages:—
"I did not woo the world by toil and justice;
God set the crown upon my head, and none
V. 1776 Will see a case in public or in private
More wonderful than mine; while as for me
I can but make return by doing right
That men may bless me after I am gone.
None must be irked by travail for my sake
In this my season for amassing treasure.
May this age prosper under my just rule,
And may my subjects' hearts be jubilant."

[1] Ardshír in the original, but *cf*. Vol. v. p. 282.
[2] Dárá in the original, but *cf*. *id*. p. 297 and *note*.

Then out of Hindústán and out of Rúm,
From every wealthy march and peopled land,
Ambassadors with gifts and offerings
Came to secure the favour of the Sháh.
    It happened that one day he went to view
The herds of horses that were running wild,
And, coming from the lowlands to the mountains,
Observed a deep and boundless lake. He gave
Commandment that from Hind and from the Rúmans
Experienced master-workmen should be brought
To open out a channel from the lake,
And send a river into all the land.
When these skilled men had set the water free
He bade them to erect a splendid city,
And, when the wall around it was complete,
They gave thereto the name of Dárábgird.
He lit the Fire upon the mountain-top,
Whereto the worshippers of Fire resorted,
And then artificers of every craft
Were summoned, and the city was adorned.
    The Sháh sent countless hosts to every quarter,
Safeguarded all the world from enemies,
Released it from the fear of any foe,
And rent in twain their hearts that wished him woe.

§ 2

How Dáráb defeated the Host of Shu'íb

It came to pass that five score thousand Arabs,
Brave, spear-armed cavaliers, marched forth.   Shu'íb—
A chief sprung from Katíb—commanded them.
The monarch of Írán led forth a host,   V. 1777
'Tis said, beyond compute.   The armies met;
The world was all in dudgeon at the troops;

The earth could not support them; none had room
To stir within that land.   The rain of arrows,
And double-headed javelins, made the soil
A cistern seem of blood.   On every side
The war-cry rose, and corpses showed in piles.
Thus for three days and nights the battle waged,
The age was straitened to the combatants.
The Arabs on the fourth day turned away,
And in the night fled from the scene of strife,
Shu'íb himself was slain upon the field
Of battle, and the Arabs' day was done.
A host of Arab steeds with poplar saddles,
A mass of helmets, spears, and coats of mail—
The havings of the fugitives—remained
With that world's lord, the offspring of Humái,
Who gave the whole thereof—the steeds and spears,
The helms and swords—in largess to the troops.
He chose a marchlord, one among the host,
Who understood the language of the folk,
And sent him to demand the tribute due
From those waste parts, that year's and last year's
      too.

§ 3

How Dáráb fought with Failakús and took to Wife his
Daughter

Dáráb marched from the desert of the spearmen
Rúm-ward to war against that prosperous land.
Now Failakús was monarch of the realm;
He and the king of Rús were close allies.
They wrote to say: "The offspring of Humái
Hath led forth countless troops."
                            On hearing this
The prince of Rúm bethought him of old feuds,

And levied soldiers in 'Ammúriya,[1]
All men renowned upon the day of battle.
The chiefs of Rúm, what time Dáráb drew nigh,   V. 1778
Abandoned all the coast and borderland,
While from 'Ammúriya marched Failakús,
He and his captains, warriors, and troops.
They fought two mighty battles in three days,
And on the fourth day when the sun arose
Both Failakús and all his army fled;
Not one retained his helm or Rúman casque.
The Íránians took the wives and children captive,
And slaughtered many with their showers of arrows.
When fleeing from Dáráb the Rúmans reached
The city but two thirds of them arrived,
The other had been slain erewhile or wounded;
The spear had been insistent at their backs.
They sheltered there within that stronghold.   Many
Sought peace.   An envoy came from Failakús,
Wise, shrewd, a bearer both of weal and woe,
With purses, slaves, and, as an offering,
Two caskets filled with royal jewelry.
This was the message : " Of the only God
I ask for guidance that we may conclude
This fight in feast.   Ne'er may we strive again,
But all be honesty and uprightness :
Dark ways and crookèd only end in loss.
If to 'Ammúriya, which is my seat,
Thou comest and art fain to capture it,
My heart will throb for honour and for fame,
And I will leave the feasting for the fighting.
Act in the manner that becometh kings ;
Thy father was, and now his son is, Sháh."
  Dáráb, on hearing this, convoked his lords,[2]

---

[1] Ancyra probably, the modern Angora, an important place on the
route from Byzantium to Armenia and Syria. There was also an
ancient Amorium in Phrygia, not far from the borders of Galatia.
[2] Reading with P.

And told before them every circumstance.
"What say ye," said he, "touching this appeal,
Since Failakús is fain to save his face?"
   The chiefs all called down blessings on the Sháh,
And said: "O Sháh, shrewd-hearted, pure of Faith!
The king of kings is greatest of the great,
Let him determine what is best to do.
That famous monarch hath an only daughter
Of cypress-height and spring-like cheek.   In Chín

V. 1779
One will not look upon so fair an Idol;
She shineth mid the others like a signet.
The king of kings on seeing will approve her,
And that tall Cypress come within his Garden."
   The Sháh called in the ambassador from Rúm,
Told him the counsel of those loyal lieges,
And said: "Go say to Cæsar: 'If thou art
So fain to save thine honour thou possessest
Within thy bower a daughter, one who is
The crown upon the head of womanhood,
A perfect picture whom thou call'st Náhíd, [1]
And settest on a golden throne.   Send her,
Together with the tribute due from Rúm,
If thou wouldst dwell untroubled in that land."
   The envoy heard and, coming like the wind,
Reported this to Cæsar.   Failakús,
And all the army, were rejoiced thereat,
Because the Sháh would be his son-in-law.
The question of the tribute was discussed,
As to how much the king of Rúm could pay,
And they agreed that in the month of Mihr
In every year the Sháh should take from Cæsar
A hundred thousand eggs of solid gold,
And with each egg a royal gem, each egg
To be two score miskáls [2] in weight, each gem

---

[1] The planet Venus.
[2] A miskál=a dram and three sevenths.

Of highest excellence. First, Failakús
Rewarded all his frontier-chiefs that dwelt
Within the peopled parts of Rúm, and then
Commanded the philosophers, and all
That had an interest in those parts, to give
Their whole attention to prepare a road.
The nobles that escorted the princess
Brought every one his present. They made ready
A golden litter, slaves, and crown of gold,
Ten camels laden with brocade of Rúm
With jewelled patterns on a golden ground,
Three hundred camel-loads of carpetings,
With other presents for the Sháh. Within
The litter sat the entrancing Rúman maid   V. 1780
With prelate and with priest conducting her.
Náhíd had sixty damsels in her train,
Each with a golden goblet in her hand.
Within the goblet there were royal gems,
And every Idol wore her crown and earrings.
The bishop gave the fair one to Dáráb,
And paid the jewels to his treasurer.
The Sháh remained no longer on the field,
But marched back to Írán. He came to Párs,
Rejoicing, with his charming spouse, and set
Upon her head the royal coronet.

§ 4

*How Dáráb sent back the Daughter of Failakús to Rúm, and
how Sikandar was born*

One night that Moon was sleeping with the Sháh,
All gems and colour, scent and loveliness,
But verily her breathing was not sweet,
And grew disgustful to the king of kings,

Who shrank and turned his head away from her
Upon the couch because her breath was foul.
The monarch of Írán was grieved thereat,
His mind was troubled and his soul all care.
They summoned skilful leeches to Náhíd,
And one of them, a shrewd and prudent man,
Examined till he found a remedy—
A herb whereby the gullet is inflamed,
Called in the Rúman tongue "iskandar."   This
He rubbed upon the palate of the queen,
And caused her eyes[1] to water lustily.
The fetor fled away, her palate burned,
Her face shone like brocade ; but though the Fair
Was sweet as musk Dáráb had ceased to love her,
The monarch's heart turned coldly from his bride,
And so he sent her back to Failakús.
She was with child but told not any one.

V. 1781   Nine months passed and from that fair dame was born
A babe like radiant Sol.   She used to call him
Sikandar[2] since he was so tall, well favoured,
And sweet of breath, for she esteemed the name
Of what had sweetened her own palate lucky,
While Cæsar told each chief: "There hath appeared
A Cæsar of my seed."
                     None named Dáráb,
Sikandar was the son and Cæsar sire,
For Cæsar shamed to say to any one :—
"Dáráb hath put away my child."
                                 What time
Sikandar's holy mother brought him forth,
And one went to his grandsire with the tidings,
There was within the stable a brown mare,
In body lusty, swift and tall, and she
That very night produced a foal all white,
Short-shanked, and breasted like a lion.   Cæsar

---

[1] Literally eyelashes.   [2] Sikandar = Iskandar.

Exulted o'er that mare because he deemed
That birth would prove a lucky sign for him.
He used at dawn to have the infant fetched,
Would have the trappings put upon the mare,
And then caress the foal on eyes and mane
Because it was coeval with Sikandar.
  The sky revolved awhile with matters thus,
And years of varied fortune passed away,
Sikandar came to have a monarch's heart,
The utterance of heroes. Cæsar held him
More dearly than a son and used to place
The due adornments on his martial breast.
He gained in wisdom, aptitude, good sense,
Weight, and intelligence. He was acknowledged
Successor on the throne to Failakús,
Who held him in regard in weal and woe.
He learned from tutors kings' accomplishments,
And thou hadst said that he was made to judge,
To found an empire, and to fill the throne.
  Now when Náhíd had gone back to her sire
Dáráb took unto him another wife,
And had by her a son of Grace divine V. 1782
And puissance, and younger than Náhíd's,
Named the same day Dárá in hope that he
Might be yet more successful than his sire.
  Thereafter, when twelve years had passed away,
The Sháh failed both in fortune and in limb;
Humái's illustrious offspring 'gan to fade,
And he was summoned to the other world.
He called to him the magnates and the sages,
Conversed at large about the throne of power,
And said to them: "Dárá, son of Dáráb,
Now will become your leader in all good.
Give ear to him, perform what he commandeth
And be his will the music of your souls,
Because this throne of kingship lasteth not,

And when joy cometh it is soon recalled.
Be instant ye, let love unite with justice,
And think on me too gladly."

This he said,
And heaved a sigh.   The colour of his cheek
Turned from pomegranate-bloom to fenugreek.

XIX

DÁRÁ, SON OF DÁRÁB

HE REIGNED FOURTEEN YEARS

ARGUMENT

After the death of Dáráb, his son Dárá ascends the throne and administers the realm. Meanwhile Failakús dies, and Sikandar succeeds him in Rúm. Dárá sends to demand tribute of Rúm, and Sikandar replies by invading Írán. He visits the camp of Dárá as his own ambassador, and is recognised, but escapes. Three great battles are fought, in which Dárá is defeated, and subsequently murdered by his own ministers. Sikandar finds Dárá mortally wounded, promises to carry out his last wishes, executes his murderers, and universally is recognised as Sháh.

NOTE

With Dárá we enter upon the historic period of the Sháhnáma.[1] In the last reign he was represented as being the younger son of Dáráb, with Sikandar for his elder brother. Historically, Dárá's prospect of ever becoming Sháh had been remote in the extreme. Artaxerxes Ochus, who had put Nectanebus to flight and conquered Egypt, was murdered in B.C. 338, with all his sons, by the eunuch Bagoas, with the exception of the youngest, Arses, whom Bagoas made Sháh. Two years later Bagoas murdered him also, and all his family, and raised a distant collateral of the royal house to the throne, who is the Dárá of the Sháhnáma and the Darius Codomanus of Greek writers. Him too in his turn Bagoas tried to do away with, but was put to death himself instead. Historically, Dárá reigned six years, not fourteen.

§ 2. When Alexander was fourteen years old, his father Philip sent for Aristotle to become his son's tutor.

---

[1] See Vol. i. p. 49.

For the tribute due from Rúm see p. 24. In the Pseudo-Callisthenes and the Syriac and Ethiopic versions the ambassadors come in Philip's lifetime and are interviewed by Alexander.[1] The golden eggs are mentioned in the Syriac, which, with the Greek, also says that the ambassadors employed a painter to take Alexander's portrait, which they presented to Darius. The Syriac makes the further addition that Darius ordered the picture to be carried to his daughter Roxana, and their several heights to be compared, after which he flung it away in scorn, but Roxana secured it, honoured it greatly, and from that time fell in love with the original.[2]

Sikandar in the text is represented as beginning his expedition to the East by the invasion of Misr (Egypt), but a good deal happened first both in history and romance. Historically, he spent the first eighteen months of his reign in Greece, and crossed into Asia Minor in the spring of B.C. 334, where, having won the battle of the Granicus, he established his power sufficiently to allow him to advance through the passes into Syria. Having encountered and defeated Darius at Issus in the autumn of B.C. 333, he proceeded to make himself master of the coasts of Syria and Palestine, the sieges of Tyre and Gaza together taking about nine months, after which he invaded Egypt. Romantically, after the Granicus and Asia Minor, Alexander sails to Sicily and Italy, where he is well received by the Romans, who present him with a jewelled crown, thence voyages to Africa, where he interviews the Carthaginians, and proceeds by way of the oasis of Ammon to Egypt.[3]

§ 3. This corresponds with the Greek Pseudo-Callisthenes[4] and with the Syriac version[5] in general, but these texts add the picturesque incidents that, after Alexander's flight from the feast, the effigy of King Xerxes, which Darius loved, fell from the wall or ceiling of the banquet-hall, and that Alexander in his flight had to cross a frozen river, on which the ice gave way as he reached the other side, his horse being carried off by the current and drowned, while the pursuing Persians were unable to follow him across.

§§ 4–6. The Syriac version only mentions one battle between Alexander and Darius, at which both were present.[6] In the Sháhnáma there are three, of which the first corresponds with the one in the Syriac. According to Tabarí, who quotes Hisham bin Muhammad, the two kings fought for a year in Mesopotamia.[7]

---

[1] MPC, Bk. i. c. 23 ; BHA, Bk. i. c. 23 ; BLEA, p. 34.
[2] BHA, *id.* and i. 36, *cf.* note on § 8.　　　[3] MPC, i. 28–31.
[4] MPC, ii. 14, 15.　　　[5] BHA, ii. 6, 7.
[6] *Id.* ii. 9.　　　[7] NAR, p. 42.

Firdausí places the scene of at least two of the battles of which he speaks to the west of the Euphrates. He was drawing probably from Arabic sources of information. The three battles cannot be regarded as in any way intended for those of the Granicus, of Issus, and of Gaugamela. The number is perhaps a tribute to the importance of the occasion.[1]

In the Sháhnáma Dárá, after his final defeat, goes to Kirmán. According to the Pseudo-Callisthenes[2] and the Syriac version,[3] he withdrew to his palace, and next is heard of locally in connexion with Ekbatana and the Caspian Gates.[4] This is more accurate historically. Arrian says that Darius, after his defeat at Gaugamela (October 1st, B.C. 331), fled towards Media, rightly supposing that Alexander would march upon Susa and Babylon.[5]

§ 7. In the Pseudo-Callisthenes Darius, in his letter, asks for the return of his wife and family, offering land and treasures in exchange;[6] in the Syriac version he is ready to surrender everything if he may have mercy shown to him.[7] Alexander's reply is softened in the Persian. In the Greek and Syriac he takes the view that he is only recovering his own, Darius having been the aggressor, and in the latter makes no reply to him. Alexander's honourable treatment of Darius' family, whom he had taken at Issus, is a matter of history,[8] and the same sentiment toward them is preserved in the Pseudo-Callisthenes.

§§ 8-9. In the Greek and Syriac versions the letter to Porus is given at somewhat greater length. Darius invites Porus to meet him with an army at the Caspian Gates, and promises him half the spoil and Alexander's horse Bucephalus.[9] Porus, of which the Arabic form Fúr is used in the Sháhnáma, is a dynastic or family name, and represents the Pauravas who are mentioned in the Mahábhárata as reigning in the neighbourhood of Kashmír.[10] The Porus of Alexander's time ruled between the Hydaspes (Jhílam) and the Akesines (Chináb), and was allied to the king of Kashmír.

With regard to the death of Darius at the hands of two of his satraps,[11] the historical account is that, after Gaugamela, he went, accompanied by remnants of his broken army, to Ekbatana (Hamadán), where he endeavoured to raise fresh forces. Alexander, in the meantime, had made himself master of Babylon and Persepolis, and, hearing of Darius' doings, advanced northward

[1] *Cf.* Vol. i. p. 349 *seq.*   [2] MPC, ii. 16.   [3] BHA, Bk. ii. c. 9.
[4] MPC, ii. 19; BHA, ii. 11.   [5] DAA, iii. 16.
[6] MPC, ii. 17.   [7] BHA, ii. 9.
[8] DAA, ii. 12.   [9] MPC, ii. 19; BHA, ii. 11.
[10] DHA, iv. 399.   [11] MPC, ii. 20; BHA, ii. 12

against him in the spring of B.C. 330. Darius did not wait for Alexander's arrival, but left Ekbatana, intending to take refuge with his cousin Bessus, the satrap of Bactria. Darius went, of course, by the well-known route that connects western with eastern Irán.[1] He had considerable forces with him, but his counsels were distracted, and his troops gradually deserted him. Alexander reached Rai by forced marches from Ekbatana, but, hearing that Darius was far ahead, abandoned the pursuit, and rested for five days. He then resumed his march, and halted in the neighbourhood of Girduni Sirdarra, which appears to be the Caspian Gates of Arrian, passed through them the second day and heard, when encamped beyond them, that Darius was a prisoner in the hands of Bessus, the satrap of Bactria, of Barsaentes, the satrap of Arachosia and Drangiana (Sístán), and of Nabarzanes, the commander of Darius' cavalry. On this Alexander resumed the pursuit, and, four or five days later, came up with the fugitives, whereupon Nabarzanes and Barsaentes mortally wounded Darius and abandoned him. He was dead before Alexander reached him.[2] This was in July B.C. 330. Nabarzanes soon after surrendered to Alexander, and was pardoned.[3] Bessus and Barsaentes escaped to their own satrapies, where the former assumed royal state and the name of Artaxerxes. Ultimately both were captured and executed.[4] Their resistance to Alexander seems to have been a more serious crime than their removal of his chief opponent. An Arabic account [5] affirms that the death of Darius was brought about with the connivance of Alexander, and although Firdausí's version naturally omits this feature, it in other respects follows the Arabic very closely with regard to the scene between the two kings. The names of the two assassins are in the Pseudo-Callisthenes Bessus and Ariobarzanes,[6] in the Syriac version Bágíz and Ánábdéh, and in the Ethiopic Háshísh and Arsalás. The names in Firdausí seem to be of his own invention. The arrangement made between the two kings that Alexander should marry Roxana or Rúshanak appears in all the versions, and is not historical. She was not the daughter of Darius, but of Oxyartes, a Bactrian chief, whose stronghold Alexander escaladed. He fell in love with her at sight, and married her,[7] B.C. 328. Subsequently, on his return from his

---

[1] See Vol. ii. p. 28.   [2] DA, iii. 19–21.
[3] HQC, vi. 5.   [4] DAA, iii. 25, 30.   [5] NAR, pp. 44, 50.
[6] Historically, there was a worthier holder of that name who, after Gaugamela, held the entrance to Párs against Alexander, and died, fighting to the last, outside Persepolis. HQC, v. 4.
[7] DA, iv. 19, cf. note on § 2.

Indian expedition, he did marry a daughter of Darius—Barsine or Stateira—at Susa in B.C. 324. Rúshanak, the Persian form of Roxana, is a diminutive from the adjective "rúshan," bright.

For the feast of Sada *see* Vol. i. p. 123. Naurúz, New Year's Day, was also the name of a feast then held. *Cf. id.* 74. For Mihr *see id.* 175 and *note*.

The corpse of Darius was sent to Párs.[1] In the Romance the punishment of his assassins follows quickly. In the Greek, Syriac, and Ethiopic versions of it, Alexander announces his intention of "exalting" the doers of the deed, and so induces the culprits to declare themselves, who thereupon are "exalted" on the gibbet, set up over the grave of Darius.[2] Firdausí's version relieves Sikandar from all imputation of sharp practice. In the Arabic account mentioned above, Alexander gives the murderers all that they bargained for, but they had forgotten to include their lives in the compact, and are put to death.

§ 10. Sikandar's proclamation to the Persians and his correspondence with the women-folk of Dárá appear in the other versions,[3] but the correspondence is reserved for the next reign. Here we have a message only. The passage about the handmaids in Firdausí's version of the proclamation runs in the Syriac: "And we command that damsels . . . shall enter into the temple of the god whom my mother Olympias worships, for the space of one year for the service of the gods; and when they have arrived at the age for marriage, they shall go forth from the ministry, and shall receive a dowry of five thousand dínárs from the treasury of the god, and shall marry." Expressions in Firdausí's version show that it came to him, in part at least, through the Arabic.

[1] DAA, iii. 22. For the accounts given in the Greek, Syriac, and Ethiopic versions, see MPC, ii. 21 ; BHA, ii. 13 ; BLEA, p. 95.
[2] *Id.*   [3] *Id.* and *seq.*

§ I

*How Dárá harangued the Chiefs and took Order
for the Realm* [1]

V. 1783 Dárá, when he had ceased to mourn Daráb,
Exalted to the sun the Kaian crown.
He was a man of action, young, and lusty:
A sword was blunt contrasted with his tongue.
He took his seat upon the throne and said:—
"Ye princes, noble chiefs, and warriors!
I want not any that hath fallen low,
Nor will I summon such to crown and state,
And if one disobeyeth my commands,
Let not his body count its head its own,
While if he hath disloyalty at heart,
That will I frustrate with the scimitar.
If others too have wealth 'tis not for me
To vex their happy hearts on that account,
And shall I wish for any as a guide,
Who am myself the guide and gladdener?
Sun, fortune, and the right to fealty
Are mine, mine greatness, kingship, and command."
  He summoned unto him a ready writer,
And held talk with him of affairs at large.
That worthy wrote a letter from Dárá,
Son of Daráb, son of Bahman.[2] Wherever
Reigned independent kings the Sháh commanded
To send a letter trenchant as a sword:—
V. 1784 "Whoever turneth him from my behest,
And rede, shall mark how I will scatter heads.
Give all obedience whether I command
To take another's life or yield your own."
  He opened up his father's treasure-hoard,

----

[1] This heading is not in the original.
[2] Dárá and Ardshír in the original. See Vol. v. pp. 282, 297 *note*.

Called out the troops, and gave allowances.
The stipend varied from four drachms to eight;
This had a cupful, that a basonful.
He gave moreover drachms, dínárs, and bards,
As well as breastplates, swords, and massive maces,
Appointing veteran chiefs to provinces,
To one among the notables the marches,
And largessing the troops with things of price.
Ambassadors arrived from every quarter,
From every man of name and potentate,
From Hind, from the Faghfúr, the Khán of Chín,
From Rúm and likewise from the provinces.
Each of them carried tribute, dues, and gifts,
For none could stand or strive against Dárá.
　　He built a city which he named Zarnúsh—
A cause of much rejoicing in Ahwáz.
He gave to every mendicant his due,
And freely unto those that came to sue.

§ 2

The Death of Failakús and Sikandar's Accession to the Throne

In those days was the death of Failakús—
A cause of trouble for a while in Rúm;
Then sat Sikandar on his grandsire's throne,
Sought virtue, and restrained the hands of evil,
For in those days there lived one known to fame
In Rúm, a joy to all that land and hight
The erudite Arastálís [1]—a man
Of wisdom, vigilance, and influence.
That sage adviser came before Sikandar,
And, as he took his place, held forth, and said:—

---

[1] Arastátális in the original. Firdausi uses both forms, and there are others.

"O ruler happy in thy full desire!
By acting as thou dost thou wilt abate
Thy fame because the royal throne hath looked
On many such as thee but will not rest

v. 1785
With any.　When thou sayest: 'I have gained
Mine end and need not any to direct me,'
Know that there is no greater fool than thou,
If thou wilt hearken not the rede of sages.
We are from dust, are destined from our birth
To go back thither, and must needs submit;
But thou wilt live in fame if thou art good,
And be successful on the throne of kings,
While from ill-doing thou wilt reap but ill,
And never pass a night of peaceful sleep.
Well-doing is a monarch's adjutant,
And none hath won good days by doing wrong."

　　Whenas Sikandar heard he was well pleased,
And used to court the speaker's company,
Did every act according as he bade
In fight and festival, in war and strife,
Bestowed new favours on him every day,
And, when he came, would seat him on the throne.
　　It chanced one day that an ambassador,
A Persian shrewd of heart and eloquent,
Came from Dárá to Rúm to ask for tribute
Due from that prosperous land.　He came and spake
About it to Sikandar who was irked
By reason of that tribute and old tax,
And said to him: "Go say before Dárá:—
'Our tribute now hath lost its hue and scent,
For since the bird that laid the golden eggs
Is dead the tribute is no more in force.'"
　　The ambassador, on hearing such an answer,
Was frighted and was seen no more in Rúm.
Sikandar summoned all his troops and told
Of what had passed.　He said: "The well-disposed

'Scape not the revolutions of the sky.
I have to tread the world's face and account
Much weal and woe, so now ye must make ready,
And banish home and country from your hearts."
    He oped his grandsire's hoards and bade his troops   V. 1786
Prepare. At dawn the war-cry rose from Rúm
Both from the city and the young king's court.
The standard that was carried after him
Was red inscribed upon a turquoise ground.
He started on his march by way of Misr,
With troops and trumpets, drums and warriors.
The king of Misr with hostile troops forthwith
Went to encounter him. The armies met
And fought for seven days, but on the eighth
Misr was o'erthrown, Sikandar cut them off,
And at a blow enough were taken captive
To paralyse the taker's hands. Of maces,
Steeds and horse-armour, jupons, Indian daggers,
Of golden girdles, silvern harness, swords
Of Misr with golden scabbards, of brocade
And of dínárs, he compassed such a store
That e'en the beasts of burden could not bear it,
While multitudes of noble warriors,
Of chiefs and cavaliers, came in for quarter.
Sikandar thence made ready to invade
Írán, took lions' hearts and warriors' hands.
Now when Dárá had heard: "A host hath marched
From Rúm and reached our borders and confines,"
So great an army issued from Istakhr,
That e'en the wind was hampered by the spears.
He purposed to advance on Rúm from Párs,
And fire the peopled parts. When he had led
His troops more many than the blades of grass   V. 1787
To the Farát he drew up on the shore,
And none could see the stream for armature.

§ 3

How Sikandar went as his own Ambassador to Dárá

Now when Sikandar heard: "The host hath come,"
He marched to meet it, and when two leagues' space
Was left between he called to him the magnates,
Who spake with him at large about Dárá
Until, outworn by his advisers' words,
He said: "There is one way and only one—
That I should go as an ambassador
To him and weigh his state."
                He bade to fetch
A girdle decked with jewels fit for kings,
And royal robe embroidered. They brought forth
A led horse all betrapped with gold. A sword
Hung from its saddle in a golden scabbard.
Sikandar chose ten Rúman cavaliers,
Men good at parleying, and left the host
At dawn with those ten famed interpreters.
As soon as he approached the exalted Sháh
He lighted from his steed and did obeisance.
Dárá, the world-lord, called him, greeted him,
And seated him below the throne. The courtiers,
Amazed, invoked the Maker of the world,
Such were Sikandar's aspect, Grace, and prudence,
His stature, limbs, and dignity! He took
His seat but rose forthwith, delivered well
Sikandar's message, blessing first the king,
And said: "For ever may the crowned head live.
Thus said Sikandar: 'O illustrious,
Whose will prevaileth everywhere on earth!
I have no wish to fight against the Sháh,
Or sojourn in Írán. Mine aim is this—
To roam about the earth a little space,
And see the world for once. My whole intent

V. 1788

Is good and honest, and especially
Since thou art now the ruler of Írán.
If thou forbiddest me to use the ground
I cannot travel in the air like clouds,
But thou, unwitting of my purposes,
Hast met me in this fashion with a host.
If thou wilt fight then I will fight with thee,
And not depart without a stricken field.
Choose for thyself the season for the fray,
And hold thereto : let not thy purpose change,
Because I shrink not from a war with chiefs,
However great their host.'"

Now when Dárá
Observed his counsel, courage, eloquence,
His Grace and bearing, so that thou hadst said :—
"It is Dárá[1] upon the ivory throne
With armlets, torque, with Grace and crown," he
        asked :—
"What is thy name and stock because thy Grace
And limbs denote a king ? Thou art no subject.
Methinketh that thou art thyself Sikandar.
Thee with thy Grace and stature, speech and face,
Heaven peradventure nurtured for a throne."
    Sikandar answered : "None hath acted thus
In peace or war, and men of eloquence—
The crown of all the sages of the world—
Are not so lacking at Sikandar's portal
That he should take a message from himself,[2]
And he so great a king, the people's head ?
Sikandar's wit is not of such a sort
That he should pass from his forefathers' ways.
This was the message that my master gave me,
And I have told the Sháh his words."

They lodged him

---

[1] Dárá = Dáráb here perhaps.
[2] Or, with stop at " portal," "How should he," &c.

In fitting state.　The monarch of Írán,
As soon as they had spread the board, commanded
The chamberlain : "Invite the ambassador."
　　Forthwith they summoned him and gave to him
The envoys' seat.　They eat and then prepared
To revel, calling out for wine and harp

V. 1789　And minstrelsy, but as Sikandar drained
The pleasant wine he lightly laid each goblet
Within his lap till as the cups and wine
Passed round and round their sum passed reckoning.
The server came before Dárá and said :—
"The guest to-day hath cottoned to the cups!"
　　The Sháh bade : "Ask him : 'Why dost thou thus tender
The wine-cups ? '"
　　　　　　　　　Said the server : "Kingly man !
Why keep these golden cups upon thy lap ?"
　　Sikandar made him this reply : "These cups,
Are, my good sir, the envoy's perquisite.
If such be not the usage in Írán
Restore them to the royal treasury."
　　The monarch smiled to hear of such a custom,
And bade to set within the envoy's hand
A goblet filled with jewels fit for kings,
And lay a ruby on the top thereof.
Just at that moment those that went to make
Demand for tribute from the land of Rúm
Came from outside within the banquet-hall,
Advancing toward the Sháh with measured tread.
He that was envoy recognised Sikandar,
Went to the Sháh, and did obeisance, saying :—
"This is Sikandar—Cæsar's self—who hath
The throne, the mace, and diadem !　What time
The Sháh commanded us to go and ask
For tribute he was wroth, entreated us
With scorn, and spake of war with thee, while we

Had to escape by night and urge our steeds.
We saw not any like to him in Rúm.
Now boldly hath he come within thy borders
To weigh thy host, thy treasure, throne, and crown."
    The Sháh, on hearing what his envoy said,
Gazed at Sikandar yet more earnestly,
Who apprehended what it was they spake
In secret to the monarch of the world,
But waited till the day was growing darker,   V. 1790
And sunlight was declining in the west,
Then gained the entrance of the Sháh's pavilion,
And mounted boldly, saying to his horsemen,
His fortunate and noble followers:—
"Our lives are now dependent on our steeds,
And if they fail us we shall grasp the wind."
    Then he and all his meiny plied the spur,
And fled forth from the monarch of the world,
Who missed Sikandar's head and coronet,
Then lost amid night's gloom, and sent his guards
At once to seek his foeman in his tent.
They went to find that wary one departed,
So sleepy was the fortune of the Sháh!
Dárá dispatched a thousand cavaliers,
Bold fighters, in pursuit as swift as wind,
But in the dark they lost their way, beheld
The outposts of the foe, and turned unguerdoned
Save with the travail of their longsome journey.
    Now when Sikandar reached his own encampment
The warriors of Rúm approached and found
Their king well pleased that night. "There is," they
        cried,
"A cup of gems before him!"
                                    Said Sikandar:—
"Hail and exult in this our glorious omen,
For this cup is the triumph of my life;
The stars themselves are subject to me now.

I have obtained the number of the foe;
Their horsemen are much fewer than we heard.
Draw, all of you, your falchions for the fray,
Advance and quit the desert and the plain.
If in this fight ye give yourselves to toil,
The toil shall both enrich you and content you.
The Maker of the world is mine ally,
And fortune's head is lying on my breast."
   The mighty men called blessings down on him,
And said: "May all the earth rejoice in Cæsar,
And may our souls and bodies be thy ransom;
To that we pledge ourselves for evermore,
For who among the kings can vie with thee
In stature, goodliness, and bravery?"

V. 1791

§ 4

How Dárá fought with Sikandar and was worsted

Now when the sun rose o'er the Raven's back,
And earth grew as it were a lamp aflame,
Dárá, the world-lord, led his army forth;
The world drew o'er its head a veil of pitch.
He marched his army on from the Farát,
And men were more than grass-blades on the plain.
Whenas Sikandar heard: "A host hath come,"
He beat the kettledrums and marched to fight.
What with the jupons and the Indian swords,
The steeds and armour both for man and horse,
The baggage and the warriors on both sides,
Earth seemed a sea, and dust rose mountain-high.
Both hosts drew up for battle, and the falchions
Flashed in the sun.   They led the elephants
Before the army, and the world became
As 'twere the river Nile.   The cavaliers
Were in the rear, the elephants in front,

And all men ceased to set their hearts on life.
Thou wouldst have said: " Air is blood-clamouring,
And earth is rocking underneath the cry!"
So loudly sounded horn and Indian bell
That all men's hearts were moved and therewithal,
What with the neighing of the steeds, the shouts
Of captains, and crash of massive maces,
Thou wouldst have said: "Earth is a mount of war,
And heaven with flying dust an Ethiop's face!"
 For one whole week those valiant warriors
Confronted. On the eighth day rose a murk
Of dust such that the sun turned azure-dim,
And veiled the Íránians' eyes, who saw but dust
Upon the battlefield. Dárá, the world-lord,
Turned with his noble host of warriors.
The army reached the banks of the Farát,   V. 1792
Retreating in confusion from the field.
Sikandar's troops pursued them: of those hosts
One was o'erwhelmed with sorrow, one o'erjoyed.
Sikandar pressed on to the river-bank;
They slew Íránians innumerable,
But turned back at the river; he forbade
To cross and occupied victoriously
The battlefield with his picked soldiery.

§ 5
How Dárá fought with Sikandar the second Time

Whenas Dárá had fled before Sikandar
He sent off cavaliers on every side
In haste and called the chieftains of Írán
And of Túrán. He gave out pay, he summoned
The commissaries and, by next new moon,
Reorganised the troops and filled with bluster
The chieftains' heads. Again he crossed the river

And ranged his army on the spacious plain.
Sikandar, hearing this, marched forth ; he went
To meet Dárá and left behind his baggage.
When those two hosts encountered, earth and time
Contended too. They battled for three days
Till all the field was straitened by the slain.
Vast numbers of the Íránians perished there,
The day was lost to the aspiring Sháh,
Who turned in anguish from the battlefield
When sun and moon alike refused him aid.
Sikandar followed swift as flying dust,
Invoking much the Maker of the world.
A proclamation went forth to the troops :—
" Ye subjects who are wandering astray !
There is no fear that I shall injure you,
And ye are no concernment to my troops.

V. 1793 Abide in safety in your own abodes,
And trust your persons and your lives to God.
Ye have escaped the Rúmans safe and sound,
Although ye have imbrued your hands in blood."
   The soldiers, quarter being granted, turned
Their faces toward the Rúmans, while Sikandar
Went on the battlefield, collected all
The spoil, and gave it to his troops. His army
Was all equipped anew. They stayed awhile
Upon the field till king and hosts were rested.
   Dárá, the world-lord, reached Chahram where lay
His treasures' key. The chiefs all came to him,
Fulfilled with sorrow, misery, and anguish.
There sire lamented, seeing not his son,
And son in like wise, seeing not his sire ;
The country of Írán was full of wailing,
And tears like hailstones were in every eye.
Then from Chahram he journeyed to Istakhr—
The Persians' glory. Envoys went on all sides
To all the chieftains and the paladins.

The soldiers mustered at the royal palace,
They set a golden throne for Sháh Dárá,
And when he sat upon that seat of gold
The nobles, faithful still to him, drew nigh,
And he harangued the Íránians: "O ye chiefs,
Ye men of wisdom, Lions, warriors !
Consider now our course."

He spake in anguish,
And wept awhile, then added : "Better die
To-day with fame than live while Rúmans triumph.
Of old our ancestors and Sháhs took tribute
Each year from them ; Rúm was submiss in all
To us ; but now the Persians' fortune loureth,
Sikandar hath possessed him of all kingship,
Become world-lord, hath compassed throne and crown,
And will not pause, but presently be here ; V. 1794
All Párs will be as 'twere a sea of blood,
Men, women, children will be taken captive,
And neither young nor old left in the land.
If ye will give me aid I will avert
This anguish, travail, and calamity.
The Rúmans used to be our nobles' quarry,
They used to be in terror of Írán,
But we are now the quarry, they the leopards,
And in each battle we forsake the field.
Yet still if ye will struggle back to back
Ye shall renew your clutch upon their land,
But if one showeth slackness in the fight,
And striveth not to hazard his own life,
Abandon hope of this world in that Rúm
Is the Zahhák and we are the Jamshíd." [1]

He spake in tears with anguish in his heart ;
His lips were livid and his cheeks were wan.
The prudent nobles rose to make reply ;
A mournful wail ascended from the court :—

[1] See Vol. i. p. 139.

"We would not have the world without the Shád.
We all will face the conflict, make the world
Strait to our foes, and bind our skirts together [1]
For conquest or the grave."
　　　　　　　　　　Of all that coast
He paid and armed the leaders and the host.

§ 6

*How Sikandar fought with Dárá the third Time, and how
Dárá fled to Kirmán*

Sikandar, ware of what Dárá was doing,
And how he had become upon the throne
The moon's own diadem, led from 'Irák
His powers while all invoked on him God's blessing.
His army had no middle and no end;
Dárá's good fortune was not young withal,
But still the Sháh prepared to meet his foe,
And led so vast an army from Istakhr
V. 1795 That thou hadst said : "The earth can not sustain them,
And heaven itself will have not room to turn!"
Both kings arrayed the forces of both realms,
They all had spear and mace and sword in hand,.
And such a shout ascended from both hosts
As split the ears of heaven.　The earth became
A sea of warriors' blood, and all the field
Of battle was o'erstrewn with headless trunks,
Paternal love itself grew pitiless,
And heaven revolved indifferent to all.
Night came, Dárá was worsted, while Sikandar
Was girding up his loins for fresh assaults.
The Sháh fell back upon Kirmán and thus
Escaped alive the clutches of his foe;
Meanwhile Sikandar reached Istakhr of Párs—

---

[1] *Cf.* Vol. iv. p. 85 and *note.*

The crown of Sháhs, the glory of that land.
A proclamation went up at the courtgate:—
"Ye noble men and showers of the way!
Whoe'er desireth quarter for his life,
And is a penitent before his God,
Shall be 'neath my protection, one and all,
And know it if they are but true to me.
All that are wounded will we recompense,
And likewise cease to shed our foemen's blood,
We will forbear the goods of private folk,
And make our wisdom manifest. Since God,
The Conqueror, hath given us Grace divine,
With greatness and the imperial diadem,
A man had better trample on the neck
Of dragons than transgress our ordinance."
 Whatever spoil was taken on the field
Sikandar shared in full among his troops.
 When from Írán Dárá had reached Kirmán
He missed the more part of the Íránian chiefs.
A wail rose from amid the troops. They saw
Not any one with helmet on his head.
Dárá assembled all the great and wise,
All those who had been with him in the fight.
They came together grievously lamenting,
And burning at the evil of their lot.
Thus spake Dárá: "We verily have brought   V. 1796
Heaven's wrath upon ourselves. None in the world
E'er hath experienced such discomfiture,
Or heard of such from statists of old time.
The wives and children of Írán are captives,
Our souls are hurt by fate, our flesh by arrows.
What are your views and what device have ye
To make our enemy repent hereof?
We have no realm, no city, throne or crown,
No kingship, children, treasury or host,
And we are ruined if God pity not!"

The chiefs that still survived wept bitterly
Before Dárá, and cried : "We all, O king!
Are stricken by the evil of the time.
The matter is beyond the host's endeavours,
The waves have risen higher than our heads.
The sire is sonless and the son is sireless,
For so revolving heaven hath decreed.
Our mothers and our sisters and our daughters
Are all within the clutches of Sikandar,
While all the ladies of thy family,
Who trembled for thy safety, all the wealth
Transmitted by thy noble ancestors,
Whereto thou wast the undisputed heir,
The royal offspring and the Kaians' treasure,
Are in possession of thine enemies.
No longer can we stand against our foe
To battle with him in the way of fight.
Complete submission is our one resource,
For none can keep the crown of majesty,
And this same turning sky is passing too
O'er him as every man of wisdom knoweth.
Present thyself in person as his liege,
And make thy court with many flatteries.
Then shall we see how matters will result,
For heaven's process is beyond our ken.
So write a letter unto him and fill
His gloomy soul with thought because the man
V. 1797   Whose tongue is bright with knowledge will make shift
To pluck up evil from its base."
                                        Dárá,
On hearing this, announced his own intent—
One in accord to royal precedent.

§ 7

How Dárá wrote to Sikandar to propose Peace

The Sháh then called a veteran scribe who brought
His paper and musk-scented ink.   The Sháh,
In pain and grief, with livid cheeks and eyes
Fulfilled with tears of blood, wrote from Dárá,
Son of Dáráb, son of Bahman, a letter
To lion-capturing Sikandar Cæsar.
He first gave praises to the Omnipotent,
The Author of his good and evil fortune,
Then said : "Assuredly the sage himself
Will not escape the process of the sky
Whereby we are made joyful and appalled,
At whiles exalted and at whiles abased.
The battles of our hosts turned not on valour,
But on the processes of sun and moon.
What was to be hath been.   Our heart is sore :
What hath yon azure vault in store for us ?
If, heart-repentant now for having sought
The fray, thou wilt consent to terms, the treasures
Both of Gushtásp and of Asfandiyár,
The earrings and the armlets and the torques,
With all that we ourselves have gained, will I
Dispatch now from our treasury to thine.
Moreover I will aid thee in thy wars,
And when thou shalt be instant will not lag.
As for my wives and children, now thy captives,
I should not deem their restoration strange.
They who would rule the world must not be vengeful,
And from revenge on women mighty kings   V. 1798
Get nothing but reproach.   The lord of wisdom,
Who hearkeneth to knowledge, having read
What I have written will improve thereon."

A cameleer departed from Kirmán
In all haste to Sikandar, the arch foe,
Who, when he had perused the letter, said :—
" May wisdom be the consort of his soul !
Whoever injureth his family,
His ladies or the children of his house,
Shall see no throne except a coffin-board,
Or dangle from the branches of a tree.
I will not trouble any in Írán,
And God forbid that we should take their treasures.
If thou returnest to Íran 'tis well ;
The sovereignty is altogether thine.
What thou commandest ne'er will I transgress,
And draw no breath unless advised by thee."
    The camel voyaged homeward vessel-wise,
Dárá was filled with anguish, heart and eyes.

§ 8

How Dárá was slain by his Ministers

V. 1799   Dárá, when he had read that answer, mused
In wonder at the process of the world.
At last he said : " 'Tis worse than to be slain
For me to gird myself before the Rúman.
A grave is better for me than disgrace,
For, as a wise man said in this regard :—
' When any river riseth in its pride
A drop of rain is viewless in the tide.'
I used to succour every one in war,
But, since disaster hath befallen me,
I see not any helper in the world,
And I have none to cry to, saving God."
    As there was no one far or near to help
He wrote to Fúr a humble, flattering letter

In deep distress and, having first of all
Praised God, said: "Ruler of the men of Hind,
Thou man of wisdom, rede, and ardent soul!
Thou surely must have heard of my misfortune:
Sikandar hath led forth a host from Rúm;
No crops or settlements or kin or children,
Or crown or throne or royal diadem,
Or treasury or host are left to us.
Now if thou wilt help me to keep away
Destruction from myself I will dispatch
So many gems to thee out of my treasures
That never shalt thou need to toil for more.
Moreover thou shalt be renowned on earth,
And held in honour by the great."

        He sent
Like wind a cameleer who came to Fúr,
The scion of the race of Fúrs.

        Sikandar,
On hearing what Dárá, son of Dáráb,
Had done, bade blow the trumpet. There arose
The din of kettledrum and Indian bell.
Sikandar from Istakhr led forth such powers
That Sol was lost in heaven. Dárá too marched
For his part, and his Grace renewed the world. V. 1800
The war-cry rose from both sides and the troops
Had little rest. Sikandar ranged his host,
The air grew dark, earth viewless. When Dárá
Led forth his troops—no army bent on strife,
But broken-hearted and grown sick of war—
The fortune of the Íránians drooped its head.
They closed not with the Rúmans hand to hand;
They were the fox, the Rúmans were the lion,
And all the chiefs asked quarter, having come
Down from their pride to deep humility.
Dárá saw, turned away, and fled lamenting.
With him there went three hundred cavaliers—

The noblest of Írán.   He had withal
Two ministers of high degree, who used
To comrade him in fight.   The name of one—
An archimage—was Máhiyár, the other
Was called Jánúsiyár.   These twain, on seeing
Their efforts fruitless and the star erewhile
So lofty, and the glory, of Dárá
Thus set, held talk and said : "This luckless man
Henceforth will see not crown and throne again ;
We needs must poniard him upon the breast,
Or smite his head with Indian sword.   Sikandar
Will give to us a province.   We shall be
A crown upon the kingdom."
                                            Both of them,
One minister, the other treasurer,
Went with the Sháh ; Jánúsiyár, the chief,
Upon the left hand, Máhiyár to right.
Night gloomed, a storm arose, Jánúsiyár
Laid hand upon a dagger, stabbed the king
Upon the breast, that famed head reached its fall,
And then the troops deserted, one and all.

§ 9

How Dárá told his last Wishes to Sikandar and died

The ministers came to Sikandar, saying :—
" O Sháh victorious and endowed with knowledge !
V. 1801 We have surprised and slain thine enemy ;
The crown and throne of chiefs are his no more."
   Sikandar, having heard Jánúsiyár,
Said thus to Máhiyár : " Where is the foe
Whom thou hast overthrown ?   Show me the way."
   The two led on.   The Rúman's heart and soul
Were filled with rage and grief.   On drawing nigh

He gazed upon Dárá and saw his breast
All blood, his countenance like fenugreek,
Gave orders to alight and set a guard
O'er those two ministers, and then, dismounting
As swift as wind himself, took on his lap
The wounded monarch's head and, tarrying
Until the stricken should begin to speak,
Chafed with his hands the visage of Dárá,
Removing from the head the royal crown,
Unclasping from the breast the warrior's mail,
While showering tears on him because no leech
Was then at hand to tend upon the wounded,
And saying: "All yet shall be well with thee:
It is thy foemen's hearts that shall be wrung.
Arise and seat thee on this golden litter,
Or, if thou hast the strength, mount on thy steed.
I will have leeches brought to thee from Hind
And Rúm, and mourn thy pain with tears of blood.
I will resign to thee the realm and throne.
When thou art better we will pack and go,
But these that thus have wronged thee will I hang
Head-downward from two gibbets presently.
When yesterday these two old men informed me
My heart flowed over, and I cried aloud,·
Because we twain are of one root and piece:
Why for ambition should we wreck our race?"
    Dárá, on hearing this, began to speak,
And said: "May wisdom alway be thy mate.
Sure am I that thou wilt be recompensed
By God, the all-holy Judge, for these thy words;
But as for what thou said'st: 'Irán is thine,
Thine are the crown and throne's seat of the brave,'
Death is much nearer to me than the throne;
'Tis quit of ruined men. High heaven so willeth,   V. 1802
Whose joy is travail and whose profit loss.
Beware of saying: 'I by mine own might

Prevailed o'er this famed people.' Know that good
And ill are both of God, and while thou livest
Give Him the praise. I illustrate my words,
And am a sign to all. What majesty,
Kingship, and wealth were mine! I injured none.
What arms, what troops withal, what noble steeds,
What thrones and crowns, what children, what allies!
Allies! My brand was burnt upon their hearts!
Then earth and time were bondslaves in my presence,
And thus it was while fortune proved my friend.
Then by this token I grew quit of good,
And captive in the hands of murderers;
I had no hope in children or in kin,
The world was darkened and mine eyes were glazed.
Of all my kindred there is none to help me;
My sole hope is in Him who giveth all.
Thus stricken am I lying in the dust;
The world hath got me in the net of ruin.
Such is the custom of this turning sky
Alike with monarch and with paladin:
All kingship too departeth in the end;
It is the quarry and the hunter death."

    Sikandar wept blood-drops upon the Sháh,
Thus stricken in the dust, who at the sight
Of all that heart-felt grief and tears o'erflowing
His pallid cheeks, said: "Weep not, tears are vain,
The smother is my portion of the fire.
He that bestowed so much on me, and fortune
That so illumed me, have apportioned this.
Now give thine ear to this my last request,
Receive and keep it wisely in thy heart."

    Sikandar said to him: "'Tis thine to bid:
Say what thou wilt; I pledge to thee my word."

V. 1803   Dárá spake quickly and recounted all
His last requests, beginning thus: "O chief!
Fear thou the almighty Ruler of the world,

For He created the heaven, the earth, and time,
The mighty and the weak. Protect my children,
My kindred, and the consorts that I love;
Ask me for my chaste daughter as thy wife,
And let her share thy throne in happiness.
Her mother used to call her Rúshanak,
And made the world both glad and fair to her.
Thou wilt have no reproaches from my child,
Nor any jibings from the ill-disposed,
For kings have nurtured her, and she is fit
In rede to be the crown upon the noble.
Thou mayst see born to her a youthful prince
Who will revive the name Asfandiyár,
Relume the altar of Zarduhsht, take up
The Zandavasta, heed the presages,
The feast of Sada and the Fanes of Fire,
With glorious Naurúz, Urmuzd, and Mihr,
And lave his soul and face in wisdom's stream,
Restore the customs of Luhrásp and follow
The doctrine of Gushtásp, maintain both high
And low in their degree, illume the Faith,
And see good days."
                         Sikandar made reply :—
"O monarch of kind heart and honest speech!
I do accept thy rede and last requests,
And I will tarry in thy borders only
To compass these good matters, and herein
Take wisdom for my guide."
                         The world-lord grasped
Sikandar's hand, began to wail, then pressed
The palm upon his mouth, and said : "Be God
Thy refuge. I resign my place to thee,
Depart to dust, and give my soul to Him."
   He spake, his soul passed, and folk wept him sorely. V. 1804
Sikandar rent his garments and strewed dust
Upon the Kaian throne. Then for Dárá,

According to the custom of his race,
And honouring his Glory and his Faith,
Sikandar built a charnel-house. They washed
The monarch's blood away with clear rose-water,
Now that the time of endless sleep was come,
And draped him in brocade of Rúm; the pattern
Was all in jewelry, the ground was gold.
The corpse was hid by camphor; none beheld
Dárá's face more. They set within the charnel
A golden throne, o'erhead a crown of musk,
And laid him out upon a golden bier,
While every eye rained blood, then lifting it
They passed it on from hand to hand. Sikandar
Preceded it afoot, went too the nobles,
Their eyes all charged with blood, and thus he fared
Until the rites were o'er, and thou hadst said:—
"His very skin hath burst!"
      When he had placed
The Sháh's bier on the throne, had gone the way
Of royal precedent, left that grand charnel,
And made the lofty portals fast without,
He set a gibbet for Jánúsiyár,
With one for Máhiyár of equal size,
And hung those miscreants alive thereon—
Those regicides—head downward. From the host
Came warriors with stone in hand and slew them
Upon the gibbet all despiteously:
So perish every slayer of a king!
 Now when the Íránians saw how much Sikandar
Was troubled for the Sháh—that noble man—
They all of them began to laud his worth,
And hailed him as the ruler of the earth.

§ 10

How Sikandar wrote to the Nobles of Írán

One left Kirmán to go to Ispahán,
Wherein the Íránian chieftains were assembled.
One too—a man of high authority—
Approached the women-folk of Sháh Dárá,
Gave greetings on Sikandar's part, recounted
All that had happened to Dárá, and then
Spake thus: "The hearts of foe and friend alike
Rejoice not at the death of lawful Sháhs.
Know ye to-day then that I am Dárá.
If he is hidden I am manifest,
And greater favours are in store for you.
There is no cause to rend your hearts with grief;
We all are born to death, both Sháh and host;
It is the sole way though thou tarry long.
Convey your havings to Istakhr and gain
New glory by affinity to us.
Írán is now as ever it hath been;
May health of body and glad hearts be yours."
    They wrote to every province, prince, and peer
As from Sikandar, son of Failakús,
The great, the lord of earth and dread of foes,
A letter to the kinglike potentates,
Brave cavaliers and ready for the fray.
He sent withal a letter to the archmages,
All brilliancy, excuse, and compliment.
This was the heading: "From the king of Kaians
To all the administrators of Írán,"
And, when the pen of Chín had dipped in ink
Gris-ambered, first there came the praise of God,
"The righteous Judge, the Maker of the world,
And things invisible and visible.

V. 1805

Both worlds were made by His creative word :
Thou canst not call in question His decree.
The sky, which thou beholdest thus revolving,
Will, while it lasteth, never scape His ken.
Whate'er He willeth is at His command ;
We all are slaves and He is sovereign.
From Him be greetings to the men of name
Above their own deserts.   Remember naught
Of all that passeth in this world of ours
Save honest fame, accomplishment, and justice.
Amid my conquests grief hath come to me,
And mourning at a feast.   I swear by Him,
The Lord of sun on high, that ne'er I purposed
Harm to Dárá's life.   They that wished him ill
Were of his household, and the act was not
A stranger's but a servant's who hath felt
God's chastisement and suffered for his crimes.
Now seek ye justice, do as I command,
And stake your lives upon your fealty
As ye would have success from heaven, would have
At my hands purses, captives, thrones, and crowns.
Mine ardent heart is woeful for Dárá,
And I shall strive to do his last behests.
Whoe'er he be that cometh to my court
Shall have drachms, honours, thrones, and diadems ;
But, if he will abide at his own house,
Let him not swerve from his fidelity.
Send ye my treasury its dues, and then
No one shall suffer either pain or travail.
Coin money with Sikandar's superscription,
Be diligent, and break not faith with him ;
Maintain henceforth your kings' seat as of old ;
Let not your marches be without a guard,
And in this matter let each show his worth ;
Take care that there shall be in each bázár
A watch to call our name continually

V. 1806

That thieves may do no harm and ye abide
In all success and joy.   Send to our bower,
To those devoted to us, from each city
A goodly handmaiden, a slave of sense
And modesty, fit for our golden chambers,
One knowing all the doctrines of our Faith,
And having no reluctance to be sent,
For wrong must not be done to any captive.
Those strangers who pass through our provinces   V. 1807
Afoot, in abstinence, heart-free from vice,
Content to live the life of mendicants,
And called Súfís,[1] distinguish from mere beggars,
And let them stand the foremost on the roll.
If any of you are unfortunates,
Afflicted by an officer of mine,
Break ye the unjust doer's heart and back,
And rase him utterly, both root and branch.
I will suspend alive that miscreant,
Who hath led fair beginnings all astray.
Enrich your hearts by alms and equity,
And make nobility your diadem,
Because your lives will pass and time account
Our every step.   Whoever doth trangress
Our will shall suffer for it in the end."

The letter having been dispatched, he went
And took serene possession of the world.
He left Kirmán and coming to Istakhr
Encrowned him with the Kaians' glorious crown.

Seek not the secrets of the world to pry,
It turneth from the seeker's scrutiny;
Make knowledge in this life thy chief pursuit,
For in the next thou wilt enjoy the fruit.

---

[1] A sect of mystics.

XX

SIKANDAR

HE REIGNED FOURTEEN YEARS

ARGUMENT

Sikandar, on ascending the throne, harangues the nobles and marries Rúshanak, the daughter of Dárá. The poet then tells of Sikandar's dealing with Kaid and Fúr (Porus) of Hind, his visit to the Kaaba, to Queen Kaidáfa (Candace), to the Brahmans, to the Western Sea, to the land of Habash and of the Narmpái, to the City of Women, to the Darkness in search of the Water of Life, and to the Angel Isráfíl. Sikandar then again turns eastward, and erects a barrier against Yájúj and Májúj (Gog and Magog), reaches the End of the World, and is warned of his own death by the Speaking Tree. The poet then tells of Sikandar's relations with Faghfúr of Chín, of his visit to Bábil, of his correspondence with Aristálís (Aristotle), and of the circumstances attending his death and burial.

NOTE

.The Vullers-Landauer text, from which we have translated thus far, does not extend beyond the reign of Dárá, and from this point to the end we have made our version from the text of Macan. Mohl's edition of the text—the alternative—is, apart from other reasons for our choice, too ponderous for practical purposes ; the volume of it containing the reign of Sikandar, for instance, measures $18 \times 13 \times 2\frac{5}{8}$ inches and weighs 17 lbs. 2 ozs. ! The principles of our translation remain the same as laid down in the Introduction,[1] but it is necessary to add that in Macan's edition there are many misprints not included in. the Errata at the end of his volumes. These misprints we have corrected in our translation, but have not thought it necessary to call attention to them

---

[1] Vol. i. p. 77.

in footnotes. The corrections for the most part are quite obvious, and sufficiently indicated in our version to any one acquainted with the original.

§§ 2–4. These correspond generally with the Pseudo-Callisthenes, Book II. chap. 22, and with the Syriac version, Book II. chap. 14. For Roxana, see p. 32.

§§ 5–11. Alexander on his arrival in India naturally came into contact with the Fakírs—the mendicant and ascetic orders which are such a feature of that country. His pilot, Onesicritus, has left an account of an embassy on which he was sent to them. He describes how he found fifteen men standing, sitting, or lying in various attitudes naked in the sun, and conversed with two of them, Calanus and Mandanes, of whom the latter was the older, the wiser, and the more generally amenable.[1] The former, however, accompanied Alexander back to Persia, where, having fallen into bad health, he was burnt to death by his own request.[2] Calanus is mentioned also by Alexander's admiral, Nearchus,[3] and by Chares of Mytilene.[4] According to Plutarch his real name was Sphinés, and Calanus was a name given him by the Greeks because in salutations he used the word *kale*, "hail."[5] The accounts in the original authorities of Calanus and Mandanes, or Dandamis—a name by which also he is known—were freely used by later writers.[6] Palladius, who was bishop of Helenopolis at the beginning of the fifth century A.D., wrote a treatise on the peoples of India and the Brahmans in which he gives an account of Calanus and Dandamis, drawn from the older authorities. This work was interpolated into Codex A of the Pseudo-Callisthenes, where it forms chaps. 7–16 of Book III., thus bringing Calanus into the Romance. Dandamis had appeared already in chap. 6. The passage from Palladius is given in the early Latin version of the Romance by Julius Valerius, but not in the Syriac translation from the Pahlaví. The first oriental mention of the Indian sages seems to be in the little Pahlaví treatise known as the Kárnámak-i-Ardshír-i-Pápakán, which will engage our attention later on in the present volume.[7] In that treatise, which dates back probably to the seventh century A.D., the founder of the Sásánian dynasty consults the wise Indian, Kait. It is true that Ardshír Pápakán lived five centuries after Sikandar, but in the Sháhnáma this would be no bar to the reappearance of the sage. Ya'kúbí, the Arabic historian, writing towards the end of the ninth century

---

[1] MF, p. 50.   [2] DAA, vii. 3.   [3] MF, 60, 71.   [4] *Id.* 118.
[5] Life of Alexander, chap. 65. There is a Sanskrit word *kalyána*, which means "lucky." See MCI, p. 386.
[6] *Id.* 392.   [7] See pp. 195, 256.

A.D., has an account of Sikandar's meeting with a wise Indian king named Kaihan. In Pahlaví the letter *t* well might be taken for the letters *h* and *n*, and these with the short vowel *a* interposed would make Kaihan.[1] The story of the Indian sage seems rapidly to have developed in oriental hands, as is evident from the account given by Mas'údí, who died in A.D. 956, of the dealings of Sikandar with the wise Indian king, Kand.[2] Mas'údí, indeed, professes to give an abridgment only; but his version, with one exception, agrees closely with that of Firdausí. The exception is the introductory matter contained in § 5, which appears to be the poet's own contribution to the story. Kaid's dreams are a veiled presentment of Firdausí's own discontent with the circumstances of his own time, and contain a fierce arraignment of Sultan Mahmúd himself.[3] Kait, Kaihan, Kand, and Kaid evidently represent the same personality, which is none other than that of the Mandanes or Dandamis of classic authors, while the sage whom he sends as one of his four gifts to Sikandar is the historical Calanus.[4] Firdausí adopted the form Kaid for rhyming purposes. Kaid, we are told in § 6, dwelt at Mílád. Historically this would be Taxila, a city situated between the Indus and the Hydaspes (Jhílam) and Attock and Rawalpindi. Omphis, the king of Taxila, who was at enmity with his neighbour King Porus, was on very friendly terms with Alexander. Both Calanus and Mandanes or Dandamis were resident at Taxila. In the Sháhnáma Sikandar's dealings with Kaid are placed correctly before the war with Fúr. In the Pseudo-Callisthenes the interpolation from Palladius[5] is inserted after the account of Alexander's interview with the naked Indian sages in Book III. chaps. 5 and 6, a passage which is an integral part of the work and will be dealt with later on, for the interview is represented both in the Pseudo-Callisthenes and in the Sháhnáma as taking place after the war with Porus (Fúr).[6] In Mas'údí and Mírkhánd the affair with Kaid also takes place after that war.[7] Their account of Sikandar's passage of wits with the sage agrees closely with that of Firdausí in § 11, save that when Sikandar returns the rusted mirror to the sage the latter makes a cup that will float of it; on which Sikandar sends it back filled with earth, and the sage returns it to him without alteration, earth being the last word in all matters. Such symbolism is common in the East, and the whole passage might be interpreted thus. The Sháh begins by suggesting that the sage had better get into training if his wits are to be of any use to his new master. The sage

---

[1] NAR, 47. [2] MM, ii. 260. [3] *Cf.* Vol. i. p. 33.
[4] NAR, 47. [5] See p. 61. [6] See p. 67.
[7] MM, ii. 260; RM, Part I. vol. ii. p. 253.

replies that they are already as sharp as needles. The Sháh retorts that, though they may be sharp they are unpolished, and the sage rejoins that on the contrary they are exceedingly bright. The Sháh then observes that he can soon take the shine out of them, and the sage retorts that he knows a trick worth two of that. At this point the Sháh, hoping to take the sage at a disadvantage, summons him and requests him to interpret what had passed between them, thinking that he may not like to put his symbolism into plain speech. The sage, however, is equal to the occasion, and on the spur of the moment gives an unexpected turn to his interpretation, and one which meets with the Sháh's approval. The true interpretation seems to be this. The Sháh by sending a bowl full of ghee indicates that already he is so charged with knowledge that he has no occasion for the sage's services. The sage, by inserting many needles into the ghee, suggests that there is room for improvement. The Sháh replies that his finer faculties have become too blunted by the cares of his station. The sage rejoins that he can amend that. The Sháh retorts that the improvement will not last, but this the sage denies. Mas'údí adds that ultimately Sikandar allowed the sage to return to his own country.[1]

A similar story is told by Hiuen Tsiang of two great Buddhist saints who lived about the first century B.C. One visited the other to hold discussion with him. The visitor was not admitted at once. The other sent a disciple to him with a begging bowl full of water, symbolising the fulness, depth, and lucidity of the wisdom of his master. The visitor said nothing but dropped a needle into the bowl. The disciple returned and reported what had happened to his master, who at once recognised the worth of the visitor and gave orders that he should be admitted.[2]

§§ 12–15. These correspond with Book III. chap. 1–4 of the Pseudo-Callisthenes and of the Syriac version of it, and like them are quite unhistorical, as will be seen from the following summary of what really happened. On quitting Taxila, Alexander marched to the Hydaspes (Jhílam), on the opposite bank of which he found Porus with his forces prepared to dispute the passage. He deceived Porus so often by feints that after a time the latter ceased to believe that Alexander's intention of crossing the river was serious; and Alexander, in a night of storm and rain, succeeded in effecting the passage—one of his most brilliant feats of arms. Immediately after the crossing he was attacked by the son of Porus with a small force, which he defeated without much difficulty, and the son of Porus was slain. The general engage-

---

[1] MM, ii. 276.   [2] BBR, ii. 210, 215 *note*.

ment with Porus himself followed. Alexander was again victorious, and Porus, who had behaved throughout with great gallantry and was wounded, surrendered after Alexander had sent several messengers to beg him so to do. Alexander treated Porus with every consideration, restored his kingdom to him, and enlarged it. The battle with Porus was fought in the late spring or early summer of B.C. 326. Alexander then continued his advance into India, crossed the Akesines (Chináb) and the Hydraotes (Ravi), and reached the Hyphasis (Beas). At this point his army refused to proceed further, and he acceded to their wishes, though with the greatest reluctance. In the Pseudo-Callisthenes such historical features as survive are adapted so as to contribute to the glory of its hero. Thus the protest of the army takes place before the battle with Porus and proves ineffective, because it was incumbent that Alexander should meet with no check. The difficulty of transporting horses across a river on the further bank of which a strong force of elephants was drawn up to oppose them, and the known antipathy of horses to elephants, suggested the device of the iron steeds. A tradition, resting on good authority, that Porus was very tall, " more than five cubits in height " according to Arrian,[1] suggested that Alexander should be made out to be very small. The death of the son of Porus may have suggested, or been mistaken for, that of his father, which naturally is represented as having been caused by Alexander's own hand.

The differences between the Pseudo-Callisthenes and Firdausí are not important and chiefly in matters of detail. In the former Porus begins the correspondence; he has wild beasts as well as elephants in his army. In branches B and C Alexander, disguised as a sutler, visits the city of Porus and has an interview with him. In the battle that ensues Bucephalus falls, in branch A by the hand of Porus. The battle lasts for twenty days, and so forth. In the latter the kingdom of Fúr is situated beyond Kannúj—a city on the Ganges—and it is there that the correspondence with Fúr takes place. After the correspondence comes the protest of the army against proceeding further. Sikandar appoints Sawurg king in Fúr's stead.

§ 16. This is derived, of course, not from the Pseudo-Callisthenes, but from independent Arabic sources. It appears in Dínawarí, who died in A.D. 896.[2] The insertion makes wild work of the geography, for it brings Sikandar back from Kannúj, according to Firdausí, to Mecca. Later on,[3] he has to go eastward again in order to interview the Brahmans.

The neighbourhood of Mecca has been a sacred spot from time

---

[1] DAA, v. 19.   [2] NAR, 39.   [3] § 24.

immemorial. The city stands in a sacred territory known as
"Harám," *i.e.* "prohibited," and contains the still more sacred
Kaaba, into the wall of which, and perhaps most sacred of all, is
built the meteorite known as the "Black Stone." The Kaaba
itself, according to the Kurán, was built by Abraham and Ishmael.[1]
The custody of the Harám—a position of great honour and profit
—was in the hands now of one, now of another, of the Arab tribes.
In Muhammad's time the Kuraish, whose ancestor was Nasr, son
of Katíb, were in charge. Previously it had been in that of the
Khuzá'. The fact that the change of guardianship is attributed
to Sikandar is an eloquent testimony to his fame.[2] Kahtán,
according to Arab tradition, was descended from Shem, and was
one of the great progenitors of the race. He was identified with
Joktan.[3]

§§ 17–23. We learn from Quintus Curtius that when Alexander
was besieging Mazaga, a city situated probably on the Swat River,
and the inhabitants despaired of the defence, their queen Cleophis,
attended by many noble ladies, came out to him, was received
graciously, and confirmed in her sovereignty. Some people, however, were ill-natured enough to say that her personal charms
rather than Alexander's humanity brought about this result. At
all events she is said to have had a son later on whom she named
Alexander.[4] Alexander's relations with Cleophis and his visit to
the Oasis of Ammon may have suggested to the author of the
Pseudo-Callisthenes the episode which is the subject of the above
sections. The story is, of course, unhistorical ; but it is easy to
see how it would suggest itself to an Egyptian, whether native or
naturalised. Both before and after the Christian era Candace
seems to have been the dynastic name of the queens, whether sole
regnant, consort, or dowager, of that part of Nubia which is
bounded by the Nile, the Blue Nile, and the Atbara, and known
as the Island or as Meroe, the latter being also the name of one
of its two principal cities, the other being Napata. Excavations
have brought to light remains of tombs and palace, and reliefs of
various queens of a pronounced negroid type. Whether Alexander
was introduced into some already existing story, told originally
in another connexion, of one of the old queens of Meroe or
whether the whole thing is the invention of the Egyptian author
of the Pseudo-Callisthenes, it is impossible to say. Firdausi's
version of the story corresponds with the Pseudo-Callisthenes,
Bk. III. chaps. 18–24, and with the Syriac version of it, Bk.
III. chaps. 8–14. The three are closely in accord in most points,

[1] RK, p. 446.   [2] NAR, 39, and *notes.*
[3] Gen. x. 25 ; 1 Chron. i. 19–20.   [4] HQC, Bk. viii. c. 10.

but there are differences in matters of detail and in the names of the characters in the story. The Kandake (Candace) of the Pseudo-Callisthenes and of the Syriac version becomes Kaidáfa in Firdausí, which shows that his account came to him through the Arabic, in which the name, in the absence of diacritical points, could be read either way. Similarly the Kandaules of the Greek, the Kandáros of the Syriac,[1] became Kaidrúsh, the story having passed from Greek into Pahlaví, from Pahlaví into Syriac, from Syriac into Arabic, and from Arabic into Persian again (modern instead of middle) before Firdausí dealt with it. In the Pseudo-Callisthenes and the Syriac version Ptolemy takes Alexander's place when Kaidrúsh is brought into court, and Alexander assumes the name of Antigonus. In Firdausí the latter becomes the name of Sikandar's chief minister (Naitkún), and the two exchange their respective positions. In the Greek and the Syriac the wife of Kandaules is taken prisoner by a hostile king, while Kandaules himself escapes to the camp of Alexander, who regains his wife for him. In Firdausí the pair are taken prisoners by Sikandar while celebrating their wedding-feast in the city of king Faryán, the father of the bride. This version is more considerate of the lady, who does not get off so easily in the Greek and Syriac. In the Greek too the scene of the action is laid in the kingdom of Semiramis, whose descendant [2] Kaidáfa is stated to be. In the Syriac the name Semiramis is corrupted into that of a people. In the Sháhnáma the scene is laid in Andalús, *i.e.* in Spain, which was conquered by the Arabs early in the eighth century A.D. In the Greek, Candace's other son, who had married a daughter of Porus, is unnamed, but is called Charogos in the early Latin version of Julius Valerius. In the Syriac he appears as Kerátór, and in the Sháhnáma as Tainúsh, who is represented there as being the eldest son, as in the Ethiopic, where he is called Kanír.[3] The Ethiopic too alone coincides with the Sháhnáma in giving the dramatic conclusion of the story—the discovery by Tainúsh (Kanír) that the ambassador to his mother was Alexander himself—from which we might conclude that both versions derived the incident from a common Arabic source. Another view, however, may be suggested. The hand of a poet is visible in Firdausí's presentment of the whole story. He enlists our sympathy by making Kaidrúsh and his wife a newly married couple, which is found in no other version, suppresses the worst of the lady's misfortunes, which is

---

[1] The *l* being read as *r.   Cf.* p. 14.

[2] Proneptis in the version of Julius Valerius, from which the Greek is restored, MPC, p. 126.

[3] BLEA, p. 206.

expressed or implied in the other versions, and makes two other consequential alterations. Tainúsh is described as being the elder instead of the younger son, because Firdausi represents him as having been longer married ; and Faryán, who stands for the abductor of the lady in the other versions, becomes her own father. Further, the Ethiopic version appears to have been a late production which came into being some time between the fourteenth and sixteenth centuries,[1] when the Sháhnáma itself had become a great authority, and it seems not unlikely that the dramatic conclusion in the Ethiopic version was derived through the Arabic from Firdausí's own handiwork.

§ 24. This corresponds with Bk. III., chaps. 5–6, of the Pseudo-Callisthenes and of the Syriac version, in both of which the order of events is the war with Porus, the interview with the Brahmans, the affair with Candace. In Firdausí the order of the last two is transposed. This is due to the interpolation from Arabic sources of Sikandar's expedition to the Kaaba, in § 16, immediately after the war with Fúr. Consequently he has to make a second expedition eastward. His interview with the Brahmans may be regarded as a literary invention based partly on the account of Onesicritus [2] and partly on some other source, which is responsible for his questions and their answers. These appear in Plutarch's *Life of Alexander*, ch. 64. That historian makes the interview take place in the course of Alexander's voyage down the Indus to the sea. The questions and answers vary in the different accounts. The question as to whether the living or the dead are the most numerous is found in Plutarch, where the answer is, the living, in the Pseudo-Callisthenes, in Julius Valerius, and in the Syriac and Ethiopic versions.

The question whether there is most land or water occurs in the Pseudo-Callisthenes and Julius Valerius. In the Syriac version the question is as to whether the land or the water is the older. In Plutarch the question is whether the earth or sea produces the largest beast. In both cases the answer is, the earth.

The question as to who are the sinners, or the most sinful, is found in the Pseudo-Callisthenes, in Julius Valerius where it occurs in the form, which is the most cunning of beasts? in the Syriac and in the Ethiopic.

Alexander's question as to what the Brahmans would have of him is found in the Pseudo-Callisthenes, in Julius Valerius, and in the Syriac and Ethiopic versions.

Several of the questions occurring in other versions do not appear in the Sháhnáma, such, for instance, as those in the Syriac

---

[1] BHA, p. lxxxix.   [2] See p. 61 ; and *cf.* NAR, p. 6.

as to whether death or life is the mightier; which existed first, day or night; and whether the limbs on the left side of the body or on the right side are the better, and so forth.

§§ 25-27. At this point the adventures of Sikandar become more romantic. In codex A of the Pseudo-Callisthenes, and in the Latin version of Julius Valerius, they form the subject of a letter, purporting to be written by Alexander to Aristotle, and come between the visit to the Brahmans and that to Candace. The letter is a long one, and is lengthier still in the Syriac version, which contains incidents no longer extant in the Greek but found in the Sháhnáma. In the Greek the letter forms ch. 17 and in the Syriac ch. 7 of Bk. III.

It may be well to quote here a short passage from M'Crindle's *Ancient India as described by Magasthenés and Arrian*, which is very apposite in the present connexion. Speaking of the ancient Greeks' conception of India, he says:—" They imagined it to be an Eastern Ethiopia which stretched away to the uttermost verge of the world, and which, like the Ethiopia of the West, was inhabited by a race of men whose visages were scorched black by the fierce rays of the sun. See Homer, *Od.* i. 23-24, where we read

Αἰθίοπες, τοὶ διχθὰ δεδαίαται, ἔσχατοι ἀνδρῶν,
Οἱ μὲν δυσομένου Ὑπερίονος οἱ δ' ἀνιόντος.

(The Ethiopians, who are divided into two, and live at the world's end—one part of them towards the setting sun, the other towards the rising.) Herodotus in several passages mentions the Eastern Ethiopians, but distinguishes them from the Indians (see particularly Bk. vii. 70). Ktêsias, however, who wrote somewhat later than Herodotus, frequently calls the Indians by the name of Ethiopians, and the final discrimination between the two races was not made till the Makedonian invasion gave the Western world more correct views of India. Alexander himself, as we learn from Strabo, on first reaching the Indus mistook it for the Nile. Much lies in a name, and the error made by the Greeks in thus calling India Ethiopia led them into the further error of considering as pertinent to both these countries narrations, whether of fact or fiction, which concerned but one of them exclusively. This explains why we find in Greek literature mention of peculiar or fabulous races, both of men and other animals, which existed apparently in duplicate, being represented sometimes as located in India, and sometimes in Ethiopia or the countries thereto adjacent."[1] Bearing this passage in mind, it is easy to understand that the original author of the Romance of

---

[1] MCAI, p. 3 and *note*.

Alexander, whose idea was to make his hero traverse the whole world, and the later redactors of the Romance, found it easy to provide a crop of marvels, of which the Persian version in the Sháhnáma furnishes a by no means exhaustive account. The Macedonian invasion may have given the Western world more correct ideas of India, but it did not prevent the Pseudo-Callisthenes from coming into being some five centuries later and flourishing exceedingly. The return of Alexander from India to Persia by sea and land along the desolate shores of Makrán (Gedrosia) naturally gave rise to a crop of marvels not all without foundation.

§ 25. The people encountered by Sikandar after leaving the Brahmans were known to Arrian as the Oritæ. They dwelt in the neighbourhood of the Pur-Ali River. He describes them as wearing a dress and using arms similar to those of the Indians, but as differing in language and customs.[1] The shore-dwelling Oritæ are responsible for one of the etymologies suggested for the name of their country—Makrán—*i.e.* " Máhí-khúrán," " Fish-eaters," " Ichthyophagi," which, even if it be not correct, is at least appropriate. Two extracts from Arrian's *Indica*, based on the account of Nearchus, Alexander's admiral, and others from modern sources, will serve to show that the habits of the shore-dwellers in that region have not altered materially during a period of over two thousand years, if we except the employment of the skeletons of whales for house-building—a custom that would be mentioned by modern travellers in those parts if it still obtained. The dwellings now consist of mats held together by poles or else take the form of mud huts.[2] " The Ichthyophagi live on fish, whence their name. Few of them indeed fish, few indeed have boats for the purpose, or know the art of fishing, but catch most at the ebb of the tide. Some even have made nets to do this, most of such a size that they stretch two stades.[3] These they make of palm-bass, which they twist like flax. When indeed the sea recedes, deserts the land, and leaves it dry, it is generally void of fish, but when the land retains the water in some deeper indentation, then they find a great abundance. Of these most are small, others large. These they encircle with their nets and take. The finer sorts they eat raw as they draw them from the water ; the larger and coarser they dry in the sun, and, as soon as they are baked through, reduce them to flour by grinding and convert them into

---

[1] DAI, c. 25.

[2] *Diary of Proceedings of the Mission into Mekran.* By Major F. J. Goldsmid, in JRGS, Vol. xxxiii. pp. 189, 198, 200, 203.

[3] Rather over 400 yards.

bread. Some make it into a paste. They even give their beasts
fish-flour instead of fodder. All the region, in the absence of
meadows, produces no herbage. They take withal in these parts
a great quantity of crabs, oysters, and shell-fish. The region
also naturally produces salt, from which they make (an equivalent or substitute for?) oil. Those of them indeed that in-
habit the desert parts, and a region productive of neither trees
nor fruit, live on fish only: a few sow a little ground, and eat
bread as a relish with their fish, for fish are their corn. They
build their houses thus. The wealthiest of them take whatever
bones of the whale the sea throws up, and use them in the place
of timber, making the largest into doors. The indigent majority
make their houses of fish bones." [1] In the following chapter Arrian
enters more into detail:—"Some of the whales are driven ashore
occasionally in various places, and are stranded when the tide
recedes; others are cast on to the land by violent storms, and
perish of putrefaction; their flesh dropping off leaves their bones
for men to employ in house-building. Their greater ribs are
selected for the beams, the smaller for the planks; the jaw-bones
are taken for doors." [2]

A modern account says:—"Nearchus . . . names the whole of
this coast, from the river Indus to Charbar, the country of the
Ichthyophagi or fish-eaters, and the inhabitants still live entirely
on fish, the cattle having much the same diet as their masters, for
the country is wholly destitute and barren, and yields no sort of
grass. Vast stores of oysters, crabs, and all kind of shell-fish are
found on the coast, of which Nearchus's description is generally
very accurate. In many places, both here and in Arabia, the
cattle are fed entirely on dried fish and dates mixed together, on
account of the great scarcity of grass in these sun-burnt and
sandy regions." [3]

A later account says:—"Fish, to this day, is the staple article
of food for those of the inhabitants living on the sea-board, and in
this respect they fully bear out the name of ichthyophagi given to
their ancestors by ancient writers." [4] And again:—"Nearchus . . .
coasted along the shores of Balochistan, and his account of the
natives he met with, and the difficulty he found in obtaining
supplies, is as credible as if the voyage had been carried on under
similar circumstances at the present day." [5]

---

[1] DAI, c. 29.   [2] Id. 30.
[3] *Notes made on a Survey along the Eastern Shores of the Persian Gulf
in 1828.* Communicated by Lieutenant G. B. Kempthorne. In
JRGS, Vol. v. p. 270, original series.
[4] HB, p. 19.   [5] Id. 178.

There is further mention of the Ichthyophagi in § 34.

The story of Sikandar's adventure with a basking whale which was mistaken for an island, with disastrous consequences to those that visited it, has not been lost sight of by the romancers and poets of later ages. In the first voyage of Sindbad the sailor, in the *Arabian Nights*, he lands upon an island "like a garth of the gardens of Paradise," but which proves to be a great fish, and sinks when fires are lighted on it for cooking purposes.[1] For the poets the reader may be referred to the passage in *Paradise Lost*, Bk. i. line 200 *seq.*, Aldine ed.[2]

The reeds mentioned are of course bamboos, of which one of the many uses is for house-building.

§ 26. Here we are introduced to the true Ethiops, who, according to Greek notions, occupied the extremities of the world both in the East and West.[3]

§ 27. The above remark applies equally to the Narmpái.[4] The story of the dragon is not extant in the Pseudo-Callisthenes or in the Latin version of Julius Valerius. It is found, however, in the Syriac version and in the Ethiopic,[5] which represent the monster as being regarded as a god by the natives. In the Syriac it is described as killing its victims by drawing in its breath, and so sucking them down its throat.[6]

The temple that Sikandar visits is that of Dionysus, and the corresponding passage in the Pseudo-Callisthenes is Bk. III. ch. 28. There is a doublet of the visit in § 31.

§ 28. Modern historical research, which is restoring to us the knowledge of the great Hittite empire once dominant in Asia Minor and northern Syria, appears incidentally to have thrown light on the origin of the legend of the Amazons. The period of the historical importance of the Hittites dates approximately from B.C. 2000 to B.C. 700; and it appears that their great goddess Ma—the prototype of Cybele, the Great Mother—was served by women "who in later centuries, on the decline of the Hittite power, at the coming maybe of the Phrygians, at first for the defence of their religion, and later separating in independent action, developed into armed priestesses."[7] In the Introductory Note to the work here quoted Professor Sayce says:—"The Amazons of Greek legend prove to have been the warrior-priestesses of the

---

[1] BAN, vi. 5.   [2] See too *id. notes,* and LAN, iii. 83.   [3] See p. 68.
[4] They are referred to in Pliny's *Nat. Hist.*, Bk. v., sect. 46, as "Himantopodes loripedes quidam quibus serpendo ingredi natura sit." *Cf.* Vol. ii. p. 55, and *note.*
[5] BHA, p. 107; BLEA, p. 166.   [6] *Cf.* Vol. v. p. 233, *note.*
[7] GH, pp. 170, 357.

great Hittite goddess." [1]   The seat of the Amazons, which legend
places on the river Thermodon, is quite in concord with the above
identification, and their legend itself extends from Homer [2]
through Herodotus and many other writers to Sir John Maundeville. [3]   As to the origin of the legend that brought Alexander
into connexion with the Amazons we are told by Arrian that
when that king was in Sughdiana he received a visit from Pharasmanes, king of the Kharazmians, who stated that his dominions
marched with those of the Colchians and Amazons, and that if
Alexander desired to proceed to those regions and subjugate the
races in the neighbourhood of the Euxine he would act himself
as guide and furnish necessaries for the troops. [4]   The land of
Kharazm is now represented by the modern Khiva, and the whole
breadth of the Caspian Sea intervened between Pharasmanes and
his nearest neighbours to the west; but the mere suggestion
seems to have taken root, and soon it was affirmed by some of the
more romantic, or less scrupulous, historians of Alexander that the
queen of the Amazons had visited him in person—the view adopted
by Quintus Curtius, who tells us how their queen Thalestris
arrived with her suite of three hundred women from the vicinity
of the river Thermodon, and spent about a fortnight with the
king. [5]   In the Pseudo-Callisthenes it is Alexander who visits the
Amazons, and the visit takes place immediately after that to
Candace, queen of Ethiopia, in which the ground is laid for it by
representing her son and daughter-in-law as being on their way
to perform religious rites in the land of the Amazons when the
lady was abducted.   Firdausí, who omits the passage about the
abduction, naturally leaves out the reference to the Amazons and
gives his account of them in another connexion. [6]   His version
corresponds with that of the Pseudo-Callisthenes, Bk. III. ch.
25-27, and with the Syriac version, Bk. III. ch. 15-17.   In
these versions and in the Sháhnáma the Amazons are represented as living on an island, and the account of their marriage-
customs in the Pseudo-Callisthenes and in the poem may owe
something to the stories of the Male and Female Islands that
no doubt were current in Egypt in connexion with the country
—southern Arabia—whence it obtained its supplies of frankin-
cense.   It seems to have been the custom of the incense-gatherers,
who were always men, to leave their wives and children at home,
which in this case would mean, among other localities, the Kuria
Muria Islands, while they themselves crossed over to the mainland for the purposes of their trade.   Sons, when grown up, would

---

[1] GH, p. ix.   [2] *Iliad*, iii. 187 *seq.*; vi. 186.   [3] AM, cap. L.
[4] DAA, iv. 15.   [5] HQC, vi. 5.   [6] See p. 153.

accompany their fathers, while the daughters would remain with the mothers. The seven Kuria Muria Islands thus became known collectively as "The Female Island," while the mainland represented "The Male Island." [1] There appears to be a reference to the same custom in Hiuen Tsiang :—" To the south-west of Fo-lin, in an island of the sea, is the kingdom of the western women : here there are only women, with no men ; they possess a large quantity of gems and precious stones, which they exchange in Fo-lin. Therefore the king of Fo-lin sends certain men to live with them for a time. If they should have male children, they are not allowed to bring them up." [2]

By the black race encountered by Sikandar on his way to the city of the Amazons the negroes seem to be intended, and the description is quite in the style of one in the *Arabian Nights :—* " Then sprang with a drop-leap from one of the trees a big slobbering blackamoor with rolling eyes which showed the whites, a truly hideous sight." [3] The bringing of frost and snow would be a great marvel in their hot country. Similarly Sarv, king of Yaman, tries to overcome the three sons of Farídún. [4]

It does not seem possible to identify the fair-haired race that Sikandar met after leaving Harúm. The type is too common and his wanderings are too vague. There is the Berber race in North Africa among which the blond type with blue eyes is not uncommon, and in northern Europe the Scandinavian. Herodotus too speaks of the Budini, whom he places north of the Palus Mæotis, as having blue eyes and red hair ; [5] and Tacitus describes in similar terms the peoples of Germany. [6] Moreover, tribes with red beards and blue eyes are mentioned in Chinese annals as living in Central Asia. [7]

The notion of " The Gloom," about which Sikandar makes inquiries, seems to have been the outcome of two distinct conceptions. One was that as the sun set in the West, and thereupon night ensued, there was a Land of Darkness in that quarter. This notion is as old as Homer, who opposes the East to the West by describing the former as being πρὸς Ἠῶ τ' Ἠέλιόν τε, "towards the dawn and the sun," and the latter as being ποτὶ ζόφον, "towards the gloom." [8] The other was based on the accounts that filtered through to the sunnier South of the dark-

---

[1] SP, p. 144.
[2] BBR, ii. 279. Fo-lin is supposed to stand for the Byzantine empire. *Id.* p. 278, *note. Cf.* too YMP, Bk. iii. c. xxxi., and *note.*
[3] BAN, i. 6.   [4] See Vol. i. p. 184.   [5] Bk. iv. c. 108.
[6] *Germania*, c. 4.   [7] BAG, i. 193, and *note.*
[8] *Iliad*, xii. 239–240; *Odyssey*, xiii. 240, &c.

ness of the North—the long sunless winters of the Arctic Circle.
Attached to each conception was the idea of an earthly paradise—
in the West the garden of the Hesperides, and in the North the
elysium of the Hyperboreans, who had their counterpart, or
original, in Indian legend which told that "towards the North,
beyond the Himâlaya, dwelt the Uttarakuri, a people who enjoyed
a long and happy life, to whom disease and care were unknown, and
who revelled in every delight in a land all paradise." [1] Hesiod knew
of the Hyperboreans. [2] There is an interesting chapter on " The
Land of Darkness " in Marco Polo. [3]

§ 29. At the close of § 28 we have the beginning of the story
of Sikandar's famous expedition into the Land of Darkness and
to the Fount of Life. This does not appear in branch A of the
Pseudo-Callisthenes, in the early Latin version of Julius Valerius,
or in the Syriac version. It is given at large, however, in branch C,
which has Christian leanings, and it is found also in the Ethiopic
version. It is obvious that Firdausí's account had passed through
the Arabic. The Arabic in its turn came from the Syriac, and the
existence of the account in the Syriac is due to the fact that
Jacob of Sarúg [4] inserted it in his metrical version of the Syriac
Christian Legend of Alexander already referred to. [5] The basis
of the whole is branch C of the Pseudo-Callisthenes, where the
account runs as follows:—" Thence Alexander set forth again
with his host, retiring to a level place in the midst whereof was a
ravine. Having thrown a bridge across he wrote thereon in
Greek, Persian, and Egyptian, and the writings signified : ' Alexander, arriving hither, built this arch, and crossed it with his
whole host, being desirous of possessing the ends of the earth,
God willing.' And in three days he came to regions where the
sun did not shine. The name thereof is ' The Country of the
Blest.' And Alexander, having left the baggage and the infantry
with the old men and the women, was minded to take chosen
youths with him to investigate and see these regions. His friend
Callisthenes advised him to make his entry with forty friends,
one hundred youths, and twelve hundred soldiers. King Alexander
set forth, instructing them to take no old man with them. An
inquisitive elder, however, who had two sons—noble and trusty
soldiers—said to them : ' Children, hearken to your father and
take me with you, and I shall be found not empty on the journey,
for I wot that in time of difficulty the old will be sought after,
and you therefore, as having me with you, will be honoured much

---

[1] MCAI, p. 24.
[2] Herodotus, iv. 32.
[3] YMP, Vol. ii. p. 483 *seq*, and *notes*.
[4] See p. 15.
[5] *Id.*

by your king. Lest, being found to transgress his ordinance, ye be deprived of life, now, bestirring yourselves, crop my head and beard ; thus altering hair and appearance I will go with you and prove of great use to you in the time of need.' So doing their father's bidding, they took the old man with them. Thus they fared with Alexander and reached a murky spot. Being unable to advance further, owing to the impassable nature of the place, they removed thence their tents. Next day, Alexander, taking with him a thousand soldiers, went to ascertain if the end of the earth were there. Going leftward he saw a part that was lighter, and fared over places waste and precipitous for half the day. This he knew not from the sun but by taking measurement of the way geometrically. Afterwards he turned back in alarm because the route was impracticable. Emerging, he was minded to go to the right because the plain was level, albeit dark and gloomy. But being in difficulties because none of the youths were willing for him to enter that dark place in that, the horses being wearied out by the glooms of that dark road, they would be unable to return, Alexander said to them :—' O noble soldiers ! ye all know now that in wars nothing is done nobly without counsel and advice, for in good sooth an old man coming with us would direct us how we ought to enter this dark region. If now there be some noble man among you let him go and bring into our camp for me an elder, and he shall have much gold of me.' Howbeit none of them was found to do this thing by reason of the length of the way and of the lightless air. Then, presenting themselves, the sons of the old man said to Alexander :—' If thou wilt hear us with forbearance, O king ! we will tell thee somewhat.' King Alexander said :—' Say what ye will, for I swear by divine Providence not to wrong you.' Forthwith they told him about their sire, and ran and brought the old man to him. Alexander, on seeing, embraced him and asked him to counsel them. The old man said : 'It is fit, O king Alexander ! for you to know this, that if horses enter you will see the light never more. Choose therefore mares with foals, and leave the foals there, going yourselves with the mares ; they will lead us thither.' [1] Alexander therefore made search among all those with him, but only found a hundred mares with foals. Taking these and another hundred selected ones, as well as many others to carry their provand, he entered according to the counsel of the old man, leaving the foals without. The old man instructed his sons that whatever they should find lying on the ground as they went they were to collect and place in their pouches. There entered with Alexander three

---

[1] *I.e.* back to the foals.

hundred and sixty soldiers, and thus advancing along the dark road for fifteen *schœni*,[1] they saw a certain place wherein was a bright fountain whereof the water flashed like lightning ; the air was fragrant and most sweet. Now Alexander, the king, becoming hungry, wished to eat bread, and calling his cook, who was named Andreas, told him to prepare a meal. Taking a dried fish he went to the shining water of the fountain to wash the meat. On being wetted in the water it came to life forthwith and escaped from the hand of the cook, who told nobody of what had happened, but took himself some of the same water in a silver vessel and safe-guarded it; the whole place indeed gushed with waters whereof all drank and partook of food. Alexander, after he had eaten, again journeyed on for thirty *schœni*, and further saw a light without sun, moon, or stars, and he beheld three birds flying, but having the aspect of men, and crying to him from aloft in the Grecian tongue: ' The land whereon thou treadest, Alexander ! is that of God alone. Return, thou wretch ! thou art not able to tread the Country of the Blest. Go back then, O man ! and tread the earth bestowed upon thee, and prepare not troubles for thyself.' Being affrighted, Alexander gave instant heed to the words spoken to him by the birds, one of which cried to him again :—' The East calleth thee, Alexander ! and the realm of Porus shall become subject to thee by conquest.' Thus saying the bird flew off. Alexander, having resigned himself to Providence, bade Antiochus to signify to the troops :—' Let each that wisheth take of what is here, be it stone or earth or wood.' To some it seemed good so to do, while to others Alexander's words appeared madness. Now as they went he said to Philon :—' Dismount and take up whatever chanceth.' Philon, dismounting, found a stone that seemed to him one of the worthless sort, and taking this he fared with Alexander. Many of the troops too took what each found from the material lying in that place, and the sons of the old man in particular, according to the bidding of their father, filled their wallets till they could walk no longer. Alexander, having guides, sent on the asses in front, marched by the Wain, and in some days arrived within hearing of the neighing of the mares, and in this manner issued from the land of night. So they came to the light where were the rest of the troops, and, looking on one another, found pearls and stones of price. When they saw this those that had taken none repented, while all those that had taken them blessed the old man and Alexander for their good counsel. Philon brought his stone to Alexander, and it was

---

[1] A measure of length varying from 60 to 30 stades. A stade = 606¾ English feet.

all gold. Then the cook told how the meat had come to life. Alexander, enraged, ordered him a terrible scourging. He said however to Alexander:—'What boots it, Alexander! to repent a past matter?' He did not say that he had drunk of the water or that he had kept some of it. This the cook refrained from confessing save as to the dried fish coming to life. Then that wicked cook going to Kalé, the daughter of Alexander and of the concubine Uné, seduced her, promising to give her to drink of the Water of the Fount of Immortality, which he did. Alexander, hearing of this, envied their immortality. He called his daughter and said to her:—'Take thy clothes and depart, for behold thou hast become a goddess, being immortal, and thou shalt be called Nereis as having immortality from water, and therein shalt thou dwell.' Weeping and mourning she departed from him, and consorted in waste places with the spirits. As for the cook, Alexander gave orders for a stone to be fastened to his neck, and that he should be flung into the sea. Being cast away thus he became a god and dwelt in a part of the sea that on this account was called Andreanticus. So much for the cook and the daughter of Alexander, who took these things to signify that the end of the earth was in those parts. When they came to the arch that Alexander had built, he engraved thereon again to this effect:— 'Let those that wish to enter the Land of the Blest fare to the right.' "[1]

This legend through the Syriac became known to Muhammad, who gives his version of it in the chapter of the Kurán known as "The Cave." Of part of the story he makes Moses the hero and of the rest Zú-'l-karnain, *i.e.* The Two-horned (Alexander the Great). In the Kurán the part of the legend concerned with the salt fish is told in connexion with Moses and, being somewhat obscure and fragmentary, has given a fine opportunity to the commentators. To elucidate the passage in the Kurán it was explained that on one occasion when Moses had made an eloquent address to his followers they were so impressed that they asked him if he knew of any one wiser than himself, and he replied that he did not. The Almighty reproached him for his vanity and told him that if he would go to a certain rock, where two seas met, he would find his master in wisdom. He was to take with him a fish in a basket and, when he missed the fish, would know that he had reached the right place. Accordingly Moses and Joshua set forth, arrived at the rock, forgot all about the fish, and fared onward. At length Moses became hungry, bethought him of the fish, and told Joshua to bring it. Joshua had to admit

---

[1] MPC, Bk. ii. cc. 39–41.

that he had forgotten all about it. The fish in the meantime had
made its way to the sea in some marvellous manner, as Muhammad
says. Moses and Joshua therefore returned to the rock, where
they met one of God's servants who by his proceedings proved his
superiority in understanding. He is identified by Muhammadans
with the prophet Al Khidr, known from the hue of his raiment as
" The Green Prophet," and the friend of the Faithful in their distress. He is familiar to readers of the *Arabian Nights*, and is a
curious development of the reprobate cook, Andreas, of the Pseudo-
Callisthenes.[1]

The angel Isráfíl, whose introduction into Firdausí's account is
another sign of his indebtedness to Arabic sources, is one of the
four archangels and the sounder of the Trump of Doom which will
slay all creatures, himself included, after which the general
Resurrection will ensue.[2]

§ 30. The legend of the iron gates built by Alexander in the
Caucasus to exclude from the civilized world the savage tribes of
the North is absent in branch A of the Pseudo-Callisthenes, in
the Latin version of Julius Valerius, and in the Syriac version.
It is found, however, in branches B and C.[3] Thence the account
passed into the Christian Legend of Alexander and thence into
the poem of Jacob of Sarúg and the Kurán.[4] In the latter the
passage is as follows :—" Then followed he (*i.e.* Zú-'l-karnain) a
route until he came between the two mountains, beneath which
he found a people who scarce understood a language. They said :—
' O Dhoulkarnain ! verily, Gog and Magog waste this land ; shall
we then pay thee tribute, so thou build a rampart between us and
them ? ' He said, ' Better *than your tribute* is the might wherewith my Lord hath strengthened me ; but help me strenuously,
and I will set a barrier between you and them. Bring me blocks
of iron '—until when it filled the space between the mountain
sides—' Ply,' said he, ' your bellows '—until when he had made
it red with heat (fire) he said,—' Bring me molten brass that I
may pour upon it.' And Gog and Magog were not able to scale
it, neither were they able to dig through it." [5]

Naturally this account appealed to the commentators on the
Kurán and to Arabic historians, and as embellished by them provided the material for Firdausí's picturesque version. Tabarí,
for instance, compares the promiscuity of the excluded races to
that of beasts, speaks of their sleeping on one ear and covering

---

[1] See on the story of the fish in the Kurán and Al Khidr, SK, ii. 116
seq., and *notes ;* LAN, i. 22, 233, ii. 420.

[2] LAN, i. 30.   [3] MPC, iii. 26 (C), 29 (B).

[4] See p. 15.   [5] RK, p. 222.

themselves with the other, and as having a thousand children each [1]—traits found in the Sháhnáma.[2] The word used in that poem for the monsters whereon Yájúj and Májúj are said to batten is " tinnín "—the same as that variously translated in the Old Testament R.V., as sea-monster,[3] dragon,[4] and serpent.[5]

It is a question as to which of the passes through the Caucasus[6] Sikandar's barrier is to be referred. The most probable, because the most exposed, is the one between the range and the Caspian, but· the description in the text, and still more in the older authorities, which describe the wall as being built .from mountain to mountain, seems to favour the pass of Dariel, where the road runs through vertical walls of rock nearly 6000 feet high.

The method of vitrifying fortifications by means of heat was known in ancient times, and was used in the new world as well as the old. The operation is said to be not difficult if the proper rocks are used for the purpose, some of the primaries fusing easily when exposed to the heat of wood-fires. There are stated to be some fifty examples of such vitrified forts in Scotland alone.[7]

§ 31. We have had already a version of the account of the corpse in the palace of jewels in § 27.

The speaking trees of the sun and moon are found in all the branches of the Pseudo-Callisthenes, in A as part of the contents of a letter from Alexander to Aristotle, and in B and C as part of the narrative.[8] They occur also in the Syriac version[9] and in Julius Valerius. The trees, which in the above versions are described as resembling cypresses, seem akin to those of the riddle propounded by the archimages to Zál.[10] In fact it is not improbable that the riddle was suggested by this passage in the Romance of Alexander. Other passages in the Sháhnáma may have been suggested similarly, the wonders, for instance, seen by Kai Khusrau during his voyage in pursuit of Afrásiyáb,[11] and the account of Asfandiyár, whom Persian tradition may have liked to regard as forestalling Sikandar, wandered over the whole world and reached the Gloom.[12] In the same chapter of the Syriac version as that mentioned above we have the account of another solar tree, corresponding to a passage in the Pseudo-Callisthenes:[13]—

" From thence we set out again and came to a river (the ocean-

---

[1] ZT, i. 521. [2] See p. 163. [3] Gen. i. 21; Job vii. 12.
[4] Ps. lxxiv. 13. [5] Id. xci. 13. [6] Cf. Vol. i. p. 16.
[7] See the article on " Vitrified Forts " in Ency. Brit., 11th ed.
[8] MPC, iii. 17, and note. [9] BHA, iii. 7.
[10] See Vol. i. p. 308 seq. [11] Id. iv. 245.
[12] Id. v. 76. [13] BHA, p. 100; MPC, p. 88.

stream ?). And upon the bank of the river there was a tree, which grew and increased from dawn until the sixth hour, and from the sixth hour until evening it diminished in height until there was nothing to be seen of it. Its smell was very pleasant. . . ." In Zál's riddle the sun only was taken into consideration. In Sikandar's case the tree has a double trunk to provide for the moon as well. The male trunk (the sun) speaks by day, the female (the moon) by night. Much has been written about these trees, but the allegory seems fairly obvious.

§ 32. Sikandar's expedition to Chín and his dealings with the Faghfúr are extant only in the Syriac version of the Pseudo-Callisthenes, whence it passed into the Arabic as Dínawarí's account, which follows the Syriac closely, shows.[1] Firdausí's is closer still and agrees with the Syriac in making the Faghfúr, though conscious of his power, fall in with Sikandar's wishes through sheer love of peace—a point omitted by Dínawarí.[2] This is the third occasion on which Alexander is represented as going as his own ambassador[3]—a notion originating no doubt with the Egyptian author of the Pseudo-Callisthenes.

§ 33. According to Firdausí's version, this is the third time that Sikandar goes to Hind. Historically, after the defeat of Porus, Alexander had some trouble with that king's nephew, who, after having sent ambassadors to Alexander out of enmity towards his uncle, became disaffected when he found that Porus was held in such great honour by his conqueror.[4] Part of Alexander's army, under Craterus, returned from India by way of Nímrúz.

§ 34. This has some correspondence with the Pseudo-Callisthenes, Bk. III. ch. 28, and with the Syriac version, Bk. III. ch. 18. In the former the priest of the sun is described as being an Ethiop, and seems to reappear in the Gúsh-bistár of the Sháhnáma. We have had Gúsh-bistárs already, in fact if not in name in Firdausí's description of the races excluded by Sikandar's barrier—

> " They sleep upon one ear,
> And use the other as a coverlet." [5]

In this connexion the following passage is of interest : " The Enôtokoitai are called in Sanscrit *Karnaprávaramás*, and are frequently referred to in the great epic poems—*e.g. Mahábh*. II. 1170, 1875. The opinion was universally prevalent among the

---

[1] NAR, p. 40; BHA, p. 109 seq.   [2] *Id. note.*

[3] Or the fourth if we include his visit to the city of Porus, which is not mentioned in the Sháhnáma. See p. 64.

[4] See p. 64.   [5] *Id.* p. 163.

Indians that barbarous tribes had large ears. . . . "It is easy," says Wheeler (*Hist. Ind.*, Vol. iii. p. 179), "for any one con versant with India to point out the origin of many of the so-called fables. . . . Men do not have ears hanging down to their feet, but both men and women will occasionally elongate their ears after a very extraordinary fashion by thrusting articles through the lobe. . . . If there was one story more than another which excited the wrath of Strabo, it was that of a people whose ears hung down to their feet. Yet the story is still current in Hindustán. Bábu Johari Dás says:—' An old woman once told me that her husband, a sepoy in the British army, had seen a people who slept on one ear, and covered themselves with the other.' (*Domestic Manners and Customs of the Hindus*, Banáras, 1860.) The story may be referred to the Himálayas. Fitch, who travelled in India about 1585, says that a people in Bhután had ears a span long." [1]

For the Ichthyophagi see p. 69 *seq.*

§ 35. The correspondence with Aristotle with regard to the succession is of course an Oriental addition which came to Firdausí through the Arabic. Dínawarí has it to the same effect, the chief difference being that he makes the matter the subject of an interview between Alexander and Aristotle at Jerusalem where, according to him, the former died.[2] The device was intended to account for the long interval—five centuries and a half—that separated the last of the Kaiánians (Sikandar) from the first of the Sásánians (Ardshír Pápakán). The Persians made it out to be much shorter.[3]

The prodigious birth that occurred on Sikandar's arrival at Babylon is described in the Pseudo-Callisthenes, Bk. III. ch. 30, in the Latin Version of Julius Valerius, and in the Syriac, Bk. III. ch. 19.

§ 36. The version of Alexander's will in the Pseudo-Callisthenes, Bk. III. ch. 33, is longest in codex A, which unfortunately is much mutilated. The corresponding passage in the Syriac version is Bk. III. ch. 22, and this agrees with Firdausí's in the following points—the request to his mother not to grieve, the instruction to the chiefs to honour her, the gift of the kingdom of Macedonia (of Rúm in Firdausí) to the son of Rúshanak, if she shall have one, and the direction that his (Sikandar's) body shall be laid in a golden coffin filled with honey, and conveyed for interment to Egypt. Most of the provisions of the will as given in the Greek and Syriac would have little or no interest for later

---

[1] MCAI, p. 75, *note; cf.* AM, p. 275.　　[2] NAR, 41.　　[3] See p. 193.

Persian or Arabic writers, or for Firdausí himself, and naturally are lacking in the Sháhnáma.

§ 37. This corresponds with the Pseudo-Callisthenes, Bk. III. ch. 32, 34, and with the Syriac version, Bk. III. ch. 21, but the latter omits the dispute of the Greeks and Persians over the disposal of Alexander's body. According to the Greek version the oracle of the Babylonian Zeus was consulted, by whose direction the corpse was conveyed to Memphis whence, at the instigation of the high priest of that city, it was taken to Alexandria and there buried. According to Firdausí the oracle was consulted at a place called Khurm, a word which means "vapour" or "exhalation." Similar emanations are said to have existed at Delphi

Alexander died at Babylon on June 13th B.C. 323. His death was no doubt a natural one, the result of a fever, but it gave rise to a legend, referred to by Arrian only to be rejected,[1] that poison was employed for the purpose by Antipater who, fearing that his position as regent in Macedonia had been undermined by the intrigues of Olympias, sent his son Cassander to bring about the death of his master. Cassander found a willing instrument in Iollas, Alexander's cup-bearer, who had injuries of his own to avenge, and the fatal draught was administered at a banquet. The Pseudo-Callisthenes repeats the story,[2] and it appears in the Syriac and Ethiopic versions,[3] but not in the Sháhnáma.

§ 38. The sentences of the sages over the corpse of Sikandar are not in the Pseudo-Callisthenes or in the Syriac version of it. They are an Oriental addition, and Mas'údí gives another version of them.[4]

§ 39. Alexander's burial at Alexandria of course is historical. His mother, according to Mas'údí, removed the corpse from its golden coffin, lest the cupidity of future kings should be aroused and the tomb desecrated. Mas'údí, who spent some of his last years in Egypt, and died about A.D. 956, states that a pedestal of white and other coloured marbles, and known as the tomb of Alexander, was to be seen at Alexandria in A.D. 943–944.[5] S. Chrysostom, however, says that the tomb was destroyed in his time (A.D. 345–407), and the annual observance at Alexandria of the day of Alexander's death abolished.[6] Perhaps there may have been some restoration of the tomb by the Arabs, to whom the personality of Alexander was of interest,[7] after their conquest of the city in the middle of the seventh century A.D.

---

[1] DAA, vii. 27.   [2] MPC, iii. 31.
[3] BHA, Bk. iii. c. 20; BLEA, p. 339.   [4] MM, ii. 251; NAR, p. 48.
[5] Id. 259.   [6] MPC, p. xxvi.   [7] See p. 15.

Firdausí says that Sikandar built ten cities. In the Pseudo-Callisthenes the number is twelve or thirteen,[1] thirteen in the Syriac version,[2] and twelve in the Ethiopic.[3] One at least of them has not become a brake of thorns, and the Romance of Alexander, which there first took literary form, has done more to extend his fame and make his name a household word than all the sober histories of him ever written.

To conclude then, in the three reigns of Dáráb, Dárá, and Sikandar, taken collectively, we have the Persian version of the Pseudo-Callisthenes which, if it does not possess a complete historical skeleton, has at least a historical backbone, some of the vertebræ of which reappear in the Sháhnáma—*e.g.* Sikandar's invasion of Írán, the defeat and death of Darius, Sikandar's accession to the throne of Írán, his marriage with an Oriental princess, his invasion of India, his defeat of Porus and inter-.course with Indian sages, his return to Írán, his death at Babylon, and interment at Alexandria. Of the elements introduced into the Pseudo-Callisthenes by its Egyptian author the Persian version reproduces two—the device of Sikandar going as his own ambassador, and the story of Kaidáfa. Of Persian and Arabic substitutions and additions, not appearing in versions of the Pseudo-Callisthenes other than the Persian, the most important are the account of the birth of Sikandar, his address to the chiefs on his accession to the Iránian throne, and his correspondence with Aristotle as to the succession. The purely Arabic are the story of Kaid, the pilgrimage to the Kaaba, the interview with the angel Isráfíl, and the sentences of the sages at Sikandar's interment.

The appended diagram may help to show the provenance of the Persian version of the Pseudo-Callisthenes.

---

[1] MPC, 151, *note.*   [2] BHA, Bk. iii. c. 24.   [3] BLEA, p. 351.

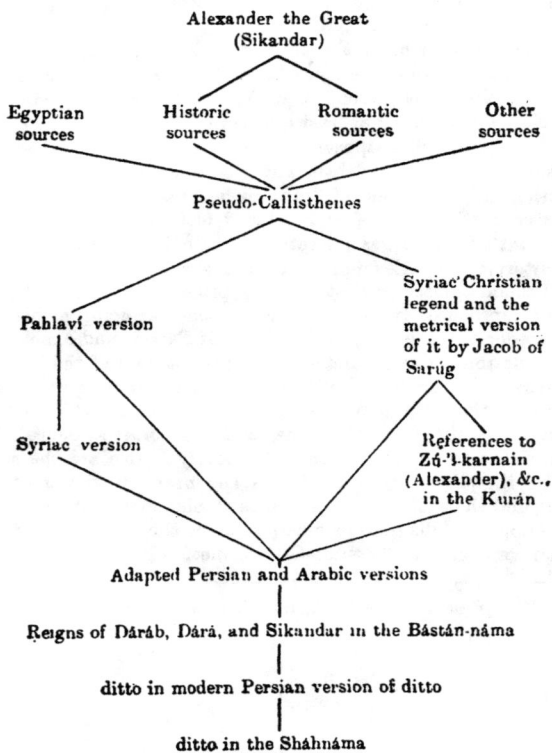

§ 1

How Sikandar sat upon the Throne of Írán

When seated on the throne, Sikandar said :—   C 1286
" Be wisdom wedded to the minds of kings,
For God is all-prevailing in the world,
And wicked is the world-lord that doth fear
Not Him.   Our good and ill beyond all doubt
Will pass and not escape time's clutch.   Whoever
Shall come to this our court and shall appeal
For justice to ourselves against ourselves,
At audience-time or midnight, shall receive
An answer to his plaint, for in that God,
Who giveth victory, hath granted us
The Grace and oped the door of conquering fortune,
My subjects all on mountain and on waste,
In city and at sea, shall share therein.
We do not ask for tribute from the world
For five years, saving from the man that saith :—
'Sikandar's peer am I.'   We will bestow
Much wealth on mendicants, but ask not aught
From him that hath."
                         At these his gracious words,
And at this union of his heart with justice,
There went up a thanksgiving from Írán
To that just-dealing monarch of the earth,
And then the assembly scattered, but the king
Sat on with his advisers, counselling.

§ 2

How Sikandar wrote to Dílárái and Rúshanak, the Wife and
Daughter of Dárá, touching the Nuptials of Rúshanak

Sikandar ordered that a scribe should come,
And called for reed of Rúm and silk of Chín.

The scribe, when he had made the kex a pen
Indited this epistle to the mother
Of Rúshanak: "The guerdon of the good
God grant to thee and mind-peace after pain.

C. 1287 I wrote to thee erewhile with more advice
Than is contained herein. What time the days
Of him who was thy spouse had reached their close,
And he was murdered by a servant's hand,
I buried him with royal obsequies,
And have accomplished all the days of mourning.
Oft-times before the war I sued for peace,
But he refused because his time had come.
His very foemen sorrowed for his blood.
May God receive him into Paradise,
The Just One give him place among the Saints,
And to his foes the bane of arrow-points.
None maketh shift to scape death's clutch; 'tis like
An autumn-blast, and we are as the leaves.
Now ye have all the world at your disposal.
Not few bear witness to Dárá's last wish,
How he gave Rúshanak to me, and said:—
'Thou hast no equal to her in thy bower.'
So send her to me, and that presently,
Escorted by her guardians and her slaves,
And by the chiefs and nobles of Írán,
To bring the light upon my darkling soul.
Make Ispahán¹ thine own as in the past,
Send out intelligencers everywhere,
And keep in office those just, modest men
Appointed by Dárá, son of Dáráb.
If ye would live not there choose where ye will,
The cities of Írán are all before you;
But be ye reconciled to me in heart,
And give me in the world the name Dárá."
  He wrote a letter too to Rúshanak,

¹ The text has the Arabic form Isfahán.

And made the pen's point eloquent. He first
Gave praise to God, the Ruler of the world,
The Wise, the All-sustainer ; then he said :—
" The stock of kings begetteth but men pious,
Attractive, well-advised, refined, and modest,
Men eloquent of speech and soft of voice.
Thy father gave thee to me ; then he died,
And bare away with him a goodly name.
When thou arrivest hither, and beholdest
My bower and palace, thou shalt be my queen,
Chief consort, the adornment of my throne,
The lustre of my Grace, my name, and fortune.
A letter have we written to thy mother
To bid her send thee hither in a fashion
Befitting issue of the king of kings,
And with an archimage of Ispahán
Preceding thee, with servants of the crown,
With elephants and litters, and with her
Who gave thee milk and honey.   Dwell within
Our house with joy—chief lady of the bower.
Now be high heaven circling to thy will,
Thy person far from foe and far from harm."
    Came, swift as flying dust-cloud, one well versed
In wisdom, and the world's king's words rehearsed.

§ 3

How Dilárái answered the Letter of Sikandar

When Dilárái heard this she heaved a sigh,   C. 1288.
And weeping for Dárá in tears of blood,
So that the dust beneath was saturate,
Called for a scribe and wrote a fair response
In well instructed terms and well inspired.
She first gave praises to the Omnipotent,
The Lord of counsel, peace, and excellence,

Then: " From the process of revolving heaven
Whence are strife, peace, and love, we used to ask
All Grace upon Dárá's behalf and made
His name the jewel of our tongues; but since
His day is over, and he is enthroned
Upon a coffin-board, it is for thee,
And thee alone, that I ask blessings, might,
With triumph, kingship, and the world's obedience:
I ask it openly without reserve,
For I have heard (may heaven joy in thy soul!)
What courteously thou hast conveyed to me
About the obsequies of Sháh Dárá,
How Máhiyár was gibbeted and how
Malevolent Jánúsiyár was punished.
Brief is his life that murdereth his master.
Thou hast sought peace, too, and passed many a day
In counsel.   Service is not for the Sháhs,
And none expecteth thraldom in the great.
Thou'rt in Dárá's place, who was king of kings,
And as the Sun hath set thou art our Moon.
Since he that was the monarch of the age
Chose thee not one will dare transgress his rede.
Next as to what he said of Rúshanak,
That wish of his which made our heart rejoice:
She is thine handmaid, and we are thy slaves;
We bow our heads to thy command and will.
She sendeth greetings and hath writ to thee
A letter like the garth of Paradise.
We have, moreover, written to the magnates,
The frontier-chieftains and the men of war,
That thy commands are as Dárá's commands,
And none will swerve from fealty to thee."
    She gave the envoy purses, slaves, and treasures
Of all kinds.   When that Rúman reached Sikandar,
And told what he had seen and heard of court, ·
Of precedents obtaining, and of throne,

Whereon thou hadst declared: "The Sháh still liveth"
Sikandar was rejoiced at what was said,
And placed the crown in peace upon his head.

§ 4

How Sikandar sent his Mother, Náhíd, to fetch Rúshanak,
and how he Married her

He called his mother from 'Ammúriya,[1]   C. 1289
Told her upon her coming what Dárá
Had said, and added: "Go to Dilárái,
And enter into gracious intercourse
With her, see Rúshanak within the bower,
And, having seen her, greet her on my part,
Take her a bracelet, earrings, torque, and crown
Of royal gems, a hundred mules with loads
Of tapestries and furthermore ten camels
With gold brocade of Rúm, and place withal
In purses thirty thousand in dínárs
Out of the treasury by way of largess,
And take with thee three hundred Rúman damsels,
Or more if more are needed.   Give each one
A goblet worthy of a queen's fair handmaid;
Take servants to escort thee and forgo
No circumstance of royal etiquette."
    The mother of the Sháh, as he commanded,
Made ready and set off upon her journey,
With her interpreters escorting her—
Ten of the honey-tongued philosophers.
Now as she drew anigh to Ispahán
A crowd of nobles went to give her welcome,
While Dilárái came forward from the palace,
She and the magnates, as their custom was,
And gave such largess in the court that treasure

---

[1] *Cf.* p. 23 and *note.*

And money grew misprized.   They held a conclave
Of counsellors within the palace; all
The chiefs attended: Dilárái the while
Prepared such wedding-gear that the bázárs
Looked busy everywhere, and league-long files
Of camels carried stuffs for clothes and carpets,
For hangings and for tapestries inwoven
With gold and silver thread, and diverse-hued.
There were such Arab steeds with golden bridles,
Such Indian scimitars with golden scabbards,
Surtouts and morions and bards withal,
With golden sparths and maces ponderous,
With stuffs for raiment cut or in the piece,
That no one in the world e'er looked on more;
Such aloe-wood, gris-amber, and pure musk,
As gave to enemies good cause to writhe.
They requisitioned servants from the palace,
And made them ready forty golden litters.
In one of them with parasol and slaves
Sat Rúshanak rejoicing.   From the halls
Of Dilárái, for half the route, the way
Was all gold, jewels, horses, and attendants.
They raised triumphal arches in the cities;
All lips were smiling, all hearts full.   They showered
Drachms on the bride's brocaded parasol,
And mingled overhead musk and dínárs.
   When that Moon reached the Sháh's own bower
      Sikandar
Much scanned her stately form and goodly face:
Thou hadst said: "Wisdom nurtured her on love."
Whenas her mother set her on the throne
Of gold he poured out all his soul to her,
And passed a se'nnight in her company,
Conversing much with her, observed her shrewdly,
And saw in her but majesty and meekness,
Discretion, modesty, and fair behaviour,

C. 1290

So that his heart was joined to her in love.
Then all the paladins throughout Írán
Called blessings down on him as Sháh, and brought
Great gifts of gold and royal jewelry,
While justice o'er the world's whole face was spread,
And everywhere the waste inhabited.

§ 5

*How Kaid of Hind had a Dream, and how
Mihrán interpreted it*

A speaker of the tongue of days of old
A tale that thou wilt muse to hear thus told:—
There was in Hind a monarch, Kaid by name,
Whose sole pursuit was knowledge and advice;
He had a sage's heart, a prince's brain,
King's bearing and the Grace of archimages.
He dreamed a dream ten nights successively—
A portent: mark it well. The men of learning
In Hindústán, the mighty both in word
And lore, the sages and the counsellors,
Met at his bidding, and he told his dreams
At large without reserve; but every heart
Was full of deep concern, each visage wan,
For there was none that could interpret them.
Then said a sage to Kaid: "O sovereign,
Memorial of the great and man of wisdom!
There is a famous one by name Mihrán,
Who hath attained his fill of earthly lore.
He will not sleep or rest him in a city,
And liveth but with cattle of the field,
Subsisting on the herbs upon the mountains,
And not accounting us as fellow-men;
His home is with the onager and deer,
Apart from habitation and mankind;

Naught in the world doth injure him; devout
Is he, and of high fortune."
                                        To the sage
Thus said king Kaid: "One must not overlook
This virtuous man."
                            Moved by Mihrán's renown
He mounted then and there upon his steed,
While, lest he should grow downcast, men of lore
Escorted him.   The monarch reached Mihrán,
Saluted courteously the sage, and said:—
"Thou devotee who with the mountain-sheep
Inhabitest the heights! hear thou with care,
And then interpret wisely, these my dreams:
Know that one night, O wise and holy man!
I slept in peace, unfrighted, undismayed,
No care at heart, no impulse in my head,
And in my chamber there was none with me.
Night's noon had passed, but dawn was not.   I saw
A habitation like a vasty palace;
Therein a huge, fierce elephant.   The dwelling
Showed doorless, but had one strait aperture
Wherethrough that savage elephant would pass
Uninjured by the straitness; its black bulk
Would pass therethrough, but leave its trunk behind.
Next night I saw the throne devoid of lord
Fair-fortuned, but upon the ivory seat
Sat one who donned the heart-delighting crown.
The third night came; I made me haste to sleep,
And dreamed that I beheld a goodly kerchief
Whereat four men tugged till their cheeks turned blue
With pulling, yet the kerchief was not rent,
Nor were the men fordone.   Upon the fourth night
I saw, illustrious sage! a man athirst
Beside a stream.   O'er him a fish kept pouring
The water, yet his droughty head was dry
Although the water followed as he moved!

How read'st thou this, good friend ? Upon the fifth night
My mind dreamed of a city by the water.
The citizens though blind seemed none the worse,
For thou hadst said : 'The whole place is afire
With liberality and trafficking !'
Upon the sixth night, honoured lord ! I saw
A city, all whose citizens were sick,
And went to question those in health, who first,
Preventing them, inquired : 'How came ye thus
With body aching and with heart o'ercharged ?'
And then the sick, whose soul had reached their lips,   c. 1292
Sought of the healthy for a remedy.
When half the seventh night had passed I saw
A horse that grazed at will upon the plain ;
It had two fore, two hind, feet, and two heads,
And cropped the grass off quickly with its teeth.
It grazed on both sides with its double mouth,
And yet its body was without a vent !
I saw upon the eighth night, holy man !
Three vases on the ground set all a-row,
Two filled with water but the central empty,
And dry for many a year.   Two worthies tried
To fill it from the others whose contents
Were minished not by pouring while the dry
Remained with lip unmoistened.   On the ninth night
I dreamed that I beheld a cow reposing
'Mid grass and water in the sun.   A calf,
Small, gaunt, and wizened, with lack-lustre face,
Was standing just before her, and she sucked it !
The cow was lusty and the calf was weak.
If thou wilt lend thine ear to my tenth dream
Thou wilt not grow aweary ere I end.
Upon a spacious plain I saw a spring
With streams and dykes about it.   All the champaign
Was watered yet the fountain-head was dry.
I prithee answer and reveal the future."

Mihrán, when he had heard this thing from Kaid,
Said : " Be not sick at heart about this dream ;
Thy fame shall fail not, ill not reach this realm.
Sikandar will lead forth a mighty host,
The chosen chieftains of Írán and Rúm,
And, if thou wouldst still rule, consort with wisdom,
And fight him not. Four things thou hast whose
    equals
None, great or small, e'er saw. One is thy daughter,
Like Paradise above, through whom thy crown
Is bright on earth ; the next thy privy sage,
Who telleth thee the secrets of the world ;
The third thy worthy leech, most famed of doctors ;
The fourth a cup wherein, if thou pour water,
That water will not heat for sun or fire,
No drinking minish it. These will defeat
All his endeavours, for when he shall come
Confide in these, and not in war, if thou
Wouldst have him gone betimes. Thou canst not face
His troops, his strategy, his realm, and treasure.
As wisely I advise thee so will I
Interpret these thy dreams. Thou didst behold

C. 1293
A dwelling and strait aperture wherethrough
Passed elephant but left its trunk behind.
Now hear the rede of the interpreter.
Know that this dwelling imageth the world,
The elephant a thankless king, unjust,
False in his words, and royal but in name,
A man of mean heart and of feeble body,
Keen in his greed and gloomy in his soul.
At length, when he shall pass away, his name
Abideth in dishonour in the end.
Thy second dream concerning crown and throne,
Which one man voided and another gained,
Illustrateth that this inconstant world
Removeth one and speedeth up another.

As for thy third dream of that goodly kerchief,
Clutched by four righteous men yet never rent
Though they that tugged thereat were never weary :
Hereafter there will come a man renowned
Forth from the desert of spear-wielding horsemen,
A holy, virtuous man by whom the Faith
Of God will come to be four-square, and, know,
'Tis imaged by that kerchief, while the four
That tug thereat tug in safe-guarding it.
One Faith is the Dihkán's who worshippeth
The Fire, and taketh not the sacred twigs
Save with a muttered prayer.[1]   Another one
Is that of Moses, which thou call'st the Jew's,
Who saith : ' None other should be praised ' ; another
That of Yúnán,[2] a good Faith making just
The great king's[3] heart ; and, fourth, the Arabian,
Pure and exalting from the dust the prudent.
Four parties thus assuming to be guardians
Tug at the kerchief in their several ways,
And, as they pull against each other thus,
Antagonize for their religion's sake.
Then, fourthly, for the droughty man who shunned
Sweet water which a fish threw after him :
A time will come when holy men will be,
Just like that fish, despised as having drunk
Of wisdom's stream ; but evil-doers' heads
Will be exalted to the Pleiades.
When one shall call the thirsty to the water
None wisely will respond, but all will shun
The wisdom-seeker and combine to curse him.
In thy fifth dream thou sawest a busy city.
The burghers spent their lives in feasting, largess,
And trafficking, but ' Fortune,' thou hadst said,

---

[1] See Vol. i. pp. 80, 81 *s.v. Dihkán, Báj,* and *Barsam.*
[2] *I.e.* Javan, the son of Japheth and the progenitor of the Greeks.
[3] Sikandar.

'Had sewn their eyes up so that none could see
C. 1294 Another.' This referreth to a time
When wise men will be slaves to ignorant,
Who will despise the erudite and these,
Their tree of wisdom fruiting not for them,
Will laud, and openly commend, the witless,
Though conscious of their own hypocrisy,
And that such service is inglorious.
As for the sixth dream, when the ailing sick
All went to question those in health : a time
Will come wherein the wretched mendicant
Will be misprizèd in the rich man's eyes,
And turn in his resourcelessness to any
Possessed of goods, who will not give him aught,
So that he will become a wageless servant,
Or else a slave without the purchasing.
As for the ventless and two-headed steed
Of thy seventh dream : a time will come when men
Will joy in wealth and never have enough.
The beggar, student, and celebrity
Will get no share from them, for they will think
Of no one save themselves and help not any.
As to thine eighth dream of two vases brimming,
And one left wholly void, two vases filled
With lucid water, and the middle one
All dry and moistureless : a time will come
Wherein the poor will grow so weak and wretched
That, though the clouds of springtide, charged with
        showers,
Shall hide the sunshine from the mendicant,
Those very showers not e'en then will descend
On him, and he will be heart-stricken.   The rich
Will lavish gifts among themselves and bandy
Their honied compliments while beggars go
With droughty lips and so pass day to night.
As for the ninth wherein a lusty cow

Sucked its lean calf: when Saturn entereth Libra
The world will be beneath the strong arm, poor
And sick fare ill, and yet the well-to-do
Will still exact from them, will never open
Their own hoards, nor abate the others' travail.
In thy tenth dream thou sawest a fountain dry,
With waters all about it savouring musk,
Yet no clear stream of water bubbled forth,
And sped to mingle with those other waters.[1]
A time is coming when the world will have
A king that is devoid of understanding,
A king whose dark soul will be full of dudgeon,
The whole world gloom beneath his tyranny,
And never good be found among his treasures.
He ever will be gathering fresh hosts
To win his crown new fame, but in the end
This monarch and his hosts will pass away,
And there will be a change of dynasty.
But our time is the epoch of Sikandar,
Who is the crown upon the heads of nobles.
Upon his coming give him these four things;[2]
Methinketh not that he will ask for more,
But, when thou dost content him, pass thee by,
For he is diligent to learn and wise."

   Kaid, having heard the matter from Mihrán,
Regained the vigour of his former years,
Came, kissed the sage's head and eyes, and went
His ways triumphant, happy, and content.

C. 1295

---

[1] Perhaps this may mean: "I have patrons among the nobles but Mahmúd is obdurate." *Cf.* what follows and Vol. i. p. 33.
[2] *I.e.* the Four Wonders. *Cf.* p. 94.

§ 6

How Sikandar marched against Kaid of Hind and wrote a Letter to him

Now when Sikandar had surveyed Írán,
And knew that crown and throne were his, he led
His host toward Kaid of Hind and, road or none,
Pursued his march, while as he went along
The people of the cities on his way
Unbarred their gates to him.   In all that coast
He found none worthy to be called a man,
And raised his helm o'er Venus.   On approaching
The mighty city, named by valiant Kaid
Mílád, they called a scribe and seated him
Before Sikandar who, like lion lusting
For quarry, wrote to Kaid : "This from Sikandar
The mighty and victorious, the lord
Of scimitar, of crown, and belt."
                                         The letter
Began with praises of the man that laveth
His heart with knowledge, "for in his desire
To eat the fruitage of his toils he chooseth
The easiest course, adoreth holy God,
And trusteth, feareth, reverenceth Him,
While knowing that we top the throne and are
The Shadow of the all-conquering Lord.   Now I
Have written thee a letter to enlighten
Thy darkling mind ; so when thy scribe shall read it
Lay it not out before thee and consider,
But, if it come by night, wait not for day,
And do my will forthwith.   If thou shalt slight
My words so will not I, but trample down
Beneath my feet thy throne and head and crown."

§ 7

How Kaid of Hind answered Sikandar's Letter and an-
nounced the Sending of the Four Wonders

Now when this letter came to Kaid of Hind   C. 1296
He interviewed the great king's envoy, praised
And favoured him exceedingly, assigned him
In courtesy a seat upon the throne,
And said: " I joy to do the Sháh's behest,
And alway will be true to him; but still
That one so great as I am should set forward
So quickly and unreadily would please not
The Maker and the monarch of the earth."
   Then calling for a scribe, for pen of Chín,
And silk of Hind, he wrote at once an answer,
And decked it like the garth of Paradise.
He gave, first, praises to the Omnipotent,
The Lord of victory and time, the Lord
Both generous and just, the Lord of manhood,
Of sense and prowess; then: " The good man's head
Will turn not from the great, illustrious king,
Nor are we well advised in keeping aught
From him who hath the army, crown, and sword.
Four things have I that none else in the world
E'er hath possessed in public or in private,
And after me none will possess the like.
. These, if the Sháh shall bid me, I will send
To give new vigour to his heart and rule,
And afterward, if he commandeth me,
Will come and slave-like do him fealty."

§ 8

How Sikandar sent back the Messenger to receive the
Four Wonders

The envoy came as swiftly as the wind,
Told all that he had heard, and gave the letter.
Sikandar said to him : " Go to, return
To that famed man, and say : ' What things are these
That none e'er had in public or in private,
For we ourselves have seen whatever is,
And heaven will not create afresh ? ' "
                                        The envoy
Went from the presence, journeyed swift as fire,
And said to Kaid : " The Sháh is fain to know
What things they are that no one else possesseth,
For seeing is believing."
                          When he heard,
Kaid cleared the court and sat with his advisers
In council, set the envoy in his presence,
And courteously entreated him, then said :—
" I have within my bower a daughter such
That if the sun on high should gaze on her
'Twould gloom contrasted with my darling's face.
Her locks are lassos of one hue with pitch,
Milk savoureth on her lips, a cypress-stem
Is crooked to her, she scattereth pearls in speech,
Her looks and countenance make wisdom fly,
Yet 'tis the food of her discourse.   When silent
She is the soul of modesty, and none
Hath seen her peer in this age.   Sprung from chiefs,
And pious, she is chaste of heart and modest.
I have a cup which thou mayst fill with wine,
Or pour therein cold water, and although
Thou sat'st with boon-companions for ten years

C. 1297

The wine would fail not; whether wine or water
The cup affordeth thee, the marvel is:
No drinking draineth it. My third possession
Is this: a youthful leech who diagnoseth
Disease by making a uroscopy.
So long as he is at the court the Shâh
Will never ail; and, fourthly, I possess,
Though privily, a sage who will foretell
The Shâh all that will chance from circling sun
And shining moon."
                          The noble messenger
Withdrew, made wind his mate, came and informed
Sikandar, and the heart of the world-king
Bloomed like a rose. He said: "If what is spoken
Be true could this world purchase all the four?
Kaid will illume my dark soul if he send them.
His country 'neath my feet I will not tread,
But with this good will hie me home instead."

§ 9

*How Sikandar sent Ten[1] Sages with a Letter to inspect the
Four Wonders of Kaid of Hind*

The Shâh made choice of Rúmans learnèd, wise,
And well disposed, then wrote a letter all
Excuse and perfume, colour and device:—
"Ten trusty chiefs of mine, world-veteran,   C. 1298
And in my confidence, wise men and modest,
Endowed with Grace and counsel, shrewd observers,
Learned and directing, lo! I have dispatched thee:
They will not deviate from thy shrewd counsels.
Exhibit those four wonders unto them,
And suffer them to stay with thee awhile.
When I receive the letter of mine ancients,
Those men expert and erudite, to say:—

[1] Nine in P.

'The four things—those whose like none e'er beheld—
Have passed before our eyes,' I will indite
A patent drawn on silk to this effect:—
'Kaid, while he liveth, is the king of Hind.'"
    So those ten Rúman sages left Sikandar,
And sped to Kaid who, when he saw those chiefs,
Had much to ask of them and heard their answers,
Received them graciously and lodged them featly.
    Next day, when heaven grew pallid and the sun
Drew forth its sword of battle, they adorned,
Although the moon requireth no adornment,
The monarch's daughter, and within the palace
Set up, and decked with ornaments of Chín,
A golden throne whereon she sat sun-faced,
Outshining Venus in the sky.   The sages,
Those ancient men, fair-spoken and observant,
Drew near.   The monarch sent them to the bride,
As bade Sikandar, son of Failakús.
The ancients, seeing the king's daughter's face
Illumining the palace, crown, and throne,
Were lost in wonder and astonishment;
Feet failed them at the sight.   They stood stock-still,
Their tongues all busied with the praise of God,
Unable to withdraw or look elsewhere,
Till one arrived to call them, since they lingered,
Before the king, who said: "Why such delay?
The owner of that face is but a human,
Endowed with goodliness by every star."
    A Rúman answered: "None, O king! beholdeth
A picture like her in his halls; so now
We each of us will send the Sháh a letter
Describing somewhat of the lady's charms."
    They all sat down with paper, ink, and pens.
Each wrote what he had noted, covering all
The paper with his words; then from [1] Mílád

---

[1] Reading with P.

They sent in haste a horseman to Sikandar,
Who marvelled as he read, for every sage
Had written some description of the lady.
He wrote to them and said : "Ye have done well,
Ye ancients! ye have looked on Paradise.
Return with those four things and ask naught else.
When ye have given the patent unto Kaid
Make ready for the way and load the beasts.
No man henceforth shall do him injury,
For I have found him just, and that sufficeth."
    The envoy quitted that green country-side,
And to those Rúman ancients' presence hied.

C. 1299

§ 10

*How the Ten Sages brought the Daughter, the Cup, the
Leech, and the Sage, from Kaid of Hind to Sikandar*

Now when those sages heard their Sháh's reply,
Brought by the toilful cavalier, they went
Forth from their palace and approached king Kaid,
And his famed court.   The king of Hindústán,
When he had read the answer to his letter—
The message of the imperious world-aspirant—
Joyed to be free from trouble with Sikandar,
And chose withal a hundred men of Hind
Of honied tongue and eloquent, unlocked
Hoards not by him amassed, and chose therefrom
Crown, throne, and armlet, and of gems withal,
And raiment in the piece, all that was best.
They brought three hundred camel-loads of raiment,
And royal jewelry; ten of dínárs,
And five score all of drachms; there was withal
A splendid litter of green aloe-wood,
Inlaid with gold and gems.   Kaid placed gold thrones
Upon ten elephants and on another,

More splendidly caparisoned, the Beauty,
Who was escorted by the sage and leech,
And showered tears of blood. A magnate bare
The cup, whose wine made all the chiefs bemused.
When that Moon reached the royal women's house
There was a crown of black musk on her head;
She had let fall her tresses o'er her cheeks,
Like mail o'er cercis-blossom, and appeared
A slender cypress 'neath the full orbed moon.

C. 1300   To gaze was perilous. Her eyes were like
To twin narcissi grown in Paradise.
Thou wouldst have said: "She is compact of charms."
Sikandar gazed upon her stately form,
Her hair, her face, and all from head to foot,
And said: "Behold the Lustre of the world!"
While privily invoking benisons
Upon the All-just, the Maker of the sky,
Who had created such a form and face.
He gave command, and all the men of lore,
And understanding, in the host of Rúm
Sat by while he demanded her in marriage,
The which he solemnised with Christian rites,
And showered dínárs upon her from above
Out of his hoards till scarcely she could move.

§ 11

*How Sikandar tested the Sage, the Leech, and the Cup sent
by Kaid of Hind*

The matter of the Cypress-tree [1] achieved,
And an abode fit for her rank prepared,
The Shán was free to find out how the sage

---

[1] The daughter of Kaid.

Would come off in a strife of wits, and so
He sent a large bowl all abrim with ghee
To that redoubtable philosopher,
And said: "Anoint thy limbs herewith, loins, waist,
Breast, back, and neck withal, repose thyself
Till thou hast shaken off thy weariness,
Then fill for me my mind and brain with knowledge."
    The sage, when he beheld the ghee, observed :—
"This should not prove a mystery to me!"
    He placed a thousand needles in the bowl,
And then returned it to the sovereign,
Who, when he saw them, summoned privily
A smith and bade him melt them to an ingot,
And fashion out of it a disk.   Sikandar
Dispatched this to the sage who furbished it,
And sent back in the place of that dull iron
A mirror free from rust and luminous.
They took this to Sikandar in the night,
Who, saying naught, exposed it to the wet
Till it grew dark and dull; then he returned it,
And thus prolonged the riddle of the iron.
The sage refurbished it to brilliancy,
And sent it back forthwith, but first applied
That which would prove preservative from damp.
Sikandar, seeing, called to him the sage
And, greetings done, assigned to him a seat
Below the throne, then spake about the bowl
Of ghee to further test that famed man's wit,
Who said: "Ghee will not penetrate the frame.   C. 1301
Thou said'st: 'I pass the sages of the state
In knowledge.' I replied: 'O mighty Sháh!
A man that is both wise of heart and pure
Will like a needle pierce both feet and bones,
Or e'en a stone if one is in the way.'
I said in fact to thee: 'My goodly speech,
My heart and soul and prudent purposes

Make use of words still finer than a hair,
And thou hast not a heart more dense than iron.'
Thy answer to me was: 'In bygone years
My heart grew rusty in the midst of bloodshed.
How shall the gloom depart, for why should I
Continue thus distraught?' I answered thee:—
'I will refurbish by celestial wisdom
Thy heart if it becometh malcontent,
And when it shineth with a brilliant lustre
How shall it rust again?'"
     His goodly words
Found favour with the Sháh whose heart grew keener
By dint of the procedure of the sage.
He ordered that the treasurer should bring
A robe, gold, silver, and a vase of gems.
These they presented to the sage who said:—
"I have a privy jewel of mine own,
Which is both brighter and immune from foes,
And not, like wealth, the mate of Áhriman.
I need not hire a watchman for the night,
And when I go abroad I fear no thieves,
Since in the night-time knowledge is my warden,
And wisdom my soul's crown when it is waking,[1]
For wisdom, knowledge, right, are necessaries
Since error knocketh at the door of loss.
The Sháh will see that I have food and raiment
Enough for public and for private uses;
Why should I joy in superfluities,
And have to safeguard all this wealth? Command
To carry back these havings, and may wisdom
Direct thy soul."
    Sikandar mused at him,
And turned the matter o'er, then said: "The Lord
Of sun and moon will find me not in fault
In future since I have thy counsel, rede,

     [1] Order of couplets as in P.

And useful talk."

He bade the leech approach
That judged diseases by uroscopy,
And asked : " Who is the greatest sufferer
Whose pangs compel our tears ? "

The leech replied :—
" The glutton, one without restraint at table.
Excessive food conduceth not to health,
And great is he who maketh health his aim.
Now will I gather herbs from every side,
And will exhibit unto thee a medicine,
One that will keep thee sound ; no need to purge ; C. 1302
Thine appetites will greaten too, and when
Thou eatest much it will not injure thee.
Heed thou my skilled advice, then blood and brain
Will wax in thee, thou wilt grow strong of frame,
Thy heart will be as blithe as jocund spring.
'Twill bring back colour to thy face and make
Thy judgment sound in all, thy flowing locks
Shall turn not grey, not soon shalt thou despond."
  Sikandar said : " I have not seen or heard
Of any king thus favoured, but if thou
Produce this noble potion thou wilt be
My guide to good, and I with mine own soul
Will purchase thee.   The malice of thy foes
Shall harm thee not."

Sikandar got prepared
A robe of honour and fair gifts for him,
And made him chief among the learned physicians.
That suasive leech departed to the mountains
Without attendants.   With his ample knowledge
He could distinguish bane and antidote,
And, having gathered many mountain-herbs,
And put the worthless by, chose such as were
Medicinal, and out of these compounded
The needed potion.   With these mountain-simples

He purged the Sháh and kept him sound and whole,
So that for nights he slept not but enjoyed
Society, affected much the Fair,
And sought their soft embraces till he ailed,
Because he tendered not himself, and so
One day the leech came, by uroscopy
Detected signs of decadence, and told him :—
"Youths surely age by intercourse with women :
Methinketh that for three nights thou hast slept not;
Speak unto me and give me a reply."

    Howbeit Sikandar answered : "I am well:
None of the ills of life is troubling me."

    Yet still the approven leech of Hindústán
Would not admit the matter to be so,
But sought that night among his books, and mixed
A medicine against that decadence.
That night Sikandar had no lovely mate.
The leech, when morning came, found him alone,
And, having ended the uroscopy,
Flung down the potion, sat in high delight,
And, taking in his hand a goblet, bade
The board be spread and wine and minstrels ordered.

C. 1303   The Sháh inquired : "Why hast thou poured away
The draught that thou hadst mixed so carefully ?"

    He said : "Last night the world-lord sought no mate
But slept alone, and when thou sleepest thus
Thou needest, sire ! no draught."

                     Sikandar smiled,
Delighted with the leech, to whom he said :—
"Ne'er may this world lack Hind, for thou wouldst say
That all the leeches and astrologers
Flock thither."

             Calling for a purse of gold,
And for a sable steed whose reins were hung
With golden balls, he gave that skilled leech both,
And said : "Be honest rede thy tongue's companion."

Then bade he, and they brought the golden goblet
Brimmed with cold water. All folk drank thereof
From morn till bed-time as in revelry,
But all the drinking did not minish it.
Then to the sage the Sháh said: "Kaid hath not
His equal in the world, and from this time
No longer shall we speak of Hindústán,
But Jádústán,[1] as being Kaid's abode.
The people are no more than other folk
In looks but wonderful in tricks and magic!"
    Then said the Sháh to that philosopher:—
"This knowledge must not be concealed from us:
How is the water in the cup renewed?
Is it the stars or Indian jugglery?"
    "Despise not, sire! the cup," the sage replied,
"For they were many years in making it,
And labours underwent in that behoof.
From all the provinces the astrologers,
Where'er there was a master known to fame,
Assisted Kaid, when fashioning the cup,
Both day and night, and passed full many a day
In noting all the aspects of the stars.
Take thou the loadstone, that wherewith a man
Attracteth iron, as an illustration.
This cup by innate force attracteth water,
Receiving fresh additions from the sky.
It catcheth water to replace the waste
Too quickly for man's eyes to follow it."
    The Sháh, on hearing that wise man's discourse,
Approved thereof; he thought the words of profit.
Thus said he to the elders of Mílád:—
"I will observe the compact made with Kaid
In honour while I live, for he is one
Before whose presence other folk should stand.
Since I have gotten from him four such things

1 Sorcerer-land.

We will not ask for more."

Now afterward
Sikandar set the goods that he possessed,
With all the treasures that he had amassed,
C. 1304   And therewithal a hundred jewelled crowns,
Upon two hundred carriers and stored
All, with dínárs and jewels in the rough,
Upon a mountain.   When they vanished there
None saw again what was reposited ;
From that time forward no one e'er beheld
That treasure and the men that hoarded it.
Sikandar only knew where, hid from sight,
Were laid those treasures on the mountain-height.[1]

§ 12

How Sikandar led a Host against Fúr of Hind and
wrote a Letter to him

Sikandar swift as wind marched from Mílád,
Abandoning his treasures, reached Kannúj
And, having led his army near to Fúr,
Bade write to him a harsh and hostile letter
As from Sikandar, king of kings, the son
Of Failakús, the illuminer of knowledge,
Of weal and woe, to Fúr, the king of Hind,
High-starred, and chief of Sind.

First praised he God,
Who hath been and will be for ever.   Then :—
"With one whom He hath made victorious
Realm, crown, and throne will last, whom He despiseth
Will be still wretched, and the sun on high
Will shine not on him.   Surely thou hast heard
What in this darksome earth all holy God
Hath given to us of victory and fortune,

---

[1] Sikandar's method of hiding his treasures bears a suspicious
resemblance to that of Captains Kidd and Flint.

Grace, diadem, and throne of king of kings,
But not for long: our day will pass; another
Will come and be partaker of these fruits,
And so I strive to leave an honoured name
In this small circle compassed by the Moon.
When they deliver this possess thy soul,
Thine unenlightened soul, with what is right,
Exchange thy throne of greatness for thy steed,
Advise not with the priests, thy counsellors,
But ask immunity from us, and practise
No craft because the crafty labour long.
If, in thy pride and thine audacity,
Thou wilt not do my bidding thou shalt rue
Thy dallying when with my cavaliers .
I come to fight with thee."
　　　　　　　　When thus these words
Had been indited, and the scribe had done,
They sealed the letter with Sikandar's signet,
And for the journey chose a prudent envoy,
Who reached the court of Fúr and held discourse
At whiles of strife, at whiles of feast and revel.
They summoned to the king that man discreet,
And by the throne appointed him a seat.

§ 13

How Fúr answered the Letter of Sikandar

Bold Fúr, when he had read the letter, raged　　C. 1305
Against that famous magnate and forthwith
Wrote fiercely in reply, and set a tree
Within the garth of vengeance.　He began:—
" 'Tis ours to fear and reverence holy God.
We will not speak so many empty words;
The boaster is a man without resource.
Art thou so shameless as to summon me?

Is wisdom to thy mind so light a thing?
If Failakús on this wise wrote to Fúr
Do thou begin too and provoke a quarrel!
But 'tis Dárá who thus hath heartened thee,
Because of him revolving heaven was weary,
And when good fortune goeth from a race
They heed not the advice of counsellors.
Thy strife with Kaid was but a merry-make;
Thou thinkest kings thy prey. No such address
Or words proceeded from the ancient Kaians.
Fúr am I and the son of Fúr. We take
No thought of Cæsars. When Dárá asked help,
And I perceived his heart and fortune failing,
I sent him mighty elephants and gave him
Words of encouragement. When he was slain
By that slave's hand the Íránians' fortunes fell,
And when earth's face was franchised from Dárá
That trenchant bane became thine antidote.
Why lose thy head because bad ministers
Ill-treated him? Talk not of war so proudly,
Because with me it is another story.
Thou shalt behold my mighty elephants
And host, which bar the wind, confronting thee.
Thy whole aim is supremacy, thy nature
One rust with Áhriman. Do not thou sow
The seed of harshness in the world, but be
In fear of misadventure and the ills
Of fortune. In this letter 'twas my part
To seek thy welfare and instruct thy heart."

§ 14

How Sikandar arrayed his Host to fight with Fúr of Hind
and made iron Steeds and Riders filled with Naphtha

C. 1306 Forthwith Sikandar, when Fúr's answer reached him,
Chose from the host chiefs fit and enterprising,

Young but mature in wisdom, and led forth
To war against that Indian such an army
That all the earth seemed sea, and thou hadst said:—
"Sikandar is sole monarch in the world." .
But all those mountains, seas, and rugged paths
Quenched in the soldiers' hearts the flame of war
The troops were all aweary of a march
By roads so grievous, steep, and profitless.
Once at a stage they gathered round the Sháh
And said: "O Cæsar and the lord of Chín! -
Earth is not able to sustain thy host.
Not Fúr of Hind, not the Faghfúr himself,
Or king of Sind, will seek to fight with thee.
Why must thou bring disaster on thy troops
By this vile country and by such a road?
We see no sound steed left whereon to fight
With vigour, and if e'er the troops turn back
From warfare neither horse nor foot will find
The way. When we have triumphed hitherto
It hath been o'er an army of our foes,
But now we are opposed by seas and mountains,
And none of us is weary of his life.
Convert not all our glory into shame;
None hath made war with water and with rocks."
    The words displeased Sikandar, and in wrath
He frustrated their scheme. "Such words," thus said
        he,
"Befit but mutineers. What time I marched
From Rúm Íránward we beheld all garden
And settlement, our Rúman slain reached not
A hundred, and our costs were small. Írán
Is yours. What better could ye ask of God?
Ill came upon Dárá from his own slaves;
No one of you hath seen one weak or wounded!
I will proceed without you and set foot
Upon the Dragon's heart. Come what come may

Of fight and feast henceforth ye shall behold me
Abandon not for good my task with Fúr.
What time I quit him I will march to Rúm,
And by my valour overcome the land.

C. 1307

With God to aid me, and Íránian troops,
I ask not I a Rúman to befriend me."
    On seeing that their words enraged the Sháh
The troops sought to excuse themselves, and said :—
" We all are Cæsar's slaves, we only walk
The earth to do his hest, will strive, and when
Our horses fail will foot it to the field
Of strife. Though foes make earth sea with our blood,
And valleys into mountains with our fallen,
None in the day of fight shall see our backs
Though sea and mountain-crag contend with us.
We all are slaves, and it is thine to bid :
In thy calamities our lives are thine."
    Sikandar, hearing this, prepared fresh strife,
And chose a hundred thousand of Írán,
Equipped for war. Behind were Rúman captains,
All clad in mail, and stalwart warriors.
Thus forty thousand veteran cavaliers
Marched in support of the Íránians.
Succeeding these came mounted men world-taking,
And falchion-brandishers, from Misr. Then Cæsar
Chose from the men of Rúm, Misr, and Barbar
Twelve thousand cavaliers efficient, martial,
For battle eager all and all renowned,
So that with this array supporting him
The dales and plains seemed heights ! He took withal
Of readers of the stars and priests three score—
Wise men well known to fame and veteran—
To choose the days for battle.
                    When Fúr heard :—
" A host hath come" he picked his battle-field,
And all his troops assembled on the plain ;

The earth was mountain-like with elephants.
The army stretched four miles with troops behind
And elephants in front.
                    Now spies arrived
From Hind before the world-lord and informed him
At large of how the elephant contendeth
In warfare: "It will rout two miles of horse.
No cavalier will dare to face that beast,
Or, if he did so, ever come again,
Because its trunk is higher than the air,
And Saturn is its helper in the sky."
    They drew a picture of an elephant,
And showed it to Sikandar who commanded
That the philosophers of Rúm should model
One out of wax for him, and then inquired:—
"Who can propound a scheme to cope with such?"
    The sages held a session and devised
A plan in all its details. Then the Shah
Assembled all the master-smiths of Rúm,   C. 1308
Of Misr, and Pars, twelve hundred men in sum,
Who made a horse, with saddle and with rider
Complete, of iron, fastening the joints
With bolts and rivets. Horse and man were furbished.
They charged it with black naphtha, and then ran it
On wheels before the troops. At sight thereof
Sikandar was well pleased for, being wise,
He felt the gain thereof, and bade to make
A thousand such and more: who e'er beheld
On chargers dappled, chestnut, black, and grey
An iron host? The matter took the month,
And then the workmen rested from their labours.
Thus led they forth on wheels an iron host
That of all things resembled horsemen most.

§ 15

How the Host of Sikandar fought with the Host of Fúr,
how Fúr was slain by Sikandar, and how Sikandar
seated Sawurg upon the Throne of Fúr

Now when Sikandar was approaching Fúr,
And from afar one host beheld the other,
On both sides rose the shout and dust of battle,
And eager for the fray the warriors
Advanced.   They lit the naphtha in the steeds:
Fúr's troops were in dismay.   The naphtha blazed:
Fúr's troops recoiled because those steeds were iron,
Whereat the elephants, when their own trunks
Were scorched, fled likewise, and their drivers marvelled.
Thus all the Indian host and all those huge,
High-crested elephants were put to flight.
Sikandar like a raging blast pursued
The foe until the air turned indigo,
And opportunity for fight was over.
   The monarch with the Rúmans in full force
Dismounted 'twixt two mountains and sent scouts
On all the roads to guard his host from foes.
Now when the ingot of the sun's crown showed,
And all the world became as 'twere white crystal,
There rose a blare of trumpets and the sound
Of fife, of cornpipe, and of kettledrum.
Both hosts made ready for the fray and raised
Their spear-heads to the clouds.   Sikandar came
C. 1309   Between the lines, with Rúman sword in hand,
And sent a cavalier to cry from far
To Fúr: "Sikandar hath come forth and seeketh
An interview with thee.   He is prepared
To name his own conditions and hear thine,
And if thy terms are just he is amene."
   When Fúr, the Indian, heard the herald's words

He rushed forth from the centre of his troops.
Sikandar said to him : " O noble man !
Our two hosts have been shattered by the fight,
The wild beasts batten on the brains of men,
The horses' hoofs are trampling on their bones.
Now both of us are heroes brave and young,
Both paladins of eloquence and brain,
Why then should slaughter be the soldiers' lot,
Or bare survival after combating ?
Let us two arm ourselves and fight it out
Since one of us must needs obtain the realm.
When one of us hath proved victorious,
The troops, the crown, and throne all will be his."
　　Fúr joyfully agreed to fight Sikandar,
For well he knew that he had lion-strength,
And rode a charger dragon-like, whereas
Sikandar was a reed-like cavalier,
Armed lightly and ill-mounted, so he said :—
" Agreed : we will engage in single combat."
　　Both took their swords and wheeled between the lines,
But when Sikandar realised the bulk
Of that mad Elephant, who rode a Mountain
And grasped a Dragon, he grew dazed in fight,
Despaired of life at heart and kept his distance,
Till, as he wheeled with Fúr upon the field,
A mighty shout arose behind the host,
Which filled Fúr's heart with dudgeon and distracted
His heart and eyes and ears.　Then like a blast
Sikandar issued from the dust and smote
The hero with his sword, clove crest, head, neck,
And from the steed the body sank to earth.
The Rúman army raised its head to heaven,
The warriors charged.　Now Fúr possessed a drum
Of lion-skin whose sound rose o'er the clouds.
That drum's din and the trumpets' blare arose,
Earth turned to iron, air to ebony,

While by that token those brave troops of Hind
Advanced to face their foes, but from the plain
Was proclamation made: "Ye righteous men,
The chiefest of the realm of Hindústán!
The head of Indian Fúr is in the dust,
His elephantine form is cloven asunder.

C. 1310   What is the purpose of this present struggle,
Such strife of scimitars, and such reluctance?
What Fúr was to you is Sikandar now,
And ye must look to him in fight and feast."
    The warriors of Hindústán assented;
They went and saw Fúr's head all dust and blood,
His body hacked up by the scimitar.
A bitter cry ascended from his troops,
Who dropped their weapons and went grieved and
      wailing
To Cæsar, dust upon their heads. Sikandar
Restored the weapons of the warriors,
Addressed them with all courtesy, and said:—
"Though Fúr of Hind is dead ye need not yield
Your hearts to grief because I will entreat you
More graciously than he did, I will banish
Both fear and anguish from them, and will give
In largess all his treasures. To my troops
These are forbidden. I will make the folk
Of Hind all wealthy and administer
The crown and throne with vigour."
                    Thence he mounted
With mingled feelings to the throne of Fúr.
  So is it with this Hostel by the way!
It never is content to let thee stay.
Enjoy, leave naught for other folks to take;
Why shouldst thou labour for another's sake?
  For two months Cæsar filled the throne and lavished
Fúr's whole wealth on his troops. There was a man
Of parts, Sawurg by name, a mighty chief

Of Hindústán; to him Sikandar gave
The throne of kingship. "Never hoard dínárs,"
He said. "Give and enjoy whate'er thou gettest,
Not glorying in the fleeting crown and throne,
For whiles it is Sikandar and whiles Fúr,
Whiles pain and wrath, whiles feast and banqueting."
　Bestowing as a present on his host
Drachms and dínárs he ordered all that coast.

§ 16

How Sikandar went on a Pilgrimage to the House of the Kaaba

Now in a little while, when all the troops
Were satiate of wealth, a sudden impulse
Came on Sikandar, and he greatly longed
To journey to the Kaaba. So at dawn
The drum-roll rose,[1] the air grew like the eye
Of chanticleer, while all the mass of spears,
And silken pennons, formed a canopy
Of yellow, red, and violet.[2] Sikandar
Departed with his diadem and treasures
To look upon the house of Ibráhím,
Who bare no little toil to build that shrine,
Which God hath named Baitu'l Harám, and there
Thou hast His perfect Way who calleth it,
By reason of its purity, His house,
And thither summoneth His worshippers,
Though needing not the world, or any place,
Or food, enjoyment, rest, or blandishment;
But still, since place had being, that hath been
A place of worship—God's memorial.
Sikandar then drew near to Kádisí,
World-conquering up to Jahram of Párs.

C. 1311

---

[1] Reading with P.　　　　[2] Couplet omitted.

When news of him reached Nasr, son of Katíb,
Who was the Grace and ornament of Mecca,
He went to meet the Sháh with warlike chiefs,
And valiant, spear-armed cavaliers. Meanwhile
From Mecca sped a horseman to Sikandar,
And said: "The famous chief now on his way,
But not in quest of treasure, crown, and host,
Is sprung from Ismá'íl, the prophet, son
Of Ibráhím, the favoured of the stars."
    When Nasr arrived Sikandar welcomed him,
Assigning him an honourable rank.
Nasr, joying, told Sikandar of his race,
And of his secret purposes. He answered:—
"Good-hearted chieftain, speaker of the truth!
Who, next to thee, is greatest, most esteemed,
And honoured in the tribe?"
                                    Nasr said: "O world-lord!
Khuzá' is master here. When Ismá'íl
Had passed away Kahtán, the monarch, came
With mighty hosts of swordsmen from the waste,
And seized the country of Yaman unjustly.
Of our race many guiltless folk were slain,
So that the day was over for our tribe.
Now this displeased the Maker of the world;
High Heaven frowned upon Kahtán; but when
He was reduced to dust Khuzá' appeared,
Unjust, audacious, and tyrannical;
All from Harám[1] up to Yaman is his,
His angle is within the sea of Misr.
He hath transgressed from justice and the way,
And hath no thought of goodness in his heart,
The world is in his clutch, the hearts of all
The race of Ismá'íl are full."
                                    On hearing,
Sikandar slew such scions of Khuzá'

---

[1] Mecca and the Kaaba.

As he could find and scalped them, sparing none
Of friend or foe, delivering Hajáz,
And therewithal Yaman, from the oppressor
By policy and by his warrior-swordsmen,
And set up of the seed of Ismá'íl
All that were worthy of supremacy.
He visited afoot Baitu'l Harám ;
The seed of Ismá'íl rejoiced in him. .
At every step of Cæsar's pilgrimage
His treasurer showered dínárs. The Shám, when he
Returned and reached the throne, bestowed on Nasr
Dínárs and treasure while the mendicant,
And they that lived by toil, grew free from want.

C. 1312

§ 17
How Sikandar led his Troops from Judda toward Misr

He led his army thence with all dispatch,
And came to Judda. He abode not long,
But bade the soldiers build abundant ships
And transports, and departed with his host
For Misr. The monarch there was named Kabtún ;
His troops exceeded all imagining.
On hearing that a conquering king had come
Forth from Harám vaingloriously, he went
To meet him with a numerous retinue,
Slaves, purses, crown, and throne. At sight of him
Sikandar joyed, and all his foemen's words
Proved wind. The Shám abode a year in Misr
To rest himself and troops.
                              There was a lady,
The queen of Andalús, and she was wise,
Ambitious, bounteous, with a countless host,
Famed and victorious through her own deserts,
And named Kaidáfa. From her warriors

She chose a cavalier, a clever draughtsman,
And said; "Go to Sikandar, naming not
This country and ourselves, mark everything
Minutely—his appearance, stature, court;
Then make a full length picture of him, showing
His favour, face, and bearing."

When he heard
He mounted, girt him to perform her bidding,
And went in courier-wise from Andalús
To Misr to eminent Sikandar Cæsar,
Observed him both upon the throne and saddle,
Brought paper out and implements of Chín,
And, having limned him to the life, returned
With all dispatch. Kaidáfa, when she saw
Sikandar's likeness, grieved, concealed her feelings,
Sighed, and thus said: "By war and policy
This man will trample on the world, and brief
Will be their lives that come to fight with him!"
While for his part Sikandar asked Kabtún :—
"Who is Kaidáfa's peer on earth?"

"O king!"
He made reply, "she is unique. None knoweth
The number of her troops without at least
Much searching of the muster-roll. In treasure,
In matters courteous and of obligation,
In counsel and benevolence of speech,
Thou wilt behold not in the world her equal.
She hath a city that is built of stone ;
A leopard could not wrest it from her grasp.
The ground it covereth is four leagues long,
And four leagues wide withal. If thou inquirest
About her treasure 'tis past measuring :
Her doings in the world are no new thing."

C. 1313

§ 18

Sikandar's Letter to Kaidáfa, Queen of Andalús, and her Answer

Sikandar, having heard that mindful man,
Bade come a scribe. They wrote on silk a letter :—
" This from Sikandar, who o'erthroweth lions
And taketh cities, unto wise Kaidáfa,
Whose name is eminent in majesty.
First, praise be to the Master of the sun,
Who lighteth up the moon and turning sphere,
The Lord that meteth justice out aright,
And granteth more than any one can ask. . . .
We have not sought thy throne by violence,
But have respected thine exalted state.
When they deliver unto thee this letter,
And light is thrown upon thy darkened counsels,
Thou wilt dispatch what we impose as tribute,
As knowing that thou canst not strive with us.
To act thus will be wise and provident;
It will be strength in thee and true religion;
Oppose and thou wilt see but change of fortune.
Draw thy conclusions from Dárá and Fúr;
Thou needest go no further for instruction."
 Whenas the wind had dried the superscription
They sealed the letter with a seal of musk.
A cameleer sped to that famous queen,
Who marvelled at the letter as she read.
In answer, first, she poured her praises forth
" To that just Judge, the Maker of the earth,
Who raised the turning sky and set therein
The seat of good and ill.   He made thee victor
O'er Fúr of Hind, Dárá, and chiefs of Sind.
Thy head hath been elated by success

C. 1314

Against those famous swordsmen ; but dost thou
Rank me with them or think by conquering me
To wear my crown when I surpass them all
In Grace and greatness, troops and royal treasure ?
Shall I obey a Cæsar, fear his threats,
And quail ? A thousand thousand warriors
Are at my gate, and kings are in command
Of each contingent. Called I all my lieges
My land would not afford them room to camp,
While treasures wait my chiefs when they go forth
To war across our marches. What vain words
Thou speakest in thus crowing o'er Dárá !"
　　This 'neath her golden signet-ring she past,
Then sent a cameleer swift as a blast.

§ 19
How Sikandar led his Troops to Andalús and took the Hold of King Faryán

Sikandar, having read the queen's reply,
Let blow the brazen trumpets and set forth.
When he had been one month upon the road
He reached the marches of Kaidáfa's realm,
Where reigned a monarch who was named Faryán,
Possessed of treasure, troops, and puissance.
He had a city well supplied with arms ;
No crane had seen the summit of its walls.
He gathered troops and garrisoned that hold,
And cavaliers patrolled the ramparts round.
　　Sikandar bade the bishops [1] bring their wains
And catapults, and in a sennight took
That lofty hold ; his noble army entered,
As did Sikandar who forbade all bloodshed.
One of Kaidáfa's sons, the son-in-law

---

[1] *Cf.* Vol. v. p. 305 and *note.*

Of king Faryán who had much joy in him,
Was there within. To him Faryán had given
A favourite daughter, and his crown had been
Exalted by the queen. The son-in-law
Was named Kaidrúsh and he was all in all
To king Faryán for whom the sky decreed
Death in the fight; his daughter and her spouse
Were taken by the hands of one Shahrgír.
Sikandar, knowing who the spouse was, thought :—
"What cure is there for this contingency ? "
Bade his wazír to come and gave to him
Authority and crown and throne. This sage
Was named Naitkún, a counsellor, a man
Of influence, to whom Sikandar said :—
"They will produce the wedded pair before thee,
And I will title thee Sikandar, son
Of Failakús. Assume the Kaian throne,
And, when I come before thee girt for service,
Bid some fierce deathsman to behead Kaidrúsh;
Then I will come to thee and intercede,
Exhibiting the lowliest submission;
Make thou the audience private and, when I
Am waxing urgent, grant me my request."
   The minister was troubled, knowing not
What was the hidden purpose of the Shâh,
Who added : "We must keep this secret. Call me,
Like other envoys, talk much of Kaidáfa,
Send me right gladly with ten horse, and say :—
'Go to, take this, and bring an answer quickly.'
Dispatch Kaidrúsh with me and hide all from him.
   Naitkún said : " I will do so and will practise
Deception at thy bidding."
                          When the sun
Had drawn its sword at dawn, and gloomy night
Had vanished in dismay, Naitkún assumed
The throne, but ill at ease, ashamed, and sorry;

C. 1315

Sikandar stood before the presence girded.
They shut the door and oped the path of guile.
Now when Shahrgír brought in Kaidáfa's son,
A captive weeping with his wife beside him,
And clinging to his hand in all her charms,
Naitkún spake hastily : " What man is this
Whose pains enforce such tears ? "

                       " Be calm," replied
The youth, " because I am Kaidáfa's son,
Kaidrúsh. Save for this daughter of Faryán's
I have no spouse concealed behind my curtains.
I went to bring her home to cherish her
As mine own life, but now the lion-taker
Hath ta'en me prisoner. The stars have smitten
My soul, and shafts my body."

                       When Naitkún
Heard what the young man said he was distressed,
His heart grew full; howbeit he showed anger,
And then addressed the deathsman : " Earth must hide
    them.
Behead them with thine Indian scimitar—
The husband and his consort in their bonds."
    Then came Sikandar, kissed the ground, and said :—
" O Sháh of Cæsar's race ! if thou wilt spare
The blood of this young couple for my sake
My head will be exalted o'er the people.
Why in thy wrath behead the innocent,
For God will not approve thee ? "

C. 1316
                       Shrewd Naitkún
Replied : " Thou hast preserved the blood of both."
Then added quickly : " Thou hast saved thy head,
Kaidrúsh ! when thou hadst lost it ! Now will I
Send him with thee to tell thy mother all.
If she shall send me tribute, it is well,
And none shall burst his skin on that account.
Tend well my worthy minister, for he

Will proffer unto her a fight or feast
With me.　Repay him for his kindliness,
For good men's hearts are moved by gratitude,
And, when he hath the answer of the queen,
Dismiss him kindly on his homeward way."
　　Kaidrúsh replied: "My heart and eyes and ears
Are his.　Oh! how shall I express myself?
I tender him as dearly as my life
Because I owe him that and world and wife."

§ 20

How Sikandar went as an Ambassador to Kaidáfa and
was recognised by her

Sikandar chose ten Rúmans, men of name,
All confidants who would respect his secret,
And said to them: "While we are on our way
Call me Naitkún."
　　　　　　　Kaidrúsh led on; Sikandar,
Put trust in him.　The chieftains spurred like fire,
And reached a mountain where the rocks were crystal.
Upon it there were fruit-trees of all sorts,
And on the top they noticed grass in plenty.
They left this mountain and kept speeding on
Toward the country where Kaidáfa dwelt,
Who eagerly heard tidings of Kaidrúsh,
And went to meet him with a mighty host,
All men of name and favoured by the stars.
He, when he saw his mother, lighted down,
And did obeisance, but she bade him mount.
They rode, hand clasped in hand.　Kaidrúsh described
All that he had gone through and paled in telling
His troubles in the city of Faryán,
Where he had lost crown, army, throne, and treasure.
The man that cometh with me," he proceeded,

"Preserved me and my consort from Sikandar,
Who else had given orders to behead me,
And burn my corpse in fire.   Do what he wisheth
With right good will and thwart not his request."

C. 1317　　Now when Kaidáfa heard her son's account
Her heart was overset by that affliction.
She summoned from the palace to her presence
The envoy, placed him in the nobles' seat,
Gave him much greeting and a kindly welcome,
Assigned to him a splendid residence,
And sent all kinds of provand, robes, and carpets.
He tarried there that night and at the dawn
Went to the court to offer his respects.
The attendants raised the curtain and allowed him
To enter through the portal on his steed.
When he beheld Kaidáfa on her throne
Of ivory, crowned with a crown of gems
And turquoise, and arrayed in robes of Chín
Inwrought with gold, the attendance of her servants,
Her face bright as the sun, her throne supported
By crystal feet, and o'er her robe a net
Of onyx of Yaman on golden thread,
Impleached with many a gem, and slaves, with torques
And earrings, standing in that rosary[1]
All arabesqued with gold, he stood astound,
Oft times invoking to himself God's name.
To Cæsar, gazing on that court, Írán
And Rúm seemed even as nothing, and he kissed
The ground like other courtiers in her presence.
Kaidáfa gazed on him, received him well,
Much questioned him, and made him sit.   Now when
Bright Sol set, and the audience-time for strangers
Had passed, she gave command to deck the palace
And call attendants, and for harp and wine.
They ranged in one hall tables made of teak

　　　　　　　　　[1] *I.e.* court.

With gold stars and designs in ivory,
Meats were provided past all reckoning,
Wine was brought forth and, when the eating ceased,
And gold and silver cups were handed round,
The company drank first Kaidáfa's health.
That noble queen gazed often at Sikandar
Amid the revel till at length she bade
The keeper of her treasures: "Bring to me
The lustrous silk with that delightful portrait,
Just as it is, and handle it with care."

    He brought it to the queen, who scanned it much
And, having scrutinised Sikandar's face,
Found the presentment just, so that she knew:—
"'Tis Cæsar, chief of yon famed army! He
Hath made himself his own ambassador,
And boldly reached this court. Imperious sir!"
She said to him, "come give Sikandar's message."

    He thus replied: "The monarch of the world   C. 1318
Thus charged me in the presence of his nobles
To say to pure Kaidáfa: 'Here below
Ensue naught but the right. See that thou shun not
My bidding but observe shrewd fealty,
For if in aught thou art perverse in heart
I will lead forth a host heart-shattering,
Rob all thine army of the breath of life,
And give up all thy kingdom to the flames.
I had some intimation of thy virtues,
And therefore was not instant to assail thee,
For thou possessest modesty and wisdom;
Thy shrewd rede is the world's security.
Thou knowest that if thou refusest tribute
Thou canst withstand me not; but thou shalt have
Naught that is not both fair and just if thou
Wilt turn from falsehood and from fraud.'"

Kaidáfa

Was wroth thereat but saw no salve but silence,

And said to him : " Return to thine abode,
And for the present rest there with thy friends.
To-morrow when thou comest we will answer,
And take fair order for thy homeward way."
　　Thereat Sikandar went back to his lodging,
And thought all night how to secure himself.
Now when the bright Lamp rose above the mountains,
And plain and upland glittered like brocade,
He went to court again with smiling lips,
But heart o'ercast with care.　The chamberlain
Saw, greeted him, and took him to the queen.
He saw a throng of strangers and a hall
Where was a crystal throne with patterns traced
In emeralds and cornelians, every boss
A royal gem.　The dais was compact
Of sandal and lign-aloe, and the pillars
Of onyx and turquoise.　The edifice,
The queen's Grace, throne, and puissance much amazed
　　him.
He cried : " This is indeed an audience-chamber !
God's worshippers behold not such another."
　　He paced toward her, and they set a seat
For him below the throne.　Kaidáfa said :—
" Why marvel at our palace thus, Naitkún ?
Is Rúm indeed so other that thou needs
Must wonder at our land ? "
　　　　　　　　　　He said to her :—
" O queen ! misprize not thine own dwelling-place.
Thy head is higher than the heads of kings
Because thine ocean is a mine of gems."
　　Kaidáfa smiled : his speech and conduct charmed
　　her.
She then dismissed her court and, having seated
The envoy graciously before her, said :—
C. 1319　" O son of Failakús ! thou art a master
In fight and festival, in good and ill.

Thou hast approached me boldly to ask tribute,
Although I know not what incited thee."
   On hearing this Sikandar's favour changed;
His soul was full of pain, his cheeks were livid.
He said: "O most wise queen! such words as these
Become thee not. I thank the All-provider
That none of all our famous chiefs are here
To tell this to the master of the world,
And take my life anon. Naitkún am I,
O mistress of the world! so call me not
The son of Failakús."
                    Kaidáfa said :—
"Dispute it not because thou art Sikandar,
And, when thou seest the portrait of thyself,
Cease to dissemble and display no wrath."
   She brought and showed to him the silk all limned
With that fair portrait and so vividly
That, given motion, it had been himself.
He bit his lips; day grew for him like midnight.
He said: "Let no one be without a dagger
Concealed about him!"
               "If thou hadst one here
Suspended from thy shoulder," she replied,
"No strength or trenchant scimitar would serve;
There is no room for fight or road for flight."
   Sikandar said: "The great are eager ever
To win the world by valour, and must shun not
The path of danger, for the faint of heart
Excel not. Had I but my weapons now
The whole house would become a sea of blood,
And I, confronted by mine enemy,
Would rend my liver's seat or slaughter thee!"

§ 21

How Kaidáfa counselled Sikandar

Kaidáfa, smiling at Sikandar's bearing,
His gallantry, and angry words, replied :—
" O monarch lion-like ! become not headstrong
In valour. It was not through Grace of thine
That Fúr of Hind, Dárá son of Dáráb,
And all those warriors of Sind were slain,
But 'twas because those world-lords' day was over,
And thy star in the ascendant. Thine own valour
Hath made thee so presumptuous as to deem
Thyself the lord of time and earth, but know
That all our blessings are derived from God,
So while thou livest give the thanks to Him.

C. 1320   Thou said'st : ' The wisdom of the world is mine.
I do not look upon thy words as true.
What profit hath thy wisdom been to thee
Since thou hast come within the Dragon's breath,
And, while still youthful, hemmest thine own shroud
By going as thine own ambassador ?
But bloodshed or a reckless strife with kings
Is not my wont. The ruler who is strong,
And justly generous, is wise withal,
For, know, the shedder of king's blood will see
But fire at last. Be easy, go rejoicing,
And in departing make a new departure,
For henceforth thou wilt do no embassies
Since all the earth will recognise Sikandar.
I know not any of the great whose portrait,
Limned thus on silk, is not in my possession,
And in a careful keeper's hands, and I
Have used the judgment of astrologers
Thereon to learn if I should trust or dread,
For when a prudent king hath been vouchsafed,
The age proclaimeth it to man and woman.

Thee will I call Naitkún while thou art here,
And by that token seat thee at a distance
That none may know thy secret, hear thy name,
Or fame. I will dismiss thee with all kindness
But thou must be a master of discretion,
And, further, promise never more to be
A foe or ill-disposed toward my sons,
My kingdom or my kindred or allies,
And treat me as thy peer."

                               Sikandar heard
And joyed, relieved from fear and slaughter, swore
By that just Judge, who ruleth all, the Faith
Of Christ, and by the sword of war, and said :—
" So long as thy dominions, thine own sons,
And potentates allied to thee, endure
I will do naught but what is good and right;
I will not think of fraud or knavery."
   When he had sworn Kaidáfa said to him :—
" I must not fail to warn thee of one thing :
Know this then that Tainúsh my son misprizeth
My knowledge and my counsel. He is wayward,
Fúr's son-in-law, and must not hear from near
Or far that thou art one skin with Sikandar,
Or friend withal, for he would fain avenge
Fúr and in battle dash down heaven to earth.
Return now'to thy house in peace and joy,
And utter naught about the world's concerns."
   Sikandar went, his heart was big within him,
For wise men think of death with seriousness.
Kaidáfa brought no frown upon his face,
And never disregarded he her counsel.
He stayed that night and early in the morn
Went from his lodging and approached the queen,
Who sat within the hall of audience,
Surrounded by a crowd of warriors.[1]

C. 1321

---

[1] " toute parée et entourée de bouquets de fleurs " (Mohl).

The ceiling was of ivory and gold,
And in the gold were divers jewels set.
In front of all the musky-scented throng
Before the queen there stood two proper sons;
One was Tainúsh, the cavalier, the other
Kaidrúsh who used to hearken to her words.
The younger son spake to his mother thus:—
" O queen well favoured of the stars and just!
Take order that Naitkún glad, well content,
And with a guide, may leave thee, so that none
May harm or treat him as a foe, forwhy
He saved my life, and as bright life I hold him."
   She said : " Mine actions shall increase his great-
    ness."
Then to Sikandar spake that noble queen:—
" Now make the secret patent to us. What
Hast thou to say ? What is Sikandar's purpose ?
What knowest thou about the Sháh, and whom
Hath he for minister ?"
                Sikandar answered:—
" Great lady ! I have tarried long. The Sháh
Said: 'Go, ask tribute from her land. If thou
Delayest I will lead the army thither,
And leave her not the kingdom, crown, and throne,
Grace, queenship, might, or fortune for her own.'"

§ 22

*How Tainúsh, the Son of Kaidáfa, was wroth with Sikandar,
and how Sikandar took Precaution against him*

Tainúsh, when he had heard Sikandar's words,
Raged like a blast, and said : " Thou worthless fool !
No man could reckon thee a man at all !

Know'st not before whose presence thou art seated ?
Assume the bond slave's pose !¹ Thy head is full
Of wrath and arrogance. Inform me who
Thy monarch is. Save for our sovereign's Grace
I would pluck off thy head as I would pluck
An orange from its bough. This very night,
Because I grieve for Fúr, will I display
Thy trunkless head in presence of the host !"
    His mother called to him, for his hot head
Was growing more distraught, and said : _" The words
Are not his own ! Address the envoy's sender,
Whose utterance they are."

She bade : " Conduct   C. 1322
Tainúsh outside the court. Thou scowling one !"
She added, " show not thy vile temper here.
He saved Kaidrúsh, thy brother, from the Sháh,
And reached our court, and yet thou railest thus
Against him and art wroth and sore displeasured !"
    The son went forth fulfilled with rage and dudgeon,
With bloodshot eyes. In private to Sikandar
She said : " Tainúsh is foolish and the tool
Of dívs. In private he must not devise
Some loss or crime. Thou seekest after knowledge,
And thou art wise. Consider what to do."
    Sikandar said : " So be it then. Thy course
Is to recall Tainúsh."

Thereat the queen
Sent for her son and set him 'neath the throne.
Sikandar said : " Imperious prince ! if thou
Wouldst have thy wish command thyself, and I
Will not oppose thee. I accept each word
Of thine. Sikandar, who is Sháh and hath
The throne and crown, hath plunged me into gloom.

---

¹ Literally " Sit not before the queen. Show not thy hands," the
proper attitude for slaves being to stand with folded arms, with the
hands under the arm-pits. In this position they cannot do mischief.

He sent me to the queen with this command :—
' Ask tribute from that famous sovereign,'
So that whatever ill grow manifest
From foes toward him may come on me.   Hear, prince
Rage not nor storm—another's due—at me,
For much have I been wronged by him myself,
And I have schemed to slay him.   To thy hands
Will I deliver him, and then the world
Will be well quit, and I fare free, of him.
Thou know'st not yet my plan and what good thoughts
I harbour.   I will go to him to-day
With my reply and will advise him finely !
If I shall grasp his hand and from his camp
Conduct him to thee, and in such a fashion
That he shall have no troops with him, and thou
Shalt look not on his scimitar, his throne,
And crown, then what wilt thou bestow upon me
Of all the realm, how recognise my service ? "

Tainúsh thereat made answer : " I have heard
Thy words, and we must act thereon forthwith,
For if thou shalt achieve this, and wilt do
Thine utmost honestly, I will bestow
His treasures and his purses, steeds, and men—
Devoted lieges—and my thanks upon thee ;
Thou shalt possess the world, know good, become
My loyal minister, and in this land
My treasurer."

C. 1323

Sikandar rose and shook
Hands on the bargain, and Tainúsh inquired :—
" How wilt thou compass this and by what spell
Effect this sorcery ? "

Sikandar said :—
" Thou must go with me, when I quit the queen,
And take a thousand horsemen of thy host,
All famed in fight.   Upon my journey hither
I marked a wood where I will put in ambush

Thee and thy soldiery, and go myself
To him, will look on that malignant soul,
And say: 'The queen hath sent so much that thou
Ne'er wilt want more.   Her elder son, Tainúsh
By name, hath brought the Sháh her salutations
And messages, but saith : "I dare not face him
Amidst his host."   Now if my lord would deign
Escorted only by his priests and sages,
To meet Tainúsh then in that interview
He could receive the goods and hoarded treasures
Of all sorts, for Tainúsh would come, on seeing thee
Without thy host, or else be free to go.'
Sikandar, when he heareth my smooth words,
Will never guess my colour and design,
But seek the shade beneath those trees, requiring
From thee those crowns and thrones.   Do thou sur-
          round him
With thy fierce troops and make the future certain ;
This will achieve my vengeance and thy wishes,
And thy fame soar by favour of the stars.
When thou hast taken him I am all thine,
And, when thou biddest, I will be thy watchman.
Then mine affairs will prosper and my market
Grow hot and brisk, for thou shalt carry off
Much wealth and slaves and steeds caparisoned."
   Tainúsh rejoiced on hearing him, appeared
A noble cypress-tree, and answered thus :—
" My hope is that his day may turn to night,
And that he may be taken unawares
Within my toils, for all the bloodshed made
By him within the world—that of Dárá,
Son of Dáráb, the warriors of Sind,
And that great man of Hind, the valiant Fúr."
   Now when Kaidáfa heard Sikandar's words,
And marked and understood his stratagem,
She smiled at his device behind her lips,

And hid those corals underneath her veil.
Sikandar left her presence in a mood
O'ershadowed by his great solicitude.

§ 23

*How Sikandar made a Compact with Kaidáfa and
returned to his Troops*

C. 1324 That livelong night Sikandar laid his plans
And, when the sun displayed its fringe of Chín,
And set its golden banner o'er the heights,
While sank night's silken robe of violet,
He visited the queen and asked for audience
From her attendants. As their custom was
They caused him to alight, and then that seeker
Of world-dominion paced before the queen.
They cleared the hall and hastened to present
The envoy. When he saw Kaidáfa throned
He said: "May Jupiter espouse thy counsels!
By Christianity, the law of right,
By God who witnesseth to what I say,
By the religion of the mighty Cross,
By a brave monarch's life and head, priest's girdle,
And Holy Ghost,[1] I promise that henceforth
The soil of Andalús shall not behold me,
Nor will I send a host to battle thither.
I will employ no colourable ruse,
I will entreat not ill thy stainless son
By act or hest of mine, but bind true faith
To thee upon my soul and no wise seek
Thine injury. Thy friend shall be my brother,
Thy throne as sacred to me as the Cross."
     Kaidáfa marked his oath, his singleness
Of heart, and honest pledge. She had the palace

------

[1] Or the angel Gabriel may be intended.

Filled with gold seats, and set forth gauds of Chín,
Called for her nobles and the well-starred chiefs,
Set them, each one, upon a seat of gold
And, having sent for both her well-loved sons
And for her kith and kin, harangued them thus :—
' It is not well that we be over-troubled
Within this Wayside Inn, and changeful fortune
Must make not battle and revenge my lot.
Sikandar still will be insatiate
Of treasure though he over-top the sky,
And for that reason seeketh war with us
Though all earth's treasures are not worth the toil.
I purpose that we do not fight with him ;
I will not bring distress upon the realm ;
But we will make a politic response,
At once exalting and exhorting him.
If after mine advice he seeketh war,
Ignoring both my Glory and my throne,
I with the host will face him so that sun
And moon shall pity him.   Still what we try   C. 1325
Will do no harm, and peace may be preserved.
What say ye ?   What respond ?   Advise me well."
     The chiefs all raised their heads and answered her :—
" O queen of counsel and of justice ! none
Can call to mind a chief like thee, and thou
Speak'st naught but good.   Oh ! fair befall the land
That hath a chief like thee !   If this great Sháh
Become thy friend, what more can good men wish ?
The Sháh will not attack thee for thy wealth ;
To vex thee would cost more than all thy treasures.
When a Sikandar cometh out of Rúm,
Converting earth to ocean with his sword,
And then departeth from thy gates with gifts,
The fact outvalueth the whole world's havings.
We cannot favour any course but peace,
For he is foolish that desireth war."

When she had heard the words of those wise men,
Of those approved and holy-hearted priests,
She oped her treasures and took out the crown
Worn by her sire, with bracelet and gold torque
(It was a crown the value of whose gems
None in the city or the country knew),
And to the messenger she said : " This crown
Is priceless ; those that others have are naught,
And, seeing that Sikandar hath deserved
This crown of chiefs, I have adopted him
As son adult."
                                    Now she possessed a throne
That was compact of seventy parts and more ;
Well gifted he that could dismember it !
The pattern was of intricate design,
And every juncture fitted curiously ;
The feet had terminals of dragons' heads.
None knew its jewels' worth, but it comprised
Four hundred royal gems, an equal sum
Of brilliant rubies, two whereof, in hue
Pomegranate-grain, weighed one miskál apiece,
And emeralds four hundred, several stones,
Bright as a rainbow, and uncut.   She added
Of raiment more than forty camel-loads ;
The lady's heart was bounteous as the sea.
There were five hundred tusks of elephants ;
What tusks they were !   Their total length reached
        miles !
There were four hundred leopard-skins and more,
The sort brought from Barbar ; of dappled deer-skins
A thousand plain or dyed, all fair to see,
Besides a hundred hounds keen in the chase,
Which sped like arrows over hill and plain.
Kaidáfa's servants then led forth before her
Two hundred buffaloes ; there were withal
Four hundred seats upholstered in brocade

And silken stuffs, the frames of ebony,
And of fresh aloe-wood four hundred more
With sunbeams saturate and golden hue.
She ordered too a thousand Indian swords
With daggers and with coats of battle-mail,
While from the plain they brought a hundred steeds,
High-bred and harnessed, with the other wealth,
Besides twelve hundred casques and morions.
.She bade her treasurer: "Now, tarry not,
Account for all these to Naitkún, and say:—
'Be ready to depart at dawn to-morrow.'"
　Whenas the morning showed its flag on high,
When heaven's violet face grew camphor-like,
When earth was fresh and height like sandarac,
A sound of drums rose from the palace-gate.
Sikandar, having leave to go, bestrode
His steed and, when the brave Tainúsh had bidden
The troops to mount, proceeded from his palace
To court, and to Kaidáfa said: "Farewell,
And, while the world shall last, may it and thou
Be woof and warp."
　　　　　　　They journeyed stage by stage
Until they drew anear the scene of action—
The camp of that famed Sháh, the fortune-favoured
Sikandar, who left baggage in the forest,
Where there were streams and many trees, and told
Tainúsh: "Here rest and, rested, take the cup
In hand. I will depart, make good my words,
And do all for the best."
　　　　　　　Sikandar reached
The encampment. All the host came forth and showed
Their gladness by their shouts, while making ready
The Kaian crown, because they had despaired
Of their aspiring lord. Who ever thought
To see his face again? With tongues all praise
The soldiers bent their faces to the ground.

C. 1326

Sikandar then selected from the host
A thousand of the Rúman men of name,
Who, warriors as they were intent on strife,
With ox-head maces and in coats of mail,
Set forward and begirt the wood about—
A line of men and weapons.   Then he cried:—
" Rash man! art thou resolved on fight or flight?"[1]
　　Repenting of his plots and cleverness
Tainúsh quaked and exclaimed: "High-minded Sháh!
Thou shouldst choose rather to be praised than blamed.
This was not thine agreement with my mother.
Didst thou not say: 'I will not quit the right'?
Display, as in the instance of Kaidrúsh,
True greatness and endeavour righteousness."
　　Sikandar said: "O prince! why hast thou grown
So feeble in this weighty enterprise?

C. 1327
But have no fears for thou art safe with me.
I will not harm one of thy kin or shun
Kaidáfa's bidding I!   'Tis ill for kings
To break their faith."
　　　　　　　　Tainúsh forthwith alighted,
And kissed the ground, displaying deep abasement.
The world-lord grasped his hand and reaffirmed
The former covenant, and said withal:—
" Be of good cheer and harbour no suspicions.
I feel no hate toward thee.   When thy mother
Sat on her throne of gold, and when I clasped
Thy hand in mine, I told thee: 'I will lay
The king of earth's hand thus within thine own.'
This very day my promise is performed,
For hasty speeches come not well from Sháhs.
I am the same Sikandar that held forth
So pleasantly to thee.   Kaidáfa knew
That very day that thou didst grasp his hand."
　　Then Cæsar bade the attendants: "Set a throne

　　　　　　　　　　[1] Reading with P.

Beneath a blossom-scattering tree."

He bade
To spread the board and call for wine and harpers.
They spent a while in pleasure and delights.
Now when the ruddy wine had made them glad
The Sháh gave orders for a royal gift
Of stuffs of Rúm, of Chín, and Persian make,
And gave it to Tainúsh with gold and silver
For his companions, crowns and belts withal
To those that merited, and thus enjoined him :—
"Stay not, this wood is distant, not thy home.
Say to Kaidáfa: 'O thou prudent lady,
Thou ruler shrewd of heart and well advised!
While life endureth I will constant be,
And have possessed my soul with love for thee.'"

§ 24

*How Sikandar went to the Country of the Brahmans, inquired
into their Mysteries, and received an Answer*

He marched thence to the country of the Brahmans
To make inquiry of their ancient rites
From those abstemious men. The Brahmans heard
News of the Sháh that he was marching thither,
And from the heights came down those devotees,
Assembling at the tidings. Then the sages
Wrote to Sikandar, chief of priests. The letter
Began with heart-felt blessings from the Lord
Of all upon the monarch of the world :—
"May the Sháh ever conquer, wax, and have   C. 1328
Both mastery, and knowledge," then proceeded :—
"God hath bestowed on thee the mighty world,
Brave king! What wouldst thou in our meagre land,
The dwelling of God's worshippers? If thou
Dost come for wealth, good sooth! thy wits are failing!

It is our part to suffer and be wise;
Yea, knowledge maketh musical our souls.
Thou canst not rob us of long-suffering,
While knowledge harmeth none. Thou wilt but see
A naked flock dispersed by wind and snow,
And fain eat grass-seed if thou tarriest!"
　　The envoy, girt with roots of grass, approached
The Sháh who, having seen him and the letter,
Resolved to act aright and do no hurt.
He halted all his host and then proceeded
Himself with the philosophers of Rúm.
Informed thereof the devotees all came
To meet him on his way with paltry gifts,
Because they had no treasure, tilth, or crops,
And blessed that noble monarch of the earth.
Sikandar marked the Brahmans' looks and talk,
How they went bare of body, foot, and head,
Their bodies barren while their souls bare knowledge,
With grass for raiment and its seeds for food,
At ease from feast and battle-day, and how
They ate, reposed, and slept on plain and mountain,
And gathered everywhere in naked troops;
Their provand all of tree-fruits and the seeds
Of grasses on the mountain-tops, their girdles
The pelts of game, their raiment ready-made.[1]
He asked them of their ways of sleep and provand,
Rest and good days and fight: "What share have ye
Of this world's good? Hath Heaven no antidote
For bane save this alone?"
　　　　　　　　　　　A sage replied :—
" O conqueror of the world! none of us talketh
Of war and strife; we need not clothes, stuffs, foods.
Man being born in mother-nakedness
Should not be dainty in his garniture,
And hence returneth naked to the dust,

---

[1] In the sense explained below.

Where all is fear, anxiety, and dread.
Earth coucheth and heaven clotheth us; our eyes,
Expectant of the ending, watch the way.
How much the ambitious striveth after things
Which, strife and all, are hardly worth a doit,
For when he goeth from this Wayside Inn   C. 1329
Behind are left his gold and crown and treasure!
But, know, his virtues bear him company
While both his head and state descend to dust."

Sikandar asked of them : " Which number most—
The hidden or the manifest, to wit
The living or the dead whose needs are over ? "

The sage replied : " Know, king! the hidden far
Exceed the manifest, for thou mayst reckon
Upon a hundred thousand dead and more
For each alive, and blest is one not outcast
In Hell. The living too must die. One goeth,
And leaveth his position to another."

The Sháh inquired : " Is there most land or water
Illumined by the sun ? "

               The Brahman answered :—
" The water is the keeper of the land."

He asked : " Who are the awakened, who the sinners
On earth ? They make a stir, and many live
Not knowing wherefore they are here at all ! "

The Brahman answered : " Know thou pure in heart
And justice-seeking chief! the awakened man
Is he whom little of this world sufficeth ;
The guiltiest, one whose wisdom hath been docked
By hate and greed. If thou wouldst know such well
Look first upon thyself, for all earth's face
Is thine, and one would say that restless heaven
Is kin to thee, yet still thou schem'st for more,
And to withhold thy wits from grimy dust,
For greed is thy soul's hell, and it may be
That these our words may cause thee to repent."

The Sháh inquired: "What is our ruling passion,
And our companion everywhere for evil?"
   The Brahman answered: "Greed—the sum of hate,
And soul of sin."
                    "What is its nature then,"
The Sháh asked, "seeing there is cause to weep
O'er this its passion for aggrandisement?"
   The Brahman made this answer: "Greed and Need
Are two dívs and long-drawn calamities.
One hath its lips dried up with poverty,
The other sleepeth not to compass more,
While both are hunted by the evil day:
How blest is he whose soul is fed on wisdom!"
   Now, when Sikandar heard, his face resembled
The bloom of fenugreek, his cheeks were pale,
Tears filled his eyes, his smiling countenance
Was drawn with frowns. The imperious Sháh in-
         quired:—

C. 1330   What would ye have of us? I will not grudge you
My treasures, nor regret what they have cost me."
   One said: "Exalted Sháh! deliver us
From eld and death."
                    "Death is inexorable,"
The Sháh made answer. "How canst thou escape
That Dragon's piercing clutch? For wert thou iron
Thou wouldst not find release, while youth, if here
It tarrieth, is not exempt from eld."
   The Brahman said to him: "O mighty Sháh,
The world-lord, sage, and one whose word is law!
Thou knowest death to be remediless,
And that there is no worse calamity
Than eld. Why seek to win the world by toil,
Why in thy madness sniff the bloom of bale?
Thou wilt but leave the product of thy travail
Behind thee and bestow what thou hast toiled for,
And treasures, on the foe. To undertake

To toil for others is both ignorance
And folly.   White hair is Death's messenger;
Why hope so much to live?"

The shrewd Sháh said :—

" If any of God's servants could escape
From His decree, I had escaped withal
By observation of the turning sky;
But neither man of lore nor warrior
Evadeth that decree, strive how he may.
Moreover they that perished in my wars,
Or had their days cut short by destiny,
Deserved their fate by bloodshed and ill deeds,
For no oppressor 'scapeth.   They have suffered
God's chastisement for quitting wisdom's way.
'Tis not in man to limit heaven's powers,
Or shun the process of the passing hours."

§ 25

How Sikandar came to the Western Sea and saw Wonders

Sikandar proffered many a gift, but none
Accepted them; the Brahmans had small greed.
He did no hurt, set off upon his march,
By that same token fared toward the West,
And from the Brahmans' country reached a spot
Whence he beheld a deep and boundless sea;
The men there had their faces veiled like women,
And went arrayed, all colour and perfume.
They spake not Persian, whether old or modern,
Or Arabic, or Turkman, or Chinese;
They lived on fish alone; there was no means
Of bringing aught by road.   Sikandar stood
Astound at them and in the Rúman tongue   C. 1331
Invoked God's name.   Then from the water rose
A rock as bright and yellow as the sun.

The Sháh desired a swift ship whence to view
The thing aright.   Of his philosophers
One said : " 'Tis not for thee to cross the Deep;
Wait till some man of lore survey the rock."
    Then thirty men, some Persian and some Rúman,
Embarked.   That bit of rock turned out to be
A yellow fish which, as they came anigh,
Drew down the vessel swiftly, dived, and vanished !
Sikandar's soldiers were aghast, and all
Invoked God's name.   A priest said to the Sháh :—
" A goodly thing is knowledge, for the man
That hath it is in this world chief of folk.
Now if the Sháh had gone and perished thus
Blood would have filled the souls of this great host."
    Departing thence he led the army on
To where a novel water came in view.
Around it there were reeds as large as trees :
Thou wouldst have said : " They are the mighty stems
Of planes."   They were above ten cubits thick,
And measured forty cubits in their height.
The houses were of reeds and built thereon.
They might not tarry in that reed-bed ; no one
Drank of its water for 'twas salt.   Sikandar
Fared thence until a deepsome lake appeared ;
The world was jocund, water honey-like ;
The soil exhaled the scent of musk.   They ate,
And set themselves to sleep, when from the water
Came writhing snakes in swarms while from the wood
Flame-coloured scorpions issued, and the world
Grew black and straitened to those slumberers.
On every side there perished multitudes,
Men great in lore and war.   On one side came
Herds of wild boars with long tusks diamond-bright,
And on the other lions that out-bulked
An ox ; none could withstand them ; so the host,
Withdrawing from the mere and flinging fire

Upon that reed-bed, set themselves to slay
Hogs in such numbers as to block the way.

§ 26

How Sikandar reached the Land of Habash, fought, and
was victorious

Departing thence the sun-like Sháh in haste C. 1332
Came to the country of Habash and saw
A land as 'twere a raven's plume with men
Black-faced with eyes like lamps. A lusty crowd
Of able-bodied folk, large-limbed and naked,
Raised, when they saw afar the army's dust,
Their war-cry to the clouds. A thousand thousand
Assembled. All turned black before the Sháh.
They came on him and slaughtered many troops,
Transfixing them with bones instead of spears.
He bade his soldiers arm. Those lion-men
Discomfited the blacks, who charged unclad,
And slew above a thousand while the rest
Turned from the fray. Earth's face seemed like the sea
Of Chín with bloodshed. When the dales and deserts
Were smirched with gore, and slain piled everywhere,
The soldiers scattered fuel on the heaps,
And then Sikandar bade to kindle them.
When it was dark the wolves began to howl:
Sikandar donned his helmet and cuirass.
A pack approached, all big as buffaloes.
Their leader, larger than an elephant,
Had on its head a dusky horn. It slew
Full many a chief and, oft attacked, ne'er showed
Its back. With arrows they made shift to kill
At last that elephant-taking iron Hill.

§ 27

How Sikandar reached the Land of the Narmpái, how he fought
and was victorious, how he slew a Dragon, ascended a
Mountain, and was forewarned of his own Death

Thence marched he quickly and invoking oft
The just World-lord. On reaching the Narmpái
He saw a countless folk who had no steeds,
C. 1333   Or breastplate, sword, or mace, and every one
Was lion-like in form. Now when the host
Neared the Narmpái the world grew black to them ;
They roared like rattling thunder, came like dívs
Upon Sikandar, running on their knees,
With martial bodies and contentious hearts,
And showered stones fiercely as the autumn-blasts
Beat on the trees. The Rúman host advanced
With sword and arrow, and thou wouldst have said :—
" Bright day is dimmed."
                        When few Narmpái were left
Sikandar rested, then led on the host,
And reached what seemed a boundless city whence
All, as their wont was, went to meet him gladly,
Asked naught but brought all kinds of tapestries,
Of raiment and of provand while Sikandar
Saluted, well received, and honoured them
According to their station. Then he bade
The common folk, the chiefs, and those star-favoured
To carpet all the plain. The sands and soil
Were tricked out with brocade. Upon the waste
They pitched the Sháh's pavilion, and the brave
Took post around. All revelled, Sháh and horsemen.
Thus, as he fleeted time with feast and wine,
Or rest, the host, inured to heat and cold,
Reposed from war. Thereafter ceaselessly
He sought a lucky day whereon to march

Sought for intelligence from all, but none
Gave him auspicious counsel. He observed
A mountain with its summit midst the stars:
Thou wouldst have said: "It will arrest the sky!"
Few were the folk thereon, and none of them
Remained at night. Of these he asked: "What way
Is there, and how must I conduct the host?"
  All blessed him, saying: "Famous king of earth!
"The way is o'er the mount if guide could go,
But on its farther side there is a dragon,
Whose grievous venom doth confound the wolf.
Thy troops can pass it not; its venom's fumes
Mount to the moon; flames issue from its maw,
And its two side-locks would avail to snare
An elephant. Our folk can not withstand it.
It needeth for its food five oxen nightly.
We buy, and drive, them on yon rocky mount,   C. 1334
Drive them with care and trouble, lest the dragon
Come hither, and our folk in numbers suffer."
  Sikandar, at the dragon's feeding-time,
Chose troops and bade to give it naught that day.
The dragon, when its hour for battening
Was o'er, came down the pass like fire. Sikandar
Bade his troops shower thereon their arrows swiftly.
That laidly dragon drew one breath and sucked
Some warriors in. The son of Failakús
Bade beat the tymbals and the kettledrums,
Enkindle mighty fires and make a blaze
In every quarter. When the mountain rang
With tymbal-din the monster feared and fled.
  When Sol ascended from the Sign of Taurus,
And soared the lark's note from the garths of roses,
The warrior-chieftain brought with him five oxen,
Procured with money from his treasury.
He slew and skinned them, heads and all; his scheme
Gave courage to his friends. He charged the hides

With bane and naphtha, and made speed toward
The dragon.   Blowing up the skins he called
Upon the Giver of all good and bade
Men pass the hides along from hand to hand.
As he drew near the dragon it appeared
Black like a cloud, its tongue was livid, its eyes
Seemed blood, its maw belched flame.   They cast the
    oxen
Down from the mountain-top and closely marked
The dragon, which engorged them, swift as wind,
Or ever they had left those warriors' hands.
Now when its frame was hide-stuffed, and the bane
Had spread throughout its body, it pierced through
The entrails and invaded brains and feet.
The dragon dashed its head on mount and rocks,
And thus a long time lapsed while all the troops
Showered arrows on it till that mountain-form,
That hunter, fell.   Thence fared the host with speed,
And left in scorn the dragon's body there.
    Sikandar led them to another mountain,
One that amazed the troops.   The keen of sight
Could mark its height from far and that its peak
Was like a scimitar-blade and thereupon,
Apart from folk and distant from the throng,
Was set a golden throne.   A hoary corpse
C. 1335   Was on it verily still full of grace
In death, palled in brocade, upon its head
A crown of gems of all kinds, and heaped round
With gold and silver.   None could pass that way,
For all that scaled the mountain-top to seek
Aught of that corpse began to quake though fearless,
Died, and returned to dust.   Sikandar clomb
The mountain-top to view the corpse with all
Its gold and silver, but he heard a voice:—
"O Sháh! thou hast accomplished thy career,
Hast voided many a monarch's throne, exalted

Thy head to heaven, and slaughtered many a foe
And friend. 'Tis time for thee to quit the world."
  Burned like a lamp the Sháh's cheeks as he heard;
He left that mount and with a heart all seared.

§ 28

How Sikandar reached the City of Women, named
Harúm, and saw Wonders there

On marching with his chiefs of Rúm Sikandar
Fared toward the city that thou call'st Harúm,
Which was inhabited by women only,
Who suffered none to come within their gates.
Their left breasts were like eager warriors',
Who don the breastplate on the day of battle,
While on the right hand they resembled women's,—
Pomegranate-like on silk. The Sháh with all
His mighty men of Rúm approached Harúm,
And wrote a letter fit and fair and worthy
Of his high birth, addressed thus : "From the king
Of Rúm and of Írán to her that is
The ruler in Harúm.
                    The letter first
Named Him who ruleth o'er the starry heaven,
Of whom are justice, love, and bounteousness,
And then went on : "Whoe'er is wise of soul,
And walketh yet alive upon the world,
Hath heard of what we have achieved on earth,
And how we have exalted sovereignty,
While he that hath refused to do our bidding
Hath no couch save dark dust. Fain would I have
No place concealed from me throughout the world.
I roam not for addition's sake but ache -
For knowledge. Be my hand withheld from gain,
And justice ever comrade of my soul.

If I approach 'tis not to fight with you;
My heart is set on peace and jollity.
If ye have any sage wise, shrewd, and clerkly,
When he hath read my letter of advice
Let all of you of worth prepare to meet me,
For none shall lose by coming."

C. 1336

                          He commanded
That a philosopher of Rúm should bear
The letter to the city of Harúm,
And added many honied words. The envoy
Was wise himself. When he arrived he saw
The city full of women and no men,
And all the people went forth to the plain
To see the Rúman. All the counsellors
In that assembly gathered round the letter
And, when a city-sage had read it over,
And grew possessed of what the Sháh proposed,
They sat, and wrote back: "O exalted Sháh!
Live ever. We have set thy messenger
Before us and have read thy letter through.
First as to what thou sayest touching kings,
Thy victories, and former fights: if thou
Shalt march against the city of Harúm
Thou wilt not see the ground for hoofs and feet
The districts of our city pass compute,
And in each one there are ten thousand women.
We sleep in arms and battle for addition.
We all are spouseless, modest maidens we.
Whichever way thou comest to this land
There is deep water to be ferried over.
When one among us hath a mind to wed
We none of us behold her face again,
And she must cross the water be the day
Fine, blusterous, or snowy. Having married,
If she shall have a daughter—one refined
And fond of hues and scents—that child of hers

Abideth ever in her native air;
But if she proveth masculine and proud
Her mother will dispatch her to Harúm;
While if the mother bringeth forth a son
He tarrieth, coming not to dwell with us.
Each night ten thousand maidens guard the river.
When one of us unhorseth in the fight
Some lion-man we set a golden crown
Upon her head and raise o'er Gemini
Her throne, and surely there are thirty thousand
Among us, wearing crown of gold and earrings,
By whose hands some illustrious warrior
Hath turned to dust upon the day of battle.
Thou art a great man, and thy fame is high;   C. 1337
Close not the door thereof upon thyself,
Else folk will say that thou didst fight with women,
And, after fighting, fled'st, and this will shame thee,
And ne'er be obsolete while this world lasteth;
But if thou, with thy famous men of Rúm,
Wilt come and go about Harúm, observing
All faith and courtesy, thou shalt behold
But mirth and kindness.   If thy choice, O Sháh!
Be other thou wilt shrink from us in battle.
We will lead forth against thee such a host
That sun and moon shall darken."
                                    When this answer
Was finished an ambassadress departed
With crown and royal raiment, and with ten
Fair cavaliers.   When she approached the Sháh
In state he sent some troops to welcome her.
The noble lady gave to him the letter,
And told the message of the valiant women.
Sikandar, having read that answer, chose
A man discreet and wise, sent this reply,
And said: "Be wisdom wedded to men's brains.
No kings or chiefs, exalted though they be

And favoured by the stars, are left on earth
That are not subject unto me. Black dust
And camphor-dust, and feast and battlefield,
Are one to me. I have not come with drums,
With elephants, with players on the tymbals,
And such a host that plain and mountain quake
Beneath the horses' hoofs, to fight with women.
I fain would see your city, and if ye
Will make approaches to me all is well.
When I have seen I will march hence the host,
And not abide here long. We will behold
Your policy and glory, how ye manage
Your steeds, your grace, and potence. Privily
Will I inquire as to your works and ways,
How women can exist, men absent, how
Death's ravage is repaired, and find the outcome."
　　The envoy went and did his embassage
At large. The magnates met and made reply :—
" We will select two thousand women, fluent,
Learned, and discreet; each hundred have in charge
Ten crowns of gold each set with many gems,
Two hundred crowns in all, and none but kings

C. 1338　Are digne of them. We will collect and heap them,
Each with its jewels weighing thirty ratl.[1]
We will go forth to meet the Sháh when we
Are ware of his approach, for we have heard
About his knowledge and his Grace."
　　　　　　　　　　　　　　　The envoy
Returned and spake those words instinct with wisdom.
Sikandar marched forth from his resting-place,
And marvelled at the conduct of those women.
He went two stages, then a storm arose,
Whose snow-drifts made all level with the hills,
And many followers perished on that day
Through cold and snow. The Sháh pursued his march

---

[1] A ratl now=1·014 lb. av.　P. reads " three " for " thirty."

Two stages farther through that grievous frost,
Then reached a burning land whence vapours rose,
And murky clouds; "The host," thou wouldst have said,
" Was marching over fire." The hauberks burnt
The shoulders of the Persians, and the earth
Glowed with the horse-shoes of the cavaliers,
And thus it was until they reached a land
Where they beheld all folk as black as night,
With pendent, slobbering lips; all lips and slobber
Were they, all slobber and lip ! Their eyes seemed
    blood ;
Flames issued from their mouths ! Their warriors
Brought many elephants and offerings
Before the Sháh, and said: "We caused this storm
And snow to harm you, for none e'er hath traversed
This route as we have seen your army do."
    The Sháh abode a month. When he and host
Had been refreshed he sped thence merrily,
His heart prepared, toward the women's city,
And o'er the stream two thousand women passed
With crowns and earrings on. There was a forest
Thick and well watered; all the place was glad,
And flourishing. The women brought a store
Of provand and bright, figured tapestries
Out to a mead and, when Sikandar reached
The city of Harúm, they flocked to him
Out of their settlements. Full many a crown
They proffered him, as well as raiment, gems,
And things both fair and sweet. These he accepted,
Received the women with all courtesy,
And gave them quarters in that charming spot.
    When night turned day he visited the city,
And occupied himself in seeing it,
Investigating all its usages
Till all had been made clear. He questioned much,
Surveyed the river. and departed westward.

He found a mighty city of brave men
With ruddy faces and with flaxen hair,
All fit for battle and the day of fight.
They came before Sikandar at his bidding
With bodies bent and hands upon their heads.
He asked their chiefs: "What wonders have ye here?"
    An elder thus replied : "Star-favoured Sháh,
And lion-capturer! there is a Deep
Beyond the city. Brighter than that water
Naught have we seen, for when the radiant sun
Arriveth there it setteth in those depths.
Beyond it all is dark and lost to sight,
While of that place of darkness I have heard
So many tales that they are numberless.
A man of lore, a worshipper of God,
Declareth that there is a fountain there,
And mine informant, who is wise and great,
Referreth to it as the Fount of Life.
That wise, discerning man said : 'How shall one
Who drinketh of the Fount of Life e'er die?
From Paradise it runneth ; wash therein
The body, and thy sins will pass away.'"
    Then Cæsar said : "As to this place of gloom,
How can beasts fare therein?"
                                    The devotee
Made answer : "Ye must ride upon young horses."
    The Sháh bade herdsmen gather to the camp
The herds at large and chose ten thousand steeds,
All four-year-olds and fit for battle-needs.

§ 29

*How Sikandar went into the Gloom to seek the Water of Life
and spake with Birds and Isráfíl*

Sikandar, summoning his prudent chiefs,
Marched cheerly thence his host and reached a city
Whereto he saw no middle and no end,
And having all things needful in abundance.
'Twas full of garths, parks, halls, and palaces.
There he dismounted and at dawn next day
Went forward unattended toward the Source
Which in his story of the hero's fortunes
The rustic minstrel calleth that of Life.
He tarried there until the sun, grown pale,
Sank in that fount of lapis-lazuli.
He saw the wonder wrought by holy God—
The Bright One's disappearance from the world—
Returned to camp, and pondered much.   That night
He prayed to God, mused on the Fount of Life,   C. 1340
First chose the most enduring of his troops,
Took with him food for forty days and more,
And went forth eagerly to look on wonders.
He camped his other troops within the city,
And sought and found a guide.   Khisr, who was chief
Among the nobles of that folk, advised him.
Sikandar did as Khisr enjoined, surrendered
Both heart and soul to his allegiance,
And said: "Shrewd-hearted man! be diligent
Herein, and if we shall obtain the Water
Of Life then we will pass much time in prayer.
He will not die who nurtureth thus his soul,
And in his wisdom refugeth with God.
I have two signets that in sight of water
Shine out at night like suns.   Take one, lead on,
And tender well thy person and thy life;

The other one shall light me on my way.
'I go amid the Darkness with mine escort,
And we will see what God omnipotent
Preserveth hidden where so much is seen.
Thou art my leader, and He is my refuge,
And showeth me the Water and the Way."
　　Now when the troops marched toward the Fount of
　　　Life
A shout rose from the desert : "God is great !" [1]
　　Khisr left that station and all food behind him,
And fared thus for two days and nights while none
Bestirred his lips to eat.　Upon the third
Two ways showed mid the Darkness, and the Shâh
Lost trace of Khisr.　What while the prophet went
Toward the Fount of Life, exalting thus
His living head to Saturn, bathed his body
And head in that bright Water, sought no guard
Save God, drank, rested, and returned apace,
More instant ever both in prayer and praise,
Sikandar reached the light and saw a mountain
Both high and bright, and on its top four columns
Of aloe-wood uplifted to the clouds.
On every column was a mighty nest,
And in each nest there sat a huge, green bird,
Which, speaking loudly in the Rúman tongue,
Hailed the victorious master of the world,
Who hurried to them when he heard.　One said :—
"O votary of toil ! what seekest thou
Within this Wayside Inn, for though thou raisest
Thy head to heaven above it will dismiss thee
C. 1341　In grief at last ?　But now that thou hast come,
Hast seen aught built of reeds or reed-baked bricks ?"
　　He answered : "Both : our dwellings are directly
Or indirectly made with reeds."
　　　　　　　　　　　　　　The bird,

[1] Alláh akbar. Properly "God is greatest." This part is very Arabic.

On hearing this reply, perched lower down,
Astonying that worshipper of God,
And asked him: "Hast thou heard within the world
The sounds of harp, of reveller, and song?"
  He made this answer: "One, whose lot it is
To have no share in joy, the glad account not
Although for them he pour out heart and soul."
  From that tall column of lign-aloe-wood
The bird flew to the ground; its musky perch
Was void. The bird inquired: "Do understanding
And right prevail or do defect and guile?"
  The Sháh made answer: "He that seeketh know-
    ledge
Is eminent in every company."
  Back from dark ground to column went the bird
And, having cleaned its talons with its beak,
Inquired of Cæsar: "Why do devotees
Dwell on the mountains?"
                            "The devout," he said,
" Find not another place so good for worship."
  The bird ran up the column to its nest.
The monarch was delighted with that fowl,
Which with its talons sharpened up its bill
In full security.   Then it instructed
Sikandar to ascend the topmost peak,
Afoot and unescorted, there to see
That which would cause the merriest to weep.
On hearing this he went toward the mountain
Alone to view the sight upon its summit,
And there saw Isráfíl, with trump in hand
And head uplifted, standing at his post,
Wind on his lips and moisture in his eye,
Till God shall bid him blow.   On seeing Sikandar
He roared like thunder: "O thou slave of greed!
Toil not so much, because some day a Call
Will reach thine ears. Be less concerned for crown

And throne.   Make ready to depart and bind
The baggage on."
　　　　　　　"It is my lot from fortune,"
The Sháh replied, "for save by stir and roaming
I may not look on sight and mystery."
　　He then descended, wailing and imploring
The Giver of all good, and, with a guide
Preceding him, advanced along that route,
Involved in gloom, which when the army entered
A cry ascended from the darksome heights:—
" He that shall take a stone up from the road
Will grieve for what he beareth in his hand,

C. 1342　And if he taketh none he will repent,
And heartily in each case seek a cure."
　　The soldiers all gave ear, and every one
Grew thoughtful at that cry since, whether they
Took stones or no, must they not count on ills?
One said : " It is the punishment of guilt
To bear repentance and the stones as well."
　　Another said : " We should take some; perchance
We may not have to savour pain and toil."
　　One man took of the stones; another left them;
A third through indolence took little ones.
When from the region of the Fount of Life
They reached the plain, emerging from the Gloom,
Each sought the truth and then perceived the trick.
One had his bosom full of jewels cut,
Another his with jewels in the rough,
And both regretted that they had so few;
Why had they passed by emeralds as vile?
But sorrier still was he that picked up none
At leaving precious gems as he had done.

§ 30

How Sikandar went to the East, saw Wonders, and built a
Barrier against Yájúj and Májúj

Two weeks he tarried and, when rested, marched.
He set forth eastward, having seen the west ;
His purpose in the world was wayfaring.
Now as he went he saw a noble city ;
" No wind or dust passed o'er it," thou wouldst say.
Whenas the drums beat on the elephants
The chiefs came out two miles to welcome him.
The Sháh, on seeing them, received them well,
Exalting them o'er circling Sol, and asked :—
" What matchless marvels have ye in these parts ? "
    They loosed their tongues and thus bewailed their
        fortune :—
" A very grievous case confronteth us,
And we will tell it to the conquering Sháh.
By reason of this cloud-capt mountain-range
Our hearts are full of anguish, toil, and grief.
Since for resistance we are powerless
Yájúj there and Májúj give us no sleep,
For when a portion of them reach our city
Our portion is all misery and travail.
Their faces all resemble those of beasts,
Their tongues are black, their eyes like blood, their
    faces
Are black, their teeth are like wild boars' ! Who dareth
Draw nigh to them ? Their bodies all are clad   C. 1343
With hair, the hue of indigo, their breasts,
Their bosoms, and their ears resemble those
Of elephants. They sleep upon one ear,
And use the other as a coverlet.[1]
The mothers have a thousand children each,

[1] See p. 80.

And who can reckon them? They herd like beasts,
They go apace and run like onagers.
In spring, when clouds roar and the green sea heaveth,
The clouds draw up great monsters from the waves,
While air is roaring like a mighty lion,
And pour them down in masses: then these folk
Come troop on troop and batten year by year
Upon these monsters and thereby grow lusty
In limbs and body. Afterward they feed
On herbage, scattering to gather it.
In winter they are pale and thin, their voices
Like doves'; but through those monsters in the spring
They are as wolves and roar right lustily.
Now if the great Sháh could devise a means
To liberate our hearts from this distress,
He will receive the praise of every one,
And will prolong his sojourn in the world.
Exert thy power and do this work for us,
For thou too needest help from holy God."

Sikandar mused at them, grew grave, and pondered,
Then answered thus: "I will defray the cost;
Your city must provide both aid and labour.
By help of God, our Guide and Succourer,
I will reduce this way of theirs to reason."

All cried: "May fortune's ills be far from thee,
O Sháh! We are the slaves of thy good pleasure,
Thy lifelong servitors. We will supply
All that thou need'st, for we have no concern
More urgent."
　　　　　　　　So Sikandar came and viewed
The heights, and took with him a troop of sages.
He ordered to bring blacksmiths, copper, brass,
And heavy hammers, mortar, stone, and fire-wood
Past reckoning, bring all things requisite.
They brought him everything that he demanded
In measureless supplies. When all was ready,

And planned, the masons and the smiths, all those
Of mastery in their trade throughout the world,
Assembled to Sikandar to assist him
In that most needful work.   From every province
The experts mustered, and he built two walls
Across the mountain-pass from base to crest,
One hundred royal cubits broad, one cubit
Of charcoal, one of iron, in between   C. 1344
Strewed copper, and showered sulphur in the midst,
Such is the craft and subtlety of kings !
He laid thus his materials course on course,
And when from top to bottom all was set,
They mixed much ghee and naphtha, poured it over
Those substances, and on the top shot charcoal
In ass-loads.   Then the Sháh bade fire the whole,
And five score thousand smiths blew up the flames,
As bidden by that king victorious.
A sound of blowing went up from the mountain,
The stars were frighted at the glowing fire.
Thus passed a season with the fire in blast,
And smiths a-toil.   They ran the substances
Together, fusing them in that fierce blaze.
Thus was the world delivered from Yájúj
And from Májúj, and earth grew habitable,
For by Sikandar's famous barrier
The world escaped the misery of strife.
It was five hundred cubits high, about
One hundred broad.   The nobles blessed the Sháh,
And said: "May neither time nor earth lack thee."
   They brought before him in abundant store
Whatever was the produce of those parts .
He would accept of naught and went his ways;
His doings filled the whole world with amaze

§ 31

How Sikandar saw a Corpse in a Palace of Jewels on the Top
of a Mountain, and the Speaking Tree, and how he was
warned of his Death

He marched one month till Sháh and troops were
    weary.
At length he reached a mount where he beheld not
A man or beast.   Its peak he saw to be
Of lapis-lazuli and thereupon
A palace built of topazes, with lustres
Of crystal everywhere, and in the middle
A fount of brackish water.   A ruby served
For lamp and lighted palace, mount, and heights ;
The light fell on the water, and the jewel
Illumed the palace like the sun.   Beside
The fount was set a double golden throne
Where lay a hapless one with human body
And with a wild boar's head—a helpless corpse
On that fine throne.   His couch beneath was camphor,
And o'er him spread a mantle of brocade.
C. 1345 Whoever went to carry aught away,
Or even trod the dust upon the floor,
Died in convulsions on the spot.   A cry
Came from that briny fount: "O slave of greed !
Be not so mad.   Much hast thou seen that none
Besides hath seen.   'Tis time to draw thy rein
Because thy life is ending, and thy throne
Of sovereignty is going all astray."
    Sikandar feared, turned him about apace,
And came back to his camp as swift as smoke.
He marched thence quickly, wailing and invoking
The name of God, then from that mountain took
The desert-route in dudgeon and concerned
About his life.   All sorrow and in tears

He went with troops behind and guides before
Till, by that desert-route, he reached a city,
And joyed to hear the voice of men. The land
Was all a garden, gladding to delight
The heart of man. The magnates of the city—
The men of valour—went to welcome him ;
All praised him, showering on him gold and gems,
And said : " O Sháh ! how blesséd 'tis that thou
Shouldst traverse thus our coasts ! No host before
E'er visited this city, none of us
E'er heard the name of Sháh, but now that thou
Hast come our souls are thine, and mayst thou be
In spirit lucid and in body hale."
   Sikandar gladdened in his heart at them.
He rested from the desert-march, and asked :—
" Of marvel what is there for me to note ? "
   The guides thus answered : " O victorious Sháh,
And pure of rede ! there is a wonder here,
Whose match none in the world of small and great
E'er hath beheld—a tree with double trunk—
A marvel manifest. One trunk is female,
The other male ; they speak, have boughs, and flourish.
At night the female yieldeth speech and perfume,
The male doth speak by day."
                    Sikandar went
With cavaliers of Rúm and native chiefs
Of whom he asked : " This tree—when speaketh it
Aloud ? " The interpreter replied : " One trunk
Will talk or ever day's ninth hour hath passed,
So that the auspicious Sháh will hear its voice.
When it is night the female trunk will speak ;
Its foliage will savour as 'twere musk."
   The Sháh asked : " When we pass the tree, good friend !   C. 1346
What marvel meet we then ? "
                       " Of going further,"
The interpreter replied, " there is no question.

There is no place beyond it, and guides call it
' The World's End.' "

     Then the blest Sháh with his Rúmans
Set forward.   When he reached the speaking tree
The ground was seething hot, and all its surface
Was hid by beasts' skins.

     " What are these, and who
Hath torn beasts thus ? " he asked of his informant,
Who said : " The tree hath many devotees,
Who, if they hunger while engaged in worship,
Feed on the flesh of beasts."

     When Sol attained
The apex of heaven's vault Sikandar heard
Aloft a cry proceeding from the leaves
Of that tall tree—an awful, boding cry.
He feared and asked of the interpreter :—
" Shrewd, trusty friend ! what say the talking leaves,
Because they bathe my heart in lymph of blood ? "

  The guide replied : " O favourite of fortune !
The leaves upon the boughs of this tree say :—
' Why doth Sikandar roam so o'er the world,
For he hath had his portion of good things,
And, when he shall have reigned for twice seven years,
Must quit the throne of sovereignty ? "

     Sikandar
Wept tears of blood ; the guide's words wrung his heart.
Thenceforth he spake to no one, but remained
All sorrowful till midnight.   Then the leaves
Upon the other trunk gave utterance.
Again the Sháh asked of his friendly guide :—
" What is it that the other branches say ? "

  Thus his informant solved the mystery :—
" The female branches say : ' Thou travailest
In this wide world for greed and for addition.
Why torture thus thy soul ?   It is thy passion
To go about the world, aflicting folk

And slaying kings. Thou hast not long to live;
Do not thyself cloud and contract thy days.' "
The great king asked of the interpreter :—
" O good, discerning man ! inquire if I
Shall be in Rúm when my dark day shall come,
And if my mother see me not alive
Will she at last enshroud this face of mine ? "
The speaking tree said to the Sháh : " Be speedy,
And bind the baggage on. Thy mother, kindred
In Rúm, and face-veiled ladies there will look
On thee no more. Death in an alien land
Will come ere long, crown, diadem, and throne
Grow tired of thee."

C. 1347

       He heard and left the tree,
Heart-stricken by the scimitar of fortune.
When he reached camp the noble native chiefs
Went home and, when they had made ready gifts,
Came hurrying to the Sháh. There were a breastplate,
Resplendent as the Nile and wide and broad
As is an elephant's hide, two elephant-tusks
Five cubits long—a toil to lift—mail-coats
And rich brocade, and, made of solid gold,
A hundred eggs, each weighing sixty mans [1]
If weighed as drachms, and a rhinoceros
In gold and gems. Accepting these he led
His host away and tears—his heart's blood—shed.

§ 32

How Sikandar marched his Army to Chín, carried his own
 Letter to Faghfúr, and returned to his Army with the Answer

He led his army thence toward Chín and raised
The chiefs' heads to the Pleiads. Stage by stage
He crossed the desert till in forty days

---

[1] The weight of the " man " varies with the locality. The " man "
of Tabriz "—the smallest— = from 7 to 7½ lbs. av.

He reached the sea,[1] dismounted there his troops
And pitched the camp-enclosure of brocade.
He ordered then a scribe to write a letter
As from Sikandar, conqueror of cities,
Bade that the letter should comprise all kinds
Of fair and foul, and, when the scribe had finished.
Went as ambassador. He chose a Persian,
A shrewd man, one with him in heart and word,
To bid him "Do" or "Do not."   Then he gave
The captain of the host charge of the troops,
And of the Rúmans took with him five sages.
.When tidings reached Faghfúr: " There is an envoy
Approaching Chín " he sent a force of troops
To meet him, and Sikandar fared in state.
He reached that spacious court.   Faghfúr beheld
That chosen troop of valiant men and came,
With mind averse and anxious, from the entry
To meet Sikandar who ran up to him,
Did him obeisance, and sat long within
The hall of audience.   Faghfúr gave greeting,
Received him well, and lodged him splendidly.
    Now when the bright Lamp rose above the mountains
They brought a horse caparisoned with gold,
And summoned the Sháh's envoy to the presence.
Sikandar spake at large, said what was fit,
Then gave the letter, and recalled what Cæsar
Had said.   The letter's superscription ran :—
" From Rúm's Sháh, who is world-lord and the prince
Of every march and land, whom other monarchs
Praise, to Faghfúr, the glory of the realm."
    The letter thus began : " Praise to the Maker
From us His slaves," and then went on to say :—
" Our will for Chín is this, that it should prosper.
Ye should not fight us ; that cut short Fúr's life.
So was it with Dárá, who ruled the world,"

C. 1348

[1] *Cf.* p. 174.

Faryán the Arab, and with other chiefs.
From west to east none hath escaped our sway.
Heaven knoweth not the number of my troops
Though Venus, Mercury, and Sol shall count them.
If thou infringest my command in aught
Thou wilt but vex the country and thyself.
Prepare thy tribute when thou readest this,
Be not aggrieved, and meddle not with evil.
If thou wilt come and see me and my host
I will regard thee as ally and friend,
Assure to thee thy throne and crown, and fortune
Shall harm thee not ; but if thou wouldst not come
Before thy lord, send to my treasury
The rarities of Chín, as golden ware,
Swords, steeds and signets, raiment, slaves, and thrones
Of ivory, rich brocade and torques and crowns—
Whate'er thou hast—as thou wouldst be unscathed
By us.   Repulse mine army by these means,
And keep in safety crown and throne and treasure.
Thou know'st both courses now : my host expecteth
Thy fall or rise.   The Maker bless thee.   Mayst
Thou ne'er have reason to recall my words!"
    The lord of Chín, on seeing such a letter,
Was wroth but showed it not and with a smile
Said to the envoy: "Heaven is thy Sháh's consort !
Tell what thou canst about his looks, his stature,
His prowess, and his speech."
                                    The envoy said :—
"O chief of Chín! know, none is like Sikandar
On earth.   In prowess, bounty, rede, and wisdom,
He passeth man's conception.   Cypress-tall
Is he, an elephant in strength, a Nile
In bounty, and in tongue a trenchant sword.
His blandness draweth eagles from the clouds."
    Faghfúr, on hearing this, took other order.   C. 1349
He bade serve meat and wine, and deck a hall

Within the garth.   They quaffed till it was dark,
And they were all bemused.   The lord of Chín
Said to the ambassador: " Be Jupiter
Thy Sháh's ally.   Tomorrow I will answer,
And make the day right glorious in thy sight."
  Now when Sol rose in Leo, and the sky
Had night alow, Sikandar drew anear,
But not with ill prepense.   Faghfúr inquired :—
" How went the night, for thou wast flushed wine-red
Yestre'en when going hence ? " then bade a scribe
To come with paper, musk, and spicery,
And wrote a warm rejoinder, and adorned,
Like Paradise, that paper wrought in Chín ;
And first he praised the Judge, the Lord of manhood,
Of justice, and accomplishment, the Lord
Of learning, self-control, and Faith, " and may
He bless the king of Rúm.   Thy courteous envoy
Hath reached us with the letter of the Sháh,
That seeker after knowledge.   We have read
Thy royal words and with the great discussed them.
For what in fight and feast befell Dárá,
Son of Dáráb, Faryán, and Fúr whom thou
Didst triumph over and become the shepherd,
With monarchs as the flock : the Lord of sun
And moon so ordered it ; impute it not
To prowess and the number of thy troops,
For when a chief's life endeth 'tis all one
To die in feast or fight.   Thou foughtest them
Upon their fated day which altereth not.
Boast not and vaunt not over them, for thou
Past doubt wilt pass thyself, though thou be iron.
Where are Jamshíd, Zahhák, and Farídún ?
They came from wind and went to wind again.
I neither fear thee nor will fight with thee.
Not, as with thee, doth bluster fill my head,
Who am not used to bloodshed, while ill-doing

Is not accordant to my Faith.   Thou call'st me
Before thee but in vain, for I serve God,
Not king.   I send thee more than thou dost ask;
Regarding largess I am not contentious."
    Upon his cheek Sikandar felt the blush
Of shame, his liver arrow-pierced with what
Faghfúr had said, and thought: "None shall behold me
Fare in disguise henceforth."
                          He left the palace,   C. 1350
Went to his lodging, and prepared to leave.
The great Faghfúr unlocked his treasury;
He grudged not bounty.   First he bade make ready
An ivory throne and fifty crowns inlaid
With gems, and load with gold and silver ware
A thousand camels and a thousand more
With silk and satins, with brocade of Chín,
With camphor, aloe, musk, and spicery.
He liveth at his ease who scorneth gold.
Of squirrel, ermine, and of sable pelts,
Of rugs, of horse-hides, and of weazel-skins,
The prudent treasurer brought forth and packed
Of every sort two thousand, brought withal
High-mettled steeds caparisoned with gold,
And slave-boys too, three hundred, with gold girdles.
They brought three hundred red-haired camels laden
With many a rarity of Chín.   Faghfúr
Chose from among the elders one of weight,
And sugared speech, and bade him go with greeting
And message to the Sháh, and bear to him
The glad news that the chiefs would do him homage
So long as he was in the coasts of Chín.
The envoy set forth with Sikandar.   Who
Would think that he was Sháh?   But when the sailors
Saw him, sprang up, and lightly spread the sails,
And when the viceroy met him with the troops,

Reporting what had chanced,[1] while all the soldiers
Praised him and bent their faces to the ground,
The man of Chín perceived : "It is the Sháh !"
And went to him afoot protesting loudly.
Sikandar said to him : "Make no excuses,
And mention not the matter to Faghfúr."
　　That night he rested and next day at dawn,
When he was set in peace upon his throne,
He gave the envoy gifts, and said : "May wisdom
Be ever thine.　Go to Faghfúr and say :—
"With us thou hast great honour.　Chín is thine,
If I may say so, and what more thou wilt.
I shall abide at present where I am ;
One cannot hurry with so large a host."
　　Back with the speed of wind the envoy hied,
And told Faghfúr what Cæsar had replied.

§ 33

*How Sikandar returned from Chín, made War against
the Sindians, and went to Yaman*

C. 1351　　The Sháh abode a month and when the troops
Were rested led them back.　From that green sea [2]
They fared by wilderness and longsome ways,
Stage after stage, until they reached Chaghwán,
And saw a fortified and prosperous city.
The magnates of the land, those famed and wise,
Came to Sikandar's presence while the chiefs
Set forward from Chaghwán with offerings,
And presents to his gate.　At once Sikandar
Began to question them : "What sights have ye
Of marvel here ? "
　　　　　　　　One said : "We know of none,
O king! worth seeing.　Beggary and toil

---

[1] Or "when Sikandar had announced the result of his undertaking."
[2] *Or* the Green Sea.　*Cf.* NAR, p. 40.

Are here, and thou wilt take naught hence but wind."
   The Sháh, on hearing what the speaker said,
Marched from Chaghwán toward Sind whose cavaliers
Went out to meet him while from Hind came help.
All those heart-stricken on account of Fúr,
Their hands all bathed in blood, brought elephants,
And Indian bells. Arose the battlecry,
And clarion's blare. The Sindians' chief was named
Bandáwa, an illustrious cavalier,
And puissant. The armies shocked together,
And earth became all mountain-like with slain.
Night came; no Sindian stayed upon that field.
Sikandar led his army in pursuit,
And captured elephants fourscore and five,
As well as golden crowns and scimitars
And treasures. Women, children, and old men
Went weeping to the Sháh while on his way,
And said: "O prudent Sháh! restrain thyself,
Burn not our land, slay not our little ones,
For thy day too will pass, and blest is he
That walketh innocently."
                          He had no ruth,
Not sparing e'en the wounded. They enslaved
A host of women, children, young, and old.
He went toward Nímrúz by way of Bust,
And purged the world of foes. Thence he proceeded,
World-conquering with his famed host, Yaman-ward,
Whose monarch, hearing, went with chiefs to meet
      him,
Selecting native gifts of price and fair,   C. 1352
As was most fit—of striped stuff of Yaman
Ten camel-loads and five of gold, ten more
Of drachms (when drachms are had hearts are not sad),
A thousand frails of saffron, with brocade
And raiment past compute. Among his treasures
He had a cup of emerald and pearls

Unpierced, in number seventy-five, besides
A cup of lapis-lazuli containing
Three score of topazes and on the top
Ten ruby signet-rings. These he delivered
To those in waiting with his benisons.
They reached the camp-enclosure of the Sháh
With all these gifts and offerings. Sikandar
Saluted and received the monarch well,
And seated him beside the throne, and he—
The monarch of Yaman—blessed him and said:—
" Be victor with thy troops.   'Twill give me joy
If thou wilt sojourn with me for two months
That Sháh and host may rest them from the road."
    Sikandar blessed him, saying: " May thy mate
Be wisdom ever."
                When the morning came
Yaman's king went his way, and all that coast
Resounded with the romage of the host.

§ 34

How Sikandar marched toward Bábil and found the
Treasure of Kai Khusrau in a City

Sikandar led his troops toward Bábil;
The air was hidden by their dust. He marched,
He and his host, a month; they saw no rest-place.
At length they reached a mount whose top was
    hidden.
A black cloud rested on it; thou hadst said:—
" 'Twas near to Saturn."   They could find no road,
And Sháh and army halted in dismay.
They scaled laboriously the craggy height,
And even light-armed troops were overworn.
When they were all exhausted by the march
A deep sea showed upon the farther side.

The host rejoiced to view sea, plain, and road.
They marched toward that deep sea, and praised the
    Maker.
The place was full of beasts; the army lived
On game. Far off a savage showed all hairy,
With mighty ears. His body 'neath its fell
Seemed indigo, his ears like elephant's
In breadth. On seeing such the soldiers seized
And bore him to Sikandar who beheld
Amazed, invoked o'er him the name of God,
And said: "What man art thou? What is thy name?
What get'st thou from the sea? What seekest thou?"

  "My father and my mother," he replied,
"Gave me, O Sháh! this name of Gúsh-bistar."[1]

  The Sháh asked: "What is that amid the water
Out yonder toward the rising of the sun?"

  "O Sháh!" he said, "for ever live renowned.
There is a city there like Paradise,
And not, thou wouldest say, compact of earth.
Thou wilt not look on palace there or house
Whose outside is not made throughout of bones,
And, brighter than the sun, within the halls
Are limned the visage of Afrásiyáb,
And that of Kai Khusrau, the combative,
His greatness, manliness, and enterprises.
All these are painted on the bones of fish;
Thou wilt see nowhere any dust or earth;
The people live on fish and naught besides.[2]
Myself I will escort the army thither
If the famed Sháh shall bid."

               Sikandar said
To him with ears: "Go to, fetch me a native
That I may look upon a novelty."

  So Gúsh-bistar set forth at once and made
All speed to go to city and to folk,

C. 1353

---

[1] *I.e.* Ear-bed. *Cf.* p. 163.   [2] See p. 69.

And gave them Cæsar's message, saying : "The Sháh,
That famed one, calleth for you."
                                        Of that city,
When young and old and high and low heard this,
There went across the water seventy men,
Possessed of wisdom or advanced in years,
And clad in silks, and some were young, some old.
The old and famed bare each a golden cup
A-brim with pearls, the young bare each a crown.
They came to Cæsar, bowed, and reverenced him ;
They held long talk with him and said : "The trea-
    sures
Of Kai Khusrau are in our custody,
And would befit a new Sháh like thyself."
    Thereat Sikandar hurried o'er the water
Toward their city, viewed it all—its marts,
And streets—and visited the treasure-house.
The hoard was all of crowns and thrones of gold,
With coronets and necklaces and girdles.
None knew its worth for none could reckon it.
C. 1354   The Sháh took all and sped to camp, rejoicing.
He stayed that night, but when cock-crow had come
Rose at his gate the sound of kettledrum.

§ 35

*How Sikandar went to the City of Bábil, wrote a Letter to
Arastális, and received his Answer*

Sikandar marched thence to Bábil ; the earth
Was hidden by his host.   He knew that death
Was near and that his day was overcast,
And thought to leave none of the royal race
To lead an army to make war on Rúm,
And set his foot upon that prosperous land.
When this thought gat possession of his brain

He wrote à letter to Arastálís,
And said: "It is my purpose not to leave
One of the royal seed. I have been round
The seven climes and taken many princes.
In sooth my death is nigh, so day hath darkened."
He bade that every one of Kaian seed
Should make him ready to appear at court,
Not dreaming of foul play. Now when they bare
The letter to the sage his heart was riven.
He answered instantly and, thou hadst said,
Made of the lashes of his eye his pen-point:—[1]
"The letter of the world's king hath arrived.
Thou must withhold thy hand from evil-doing,
Abandon this ill purpose, expiate
The thought by giving alms, restrain thyself,
Commit thyself to God and in the world
Sow only seed of good. We live for death,
For die we must past help. None hath borne off
The kingship with him, but hath gone and left
His greatness to another. So be ware,
Shed not the blood of princes else a curse
Will be upon thee till the Resurrection.
Again, when for the Íránian troops no Sháh
Shall sit upon the throne hosts will arrive
From Turkistán and Hind, Sakláb and Chín,
Arrive from all sides, and 'twill be no marvel
If they that take Írán shall war with Rúm.
Not e'en a breath must harm the Kaian-born.
Convoke the Rúman and Íránian chiefs
To merrymake, feast, conference, and banquet.
Appoint to every chief a fitting province,
And start a new roll with the names of Rúman
And of Íránian chiefs at whose expense
Thou hast obtained the world, but give to none

C. 1355

---

[1] *I.e.* either "with the tears running down his pen" or "with great subtlety."

The lordship o'er another and withal
Call none of them the Sháh, and let these Kaians
Serve as the shields of thine own land if thou
Wouldst have not Rúm invaded."

                      When Sikandar
Received this answer he made haste to change
His purpose and bade summon to his court
The Rúman and Íránian notables
That were possessed of valour, ranked them duly,
And drew the patents so that none should seek
The least addition to the share assigned him.
To these renowned and independent princes
They gave the name of "Tribal Kings."

                          The night
Whereon Sikandar reached Bábil, and saw
The chiefs right glad to look on him again,
A woman bare a child that filled beholders
With wonderment. It had a lion's head
With hoofs for feet, an ox's tail, the breast
And shoulders of a man. The monster died ᴠ
At birth but, though such things are best forgotten,
They bare it to the Sháh forthwith who gazed
Thereon with horror, held it ominous,
And said : "Let this be hidden by the dust."

   He summoned many readers of the stars,
And held discourse at large of that dead child.
In great dismay they veiled their views thereon
From that fair-fortuned Sháh who ráged, and said :—
"If aught be hid forthwith I will behead you,
And naught but lions' maws shall be your shroud!"

   The Sháh being wroth, they told him : "Famous king !
That thou wast born beneath the Sign of Leo
Was patent both to archmage and to chief.
Thou seest the lion-like head on this dead child ;
So will the head of thine own empire droop.
All thine astrologers have said as much

Already and adduced the signs."

                              Sikandar,
On hearing this, was grieved; his wits and counsel
Failed, and he said: "Death is past cure. My heart
Is not concerned thereat. No longer life
Is mine. Our period waxeth not nor waneth."
  He sickened at Bábil that very day,
Knew that calamity was near and called
A veteran scribe before him to impart
The dispositions that he had at heart.

§ 36

Sikandar's Letter to his Mother

He bade to write a letter to his mother,   C. 1356
And said to her: "One cannot blink Death's presage!
In this world I have had the appointed share,
And waned life waxeth not. Grieve not at all
About my death, for death is no new thing:
Royal or base whoe'er is born must die.
I will instruct the Rúman chiefs that when
They quit this land they must consult thy pleasure
In all things and obey thee loyally.
On every prince among the Íránians,
That might have caused calamity to Rúmans
I have bestowed a province. Now when each
Of these hath entered on his government,
Good sooth, he will have no desire for Rúm;
Our marches and our land will rest from foes.
Embalm me dead upon the soil of Misr,
And spill no word of mine. Of my dínárs
Bestow one hundred thousand every year
Upon the husbandmen; and should a son
Be born to Rúshanak his father's name
In truth will live, and Rúm must have no king

Save him, for he will renovate that land;
But in her travail if she bear a daughter
Espouse her to the son of Failakús;
Call him my son, not son-in-law, and keep
Within the world through him my memory green.
Send back too scathless to her sire in state
Kaid's daughter with her own devoted slaves,
And purses. Furnish litters for the journey;
Send too the crowns and gems, the gold and silver,
Brought by her from her sire, to Hindústán
Whene'er she would depart. I have achieved
All that I purposed here and now perforce
Must think of death. List to my last requests,
And add not thereunto. First fashion me
A golden coffin. Let my shroud be made
In worthy fashion of gold cloth of Chín,
And saturate with ambergris, and let
No pains be spared for me, but seal my coffin
With pitch and camphor, musk and spicery.
First pour in honey, let it be above,
And let there be brocade of Chín below;

C. 1357　Then let my corpse be laid inside the coffin,
And, when ye veil my visage, there an end.
O my wise mother! keep in mind my counsel
While life endureth. All that I have gathered
From Hind, Túrán, Makrán, Írán, and Chín,
Keep thou, but give thy superfluities,
What thou canst not enjoy thyself, away.
'Tis my desire for thee, my loving mother!
That thou be watchful and serene of soul,
And not too toilful, for none tarrieth here
For ever. Surely when thy day is done
Our souls will meet again. 'Tis nobler far
To suffer than to love, and 'tis the mean
That yield to passion. Since my body once
Was all thy care for months and years, now pray

To God for my pure soul and help me thus,
For prayer is all in all. Behold and see
If there be any in earth's round whose soul
Is stricken not at death."
                    He sealed and closed
The letter, and bade men on speedy steeds
Convey these tidings from Bábil to Rúm :—
" The Grace of king of kingship is bedimmed ! "
   Now when the army was aware thereof
The world was darkened to the chiefs, who set
Their faces toward the throne of majesty,
And all the world was full of hue and cry.

§ 37

How Sikandar's Life ended and how they carried his Coffin to Iskandaríya

On hearing how the army was bestead,
And knowing that his time was near, Sikandar
Bade carry from the palace to the field
His throne. The troops bewailed his malady
When they beheld the Sháh's pale face. The plain
Was one great cry; they seethed as on quick fire.
All said : " What misadventure for the Rúmans
To lose their king ! Ill fortune is upon us,
And field and fell henceforth are desolate ;
Our foes have won their wish and gained their goal ;
The world becometh bitter to us now ;
In public and in private we shall wail ! "
   With failing voice said Cæsar : " Be devout,
Wise, modest, and heed all my last requests,
If ye would prosper both in soul and body.
When I have gone the work is left for you,
And fortune is not dealing ill with me."*

C. 1358

He spake, his life departed, and that Sháh

So famous, that host-shatterer, passed away.
A cry went up from all the host and split
The ears of heaven. The soldiers all strewed dust
Upon their heads and strained their hearts' blood
    through
The lashes of their eyes. They fired his palace,
And docked a thousand steeds, reversing all
Their saddles. Thou hadst said: "The earth lamenteth!"
They bore the golden bier out to the plain,
And wailing pierced the sky. A prelate laved
The corpse with clear rose-water, and besprinkled
Thereon pure camphor. Of gold-woven brocade
They made his winding-sheet, while all bewailed him,
And, having shrouded thus that noble form
Beneath brocade of Chín, they covered it
With honey to the feet and then sealed down
The lid of that strait coffin: passed away
That Tree so fruitful and so shadowing!
Thou bidest not within this Hostel. Why
Toy then with crown or cling to treasury?

    Now when they raised the coffin from the plain,
And passed it on from hand to hand, two voices—
A Rúman and a Persian—rose, and all
The talk was of the coffin. All the Persians
Said thus: "He should be buried in Írán
Where are the ashes of the kings of kings:
Why should ye speed the coffin round the world?"

    One of the Rúman counsellors replied:—
"It is not fitting here to bury him.
If ye will hear my rede aright Sikandar
Should pass back to the soil wherefrom he sprang."

    A Persian said withal: "Howe'er ye talk
This will reach no fair ending. I will show you
A field commemorating Sháhs of old.
Wise ancients call it Khurm. It hath a lake
And forest, and in answer to thy questions

A voice, which every one may hear, will speak
Out of the mountain. Thither bear some ancient
In his decrepitude, and there too stay
The coffin. Let him ask. Then if the mountain
Reply 'twill rede you well."

       Like mountain-sheep
They hurried to the wood that he called Khurm,
They asked their question and this answer came:—
" Why long delay the coffin of the Sháh?
Iskandaríya, which he built in life,
Is destined to contain Sikandar's dust."

 The soldiers heard the voice and bare away
The coffin from the wood without delay.

§ 38
How the Sages and other Folk lamented Sikandar

Now when they brought him to Iskandaríya   C. 1359
Another dispensation ruled the world.
They set his coffin on the plain; all earth
Was full of hue and cry. Men, women, children,
Above a hundred thousand had one reckoned,
Flocked to Iskandaríya to the coffin.
The wise Arastálís stood forth; a world,
With eyes all tears of blood, was watching him.
He laid his hand on that strait coffin, saying:—
"God-fearing Sháh! where are thy prudence, knowledge,
And rede that this strait coffin should become
Thy home? In youth's day, after these few years,
Why hast thou chosen the dust for pillowing?"

 The Rúman sages all assembled there:
One said: "O brazen-bodied Elephant!
Who overthrew thee? Who desired thy place?
Where now are all thy shrewdness and wise counsel?"

Another said : " Thou laidest up much gold :
Why now is gold embracing thus thy body ? "
Another said : " No man escaped thy hand,
But why, O Sháh ! didst thou rub hands with Death ? "
Another : " Thou hast rest from pain and toil
Ɛ ·ll as from the quest of rule and treasure."
Another : " When thou goest before thy Judge
That which thou sowed'st thou shalt reap withal."
Another : " Impotent is he that used
To shed the blood of kings."
                            Another said :—
" Soon shall we be as thou art, thou that wast
An uncut gem."
                    Another said : " The Master,
On seeing thee, will teach thee things forgotten."
Another said : " Since he hath been death-smitten
We should not clutch at self-aggrandisement."
Another said : " O higher than moon and sun !
Why hidest thou from all thy goodly face ? "
Another said : " A man of many parts
Is fain to cover him face-deep in gold,
But now, O man of such accomplishment,
And brave ! the yellow gold hath whelméd thee ! "
Another said : " Thou hast put on brocade,
And veiled to us therewith thy lovely looks.
Now lift thy head therefrom, for crown and armlet,
And ivory throne, of thee are all in quest."
   " Thou hast been severed from thy moon-faced
            youths,"
Another said, " and thralls of Chín and Rúm,
And huggest gold to thee. Oh ! deal not thus,
'Tis not kings' usage, with brocade and gold."
C. 1360   Another said : " What well advised reply
Will come to thee now that the Questioner
Will question thee, and say : ' Why didst thou shed
The blood of great men, and with so much stress

Didst struggle after treasure? Didst not see
How many of the great have died and borne
Naught from the world with them except the fame
Of their good deeds?'"
                    Another said: "Thy day
Is over-passed, thy tongue hath ceased to parle.
Now wilt thou see a mighty Court—a world
Wherein the sheep is parted from the wolf.[1]
The observer of thy throne and crown should turn
His reins from greatness for, as 'tis with thee,
It will abide with none. The tree of greatness.
Should not be planted!"
                    Said another: "Thy deeds
Are turned to wind, the chiefs' heads quit of thee."
   Another said: "Why in this Wayside Inn
Laboriously didst thou employ thyself,
Since this is all that thou hast gained by toil?
A narrow coffin is thine only wealth.
Thou seekest not the trumpet-call but choosest
The bondage of a bier?"
                    Another said :—
"What time thy troops depart thou wilt remain
All by thyself on this wide waste, good sooth!
With longing eyes pursue them as they go,
And mourn thine own lost life with boundless woe."

§ 39
How the Mother and Wife of Sikandar lamented him

Then came Sikandar's mother hurrying,
And long while pressed her visage over him.
She said: "O thou illustrious king of kings,
Lord of the world, star-favoured, and devout!

---

[1] Reading with P.

Near as thou art, thou art yet far from me,
Far from thy host, thy kingdom, and thy people.
May my soul wait on thine, and be their hearts
Plucked out that joy hereat."
                                            Then Rúshanak
Came full of anguish, saying : "Noble Sháh !
Where are Dárá, son of Dáráb, the master
And up-stay of the world,[1] and all the kings
Whose head the blast sent dustward on the day
Of battle ?   Like a fierce cloud charged with hail
Wast thou and safe, I would have said, from death.
With so much warfare, combating, and bloodshed
In single action and in stricken field,
I would have said that fate had given thee
Safe conduct, and thou keepest from thy men
The secret, yet hast thou, when thou hadst voided
The world of chiefs, cast off the imperial crown,
And when the tree which thou hadst planted bore
I see thee with the dust to comrade thee !"
    Now when the Crown of heaven had set, and when
The mighty men had had their fill of talk,
They hid Sikandar's coffin in the dust.
    To do such things the world is not afraid ;
It merely giveth back what it conveyed
From wind at first, and this I hold to be
Not clearly justice yet not tyranny.
To thee the how and why are hidden things,
And past the reach of subjects and of kings.
Yet beauty, kindness, generosity,
With good and joyance, still are left to thee ;
And, be thou chief or subject, with such store
I see not aught that thou canst wish for more ;
But if thou leavest here a name for vice
Thou'lt lose God's grace and jocund Paradise.[2]
    The ancient Hostel's wont is still the same ;

C. 1361

---

[1] Couplet omitted.   [2] Reading with P.

Sikandar went, but left behind him fame.
Though able six and thirty kings to slay
Where is his portion in the world to-day?
Ten cities were erected 'neath his sway,
All splendid, but ten thorn-brakes now are they.
He sought what no man ever sought before,
And wide-spread fame is left him but no more,
Yet fame is good for fame will not decay
Like some old dwelling weather-worn away.

The barrier of Sikandar we have past,
May all be well and of auspicious cast,
And may the monarch of the world [1] be.still
Of joyous heart and free from every ill.

§ 40

Firdausi's Complaint of the Sky and Appeal to God

High-springing arch of heaven! Oh! why dost thou,
   When eld is on me, keep me thus forlorn?
Thou madest much of me in youth but now
   Thou passest my decrepitude with scorn.
The pampered blossoms take a sallow hue,
   The pictured silk is cheapened by much stress,
The dainty cypress-tree is bent in two
   Within the garth, the bright lamp lustreless,
The mountain-top once black is capped with snow,
   The soldiers mark the Sháh's deficiencies:
Thou wast a mother to me long ago,
   Who needs shed blood-drops at thy tyrannies.
I find no wisdom or good faith in thee;
   Thy dark proceedings aggravate my lot:
Oh! would that thou hadst never nurtured me,
   Or, having nurtured, persecuted not!

[1] Mahmúd.

Whene'er I quit this gloom I will arraign
  This tyranny of thine before the Just,
Of thee before the All Holy One complain
  With clamourings and head bestrewn with dust.

C. 1362   Time saw how eld increased my misery,
But laid the more part of the blame on me,
And thus to me high heaven made reply:—
"O thou that art not wronged and yet dost cry!
Why lookest thou to me for good and ill?
  Do such complaints as thine become the sage?
In everything thou betterest me still,
  And canst the famine of thy soul assuage
With knowledge. Food, sleep, choice of home are thine;
  To good and ill 'tis thine to seek the path;
All that thou chargest is no fault of mine,
  For neither sun nor moon such knowledge hath.
Ask Him that made them to be Guide to thee,
  Made day and night, religion, law, who saith:—
Be,'_and all is as He would have it be.
  A fool is he that knoweth other Faith.
In His creation I am but a thrall,
  A servant unto Him who fashioned me;
To do His bidding is mine all in all;
  I never swerve from His authority.
Turn then to God, to Him for succour fly,
  Imploring no unconscionable boon,
And own that none is master of the sky
  Save He that kindled Venus, Sun, and Moon.
His blessing on Muhammad's spirit be,
And on his comrades all increasingly."[1]

[1] See p. 196.

III

THE ASHKÁNIAN DYNASTY

XXI

THE ASHKÁNIANS

THEY REIGNED TWO HUNDRED YEARS

ARGUMENT

THE poet praises Sultán Mahmúd and then, having no subject-matter in connexion with this dynasty, proceeds to narrate the story of the rise of the race of Sásán in the person of Ardshír Pápakán and of his triumph over Ardawán, the last of the Ashkánians. He then goes on to tell of Ardshír's campaign against the Kurds, and of the strange case of Haftwád and the Worm.

NOTE

The abridgment of the epoch of the Ashkánians to 200 years is more drastic even than that of other Oriental writers. Mas'údí's curious explanation of this matter will be found later on.[1]

In one respect at least the Sháhnáma presents a remarkable analogy to the land of its origin: the central portion of both is a barren waste. Of the five centuries and more that intervened between the day of the death of Sikandar (Alexander the Great) and that on which Ardshír Pápakán (Artaxerxes I.) was acclaimed King of kings by his victorious troops on the battle-field of Hurmuzdagán,[2] that is to say between June 13th B.C. 323 and September 26th A.D. 226, Firdausí knew absolutely nothing save a few names and the semi-mythical circumstances attendant on the coming into being of the second Persian or Sásánian Empire. Consequently, for convenience sake, the period covered by the Ashkánian dynasty has come to be regarded merely as a single reign—the twenty-first in the long series of the fifty Sháhs. After all, however, this dearth of subject-matter in the core of the poem is not so complete as it seems. Firdausí took his

---

[1] See p. 251. [2] *Id.* p. 199.

authorities as he found them, and long before his days Íránian tradition already had assigned all of heroic or noteworthy that had remained in memory of Ashkánian times to the mythical epochs of the Pishdádian and Kaiánian dynasties. He spoke of the ancient tongue (Pahlaví) and of the paladins (Pahlaváns), he told at large the gests of Káran, Gúdarz, Gív, Bízhan, and óthers, but had no notion that he was dealing with words, names, personalities, and subject-matter, that had originated in a period dismissed by him in a few couplets as a legendary blank.[1] Again, apart from those heroes of secondary importance, there can be little doubt but that to the invasion of the Sacæ, which took place in Parthian times,[2] we owe the Personification of that warrior-race, Rustam himself, the great paladin of paladins. The importance of the Ashkánian dynasty in the provenance of the subject-matter of the Sháhnáma therefore is much greater than superficially is apparent, and if all the legendary material of the poem could be replaced in its proper setting there would be no longer such discrepancies in length and interest between this and the two preceding dynasties. Historically of course it synchronises with one of the most important periods in the world's history, that of the successors of Alexander the Great, of the Parthian dynasty, and of the dominance of Rome. No one, least of all a translator, would wish that the Sháhnáma were longer, but one may regret that the misplaced material, which so inordinately prolongs the Kaiánian dynasty, was not kept in its proper connexion in the Ashkánian. As things stand the latter is a mere prelude to the Sásánian dynasty, and is concerned with the rise to power of Ardshír Pápakán, its founder, between which and that of Cyrus the Great there is a remarkable resemblance. In both cases there had been a previous incursion of nomads which had resulted in the establishment of their supremacy in western Írán. In the first case it was the Manda who, being confounded with the Madá or true Medes,[3] brought about the establishment of the so-called Median Empire under which the dynasty of the Achæmenids occupied a subordinate position in Elam and Párs till the successful rebellion of Cyrus, king of Elam, against his over-lord Astyages, and his other conquests, reduced all western Asia underneath his rule. In the second case it was the Parthians, also nomads, who established a like empire over the same regions, and under whom the rulers of the house of Pápak or Sásán similarly occupied a subordinate position in Párs. As in the case of Cyrus, so Ardshír, the son of Pápak, successfully rebelled against his over-lord, and founded a great

---

[1] *Cf.* Vol. iii. p. 8 *seq.*   [2] See Vol. i. p. 19.   [3] *Id.* 17.

Persian empire. Again, the rise to power of Cyrus and Ardshír was embellished in each case by legend. In that of Cyrus two distinct accounts have come down to us, from Herodotus and Ctesias respectively. The former is that given, *mutatis mutandis*, by Firdausí in his story of the early years of Kai Khusrau,[1] the latter was transferred in Íránian legend from Cyrus to Ardshír as Gutschmid pointed out, who says, speaking of the fable that forms the kernel of the story :—" The hero is a Persian shepherd's son; from dreams shared by his parents the dream-interpreters predicted his future greatness; in his youth he came to the Median Court and there, through a strange fatality, has to do hard service; the crisis comes at last, and with it the flight of the hero to his home in Persis. Directly he has fled the astrologers declare that unless he be brought back in a given time he certainly will gain the kingdom, which comes to pass. This in a short sketch is the story of Ardshír; it is, however, exactly that of Cyrus, translated by Median hands but founded on Persian national sagas as given by Ctesias. The resemblance extends even to trifles; from the stable, where he has to do the most menial work, Ardshír starts on the flight which is to end in his gaining the sovereignty; at the moment when Cyrus resolves to break with Astyages he is met by a Persian slave, Hoibaras, carrying horse's dung in a basket, and that is interpreted as a good omen, horse's dung signifying riches and might (Nicolaus of Damascus, fr. 66, by Müller, iii. p. 400). So great a similarity certainly is not accidental, rather we recognise in it an old national saga transferred from the founder of the old Persian kingdom to the founder of the new."[2]

The Íránian version of this legend, as applied to Ardshír, is extant in the Sháhnáma and in a Pahlaví text very similar in provenance and character to the Yátkár-i-Zarírán with which we were concerned in the previous volume of this translation.[3] The work in question begins, after an invocation to Urmuzd, thus :—" In the history of Ardshír, son of Pápak, the following is written." The word for " history " in the original is " kárnámak," which is used now as the title of the extant work, and not of the one, now lost, from which it was taken. Our extant Kárnámak appears to date from the seventh century A.D., and is separable

---

[1] See Vol. ii. p. 190.   [2] GKS, iii. 133.

[3] See Vol. v. p. 24. The reader may be referred to the remarks there made as to the position of such works as the above as contributories to the main stream of Íránian legend.

into portions each of which once, in all probability, formed an
independent legend. Thus we have

1. The adapted Cyrus legend.
2. Ardshír's war with the Kurds.
3. The story of the Worm.
4. The two stories of Shápúr.

These are strung loosely together as illustrations, each in its
degree, of the process that led to the restoration of Íránian unity
at the hands of Ardshír Pápakán and his immediate successors.
The subject-matter of the Kárnámak corresponds with §§ 3–16
of the Ashkánians, and with §§ 1–6 of Ardshír Pápakán, but, like
the Yátkár-i-Zarírán in Dakíkí's case, it is not the actual authority
followed by the poet but a collateral one. This is clear from the
fact that it omits a very important passage given by Firdausí,[1]
while it contains a somewhat touching episode which is not in
the Sháhnáma, though it seems incredible that the poet should
have made no use of it had he known it.[2] The episodes of the
self-mutilation of Ardshír's minister,[3] and of the game of polo,
whereby the Sháh recognised his son, also are lacking in the
Kárnámak, though the polo-episode is found there in another
connexion.[4] Other differences are due to Firdausí's more poetical
and artistic way of looking at things, and to the toning down
of the somewhat pronounced Zoroastrianism that appears in the
Pahlaví original, but he may have found this already done in
the version that he followed, which was, in all probability, that
contained in the modern Persian tenth century prose Sháhnáma.[5]
The compilers of that work seem, however, on the whole to have
preferred, or at all events for the most part to have followed,
the Arabic versions, and this preference is reflected in the poem.

Wherever in the following notes a comparison is instituted
between the Kárnámak and Firdausí the former will be referred
to as K and the latter as F.

§ 1. In the text of C this forms the concluding portion of
§ 40 of the previous reign. We follow the arrangement in P.

For Nasr, who is referred to again under the title of Abú'l
Muzaffar just below, see Vol. i. p. 100.

At first sight there seems to be a chance here of our being
able to determine at what date this passage was written, owing
to Firdausí's reference to some occasion on which Mahmúd
remitted a year's land-tax, but the fatality which attends all
matters of date in the poem is operative even here, and there
appears to be no account of this remission elsewhere.[6]

---

[1] See p. 205. [2] *Id.* p. 255. [3] *Id.* p. 261 *seq.* [4] *Id.* pp. 257, 271 *seq.*
[5] See Vol. i. p. 67 *seq.* [6] *Id.* 24, and NIN, p. 50, *note.*

§ 2. As to who the thane (dihkán) of Chách was nothing more seems to be known.

It is the fashion of Íránian legend to connect the dynasties by means of fictitious genealogies. Accordingly the Ashkánians are represented as being descended from Kai Árash, the second son of Kai Kubád, the words Ashk and Árash being sufficiently alike to have suggested the connexion. Ashk is a word expressive of kingly virtues such as "wise," "pure," "holy." In the West it took the form of Arsaces. In the Oriental lists of the kings of the Ashkánian dynasty the other names here mentioned by Firdausí occur, sometimes more than once. There are two Ashks, one Shápúr, several of the name of Gúdarz, one or two Bízhans, two or three Narsís, one or two of the name of Urmuzd or Hurmuz, no Árash, who perhaps is inserted in the Sháhnáma to keep up the nominal connexion with the second son of Kai Kubád, and three or four Ardawáns.[1] The one here mentioned by Firdausí is the last of that name, and the poet, it appears, considered that his real name was Bahrám, but in the lists there is only one so called, and he is placed much earlier. Some account of Bahrám, Gúdarz, and Bízhan, in this connexion, has been given already.[2]

In the last reign we had Firdausí's story of the establishment by Sikandar of the system of Part or Tribal Kings and his motives in so doing.[3] Though Sikandar's share in the matter is of course wholly unhistorical, the view taken in Íránian legend of the political system that obtained after his death is, broadly speaking, fairly correct. Írán never again was organised under one supreme head, as it had been in the days of the first Persian empire, till the establishment of the second empire five and a half centuries later. The death of Alexander was followed by long wars due to the rival ambitions of his generals and their descendants. Later on came wars with Rome and the rise of the Parthian power, which remained for centuries the great bulwark of the East against Roman aggression. The system of Parthian rule, however, was a nomad one. It originated in the victories of a nomad tribe, and it was to the nomads that the Parthian kings turned for succour in their hours of need. They called themselves indeed by the title of King of kings, as the Achæmenids did before them, and some of them at all events professed the same religion, but national Íránian tradition never recognised their right to use the ancient Persian title of supreme ruler though, in a sense, it was more applicable to them than to their pre-

---

[1] See the lists in GKS, iii. 24. [2] See Vol. iii. p. 9 *seq.*
[3] See p. 178 *seq.* |

decessors. With the Achæmenids it was a claim to universal sovereignty, with the Arsacids a claim to the suzerainty of Írán. The geographical extent of the lands ruled by themselves, or by their governors on their behalf, was not very great, and the remainder of their empire consisted of kingdoms that retained at least a semi-independence under native rulers. Such, for instance, were the kingdoms of Osroene, Gordyene, and Atropatane (Azarbáiján) in the north, Elymais (Elam) and Párs in the south, and Sístán and Bactria in the east. Further, in the case of Párs, as we learn from Tabarí, and, we may presume, elsewhere also, these Part or Tribal Kings had under them small local kings or princes. In the days of Firdausí's Ardawán, the last Parthian Great King, there seem to have been four such rulers in Párs, one of whom was Pápak, under his immediate over-lord, the Part or Tribal King who ruled at Istakhr. Thus in Parthian times Írán was split into two great divisions, one under the Parthian Great King and organised into eighteen provinces administered by satraps directly responsible to him; the other under semi-independent potentates who held the same position with reference to their regal underlings as he held towards them. According to the Kárnámak there were in all 240 kings, according to Arab authorities there were 90,[1] so the Parthian over-lord was entitled to describe himself as King of kings.

§§ 3–9. Tabarí's account of the rise of the Sásánian dynasty is briefly as follows :—Ardshír was the son of Pápak, king of Khír, and was born at a village named Tírúdih in the same neighbourhood. His grandfather, Sásán, was the superintendent of a Fire-temple in Istakhr. His grandmother, Sásán's wife, was of the royal house of the Bázrangí, and was named Rámbihisht. Pápak succeeded his father, and to him was born Ardshír. The king of Istakhr at that time was of the race of the Bázrangí, and his name was Gúzihr. He had a eunuch called Tírí whom he made commandant of Dárábgird. When Ardshír was seven years old his father Pápak took him to see Gúzihr, who lived at Baidá,[2] and asked him to allow Tírí to bring up Ardshír, who ultimately was to succeed Tírí at Dárábgird. Gúzihr assented, and Ardshír in course of time succeeded Tírí as had been arranged. For a while he remained free from ambition till it was roused in him by the predictions of astrologers and the

---

[1] NK, p. 36, and note.

[2] I.e. "The White"—an Arabic translation of the Persian name of the hill-fort (now Bardi ?) of which a description will be found in Vol. i. p. 236, note, but Professor Nöldeke places it only six German miles north of Shíráz. NT, p. 5, note.

announcement to him by an angel[1] in a dream, that he was destined to rule Írán. Thereupon he began to assert himself by attacking and slaying three local kings in Párs, and setting up adherents of his own in their stead. He then wrote to his father Pápak, urging him to rise against Gúzihr at Baidá. Pápak did so, slew Gúzihr, and took his crown. Then Pápak wrote to Ardawán for permission to crown his (Pápak's) son, Shápúr, with the crown of Gúzihr. Ardawán replied that Pápak and Ardshír had acted as rebels. Pápak died, his son Shápúr became king and summoned his brother Ardshír to court. Ardshír refused to come, Shápúr marched against him, but on the way to Dárábgird was killed by the fall of part of one of the buildings of Humái.[2] On this Ardshír went to Istakhr and, with the assent of his other brothers, became king. However, on the pretext, or in consequence, of a conspiracy on their part against him, he put many of them to death later on. He then reduced Dárábgird, where the people had taken the opportunity of his absence to rebel against him. Next he conquered the king of Kirmán, and annexed that district, of which he made one of his own sons governor. After this he slew Astawadh, a king on the coast of the Persian sea. Next he conquered Mihrak, a king in the district of Ardshír-Khurra, where he founded the town of Gúr, and, while thus engaged, received a hostile letter from Ardawán, which he answered in a similar tone, and returned to Istakhr. After this he made three distinct expeditions from Párs. In the first he subdued Ispahán, Ahwáz, a district on the small Tigris,[3] and other places. In the second he went to Ahwáz by way of Girih and Kázirún and on to Maishán where he built the town of Karakh-Maishán. In the third he encountered Ardawán at Hurmuzdagán, slew him, and the same day was hailed King of kings. The date of this battle seems to have been September 26th, A.D. 226, but the actual site, according to Professor Nöldeke, is unknown, and he is of the opinion that the three expeditions of Ardshír from Párs, mentioned above, correspond with the three battles that, according to Western writers, took place before Ardawán was disposed of for good and all.[4] The plain of Rám Hurmuz, south of Shúshtar, has been suggested as the probable scene of the decisive battle.[5]

§ 3. In the Sháhnáma the Sásánian dynasty is connected with the Kaiánian by a double genealogy, one already given under

---

[1] No doubt, as Professor Nöldeke suggests, Surúsh in the original Pahlaví. NT, 6, and *note*.

[2] See Vol. v. p. 293. [3] The Kárún.

[4] NT, pp. 1-15, and *notes*. *Cf.* RSM, 35 *seq.* [5] *Id.*

the reign of Bahman,[1] the other here. Both are fictitious, Tabarí's account making it clear with regard to the latter that Ardshír was the son, not the grandson on the female side only, of Pápak.[2] In Tabarí also two genealogies are given, both of which serve to connect the line of Pápak with the Kaiánians. They run as follow :— [3]

I	II
Kai Manush (Minúchihr ?)	Luhrásp
Kai Ugí (?)	Gushtásp
Luhrásp	Asfandiyár
Gushtásp	Bahman
Asfandiyár	Sásán
Bahman	Biháfridh
Sásán	Zarár
Mihrmas	Pápak
Pápak	Sásán
Sásán	Pápak
Pápak	Ardshír
Sásán	
Pápak	
Ardshír	

Two similar genealogies, tracing back the line of Ardshír to Luhrásp, are given by Mas'údí.[4] Neither he nor Tabarí credits the legends, found in the Kárnámak and in the Sháhnáma, that Sásán was a shepherd in the employment of Pápak, who adopted him and gave him a daughter in marriage. In Firdausí Pápak is called the son of Rúdyáb, but as the poet makes that name a rhyme-word it is open to suspicion apart from the fact that it does not appear in any of the above-mentioned genealogies. The same reason, probably, led Firdausí (F) to put the visit of the master of the herds (ramah) to Pápak in the winter-season (damah)—a touch not found in the Kárnámak (K). In K Pápak has three dreams. The first of them, in which he sees the sun

---

[1] See Vol. **v**. p. 290.   [2] See p. 198.
[3] NT, p. 1.   [4] MM, ii. 151.

illuminating the whole world from the head of Sásán, is not in F. In K too the three Fires are Frúbá, representing the priestly class, Gushasp, the warrior-class, and Mihr Barzin, the agricultural.[1] The sending of Sásán to the bath, doubtlessly a very necessary preliminary, is not in the more primitive K.

§ 4. Ardawán, the Artabanus III. or IV. of Western writers, the last ruler of the Parthian dynasty, was regarded in Persian historical tradition as being himself the chief Tribal or Part King, the *primus inter pares*, not as the general suzerain, and as having Media Magna as his territory. Hence F assigns him Rai as his capital.[2]

K adds chess to the accomplishments learnt_by Ardshír at Court, but F tells us further on, under the reign of Núshírwán, the story of its introduction into Persia.

The present of money that accompanied Pápak's reply to Ardshír is not mentioned in K.

§ 5. The details of the slave-girl's descent by means of a lasso in order to visit Ardshír, and her name, are not in K, which omits too the mention of Pápak's death and Ardawán's appointment of a successor, and makes Ardawán the Part King over Ispahán, Párs, and the neighbouring lands, and Pápak himself the prince of Párs.[3]

The account of the astrologers working out their calculations in the house of the slave-girl, and her over-hearing them, is lacking in K, which gives no reason for her knowledge in the matter. On the other hand the pronouncements of the astrologers are more elaborate and technical in K, where also they state that the servant who escapes from his master in the course of the next three days will supplant him.[4]

§ 6. In K the fugitives arrive at a village, where they are afraid to stop, and are met by two women who tell Ardshír to fear not, and to hasten to the sea where he will be safe. In F the fugitives reach a pool where they want to drink and rest, but are warned by two young men to hasten on. In K Ardawán thrice in the course of his pursuit inquires of those whom he meets as to how far the fugitives are ahead. On the third occasion it is a caravan that he comes upon. F omits the caravan passage.

For the mountain-sheep see Vol. i. p. 374.

§ 7. F is more detailed here. In K the corresponding passage runs thus:—"Then he (Ardawán) sent an equipped army to Párs,

---

[1] See Vol. i. pp. 7, 130, 132.   [2] NT, p. 7, *note*.
[3] NK, p. 36.   [4] NK, i. 42. *Cf.* p. 195.

under his own son, to take Ardshír prisoner.[1] In the meanwhile Ardshír went his way to the coast. As he proceeded, some of the men of Párs, who were hostile to Ardawán, handed over to him goods and chattels and their own persons, and promised him fealty and obedience."[2]

The city founded by Ardshír was called Rív-Ardshír.[3]

§ 8. In K we have Banák of Ispahán with six sons for the Tabák of Jahram with seven sons of F. The Persian for "seven" comes in handily as a rhyme-word; hence the change. In K it is stated that Ardshír called the district where he first met Banák "Rámishn-i-Ardshír," *i.e.* "Joy of Ardshír," and founded a city there of the same name and also known as "Rám Ardshír," *i.e.* "Happy Ardshír."[4] It was natural that he should, or be thought to, have founded a Fire-temple there, and this may be the origin of F's Rám in that connexion.

The account of Ardshír's battle with Bahman, son of Ardawán, is not in K.

§ 9. Firdausí's description of this battle is in his usual style. The corresponding passage in K may be read to indicate three battles or campaigns.[5] It runs as follows:—"Then he (Ardshír) began war with Ardawán, slaughtered his whole army, and took from him his goods and chattels, houses, and property. Then he settled in Istakhr, and assembled from Kirmán, Makrán, Ispahán, and the different regions of Párs, a very great host. Then he began another war with Ardawán. For four months there were daily much fighting and slaughter. Ardawán collected from various regions—Rai, Damáwand, Dílamán,[6] and Patash-wárgar[7]—armies and horses; but as the Majesty of the Kaiánians had descended on Ardshír he was successful, killed Ardawán, and all his possessions came into Ardshír's hands. He took Ardawán's daughter to wife and went back to Pars."[8]

§§ 10, 11. Here we have the account of an "unfortunate incident," and shall meet, later on, with others that befell Ardshír after his triumph over Ardawán. He still had to fight hard to make good the title of "King of kings" conferred on him by his troops on the field of Hurmuzdagán.[9] Naturally this would be so. A dynasty that had endured for centuries could not fail to have many adherents and dependants; Ardawán had left sons; Chosroes, the king of Armenia, was either his brother or at

---

[1] According to F Ardawán's eldest son, Bahman, was established already as ruler in Párs. See p. 218.

[2] NK, p. 46.   [3] NT, p. 19, and *note*.   [4] NK, p. 46.
[5] *Cf.* p. 199.   [6] Gílán.   [7] Tabaristán or Mázandarán.
[8] NK, p. 47, and *notes*.   [9] See p. 199.

all events had been set on the throne by him ; the Part Kings
too had everything to lose by Ardshír's success, for it was
manifest that he had no intention of leaving them in the semi-
independent position that they had enjoyed under Parthian
suzerainty ; his view with regard to them was, as we have seen
already, that "stone dead hath no fellow."[1] Ardshír followed up
his success over Ardawán by striking at the heart of that king's
power which, according to Íránian tradition, lay in Media, and
here is recorded for us in the account of his expedition against
the Kurds, by whom the people of Media are meant, for in K
the name of the Kurd king is Mádík, which simply means "the
Mede."[2] These, so far as Media Magna was concerned, Ardshír
seems to have conquered, but Tabarí's statement that he subdued
Ázarbáiján and Armenia appears to be an exaggeration. The
case of Ázarbáijan is doubtful, but Armenia, whither some of the
Arsacid princes had fled for refuge, succeeded with the help of
Rome in maintaining its independence.[3]

§§ 12-16. To the exegesis of this strange story, as Firdausí calls
it, three great authorities—Mohl, Darmesteter, and Nöldeke—
have contributed. The two latter see reason to connect it with
other more ancient Indo-European myths of dragons, such as
Indra with Vritra, Apollo with the Python, &c., and Darmesteter
quotes an interesting Scandinavian parallel which he considers
more primitive and unaffected by industrialism :—"Le comte
Herraudr a donné à sa fille, la belle Thora, un serpent qu'il a
trouvé dans un œuf de vautour. Le serpent plaît à Thora qui
lui fait un lit d'or dans un coffret. Le serpent grandit, *l'or
grandit avec lui*, le coffre devient trop étroit pour lui, et même
la maison de la jeune fille qu'il enveloppe de son corps. Il était
méchant et malicieux : nul n'osait l'approcher que l'homme qui
lui apportait chaque jour sa nourriture, consistant en un bœuf
entier. Le comte promet sa fille et l'or à qui tuera le dragon.
Ragnar, âgé de quinze ans, se fait un vêtement garni de poix
(pour se garder du poison du serpent), surprend le monstre et le
tue de la pointe de son épieu qu'il lui laisse dans la gueule. Il
se retire sans dire son nom et plus tard se fait reconnaître
publiquement au manche de son épieu : il reçoit Thora en mariage."[4]

Still more to the point are Mohl's explanation and illustration,
which are as follow :—"Je suis disposé à croire que ce conte est
un vague souvenir de l'introduction du ver à soie en Perse et de
la prospérité que cette nouvelle industrie devait avoir répandue.
On me permettra peut-être de citer à l'appui de cette supposition

---

[1] See p. 199. [2] NK, p. 48, and *note*.
[3] NT, p. 15, and *note*. *Cf.* RSM, p. 37 *seq*. [4] DEI, ii. 83.

un conte analogue et presque aussi étrange, qui date de nos jours. Je me rappelle avoir vu, il y a une trentaine d'années, au ministère du commerce, un rapport du préfet d'un des départements de la Bretagne au sujet de la détresse que répandait dans la campagne l'introduction du fil de lin produit par les machines, et de la difficulté que les fileuses à la main trouvaient à lutter contre cette concurrence. Le préfet raconte, à cette occasion, que ces pauvres femmes avaient fini par composer une légende, selon laquelle il y avait une fée, appelée *Machine*, qui avait sept doigts d'acier et pouvait ainsi filer plus et plus vite qu'elles ne pouvaient le faire avec leurs cinq doigts humains." [1]

The full process of silk manufacture from the worm (*Bombyx mori*) to the finished fabric was known in China from time immemorial, and the secret was guarded very carefully. Long before the Christian era the raw silk had begun to be imported into Europe, and a famous manufactory for weaving it was established in the island of Cos in the Ægean Sea. The secret of the method of the production of the raw material itself was kept till much later times, sufficiently, at all events, for the maintenance of the Chinese monopoly, though Aristotle in his *History of Animals*, Bk. V., ch. xvii., sec. 6, ed. Schneider, speaks of a certain great worm with horns, as it were, which produces bombycina or cocoons which the women use in weaving. Aristotle's knowledge probably came to him as one of the results of Alexander's expedition to the East. The silk-worm itself, of which the secret had spread during the fourth century A.D. through India to Írán and the West, was brought for the first time into Europe by two Persian monks, at the special request of the Emperor Justinian, in A.D. 550. They smuggled the eggs from China in the hollow of a bamboo, and thus founded the Western silk industry. Justinian's object was to break the monopoly of the silk-trade then, by land and sea alike, in Persian hands.[2]

Two reasons may be suggested why the scene of our story was laid on the shores of the Persian sea. One is that a Part King of that region, *e.g.* of Hurmuz (Ormus), may have grown rapidly rich in the latter days of the Parthian dynasty by means of the silk or cotton trade of the Persian Gulf, and suffered for his prosperity at the hands of Ardshír Pápakán. The other is to be found in the popular etymology of the word Kirmán—a region

---

[1] P, Vol. v., Préface.

[2] See GDF, v. 56 *seq.*; *Ency. Brit.*, 11th ed. *s.v.* " Silk"; and SP, pp. 179, 263.

more famous for its date (khurmá) than for its silk. In Persian, however; it so happens that "kirm" means "worm," and in fact is the same word. Kirmán was supposed to mean "The Land of the Worm," and thus to be a suitable scene for some ancient Dragon-myth,[1] or a story may have been invented to account for the name. Both in K and F, it should be noted, Ardshír, after killing the Worm, proceeds to conquer Kirmán, so that we have the romantic and historic accounts of the same event put side by side, the former given at large and the latter very shortly. In Tabarí too we have the historic version and two brief rationalised versions of the romantic side of the story. He informs us that Ardshír subdued Kirmán, slew its king Balásh (Vologeses, an Arsacid), and made his own son ruler. This is represented as taking place before the war with Ardawán. Then (here begins one of the romantic versions) he went against a king named Astawadh, who lived on the coast of the Persian sea, and to whom divine honours were paid, killed him, cut him in two with his sword, slew also his retinue, and brought out from his treasure-house, and carried off, much treasure that was stored there.[2] Astawadh, Professor Nöldeke notes, is a corruption by misreading of the Pahlaví name,[3] which becomes Haftwád in the Sháhnáma. According to the other account there was in Alár, a village in the province of Kujárán, which belonged to the coast-land of Ardshír-Khurra (Gúr), a queen who enjoyed divine honours and possessed great wealth and many soldiers. Ardshír, toward the end of his reign, killed the queen and captured much gold and treasure which she had.[4]

In these accounts divine honours are transferred, in the first, from the dragon to Haftwád and, in the second, to his daughter.

§ 12. This passage is not found elsewhere, but there is no reason to assume that the poet invented, though very likely he embellished, it. From what we can gather of Firdausi's literary methods, he would not have introduced such a string of incidents without authority for so doing. When "gravelled for lack of matter," he does not "take occasion to" invent, but passes on as we see in the case of the present dynasty, where he had an unequalled opportunity for the exercise of his imagination had he been disposed to avail himself of it. The absence of the passage in the Kárnámak and in the Arabic may be accounted for easily. In the former, Haftwád (Haftánbúkht) is introduced quite abruptly,[5] and the story of his rise to power was omitted not

---

[1] DEI, ii. 81.   [2] NT, p. 10.   [3] See p. 206.   [4] NT, p. 19.
[5] "But the army of Haftánbúkht, the lord of the Worm, attacked him (Ardshir)," &c. ; NK, p. 49.

because it was well known or unknown, but because it was foreign to the purpose in hand, which was to show by what steps Ardshír rose to supreme power, effected the unification of Írán, and founded a new dynasty. From this point of view the destruction of Haftwád and the Worm was of importance, but not their genesis. In the latter we have a much more drastic system of lopping in the interests, apparently, of rationalism. In the second of Tabarí's versions we get a hint that it was the one which, in its unrationalised state, Firdausí followed. The queen there is the daughter here.

The name of Ardshír's opponent in K—Haftánbúkht, which does not scan—becomes Haftwád in F, as it may be so read in the Pahlaví if the central letters are omitted. Haftánbúkht, according to Professor Nöldeke, means "The Seven have redeemed" with reference to the seven planets which, as creations of Áhriman [1] might be expected, from the orthodox Zoroastrian point of view, to watch over the fortunes of Haftánbúkht and the Worm. In Professor Darmesteter's opinion, however, Firdausí's etymology is correct, though based on a misapprehension. The word "wád" was due to a misreading of the Pahlaví, but the word "búkht" does mean "son," and the seven sons are the sevenfold coils, or the seven heads, of the dragon. Both agree that in the original form of the story Haftánbúkht was the dragon.[2]

According to K, Haftánbúkht's seat was at Gulár in Kujárán. In Tabarí, Haftánbúkht becomes Astawadh, and Gulár, in the version which substitutes a queen for a king, becomes Alár.[3] The situation of Kujárán is unknown.

In K the food of the dragon is the blood of sheep and bullocks,[4] not rice, milk, and honey, as in F.

§ 13. In K the army of Haftánbúkht is represented as the aggressor. The forces of Ardshír, who is not present, are attacked after his return from his victory over the Kurds. This preliminary engagement is omitted by F. Haftwád's son crossed over from Arabia to help his father.[5] The water behind Ardshír was probably the sea, but the Persian word is a vague one.

§ 14. In K the older form Mithrak is preserved. According to Tabarí, who places Ardshír's war with him before the defeat of Ardawán, he lived in a district of Ardshír-Khurra."[6]

§ 15. In K Ardshír, after his defeat by Haftánbúkht, reaches the shore of the sea quite alone and almost abandoned by the

---

[1] See Vol. i. p. 52.   [2] *Cf.* NK, pp. 29, 49, and *note*; DEI, ii. 82.
[3] NK, p. 50; NT, pp. 10, 19.   [4] NK, p. 56.   [5] *Id.* 49–52, and *notes*.
[6] NT, p. 11.

divine Grace, but then it stood in front of him and led him out
of danger to the village where the two brothers, named Burjak
and Burjátur, dwelt.[1]

In K Ardshír gets admitted into the castle with the two young
men of the village only. In F he takes seven men with him.
Seven is a favourite number in Persian story, and if, as we have
seen above, one of the legends told of Cyrus the Great could be
transferred to Ardshír, there seems no reason why a fragment of
the legend of the Seven, who made the famous expedition against
the stronghold of the mage Gaumata—the false Smerdis—in the
days of Darius Hystaspis, should not be transferred here in like
manner.[2] In K Ardshír appoints, for some reason not clear to
us, the 27th day of the month as the one for decisive action, and
Haftánbúkht appears to have perished in the fight, not afterwards
by formal execution as in F.[3]

§ I

The Praise of Mahmúd

Now be the monarch of the world our theme
As one in feast and fight and lore supreme—
The great Mahmúd ; much prosperous rede hath he
And doth uphold the fame of majesty,
A king, Abú'l Kásim ! most sage and wise
Beyond e'en wisdom in his policies.
Glad be his heart for evermore and free
From toil and trouble. King of kings is he
Both of Írán and of Zábulistán,
And from Kannúj [4] up to Kábulistán.
On him, upon the troops of his command,
On his allies, his kindred, and his land,
On that world-lord and chief, Nasr the amír,
A source of joyance to time's circling sphere,
Be praise, while o'er the moon the army's head
Ascendeth by Abú'l Muzaffar led ;

---

[1] NK, p. 53.   [2] *Cf.* Vol. i. p. 58 ; DHA, vi. 201 *seq.*
[3] NK, p. 56. and *note.*   [4] *Cf.* Vol. i. p. 99.

By fortune and by name victorious he,
Whose arrows in their flight out-top the tree.
Oh! may the Sháh live scathless evermore,
And be his seat upon his treasury's store,
And may his general be happy too,
In heart illumed, in treasure well to do.
Thus while revolving heaven maintain its place
Ne'er may its love be severed from this race,
But be it ever a victorious one,
And crowned from sire to sire and son to son.
Upon this day, the fourteenth of Shawwál,
May benediction on our sovereign fall

C. 1363
For this good news about the tax—that he,
The Sháh with Grace and crown, hath made decree
To claim no contribution for a year
From men of ardent Faith and godly fear.
The age of Núshírwán hath come anew,
And all hath been transfigured to our view.
When on this wise no little time hath sped,
And when the robe of right shall be outspread,
Thou'lt see him (such his justice and his love!)
Receive the robe of honour from above—
One that upon him ne'er will wear away,
While on his head the imperial crown will stay.
May his head flourish, harm approach not near,
His magnanimity transcend heaven's sphere.
One telling o'er the years and months that I
Have lived will not despise my prophecy.
Look well, because this book a flag will be
O'er sages' heads to all eternity,
And, in original, will seem to spring
From Gaiúmart whose praise all people sing.
Thus Núshírwán, son of Kubád, once said:—
"When any monarch turn from right his head
Heaven will black out the patent of his reign,
The stars acclaim him not as king again.

Injustice is the notice to depart
To kings that vex the blameless to the heart." [1]
  For ever may this family, endued
With worth, with wisdom, and with rectitude,
Continue.   Lasting foothold here hath none,
But his good name will last when he is gone.
Where now are Farídún, Zahhák, Jamshíd,
The chiefs of Arab and of Persian breed ?
Where are the great of the Sásánians,
Those of Bahrám's race, and the Ashkánians ?
Zahhák the Sháh was most reviled, for he
Was all injustice and impurity,
While glorious Farídún approval won ;
He died, and his renown still liveth on.
In this world fame is our memorial—
A better thing than gems imperial !
The man unjust, whose joyance was in throne
And treasure, never hath made praise his own ;
His reputation in the world is naught,
And none is fain to pleasure him in aught.
Because of our foe-quelling king's decree
May he still throne it in felicity.
Forth from their homes the people plain-ward hied,
With praise transcending heaven, and thus they cried :—
" Aye may he live, the crowned head of our state,
And may time's course to him prove fortunate ;
Here may he look on naught save what doth please,
His name be graven on the palaces,
And may our benisons withal embrace
His kin, host, land, his royal form, and face."

---

[1] Similar sentiments were attributed to Ardshír Pápakán. See p. 283.

§ 2

The Tribal Kings

C. 1364   O thou that singest in extreme old age!
Now let the Ashkánians' times thy thoughts engage.
What hath the author of the history
Still left to tell us from the legendry?
What mighty chieftains hath he to enthrone
Upon the world, Sikandar being gone?
   The thane of Chách, mine author, saith that none
Thenceforward had the throne and crown, but princes,
Brave, headstrong, proud, and scions of Árash,
Each in his corner made himself a realm
Out of some portion of the provinces,
And when they sat rejoicing on their thrones
Folk called them "Tribal Kings." Two centuries
     passed,
And thou hadst said: "There is no Sháh." These
     princes
Regarded not each other, and earth rested,
Sikandar having ordered matters thus,
To guard the land of Rúm. The first was Ashk,
Sprung from Kubád, while others were Shápúr,
A royal warrior, Gúdarz the Ashkánian,
Bízhan of Kaian lineage, Narsí,
The great Urmuzd, Árash a warrior famed,
And after him the noble Ardawán,
Wise, prudent, and of ardent soul, for when
Bahrám, the Ashkánian, sat upon the throne
He lavished treasure on the poor, but folk
Were wont to call him Ardawán [1] the Great
Because he kept the wolf's claws from the sheep.
He governed in Shíráz and Ispahán,

---

[1] *I.e.* arta = great, and wán or bán = a guardian.

Which scholars call the "Marches of the princes."
He set up in Istakhr Pápak [1] as ruler,
Whose thumb-stall used to make the monsters [2] yell.
How all these princes perished, root and branch,
Their time-worn chronicle narrateth not.
Naught have I heard of them except the name,
And in the Book of Kings seen but the same.

§ 3

How Pápak saw Sásán in a Dream and gave him a
Daughter in Marriage

Now when Dárá had perished in the war,   C. 1365
And all his family had had their day,
He left one son behind—a potent prince,
A wise and valiant man by name Sásán,
Who, when he saw his father slain, and fortune
Averse from the Íránians, fled before
The host of Rúm and 'scaped the net of bale.
He died in wretched plight in Hindústán,
And left a little boy. Thus every sire
Throughout four generations gave his son
The name Sásán. They all were camel-drivers,
Or shepherds, and hard workers all their years.
The youngest of the race came to Pápak,
Beheld his master-shepherd on the plain,
And said: "Hast thou employment for a hireling,
Whose life is being spent in sore distress?"
    The master-shepherd took that luckless one,
And worked him day and night. His industry

---

[1] In the text the Arabic form of the word "Bábak" is used,
but the proper Persian form is Pápak, which we have adopted
throughout.

[2] The word is the same as that used in the previous reign to
describe the monsters on which Yájúj and Májúj fattened in the
spring. See p. 164.

Found favour, and he rose to be chief shepherd.

Pápak, son of Rúdyáb, one night thus dreamed :—
He saw upon a mighty elephant
Sásán and in his hand a Indian sword,
While all that came to him saluted him,
And did him homage ; he addressed them kindly,
And purged their gloomy hearts of grief.   Next night,
When sleeping much perturbed, he dreamed about
Fire-worshippers who bore three blazing Fires,
Such as Ázargashasp, Kharrád, and Mihr,[1]
Bright as Sol, Mars, and Venus ; all blazed up
Before Sásán, their fuel aloe-wood.

Pápak awoke, his soul and heart possessed
By care.   Those skilled in dreams and in that lore
Puissant, magnates, sages, counsellors,
Assembled in the palace of Pápak,
And as he set forth what had chanced, and told
His dreams to them at large, the adviser mused,
The interpreter gave ear, and in the end
Said : "O exalted king ! this must be scanned,
For one whom thou beheldest thus in sleep
Will raise his head above the sun as Sháh,
Or, if the dream be not of him, his son
Will have the world."
                              Pápak rejoiced on hearing,
Rewarded each according to his rank,
Then bade his master-shepherd to forsake
The flock and come.   It was a winter's day.
Wrapped in his cloak, its wool was thick with snow,
His heart with fears, he came in haste.   Pápak
Dismissed all strangers, slave and counsellor
Went, and he graciously received Sásán,
Assigning him a seat beside his lord,
And asked him of his quality and birth.
The herd, through terror of him, answered not,

C. 1366

---

[1] The names of Fire-temples.

But said at last: "O prince! if thou wilt give
A promise to respect thy shepherd's life
I will inform thee of my quality
When thou shalt grasp my hand and pledge thyself
To harm me not in public or in private."
　　Pápak, on hearing this, loosed his own tongue,
Invoked the Giver of all good, and said :—
"I will not harm but make thee glad and honoured,"
　　　Then spake the youth: "I am, O paladin!
Son of Sásán and sprung from Sháh Ardshír,
Whom chroniclers call by the name Bahman,
The great son of the brave Asfandiyár,
Who was Gushtásp's memorial."
　　　　　　　　　　　　　　Pápak
Wept from those shrewd eyes that had seen the dream,
Then brought the raiment of a paladin,
And steed with royal trappings, saying thus :—
"Go to the bath what while they fetch fresh raiment."
　　He raised Sásán o'er that chief shepherdship,
Prepared for him a noble residence,
And, having lodged him there, provided slaves,
Both boys and girls, to wait on him, bestowed
Addition by all means, set him past need
Of wealth, then gave the Crown on his own brows—
A daughter well beloved—to him as spouse.

§ 4

How Ardshír Pápakán was born, and of his Case with
Ardawán

When nine months had elapsed the beauteous dame
Brought forth an infant like the radiant sun,
The image of illustrious Ardshír,
A growing, glorious, heart-delighting child.
His sire withal, who joyed to gaze upon him,　　　　C. 1367

Named him Ardshír and fostered him through all
His years of need. A long while thus elapsed.
(The learned now call him Pápakán Ardshír.[1])
They taught him all accomplishment, wherein
He bettered e'en the promise of his birth.
He was so wise and goodly that the sky,
Thou wouldst have said, was luminous through him.
News of the youth's intelligence and knowledge
Reached Ardawán: "He is a savage Lion
In fight," it ran, "and like Náhíd in feast."

    The king wrote to that famous paladin,
Pápak, and said: "O counsellor of mine,
Wise, trusty, eloquent, and good! thy son,
Ardshír, is, I have heard, a cavalier
Of eloquence and heed. On reading this
Be pleased to send him unto us forthwith.
I will supply his every want, advance him
Among the chiefs and, when he is associate
With mine own sons, deny him not my kinship."

    Pápak, on reading this, wept tears of blood;
He bade a writer, and that rising youth,
Ardshír, attend, and said: "Peruse this letter
Of Ardawán's and let thy clear mind scan it;
Behold, I write an answer to the king,
And send it by some friend to this effect:—
'Lo! I have sent to thee a gallant youth,
One much approved, who is my heart and eyes,
And whom I have advised. When he shall come
To thy high court treat him right royally,
And suffer not the blast to blow upon him.'"

    Then swift as wind he oped the treasury-doors,
And gratified the youth with various gifts
Of golden harness, swords, and iron maces;
There was not aught that he refused the boy.

---

[1] He is generally known as Ardshír Pápakán, *i.e.* Ardshír of the family
of Pápak.

The treasurer brought forth brocade, dínárs,
Steeds, slaves, with stuffs of Chín and cloth of gold,
Such as kings wear, and gave them to the youth
What time he went to wait on Ardawán.
The favoured youth, departing from his grandsire,
Went to the court of Ardawán at Rai,
Who, hearing of his coming, graciously
Received him, spake at large about Pápak,
Assigned Ardshír a place beside the throne,   C. 1368
Lodged him near by, fed, clothed, and furnished him.
Now when the sun sat on its throne, and when
The world became fair as a Rúman's face,
Ardshír called for a servant and therewith
The gifts of obligation, and dispatched
The envoy of Pápak, the paladin,
To Ardawán, the king, who viewed the gifts;
They pleased him, and the young man profited
Thereby: the monarch held him as a son.
A while passed well with him.   The twain consorted
In revel, feast, and at the chase.
                              One day
It happened that the escort of the king,
And his own sons, were scattered in the chase.
Ardshír himself attended Ardawán,
Who found that gallant youth acceptable.
Now Ardawán had four sons of his own,
Each king-like.   Onager had come in sight,
And that great company was all astir.
They urged their wind-foot steeds and mixed the dust
With sweat.   Ardshír pressed on in front and, nearing
The quarry, placed an arrow on his bow,
And struck an onager upon the haunch.
The arrow-point and feather went right through.
Anon came Ardawán who, when he saw
The strength of that young archer, cried: "May he
That shot possess a soul to match his hand."

Ardshír replied: "I shot the onager."
A son said: "It was I that brought it down,
And I am looking out for one to match it."
Ardshír retorted: "Well the plain is broad,
And there are onagers and arrows too.
By that same token slay another such:
It is a sin for noble men to lie."
Now Ardawán was angry with Ardshír
Thereat and roared at him: "Mine is the blame,
Because this bringing up is all mine own.
Why should I have thee in my company,
Both in the banquet and the hunting-field,
In order that thou mayst surpass my sons,
And show off thine address and excellence?
Begone. See to mine Arab steeds and choose

C.1369

A handy residence. Be stable-master,
And keep all companies."
                              Ardshír in tears
Went to be keeper of the Arab steeds,
And in his wretchedness and discontent
Wrote to his grandsire thus: "In what a way
Hath Ardawán dealt with us! Anguish take
His body, care his soul."
                              He told the matter,
And why king Ardawán was wroth with him.
Pápak was troubled when the letter came,
But held his peace, and from his treasury
Dispatched ten thousand to his son in gold
By camel and by cavalier, commanded
A scribe to come, and wrote: "O foolish boy!
When thou wast hunting game with Ardawán
Why didst thou pass his sons although thou art
His servant, not his kin? He wronged thee not
In malice; 'twas thine own insensate deed.
Now strive to make him pleased and satisfied,
And do his will in all. I have dispatched thee

Gold and this letter of advice withal.
When thou hast spent the money ask for more
Until the times shall change."

The dromedary

Sped with the ancient veteran to Ardshír,
Who when he read the letter was content,
And plotted and dissembled, chose a lodging
Near to his steeds, though one not worthy of him,
Provided it with carpets, food, and raiment,
And spent his days and nights in revelry,
Companioning with wine and minstrelsy.[1]

§ 5

*How Ardawán's Slave-girl fell in Love with Ardshír and
how he fled with her to Párs*

Now Ardawán possessed a lofty palace,
Wherein there dwelt a favourite slave of his.
She was a Moon-face hight Gulnár [2]—a picture
All jewelry and colour and perfume.
She ministered to Ardawán and kept
His treasury. He loved her more than life,
And joyed and smiled to look on her.[3] One day,
When she had mounted to the palace-roof,
And gladdened at that mirth,[4] she saw Ardshír;   C. 1370
His lips were smiling, and he won her heart.
She waited till the eve or rather night,
Then tied a lasso to the battlements
With many a knot. She proved it with her hand,[5]
And then, invoking Him who giveth good,
Descended boldly. When in all her gems,

---

[1] Following the division of the text in P.
[2] *I.e.* Pomegranate-bloom.
[3] In C the section ends here.
[4] See above.
[5] "la lança avec sa main " (Mohl).

And savouring musk and other spicery,
She reached Ardshír she raised his head, which lay
Upon the pillow of brocade, and clasped him,
When he was wakened, tightly to her breast.
The young man marked that lovely one, her face,
Her hair, and scented bravery, and said :—
"Whence hast thou sprung to grace my troubled heart?"
    "A slave am I and love thee, heart and soul,"
She answered.   "I am Ardawán's beloved,
His treasurer, his darling, and delight,
But, if thou wilt accept me, thy slave now
To live but in thy sight and visit thee,
Whene'er thou wilt, and brighten thy dark days."
    A while passed thus and then mishap befell
Ardshír's inspirer.   Veteran, shrewd Pápak
Died and resigned this ancient home to others.
When news reached Ardawán he sorrowed much ;
His soul grew dark.   The chiefs all asked for Párs,
But he bestowed it on his eldest son,[1]
Bade bring the drums and march forth to the waste.
As for Ardshír the world gloomed to his heart
For his protector's sake, old, shrewd Pápak.
He loathed his service under Ardawán,
And, when those tidings came, formed new designs,
For he was rash through grief and fain to flee.
    Anon king Ardawán brought to his court
Some shrewd men of the readers of the stars
To learn his future, to direct his course,
And find whom fortune would inspire thereafter.
He sent them to the mansion of Gulnár
To make their observations of the stars.
They worked for three days at his horoscope,
The treasuress could hear the talk thereon
And other secrets, and spent all the days
And three-fourths of the night in listening

C. 1371

---

[1] Bahman, as we learn later on, pp. 225 *seq.*, 259.

With longing heart and sighs upon her lips,
But very mindful of each word that passed.
Upon the fourth day these shrewd men set out
To tell the secrets to king Ardawán,
And with their magic tablets at their breasts
Went to him from the damsel's dwelling-place.
They told the secrets of the lofty sky,
To whom it turned, the time, and the degree :—
"A thing will happen at no distant date—
A matter that will wring the monarch's heart.
The least among his magnates will take flight,
A chieftain of high birth, a warrior,
And afterward become a mighty king,
A world-lord fortunate and fortune-giving."
　　The heart of that renowned and prosperous prince
Was in great dudgeon at their words.
　　　　　　　　　　　　　　　The damsel,
When all was black as pitch, went to Ardshír.
That youth was troubled like the sea and could not
Rest for one day because of Ardawán.
She told him what those shrewd men had apprised
The famous king, whereat Ardshír grew calm
And silent yet his heart was moved thereat.
He thought of flight and asked : "If I quit Rai
And seek Írán, the country of the brave,
Consider whether thou wilt go with me,
Or tarry with the king. If thou wilt go
Thou shalt be great, the Crown of all the realm."
　　She said with many a sigh and bitter tears :—
"Thy slave am I, and death alone shall part us."
　　Ardshír replied : "We must escape to-morrow,"
And she went back resolved to risk her all.
　　As soon as earth was gilded by the sun,
And dark night had been taken in the noose,
She oped the treasury and made her choice
Among the royal gems, took what dínárs

She needed, went back to her home, and there
Secured the jewels, waited till the night
Rose o'er the hills, till Ardawán was sleeping,
The coast all clear, then quitting arrow-like
The palace, took the jewels to Ardshír.
She found the atheling with cup in hand,
And all the equerries in drunken sleep.
He had picked out two noble steeds, and these
Were feeding ready saddled in their stalls.
When he beheld Gulnár, the gold, and rubies,
He laid the cup aside and forthwith bridled
The Arab steeds, put on his armour, mounted,
And grasped a watered sword.   The lady rode
The other steed, and so they fled together
Toward Párs with gladsome hearts.
                                        Now Ardawán
Was never happy either day or night
Without the fair Gulnár and would not quit
His couch unless in her auspicious presence.
When it was time to rise and have the throne
Draped with brocade, and still the damsel came not,
He was both angry and aggrieved at her.
    The guards were posted at the gate without,
Throne, crown, and palace were in readiness
While from the court-gate rose the chamberlain,
Approached the famous king, and said : "There wait
The chief men of the kingdom at the gate."

§ 6

How Ardawán heard of the Flight of Ardshír with the Dam
and pursued them

The monarch asked the slaves: "Why doth Gulnár
Neglect the rule and come not to my pillow ?
Is she offended with me ?"
                                        Thereupon

The chief scribe entered, saying: " Yesternight
Ardshír went off incontinent and took
A grey steed and a black steed from the stables—
The riding horses of the illustrious king—
Companioned by thy well-loved treasuress."
    The warrior-king much moved bestrode his bay,
Escorted by a host of gallant horsemen:
Thou wouldst have said: " He goeth over fire."
    Upon the road he saw a place of note
With many men and cattle, and inquired:—
" Did any hear the sound of hoofs ere day?   C. 1373
Did two pass on a grey steed and a black?"
    One said: " Two passed on two steeds desertward,
And at their heels a goodly mountain-sheep,
Which kicked the dust up horse-like."
                           Ardawán
Said to his minister: " Why ever went
The mountain-sheep with them?"
                         He made reply:—
" It is his Grace—the wings that will exalt him
To kingship through the favour of the stars.
If this sheep followeth him our task is lengthened."
    There Ardawán dismounted, ate, and rested,
Then hurried on. They followed up Ardshír,
And Ardawán in person led the way
With his wazír. Swift as a blast the youth
Rode with the damsel with no moment's pause,
But he who hath high heaven for his ally
Will take no harm from any enemy.
Ardshír at length, exhausted by the ride,
Beheld a pool of water from the height,
And as he rode said to Gulnár: " Since we
Have wedded toil, dismount we by this pool,
For steed and rider are alike fordone.
Repose we here and drink and start refreshed."
    Now when the twain had drawn anigh the water

Their visages as yellow as the sun,
And when Ardshír was fain to light him down,
He saw beside the watering-place two youths,
Who called out quickly: "There is need to ply
The reins and stirrup still for thou hast 'scaped
Thus far the breath and gullet of the Dragon,
And to drink water now will cost thee dear,
Yea even thy life."
          Ardshír, on hearing this,
Said to Gulnár: "Attend to what they say."
   He pressed his stirrups, gave his steed the reins,
And laid his glittering spear upon his shoulder.
Behind them Ardawán like rushing wind
Continued the pursuit with soul all gloom.
When half the day had passed, and while the
    orb—
The lustre of the world—still paced the sky,
He saw a city—one in goodly case—
Whence many flocked to meet him, and he asked
The archimages: "When passed two on horse-
    back?"
    Their leader said: "O prosperous, prudent king!
Just as the sun was growing pale, and night
Spread out the cloak of lapis-lazuli,

C. 1374 Two hurried through the city, soiled with dust
And parched with thirst, while after one of them
There came a mountain-sheep, and I have seen
None like it pictured in the palaces!"
    Said the wazír to Ardawán; "Stop here,
Unless thou wilt return and get thee ready
Both soldiers and the implements of war,
Because the fashion of this strife hath changed
In that his fortune backeth him; to follow
Is but to grasp the wind. Write to thy son,
And tell him all. Perchance he may discover
Trace of Ardshír whom we must suffer not

To milk this mountain-sheep."[1]

                            Now Ardawán,
On hearing this, knew that it was too late,
And so alighting at that city prayed
To God—the Giver of all good—for aid.

§ 7

How Ardawán wrote to Bahman, his Son, to take Ardshír

At dawn the monarch bade the host return,
And pale as reeds re-entered Rai by night.
He wrote a letter to his son and said :—
Deceit hath taken action, and Ardshír
Hath left me quicker than the shaft the bow,
And gone to Párs. Seek for him privily,
But say no word to any."

                          For his part
Ardshír approached the water and thus prayed :—
"O Thou who art our Helper! Thou hast saved
Me from my foeman : never may he prosper."
  Now when he had reposed he called a boatman,
And spake much of the past. The shrewd, old sailor
Observed Ardshír's high stature, mien, and breast,
Knew: "He can be but of the Kaian stock,"
Rejoicing in his Grace and Majesty,
Then hasting to the water sent his boats
To every part. At news of famed Ardshír
A host assembled by the water-side,
While in Istakhr the kindred of Pápak
All gloried at those tidings of the Sháh,
While those too of Dárá, who dwelt resigned
About the realm, exulted and grew young
Of heart though old, while troop on troop the folk ·

---

[1] Or, reading with P, " We must not let this mountain-sheep turn lion."

Flocked to the youth from mountain and from sea,
And from each city counsellors and sages
Assembled round that claimant of the world.
The young Ardshír loosed tongue and said: "Ye chiefs
Of ardent soul! of all this noble throng
There is no sage or counsellor but knoweth
What shame the infamous Sikandar [1] wrought
Upon the world, slew all mine ancestors,
And laid his hand on it unrighteously.
Now I am one sprung from Asfandiyár,
Yet Ardawán is king! We may not speak
Or think of this as just. If ye will help me
I will not yield the crown and lofty throne
To any. What have ye to say hereto?
Give me a fair reply."
          Then all the assembly,
Both warriors and counsellors, stood up,
And, speaking from their hearts, made answer thus:—
"All we that are the kindred of Pápak
Rejoice to see thy face, and we that are
Descendants of Sásán will gird ourselves
For vengeance. We are thine both soul and body,
Our joys and griefs, our less and more, are thine.
Thy quality from father and from mother
Surpasseth ours, the sovereignty and sway
Are thine of right, and we at thy command
Will turn the hills to plains, and with our swords
Make streams run blood."
          Ardshír's head, when he heard
That answer, rose o'er Mercury and Venus;
He blessed the chiefs and mused upon revenge.
He founded by the water-side a city
To be his seat of power. An archimage
Said: "Well-starred Sháh who winneth over hearts!
Thou fram'st anew the head of sovereignty,

---

[1] Observe the Sásánian view of Sikandar. *Cf.* p. 15.

But must clear Párs of Weeds and afterward
Make war on Ardawán, whilst thou and fortune
Are young, because in treasure he surpasseth
The other Tribal Kings; 'twill tax thy strength
To fight with him, but when thou hast cast down
His throne none else will hold his own with thee."
   Whenas the illustrious Ardshír heard this
The words approved themselves and pleased his heart,
And when the sun rose from the mountain-tops
He set forth from the water toward Istakhr.
News reached Bahman, the son of Ardawán,
And filled him, heart and soul, with grief and gloom.
He tarried not upon the throne of might,
But gathered troops and weapons for the fight.

§ 8

*How Tabák helped Ardshír, fought with Bahman, and
conquered him*

There was a noble hight Tabák, possessed   C. 1376
Of arms, of soldiery, and prudent counsels,
The ruler of the city of Jahram,
A veteran sage and one whose word was law.
He had seven noble sons, and at the news
About Ardshír went from Jahrám to him,
With tymbals and a host, prepared for battle,
Abandoning Bahman. When he beheld
Ardshír he lighted as the custom was,
Ran to him, kissed his feet, and spake at large
Of the Sásánians. The atheling
Showed him much favour, setting store upon
That speedy coming, yet suspected somewhat,
And dreaded that old man and watched him well
Upon the march because his force was great.
The veteran was shrewd, knew what Ardshír

Thought, and came with the Zandavasta, saying :—
" May God cut off Tabák's all worthless life
If in my heart be aught but honesty.
As soon as I heard news of Sháh Ardshír,
How he had reached the water with his host,
I loathed king Ardawán as young men loathe
An agéd spouse.   Know that I am thy slave
To love and prosper thee, to serve thee well,
And keep thy secrets."
                                Thereupon Ardshír
Began to estimate him differently,
And treat him like a sire, appointing him
Chief of the men of name, ceased to suspect,
Went to the temples of Kharrád and Rám,
And prayed to God to guide him to all good,
To give him all success and make his tree
Of majesty bear fruit, then sought his tent
Where both the counsellors and muster-master
Appeared before him, and he numbered all
The host, both horse and foot, and ascertained
Who were the leaders and the warriors,
Became acquaint with each, inquired his name,
And was rejoiced at such a mighty host.
C. 1377   He gave his soldiers pay, accoutred them,
Called on the just Bestower of all good
And, when the host was like a fierce pard, went
To fight Bahman, the son of Ardawán.
The armies met, the heroes sought the fray,
The troops drew up, lance, sword, and dart in hand.
    Whenas the Azure was unveiled the host
Led by Tabák advanced, like warrior-lions
Closed with the foe, and poured blood streamlike. Thus
Dust filled the air, and men the earth, till sunset.
Arose a blast with pitchy clouds of dust,
And from the army's centre came Ardshír.
Whereat Bahman, the son of Ardawán,

Fled pierced with arrows and his soul all gloom,
While Sháh Ardshír was instant in pursuit,
With blaring trumpets and with arrow-rain,
Until they reached the city of Istakhr,
Seat of the fame and glory of Bahman.

The Sháh's fame filled the world, and countless troops
Flocked to him. He was shown the many hoards
Of treasure that Pápak had toiled to gather.
Ardshír gave them in largess. When at length
He marched from Párs it was with growing strength.

§ 9

*How Ardawán led forth his Host for Battle with Ardshír
and was slain.*

When news reached Ardawán fear filled his heart,
And gloom his mind. He said : " A lord of counsel
Told me this secret of the lofty sky,[1]
But can one 'scape by pains unthought of ills ?
I did not fancy that Ardshír would prove
To be ambitious and a lion-taker."

He oped his treasury, gave rations out,
Bound on the baggage, and led forth the host ;
Contingents came from Gíl and from Dílam :
The army's dust rose moon-ward while the Sháh [2]
Led forth a host that barred the wind. Two bow-shots
Divided power from power ; snakes found no rest,
Such was the din of drum and clarion,
The clangour of the gongs and Indian bells.
The armies shouted and the banners waved,
While blue steel falchions scattered heads around.

The battle lasted thus for forty days,
The world was straitened to the common folk,

---

[1] See p. 219.   [2] *I.e.* Ardshir.

C. 1378   The plain grew mountain-like with all the slain,
The wounded were aweary of their life.
At last there rose a mighty, sable cloud,
And men could strive no more.   A frightful storm
Succeeded, and the warriors lost all heart.
The mountains echoed and the plain was rent
While air reverberated.   Then the troops
Of Ardawán were frayed and all exclaimed
With one consent: " This storm hath come from God
On Ardawán; this host will need our tears.".
   So all the wise one day, when fight was fiercest,
Asked quarter, and Ardshír charged from the centre ;
Arose a clashing while the arrows showered.
Amidmost of the mellay Ardawán
Was ta'en, and for his crown gave up sweet life.
The hand of one Kharrád seized on his bridle,
And bare him captive to the atheling.
Ardshír saw him from far.   King Ardawán
Lit from his steed, his body arrow-pierced,
His soul all gloom, and Sháh Ardshír commanded
The deathsman : " Go, seize on the great king's foe,
Cleave him asunder with thy sword, and make
Our evil-wishers quail."
                                   So did the deathsman :
That famous monarch vanished from the world.
   Such is the usage of the ancient sky !
The lot of Ardawán Ardshír too found ;
   Him whom it raiseth to the stars on high
It giveth likewise to the sorry ground !
   Two sons of him by whom Árash's seed
Thus had been brought to shame were taken too.
The noble Sháh Ardshír imprisoned them
With fetters on their feet.   Two elder sons
Succeeded in escaping from the fight,
And were not taken in the net of bale.
They went in tears to Hindústán, and thou

Mayst well narrate a tale concerning them.[1]
The battle-field was full of reins and girdles,
The weapons of the host, and gold and silver,
Which were collected by the Sháh's command,
And given to the troops.   Among the chiefs
Tabák was most concerned to cleanse the corpse
Of Ardawán from blood, lamenting while
He washed away the dust of fight, and built
A charnel as the royal custom was.
He robed the wounded bosom in brocade,
He placed a crown of camphor on the head,
And none of all the troops that went to Rai
Might tread the palace-dust of Ardawán.[2]

Tabák thereafter came before Ardshír,
And said : "O Sháh who seekest after wisdom !
Demand the child of Ardawán to wife,   C. 1379
For she hath Grace and beauty, crown and throne.
Then will this diadem and all the treasures
That he collected with such toil be thine."

He listened to the words of wise advice,
And asked the daughter for his spouse forthwith,
Then stayed a month or twain within the palace,
A mighty leader with a mighty host.

From Rai the aspirant went toward Párs and rested
From travail and dispute.   He built a city,
All palaces and gardens, and therein
Were fountain, plain, and dale, and to this day
The noble, ancient thane[3] doth speak thereof
As Khurra-i-Ardshír.[4]   Within, a spring

---

[1] Firdausí does so later on. See p. 259.

[2] As a rule the belongings of a fallen king or minister were given up to spoil, and this is implied in C, but the context seems to show that the reading of P, followed in the translation, is correct. *Cf.* Vol. iv. p. 212 *seq.*   Tabarí's account, however, favours C. See p. 255.

[3] The thane of Chách mentioned above, p. 210.

[4] Khurra-i-Ardshír, "The Grace of Ardshír," was the name given by him to the district and city of Gúr, not Zúr as in the text, now Fírúzábád. See NT, p. 11 and *note*.

That never failed gave water for canals.
Beside it he set up a Fane of Fire,
Revived the feasts of Sada[1] and Mihrgán,[2]
And round it splendid edifices raised,
With pleasances and parks and palaces.
(When that wise Sháh of Grace and might was dead
The border-chieftain named the city Zúr).
He founded villages all round about,
And there he settled folk when all was ready.
He saw within one quarter a deep lake,
But needs must pierce a height that intervened.
They brought picks and artificers, and clove
The mountain with a hundred water-ways.
He led them thence to Zúr. It was a seat
Abounding both in dwellings and in neat.

§ 10

How Ardshír fought with the Kurds and was defeated

Then Sháh Ardshír led from Istakhr a host
Innumerable to war against the Kurds,
Who, when he came anear, encountered him
In numbers numberless. What seemed a trifle
Became of moment, for the country round
All sided with the Kurds who both outnumbered
And hemmed the Sháh's host in. All day till night
The fight raged, then the world-lord's forces fled,
The field was straitened by the killed and wounded.
No man of name survived except the Sháh,
And some few troops whose tongues were cracked with
    thirst
Through blazing sunshine and the clouds of dust.
   When night had reared its flag, and ended strife
And stir, the Sháh marked on a mountain-side

[1] See Vol. i. p. 123.   [2] *Id.* 175 and *note.*

A fire, and went toward it with his men.
He found there hinds in charge of sheep and goats.   C. 1380
He and his men alighted with their mouths
Filled with the dust of fight.   He asked in haste
For water which they brought and curdled milk.
He rested, ate of what he found, took off
His breastplate, used it as his fittest couch,
And made his royal helmet serve as pillow.

   When dawn rose from the deep, and he awoke,
The chief hind visited his couch and said :—
"Be evil far from thee both day and night.
What ill hath caused thy journey hitherward,
And made thee make a couch of thy cuirass ?"

   The Sháh then questioned him about the way :—
"Where can I shelter next ?"

                              The chief herd said :—
"Thou wilt not find a habitable place,
Without a guide, but wilt, with one to lead thee,
Discover such, four leagues away, and thence
The villages, each with a well-known chief,
Are frequent."

                     So he took old herds as guides.
When he arrived the head man of the village
Came out at once to meet him.   He sent horsemen,
Both young and old, to Khurra-i-Ardshír ;
The host at news of him set forth rejoicing.
He sent men also to spy out the Kurds.
These men went forth, returned, and said : "They all
Are boasting of their deeds and making merry ;
None recketh of the Sháh, regarding him
As out-worn in Istakhr with ageing fortune."

   The Sháh rejoiced and deemed the past mere wind,
Chose from his famous host three thousand horsemen
With scimitars, and took in company
A thousand archers with artillery.

§ 11

How Ardshír attacked the Kurds by Night and
overthrew them

C. 1381   He led the host forth as the sun grew pale,
Left all the unfit behind, and in the dark
And dead of night came on the Kurds, and saw
Earth strewn with sleepers while his own troops raged.
The chieftain reached the pillow of the Kurds,
He gave his fleet steed rein, unsheathed, and charged.
He crowned the grass with blood.   The plain was all
The heads and hands of Kurds who strewed earth's face
By scores, and countless of them were made captive:
Their truculence and folly were brought low.
He gave their lands to spoil, to all his troops
Both crowns and purses, and from that time forth
If some old man had borne upon his head
A tray of gold across those deserts, none
Would e'en have glanced thereon, such was the fortune
And justice of the Sháh!   He tarried not
To celebrate his victory but marched
Back to Istakhr and issued these commands:—
" Repose your steeds, repair your arms, and cheer
Yourselves with feasts, for ye may have to think
Of war ere long."
                           The warriors fell to eating,
But when their waists had rested from their girdles
Ardshír devised new warfare.   Mind it well,
This tale, when thou shalt hear, of what befell.

§ 12

The Story of Hajtwád and the Case of the Worm

Now mark this strange, eventful history
Of Kujárán, a city on the sea

Of Párs, told by a rustic bard for he
Hath dealt at large with Persian legendry.
   There was a city strait but full of men,
Who all must work to eat, and many girls
Therein were poor and earned their bread withal.
On one side was a mountain near at hand
Whereto the damsels all were wont to fare,
Each with her distaff-case of poplar-wood,
And with her weighed-out stint of unspun cotton.
They used to gather at the city-gate
Before they started and to club whatever   C. 1382
They brought of provand, but their talk ne'er ran
On resting or on eating; their concern
Was cotton which at night they brought back spun.
   There dwelt within that city, one Haftwád,
Who was so named because he had seven sons,[1]
A man of cheerful turn but indigent.
He had too one dear daughter and no more,
But daughters he esteemed of no account.
   One day it happened that the troop of girls
Sat at their spinning on the mountain-side.
They clubbed together all the food they had,
And during meal-time laid their distaffs by.
'Twas then it happened that this lucky girl
Beheld a windfall lying on the path,
An apple which she picked up hastily.
Now list to this strange tale. When that fair maid
Had bitten the fruit she saw a worm inside.
She picked it from the apple and then gently
Transferred it to her distaff-case, and said,
As she resumed her spinning: " In the name
Of God who hath no partner and no peer,
I'll show you wondrous spinning done to-day
All through the good luck of an apple-worm ! "
   The girls grew merry and began to laugh,

[1] See p. 206.

Grew blithe of blee and showed their silver teeth.
That day she spun a double quantity,
And marked the sum thereof upon the ground,
Then hurried home like smoke and showed her mother
The yarn. Her mother praised her fondly, saying:—
" Thou hast done well, thou Moon with sunlike face!"
    Next morning, having measured off the twist,
She took a double stint, and all agog,
Heart, soul, and body, on her spinning, joined
That busy band and told those fair-famed girls:—
" Ye moon-faced and well favoured by the stars!
By this worm's fortune I have spun so much
That never I shall want!"
                She spun that stint,
And might have dealt with more. She carried home
What she had spun, whereat her mother's heart
Became like jocund Paradise. Each morning
The pretty damsel gave the worm some apple,
And spun off all the cotton howsoever
The tale might be increased, the little witch!
    One day the parents asked their worthy daughter:—
" Hast thou obtained a fairy for thy sister
That thou dost spin so much, thou goodly one?"

C. 1383   Forthwith the fair maid told her mother all
About the apple with the little worm
Concealed therein, and showed the glorious creature
To both her parents who rejoiced the more.
Haftwád, who took it for an augury,
Gave up his work; he talked of nothing save
The luck of the Worm. His fortune which had aged
Grew young. Thus time passed and his prospects
    brightened.
They did not slight the Worm but fed it well.
It grew in size and strength, its head and back
Were beautifully hued, and it outgrew
The distaff-case. Its coat, which turned as dark

As musk, had saffron spots throughout. Haftwád
Prepared a goodly, sable cabinet,
And lodged the creature there. It came to pass
That in that city everybody looked
For counsel and for justice to Haftwád,
Who grew in honour, consequence, and wealth,
And all his seven sons were rich as well.
The city had a governor—a man
With rank, renown, and soldiery—who sought
Occasion to deprive Haftwád, the base-born,
Of his dínárs, but many of the nobles
Took sides with him and his seven warlike sons.
The trumpet-call was heard in Kujárán:
They marched out with their spears, and swords, and
     arrows,
Led by Haftwád who played the man in fight,
Seized on the city, slew the governor,
And captured all his jewels and his treasures.
   A crowd of folk assembled round Haftwád.
He went from Kujárán toward the mountain,
Upon whose top he built a hold whereto
The citizens migrated in a mass.
He fitted up the hold with iron gates;
'Twas serviceable both in peace and war.
Upon the mountain-top there was a spring,
Which by good fortune rose amidst the hold;
Around he built a wall of viewless height.
   Now when the Worm outgrew its cabinet
They made a tank of masonry¹ and, when
The air had dried it, tenderly disposed
The Worm within. Each day at dawn its keeper
Would hurry from Haftwád to dress its food—
A cauldronful of rice. The growing Worm
Consumed it all. Years passed; its neck and limbs
Grew large as elephant's, and then Haftwád   Ϙ. 1384

_____
¹ Reading with P.

Surnamed the hold Kirmán,[1] his own bright daughter
Became the guardian of the Worm, and he
The leader of its troops.   Wazír and scribe
Attended it; it fed on rice, milk, honey,
While at its door Haftwád, the chieftain, stood
To answer for it both in bad and good.[2]

§ 13

How Ardshír fought with Haftwád and was worsted

Now when Ardshír heard of Haftwád the news
Displeased him, and he sent against that chief
A host of valiant, high-starred warriors.
Haftwád, on hearing of them, took it lightly.
He set an ambush in a mountain-coign,
And went himself to combat with his troops.
Now when the battle raged, and while the soldiers
Plied mace and battle-ax, the force in ambush
Advanced, earth gloomed to those Íránians,
For none knew head from foot, and thou hadst said:—
"Earth manacled their hands."   Such were the slain
On desert, dale, and mountain that the victors
Tired of the slaughter.   The survivors sped
Back to the Sháh.   Now when renowned Ardshír
Heard of the fight, the slaughter, and the plunder,
He sorrowed, summoned to him all his host,
And hasted to distribute arms and pay.
He set forth wrathfully against Haftwád;
The head of that base-born one rose to heaven;
He brought forth arms and treasure from the hold,
Misprizing both that army and the war.
Now when his eldest son, then far away,
Heard that his father was engaged in strife
ꜜHe left ease, feasting, and repose, and crossed

---

[1] See p. 204.   [2] Six couplets omitted.

The water in a boat.   That atheling,
An ill-conditioned youth, was named Sháhwí.   C. 1385
He thus rejoined Haftwád who joyed but kept
The right wing and the chief command himself.
Both hosts were goodly, furnished, well equipped,
And combative.   The young Sháh's heart grew old
With trouble at the sight.   They ranged their ranks,
The scimitars flashed out, the reek went up,
And when the drums beat on the elephants
Folk deafened two miles off.   The trumpets blared,
The world re-echoed with the brazen cymbals,
While earth reeled 'neath the horse-shoes and the
     nails;
The air was tulip-hued with flags of chiefs,
The crash of axes on the crests of helms,
Reverberated from heaven while the rush
Of wind-foot chargers rent the ground asunder,
And pass and plain were full of headless corpses.
Such was Haftwád's host that thou wouldst have said:—
"The sea is wind-tossed."   Ant and fly were cramped
For room, those armies so fulfilled the plain.
Thus was it till day waned and night outspread
Its cloak of lapis-lazuli.   Ardshír
Drew in his troops.   Behind him was the sea.
Now when eve's rusty livery grew dark,
And when the scouts went out from both the hosts,
The soldiers of the Sháh became the prey
Of hunger for his foeman barred the way.

§ 14

How Mihrak of Jahram sacked the Palace of Ardshír

Lived at Jahram a man of low degree [1]—
Mihrak son of Núshzád—who, when he heard

[1] Of Kaian race, according to P.

About the expedition of Ardshír,
His tarrying by the sea, and how his host
Was starving, with communications barred,
Marched on the palace of the Sháh, assembled
Troops past all count, and sacked it, lavishing
No stint of crowns and purses on his soldiers.
The Sháh received the tidings by the sea,
And said in grief: "Why did I leave my home
Defenceless and attack an alien foe?"
Called all the chiefs, spake of Mihrak at large,

C. 1386

And said: "What think ye, leaders of the host!
Of such an impasse? I have tasted much
Of fortune's bitterness, but reckoned not
On trouble from Mihrak!"

                    They cried: "O Sháh!
Ne'er may thine eyes behold ill-luck. Why take
Things ill because Mihrak hath proved thy foe
In secret? Thou hast greatness, and the world
Is thine. Thy slaves are we; 'tis thine to bid."
  He gave command to have the tables set;
They called for wine and cups and minstrelsy.
They served up divers lambs[1] upon the board,
And all the guests disposed themselves to eat,
But when Ardshír himself took bread there came
A pointed shaft and deeply lodged itself
Within the dainty plumpness of a lamb,
Whereat those brave, wise chiefs forbore to eat.
All sorely grieved. One drew the arrow forth.
They saw that there was writing on the shaft;
Those that were clerkly of the magnates read it;
The writing on the arrow was old Persian,
And thus it ran: "If thou wilt hear, wise Sháh!
This issued from the hold's top which is safe
Through the luck of the Worm. Had I directed it

---

[1] Lambs are still served up whole at feasts in Persia. C. J. Wills,
Land of the Lion and the Sun, p. 91.

Against Ardshír the feathers would have pierced him.
No monarch, such as he is, in our days
Can overthrow the Worm."
           Then to the archmages
The Sháh read out the script on that sharp arrow.
The hold was two leagues off! The nobles' hearts
Were straitened, but they all evoked upon
The Glory of earth's king God's benison.

§ 15

How Ardshír heard about the Worm and made
Shift to slay it

The Sháh mused much that night about the Worm
And, when the sun displaced the moon, set forth
With all his army from the sea and hurried
Toward Párs. The foe pursued him, seized the roads,
And slaughtered all the chieftains, but the Sháh
Escaped with his own meiny while behind him
The foe cried: "May the Worm's luck light its throne."
    All said; "A marvel—one for all to ponder!"   C. 1387
Now as he fled in fear o'er hill and plain
He saw a spacious city, and they urged
Like wolves their steeds. As he approached he saw
A house and at the door two stranger youths.
There halted he and his. The honest pair
Asked him: "Whence come ye so unseasonably,
So dusty from the road, and travel-worn?"
    He said: "Ardshír hath come this way, and we
Lagged on the route. He fleeth from the Worm,
Haftwád, and that base man's ignoble crew."
    The youths had ruth upon him; they grew sad
And dark of soul, made him dismount and greeted
His nobles well, prepared him pleasant quarters,
And furnished food that was acceptable.

The mighty men sat with the Shâh at meat
While those two youths began to entertain him,
And said aloud: "Exalted one! no grief
Or joy will last. Mark what Zahhák, the tyrant,
Brought on the throne of kingship, how kings' hearts
Ached through malevolent Afrásiyáb,
And how Sikandar, in these latter days,
Slew all the monarchs of the world; all these [1]
Have passed away, have left an evil name,
And not attained to jocund Paradise.
'Twill be thus with Haftwád; that miscreant
Will writhe at last."
                              The Shâh's heart at their words
Became as fresh as roses in the spring.
The speech of those two gracious ones consoled him,
He told his secret, and, declared himself.
"I am," he said, "Ardshír, son of Sásán,
And am in need of comforting advice.
How deal we with this Worm and with Haftwád?
May both his name and lineage cease on earth."
      Thereat the two young men did homage, saying:—
"All hail!   Be ill's hand ever far from thee.
Be we thy bond-slaves both in soul and body,
And thou confirmed in spirit evermore.
As for the matter that thou askest us
We will advise thee well that thou mayst use
Craft from the first.   In battle with the Worm,
And with Haftwád, thou wilt not be approved
Unless thou shalt adopt the proper course.
They have their seat upon the mountain-peak;
Within it are the Worm, the troops, and treasure;
C. 1388 Before it is the city and behind
The sea, the hold is on the mountain-top,
And access difficult.   The Worm withal
Deriveth from the brain of Áhriman—

---

[1] *I.e.* Zahhák, Afrásiyáb, and Sikandar. *Cf.* pp. 15, 224 and *note*, and Vol. i. p. 59.

The foeman of the Maker of the world.
Thou callest it a Worm, but in its skin
There is a combative, blood-thirsty dív!"
    Ardshír, on hearing this, which won his love
And pleased his heart, replied: "So be it then,
And ye shall have the credit or the blame."
    The young men's answer pleased his prudent heart:—
"We stand before thee ever as thy slaves,
And guides to good."
                        Made happy by their words
He fared triumphant and with heart all justice,
And, when he left, the youths companioned him.
He went with ardent heart and full of heed,
With head held high to Khurra-i-Ardshír.
Troops, magnates, men of lore, and counsellors
Flocked to the Sháh, who rested for a while,
Gave out supplies, then marched against Mihrak,
Son of Núshzád, to whom the world grew dark
And strait because he dared not fight; that traitor
Hid when the great king drew anear Jahram.
The great king's heart was wrathful. He abode
Until Mihrak was taken, then smote through
His neck with Indian scimitar, consigned
The headless body to the flames, and put
All captives of his kindred to the sword.
Howbeit one daughter was concealed despite
The hue and cry for her throughout the city.
    Thence he departed to attack the Worm,
As all his host desired, and took with him
Twelve thousand horsemen proved and veteran.
When he had concentrated all his troops
He led them to a spot between two mountains.
A prudent man, Shahrgír by name, commanded
The host of Sháh Ardshír, who said to him:—
"Remain here on the watch with outposts, set
Both day and night, shrewd cavaliers and guides,

And furthermore both day and night employ
Patrols and sentries to safe-guard the host.
For my part I shall use a stratagem,
As did mine ancestor Asfandiyár,[1]
And if the watch should see a smoke by day,
Or in the night a blazing like the sun,
Know ye that all is over with the Worm,
Its luck and traffic gone."

C. 1389
He chose seven men,
All brave and Lions on the day of battle,
Among his chiefs. Those in his confidence
Ne'er breathed a word. He chose too many a gem
Out of his hoards, brocade, dínárs, and goods
Of every kind, and wisely spared not wealth.
He packed two boxes full of lead and solder,
And added to the load a brazen pot,
Because he was a master of his craft.
When all the baggage was in readiness
He ordered his chief equerry to bring
Ten asses, put a driver's blanket on,
And chose the gold and silver as his load.
When anxiously they started for the hold
He took with him the two young country-folk,
Who had received him on a former day,
As friends and counsellors. When near at hand
They rested on the mountain and drew breath.

The servants of the Worm were sixty men,
And every one was busy at his work.
One saw the company and called to them :—
" What is there in these packs ? "

The Sháh replied :—
" All sorts of goods—clothes, gold and silver, trinkets,
Brocade, dínárs, silk stuffs, and jewelry.
I am a merchantman of Khurásán,
And have no rest from toil, am well to do

---

[1] When taking the Brazen Hold. See Vol. v. p. 143.

By favour of the Worm and now have come
Rejoicing to its seat.   It blesseth me,
And, if I may but serve it, all is well."
   Thereat the servants of the Worm flung back
The castle-gate.   When they had brought the loads
Inside, the noble Sháh took charge, undid
A pack forthwith, and made the needful gifts.
He spread before the attendants of the Worm
The leathern table of the traveller,
And stood as slaves are wont, unlocked the chests,
Brought and filled cups with wine, but those whose
      turn
It was to feed the Worm with milk and rice
Refused to drink ; their duty kept them sober.
Now as they sat Ardshír sprang up and said :—
" Abundance both of rice and milk have I
And, if the Worm's chief servitor permitteth,
Will gladly feed.it for three days myself;
Fame may ensue, and I shall share its luck.
For three days then be merry and drink wine,
At sun-rise on the fourth I will erect
A spacious warehouse higher than the walls,
For as a chapman seeking purchasers
I fain would curry favour with the Worm. "
   This gained his end.   They said : " Do thou provide."
So that ass-driver undertook the toil,
While sat the servitors with wine in hand,
And feasted and grew drunk, and came to be
The servitors of wine, not of the Worm.
Now when the wine-cup had bemused their minds
The master of the world came with his hosts,[1]
Brought forth the metal and the brazen pot,
And lit a fire by daylight.   When 'twas time
To feed the Worm its food was of boiling lead.
He bore the molten metal to the tank,

C. 1390

---

[1] *I.e.* his former entertainers—the two youths.   See p. 239.

Whence that tame creature raised its head.   They saw
Its tongue thrust out, just like an Arab cymbal,
As when it used to eat the rice.   The youths
Poured down the molten stuff and quelled the Worm.
There came a rumble from its maw and shook
The tank and ground.   Came like the wind Ardshír
With those two youths; they plied sword, mace, and
    shaft,
And none among those drunken servitors
Escaped their hands with life.   Ardshír sent up
A black smoke from the castle-roof to tell
The exploit to the captain of the host,
To whom the look-out hurried to announce:—
" Ardshír hath won ! "
                          Shahrgír made no delay,
But marched to meet the Sháh with his array.

§ 16

How Ardshír slew Haftwád

Now when Haftwád was ware thereof his heart
Grew full of anguish and his head of sighs.
He came to repossess the hold.   The king
Ascended to the walls in haste.   Haftwád
Strove but to small result, for on the ramparts
There was a Lion's foot.[1]   The Íránian host
Came mountain-like, but halted seared and sore.[2]
Then Sháh Ardshír cried from the battlements:—
" O valiant lion-catcher ![3] fall upon them,
For if Haftwád escapeth from our midst

---

[1] Persian etymology derives Ardshír from " ard," anger, and " shír,"
a lion.   The true is " arta," great, and " khshathra," king.
[2] Their previous experiences with Haftwád had been unfortunate.
Cf. p. 236 *seq.*
[3] The name of Ardshír's general was Shahrgír—*i.e.* City-taker.
Ardshír addresses him as Shírgír, *i.e.* Lion-taker.

Thou wilt have naught in hand but toil and wind.
I have given the molten metal to the Worm;
Gone is its luck, its fierce career abated."
    The troops all heard the Sháh's words, donned their
        helms   C. 1391
And, grieved at past discomfiture, took heart,
And girt their loins for vengeance. Then the wind
Turned on the Worm's troops. Soon Haftwád was taken,
As was that knave Sháhwí—his eldest son
And general. Ardshír descended quickly;
Shahrgír met him afoot. They brought a steed
With golden trappings, and the famed king mounted;
Then ordered to set up beside the sea
Two lofty gibbets and suspended thence
His two opponents living and woke up
The heart of all his foes. As for the twain,
He came forth from the centre of the host,
And put them both to death with showers of arrows.
He gave the wealth to spoil and thus enriched
His troops. The servants brought down from the hold
All that there was. Such of the wealth as pleased him
He hurried off to Khurra-i-Ardshír.
The Sháh set up a Fire-fane on the mountain,
Restored Mihrgán and Sada, and bestowed
Upon his lucky hosts[1] crown, throne, and province,
And thence departing, triumphing and glad,
Spread justice over Párs. When man and beast
Had rested he led on his host to Zúr,
Sent to Kirmán an army, and a man
Fit for the crown and throne, proceeded thence
To Taisafún and brought his foe's throne down.
    Of this our whirling world it is the way
To keep concealed from thee its mystery.
Conform to it, 'twill not conform to thee,
    Because its favour changeth every day.

             [1] *Cf.* p. 243, *note.*

IV
THE SÁSÁNIAN DYNASTY

IV

THE SÁSÁNIAN DYNASTY

ARGUMENT

The poet, in this the concluding dynasty of the Sháhnáma, tells of the rise, progress, and fall of the Sásánian empire from the days of its founder, Ardshír Pápakán, to those of Yazdagird, the last Sháh of the dynasty. He commemorates the reigns of its twenty-nine Sháhs, for the most part very briefly, but in some instances at great length, as in the cases of Bahrám Gúr, Núshír-wán, and Khusrau Parwíz. He records, so far as Íránian tradition kept such things in memory, the foreign relations of the empire with other kings, races, and peoples, its internal administration and domestic concerns, the adventures that befell and the wisdom that was uttered, the invention of chess and the coming of the Gipsies. He then describes the conquest of Írán by the Arabs and ends with a short passage of personal reminiscence.

NOTE

Having passed, as Firdausí says, " Sikandar's barrier "[1] and the great historic void of five centuries and more, peopled for us in the Sháhnáma by a few shades of names only, we alight at length on the authentic but unstable soil of the Sásánian dynasty; for even here the information presented to us is by no means con-sonant with modern Western canons of accuracy. The names are historic, and so are many of the events recorded, but there are no dates, and often what is historic is misplaced chronologically and attributed to the wrong actors and the wrong causes, sometimes very trivial ones—those, for instance, assigned by the street story-teller. Of many of the Sháhs only the facts of their acces-sion, the length, often wrongly given, of their reigns, their inaugural speeches, and deaths are recorded. The occurrence, more than once, of a whole series of such reigns has a somewhat depressing effect on the reader and gives an appearance of truth

---

[1] p. 189.

to Atkinson's view that the interest of the Sháhnáma ends with the reign of Sikandar.[1] From this it might be thought that the poet, weary with his long labours and soured by hope deferred, had hurried over or scamped the concluding portion of his vast undertaking. It might be thought that even in the places where material is abundant his version of it had not the technique and attractiveness found in the earlier dynasties. In the opinion of the present writer such views are not justified by the facts of the case. It is true that here the visions of the childhood of the world fade into the light of common day, and the superhuman gives place to the human, but there is a measure of compensation in that very fact, and the study of the history of a whole epoch as it was conceived, interpreted, and handed down by popular tradition, cannot fail of interest and instruction. It must be remembered too that no other great poet ever imposed such strict limitations on himself, or so sternly adhered to them, as did Firdausí. He puts himself at the mercy of his authorities, and where they fail him, as they do sometimes in this portion of the Sháhnáma, he makes no attempt to invent incidents, but leaves a blank and passes on. This is a proceeding for which the poet should be praised rather than blamed. He was engaged in a high task, no doubt believed in the tales that he retold, just as his countrymen believe in them still, and he refused to add to the sacred story of his race as he found it in tradition. In cases, however, where his authorities offered him an opportunity he shows no falling off in vigour, as the reign of Bahrám Gúr, which will be found in the next volume, is in itself sufficient to prove. In it we seem to discern the soil and the seed whence sprang in after ages the well-beloved Nights called Arabian, but certainly of Persian origin, for we have the Sháh roaming disguised, or at least unrecognised, among his subjects of all classes, the freaks of despotic power, the humorous exaggerations, the Rabelaisian tale, and the clash of the cymbals of the Brides of the Treasure. Finally, in the story of Bahrám Chubína, which Macan admired so much,[2] the Sásánian dynasty possesses a historical romance both admirable in itself and admirably set forth by the poet. It remains to call attention to a few other points in connexion with this dynasty.

Ardshír Pápakán laid it down as a fundamental principle of government, if Íránian tradition may be credited, that the Throne and the Faith were interdependent. The Faith could not exist without the Throne, nor the Throne without the Faith. The two

---

[1] AS, p. 510.　　　　　[2] C, Vol. i. p. xxxvii.

were brothers; they wore one cloak; they were two pieces of brocade interwoven; the slanderer of the Throne and the persecutor of the Faith were alike impious.[1] Whether Ardshír really spoke to this effect or not matters little. If he did not say so in word his deeds said it for him, and most of his successors followed his example. Later ages, noting this marked feature of the dynasty—the close union between the Throne and the Faith—naturally may have attributed corresponding sentiments to its founder. Accordingly the religion of Zoroaster, as represented by its official priesthood and supported by the throne, obtained during Sásánian times a position of influence and dignity such as it never previously had enjoyed, at all events since the semi-mythical epoch of Gushtásp and of Asfandiyár. Even with all its official advantages, however, the priesthood had much ado to maintain itself, amid the religious ferment of those centuries, alike against the antagonism of rival Faiths without and heresy within.[2] Orthodox Zoroastrianism was more than once almost in the position of an *Athanasius contra mundum*.[3] The Sásánian Sháhs, for the most part, seem to have done their best to support the priesthood, and the latter showed its gratitude by a deep and loyal devotion to the House of Sásán. This loyalty to the throne, coupled with aversion from all that was heterodox or unorthodox, was reflected in the national tradition as handed down by the chroniclers of the time, who for the most part were Zoroastrian priests themselves. Consequently in this part of the Sháhnáma the reader will find a strong legitimist feeling, expressed by occasional remarks or asides, running like a thread through the poem. This feeling takes the form of devotion to the House of Sásán as a whole, with the exception of Yazdagird, son of Shápúr, " The Wicked," and to the interests of the supposed rightful Sháh or heir for the time being as against usurpers or other claimants of the throne. These little outbursts certainly are not expressions of the poet's own personal views on such matters ; he found them in his authorities and reproduced them. This remark also applies to passages of religious polemics. The poet's own views on such matters probably may be found in the parable of the kerchief.[4] These polemics represent the devotion of the Zoroastrian priesthood to orthodoxy, as they understood it, just as their legitimist outbursts expressed their loyalty to the throne, provided that it was occupied by rightful and orthodox Sháhs of the House of Sásán.

A curious instance of this close union between Church and State

---

[1] See p. 286.
[2] *Cf.* pp. 327, 358.
[3] *Cf.* Vol. v. p. 16, *note*.
[4] See pp. 92, 95.

in Sásánian times is given by Mas'údí in his "Book of Indication
and Revision," but a few words may be said by way of preface.
According to Zoroastrianism there are to be twelve millennia, at
the expiration of the last of which—the present one—will come
the Restoration of all things. Now the tenth millennium began
on the day when the Revelation came to Zarduhsht,[1] and in the
Dínkard we find a prophecy, after the event, that the last two
centuries of that particular millennium would be periods of great
misery and wretchedness.[2] The Dínkard was compiled during the
ninth century A.D., and Mas'údí flourished during the first half of
the tenth. This is what he tells us : — "There is a great difference
between the opinion of the Persians and that of other people with
reference to the epoch of Alexander, which most folk have not
noticed. It is one of the secrets of the religion and royal policy
of the Persians and is known only to the most erudite among the
priests, as we have seen for ourselves in the province of Párs,
Kirmán, and other countries where the Persians rule. It is not
found in any of the books on Persian history or in any chronicle
or annals. It is this. Zoroaster . . . in the Avasta—the book
revealed to him—announces that in three centuries the empire of
the Persians will experience a great revolution, without destruction to the religion, but that at the end of a thousand years,
starting from the same epoch, that of Zoroaster, the empire and
the religion will perish together. Now between Zoroaster and
Alexander there is about three hundred years, for Zoroaster
appeared in the time of Gushtásp . . . Ardshír, son of Pápak,
possessed himself of the empire . . . about five hundred years
after Alexander. We see then that there remained not more than
two hundred years or thereabouts before the completion of the
thousand years of the prophecy. Ardshír wished to augment by
two hundred years this space of time . . . because he feared that
when a hundred years should have elapsed after him men would
refuse aid to the king, and to repulse his enemies, owing to their
belief in the truth of the tradition relating to the future ruin of
the empire. To obviate this he retrenched about half the time
that had elapsed between Alexander and himself, and accordingly
only made mention of a certain number of the Part Kings, who
had occupied this period, and suppressed the remainder. Then
he took pains to disseminate in his empire that he had made his
appearance and possessed himself of the rule two hundred and
sixty years after Alexander. Consequently this period was
recognised and spread among men. For this reason there is a

---

[1] See Vol. v. p. 16.   [2] WPT, v. 94 *seq.*

difference between the Persians and other nations with respect to the era of Alexander, and this is why confusion has been imported into the annals of the Part Kings." [1] Whatever we may think with regard to the historical value of this explanation the fact remains that the duration of the epoch between Alexander the Great and Ardshír Pápakán is reduced by Oriental historians generally. Its standard length may be put, as given by them, at 266 years. The above account makes Ardshír strike out 288 years of the actual historical number of 548 years.

In the notes to the various reigns of this dynasty no attempt will be made to present a complete historical sketch of the Persian history of the period by adding details and filling up the frequent *lacunæ* from other sources. Such history as the poem offers will be dealt with, but such as it ignores, *e.g.* many of the wars with the Eastern Roman empire, will be passed over in silence save where reference to some omitted historical event is needed for the better understanding of what has been included but misrepresented. Readers that desire to supplement the Sháhnáma will find ample material in the late Professor Rawlinson's "Seventh Great Oriental Monarchy," and in the Bibliography appended thereto, especially if they add Professor Nöldeke's "Geschichte der Perser und Araber zur Zeit des Sasaniden," which was published three years later and is invaluable.

The form of the names of the various Sháhs, taken from Professor Rawlinson, and the duration of their respective reigns, as calculated by Professor Nöldeke, are given between brackets.

A genealogical table of the Sásánians, according to the Sháhnáma, will be found at the beginning of the volume.

---

[1] MM, ix. 327.

XXII

ARDSHÍR PÁPAKÁN

HE REIGNED FORTY YEARS AND TWO MONTHS

ARGUMENT

Ardshír, having become King of kings, marries the daughter of Ardawán, who attempts to poison him and is saved by Ardshír's minister. Shápúr is born and recognised by his father Ardshír. Ardshír consults Kaid about the future. Kaid's reply. The adventure of Shápúr with the daughter of Mihrak. The birth of Urmuzd, who is acknowledged by Ardshír as his grandson. Account of Ardshír's administration. He counsels Shápúr and dies. The poet ends the reign with praises of Mahmúd.

NOTE

§ 1. The forty years and two months assigned by Firdausí to the reign of Ardshír (Artaxerxes I., A.D. 226–241) is much too long. Tabarí makes it, from the fall of Ardawán, fourteen years or, according to some of his authorities, ten months longer.[1] No doubt Ardshír was a king, with his seat of government at Párs, from soon after the death of his father Pápak.[2] Probably he served, and won his spurs, in Ardawán's war against the Romans which was ended by the peace of Nisibis in A.D. 217. Nine eventful years followed and he became King of kings in A.D. 226. Firdausí, according to the text of C, makes him seventy-eight, according to the text of P sixty-eight, at the time of his death.[3]

There had been a city of Baghdád in Babylonian times, but the Arab city of that name was not founded till the days of the Khalífa Al Mansúr in A.D. 762. The city here meant is Bih-Ardshír, the Seleucia newly founded by Ardshír.[4]

We have two accounts of the assumption of the title "King of kings" by Ardshír. For the other see p. 273. From Firdausí's

---

[1] NT, p. 21.   [2] See p. 199.   [3] Id. p. 286.   [4] NT, p. 16, and note.

wording it might be held that the former was the popular, the latter the official, ascription of the title. For its import in connexion with Ardshír see p. 197. *Cf.* too p. 199.

§§ 2, 3. Firdausí's account agrees partly with the Kárnámak and partly with the Arabic versions, showing clearly that the former was not his direct authority. According to K two of Ardawán's sons had fled to Kábul and thence incited Ardawán's daughter, whose name is given as Zijának, to poison Ardshír, her husband. One day accordingly, on his return from the chase, she presents to him a cup of roast meal and milk with which she has mingled the poison. As he was about to drink, the sacred Fire, Frúbá, descended on the cup and it fell from his hand. A cat and dog ate the spilt food and died on the spot. Ardshír at once ordered the high priest (the chief múbid) to have Zijának put to death. Instead of so doing, however, he concealed her in his own house, where she gave birth to a son whom she called Shápúr, *i.e.* son of the king, and brought him up till he was seven years old. The story of the self-mutilation by the high priest is omitted.[1] One day Ardshír went to the chase and followed a female onager, whereupon the male came towards Ardshír and exposed himself to death in her stead. Ardshír spared him and rode after the colt, whereat the female onager came up and offered herself to be slain in her young one's place. Ardshír, reflecting on his own conduct to his wife, whom he knew to have been with child at the time when he ordered her to execution, wept. The high priest seized the opportunity to tell Ardshír the real state of the case, and Shápúr is presented to him. Ardshír in great joy bounteously rewards the high priest and founds the city of Rás-Shápúr and a sacred Fire in commemoration of the occasion.[2] According to Tabarí, when Ardshír had obtained the sovereignty he destroyed utterly, in accordance to an oath sworn by his grandsire, the elder Sásán, the royal race of the Arsacids[3] with the exception of one girl, Ardawán's daughter, whom he found in the royal palace. She was very beautiful, and, as she gave herself out to be merely the handmaid of one of Ardawán's wives, he married her. Later on, thinking herself secure, as she was with child by him, she told him who she was. On this he ordered his minister, an

---

[1] A similar story is told by Lucian in his treatise on "The Syrian Goddess" of Seleucus Nicator, his queen Stratonice, and one of his favourites—a handsome youth named Combabus—and by Hiuen Tsiang of the younger brother of a king of K'iu-chi who was left in charge of the government while the king himself went on pilgrimage. BBR, i. 22.

[2] NK, pp. 57 *seq.*   [3] Historically this is incorrect. See p. 202.

aged man, to put her to death,[1] and then follows the rest of the story as told in the Sháhnáma. All these accounts make Shápúr much too young. According to Tabarí he was present at the battle of Hurmuzdagán and slew with his own hand Ardawán's secretary.[2] Tabarí thus appears to contradict himself, but the reader should bear in mind that it is the custom of Oriental historians to give several versions, derived from different sources, of the same event or person, not to digest such versions, as a Western writer would do, into a single narrative.

A similar account of the rewards bestowed by the grateful Ardshír on his faithful minister is given by Dínawarí and in some versions of the Persian translation of Tabarí, but there is no evidence that the statement that Ardshír had his minister's head engraved and stamped on the coinage is historically correct. It is true that another head besides Ardshír's appears on his earliest and some of his latest coins, but the heads are those of Pápak and and of Shápúr respectively.[3]

The Jund-i-Shápúr of F appears to be the equivalent of the Rás-Shápúr of K.[4]

§§ 4–6. This is both in K and in the Arabic versions. In F the wise Indian king of the days of Sikandar—Kaid, the Kait of K— reappears, takes the place held by the astrologers in Tabarí, and, in K, declares that only two races can hold sway in Írán—that of Ardshír and that of Mihrak.[5] F more poetically puts it that the Sháh can only find peace by the *union* of his family with that of Mihrak. On this Ardshír, aware that one daughter of Mihrak had escaped the previous massacre, tries in vain to find her. It seems worth suggesting that, in the primitive form of the legend, Ardawán, Mihrak, and Máhdik were one and the same personality. Mihrak is Mithrak in K, a very Parthian name, and Mádik or Máhdik is the king of the Kurds. Máhdik merely means "the Mede" and thus symbolises the Parthian power which, according to Íránian tradition, had its headquarters in Media Magna. In this view Ardshír's expeditions against the Kurds and Mihrak would be mere variants of his advance into, and conquest of, Media after the decisive battle of Hurmuzdagán when doubtlessly he put to death all that he could find of his late rival's family. That he wittingly spared any of them, male or female, is most unlikely, and a legend given in Tabarí[6] had to be invented to explain how it came about that he married Ardawán's daughter, the story of this marriage being a later device, as here in Shápúr's

---

[1] NT, pp. 25 *seq.*   [2] *Id.* 14.   [3] *Id.* 30 *note*, and RSM, pp. 65 *seq.*
[4] NK p. 63.   [5] NT, p. 43; NK, p. 64.   [6] See p. 255.

case, to connect the Sásánians with their predecessors. It is worth noting too that in the Arabic historian Hamza the daughter of Mihrak is called Kurdzád, *i.e.* "the child of the Kurds." [1] This explains the words of Kait's prophecy in K and, what is hard to understand otherwise, why such great importance should be attached to Mihrak and his family in the various versions of the legends unless we regard them as all originating from a single historical incident in Ardshír Pápakán's career. F's insight in varying the form of Kaid's prophecy brings out the historical truth that Írán could be restored to internal peace only by the voluntary union of the old and new political dispensations.

The scene at the well between Shápúr and the daughter of Mihrak is not found in the Arabic versions. In Tabarí the girl takes refuge with shepherds and provides Shápúr with water one day when he is hunting. He falls in love with her and takes her in marriage, after which she tells him of her parentage. The Arabic versions, both in this case and that of Ardshír, represent the marriage into the enemy's family as having been made through ignorance.[2]

The recognition scene on the polo-ground, which we have had already in connexion with Shápúr,[3] here occurs, as in K, in its proper place. F adds the touch of Ardshír's unexpected return from the chase and consequent discovery. In Tabarí it is brought about by a sudden visit paid to his son's palace by Ardshír who thus encounters Urmuzd.[4]

At this point K, after giving a brief and exaggerated account of the reign of Urmuzd, comes to an end.

§§ 7, 8, 10. In addition to K there was once in existence a Pahlaví work known as the "Ahdnámak" or "Andarznámak" *i.e.* "Book of the Exhortations" *sc.* of Ardshír. In all probability its contents much resembled the subject-matter found in these sections.[5]

Tabarí states that Ardshír himself crowned his son Shápúr,[6] and the incident seems to be recorded in a bas-relief of Ardshír's at Takht-i-Bústán and in some of his later coins.[7] Mas'údí says that Ardshír became a religious recluse.[8]

The duration of the Sásánian dynasty was 425 years—A.D. 226–651. *Cf.* with Ardshír's prophecy the account of Mas'údí on p. 251, and for the length of his reign p. 254. Tabarí[9] credits him with the foundation of eight cities.

---

[1] NK, p. 65, *note.*   [2] NT, pp. 26, 44.   [3] p. 263.
[4] NT, p. 44.   [5] NK, pp. 26, 27.   [6] NT, p. 19.
[7] RSM, pp. 64 *seq.*   [8] MM, ii. 159.   [9] *Id.*

§ I

How Ardshír Pápakán sat upon the Throne in Baghdád

Now at Baghdád Ardshír assumed his seat
Upon the ivory throne and donned the crown
That maketh glad the heart, with girdle girt,
The sceptre of the Sháhs in hand, the palace
Prepared. Thenceforth folk called him "King of
    kings,"[1]
And no one knew him from Gushtásp.   Whenas
He donned the crown of majesty he spake,
Victorious and glad, upon the throne
Thus: "Justice is my treasure in this world,
Which is reviving 'neath my busy hands,
A treasure this that none can take from me ;
Ill-doing 'tis that bringeth ill on men.
All-holy God, if I find favour with Him,
Will not begrudge to me this sombre earth.
The world is wholly under my protection,
My policy is to approve of justice.
None—friend or foe—must slumber with his heart
All care through act of any officer,
Or chief, or warrior-cavalier of mine:
This court is free to all, both foe and friend. "
    The whole assembly blessed him and exclaimed :—
"Oh! may thy justice make earth prosperous !"
    Where there were hostile chiefs he sent forth
    troops
To bring them to submission or make known
The usage of the scimitar and throne.

C. 1392

---

[1] *Cf.* pp. 193, 197, 199, 254, 273.

§ 2

The Case of Ardshír and the Daughter of Ardawán

Now when the Sháh slew Ardawán, thus winning
The world, he took to wife the slain king's daughter
To tell him where her father's hoards were hidden.
There were two sons of Ardawán in Hind,
Companions in distress, and two in ward
With full hearts and with weeping eyes. The eldest
Of these—Bahman—who was in Hindústán,
Perceiving that the realm was lost to him,
Chose a discreet and prudent messenger,
A youth who was possessed of ears to hear,
Gave him some poison secretly, and said :—
" Go to my sister, tell her : ' Seek not thou
Our foe's affections, for in Hindústán
Thou hast two brothers, exiles both, and two
Bound in the prison-house of Sháh Ardshír.
Our sire is slain, his sons are pierced, by arrows,
And thou, as it would seem, hast ceased to love us !
How can the Maker of the sky commend it ?
As thou wouldst queen it in Írán, and win
In this world the approval of the brave,
Take thou this mortal Indian bane and use it
Forthwith upon Ardshír.' "
                              The envoy came
At eve and gave the noble girl that message.
Her soul and heart burned for her brother's sake,   C. 1393
Her heart was all a-flame. She took the bane
To do his will. Now Sháh Ardshír one day
Went forth to hunt and shoot the onager,
Returned at noon and visited the daughter
Of Ardawán. That moon-faced lady ran,
And proffered to the Sháh a topaz cup
Full of cold water, sugar, and fine meal,

And mixed therewith the bane to please Bahman.
As Sháh Ardshír received the cup it fell
Out of his hand and shivered on the ground.
The queen shook with affright, her heart was riven.
Her agitation made the Sháh suspect,
Who, doubting what the turning sky would bring,
Enjoined a slave to fetch four fowls.   They thought
That his surmise was false, but when the birds
Were put down to the meal they ate and died!
Thus certified the pious monarch summoned
An archimage—his minister—and said:—
"If thou shouldst seat a foe upon thy throne,
Who by thy kindness groweth so bemused
As rashly to lay hand upon thy life,
What is the punishment for one so raised,
How shall we remedy our own default?"

The archimage replied: "If any subject
Attempt the world-lord's life thou must behead
The guilty and accept no other counsel."

Thereat the Sháh commanded: "Make the daughter
Of Ardawán a corpse."

                 The archimage
Went out behind the queen, who quaked convicted,
But said: "O sage! my day and thine will pass.
I cannot say thee nay if thou wilt slay me,
But—I am now with child, and by Ardshír;
So if 'tis right to cause my blood to flow,
And gibbet me on high, wait till my babe
Be born, then carry out the Sháh's behest."

The shrewd archmage returned and told his master,
But he made answer: "Hearken not to her,
But do my bidding."

C. 1394
                      "'Tis an evil day,"
The archimage reflected, "when such orders
Come from the Sháh!   We all, both young and old,
Must die, and he is sonless!   Though he live

To count unnumbered years yet when he dieth
A foe will have his throne.   Well may I dare
To substitute high policy for such
A feckless action.   I will save her life.
I may induce him to repent or else
Can do his bidding when her child is born."

  He got apartments ready in his palace
That he might tend her as his soul and body,
And told his wife : " I would not have a breath
Of air behold her."

               Then " I have," he thought,
" Foes and to spare, and doubts for good or ill
Attach to every one, so I will take
Such order that no slanderer shall foul
My stream."

          He went his way and gelt himself,
Used cautery and drugs and bandages,
Then put his genitals in salt forthwith,
As swift as smoke enclosed them in a casket,
And sealed it up.   With pallid face and groaning
He came before the lofty throne, laid down
The casket closed and sealed, and said : " Now let
The Sháh entrust this to his treasurer
With an inscription thereupon to state
The matters appertaining and the date."

§ 3

How Shápúr was born to Ardshír by the Daughter of Ardawán,
and how after seven Years Ardshír heard of his Son and
acknowledged him

Now, when the time of birth drew near, the archmage
Told not the secret e'en to the air.   The daughter
Of Ardawán brought forth a son—one ardent
And with the royal mien.   The minister

Excluded all folk, named the babe Shápúr,[1]
And hid him seven years till he became
A king in looks, in mien, and Grace.   It chanced
One day that the wazír drew near, perceived
Tears on Ardshír's face, and addressed him thus:—
"O Sháh! successful art thou yet thy soul
Is fed on care!   In this world thou hast gained
Thy full desire and cast thy foeman's head
Down from the throne.   Now is the time for mirth
And quaffing wine, not for solicitude.

C. 1395Earth's seven climes are 'neath thy sway, and thine
Are troops and state and policy."

He answered:—

" O holy archimage and confidant !
Our scimitar hath justified the age,
Grief, travail, and distress have passed away.
My years amount to fifty-one, my hairs
Once musk are camphor, and my roses gone.
I ought to have a son before me now,
A joy of heart, a source of strength, a guide.
A sonless sire is like a sireless son,
And taken only to a stranger's breast.
A foe succeedeth to my crown and wealth,
And all my gains are travail, pains, and dust."
    Then thought that shrewd old man: " 'Tis time to
        speak."
He said : " O Sháh! who cherishest thy lieges,
Magnanimous, shrewd-hearted, and supreme !
If thou wilt promise me to spare my life
I will remove my lord's distress."

The Sháh

Replied : " O sage! why shouldst thou fear for that ?
Say what thou knowest and enlarge thereon,
For what is better than a wise man's words ? "
    He made reply : " Pure and shrewd-hearted Sháh !

---

[1] *I.e.* Sháh's son.

I gave a casket to thy treasurer:
Now let the Sháh vouchsafe to ask for it."
    The Sháh said to his treasurer: "He asketh
For that which he consigned to thy safe keeping.
Restore it that we may examine it,
And haply cease to live a life of care."
    The treasurer produced and gave the casket
Back to the minister. The Sháh inquired:—
" What is there in it under lock and seal?"
    He made reply: " The blood of mine affliction,
And parts of shame dissevered by the roots.
To me thou gavest Ardawán's own daughter
Until thou shouldst require her corpse of me.
I slew her not because she was with child,
And I feared God, but sacrificed my manhood,
When thou didst give that order, and cut off
My parts of shame that none might slander me,
Or plunge me into infamy. Thy son
Hath been in keeping of thy minister
Seven years. No other king hath son like him,
And his sole semblance is the moon in heaven.
In love I gave to him the name Shápúr,
And may his fortune jubilate the sky.
His mother too is with him, educating
The prince her son."
                    The world's king marvelled at him,
Began to muse upon that child, then said:—
" O shrewd of heart and well advised! much toil   C. 1396
Hast thou endured! I will not let it age
With thee. Select a hundred of his years,
Like him in face and stature, breast and limb,
And all in like garb, neither worse nor better.
Send them to play at polo on the ground,
And furnish balls. When those fair youths are there
My soul will yearn for love upon my child,
My heart will be a witness to the truth,

And make me know my son."

At break of day

The minister arrived and brought the boys
In dress, in stature, and in mien so like
As not to be distinguished. Thou hadst said :—
" A holiday is toward in the park,
And prince Shápúr is in the thick of it,"
For when the youth began to play he bore
The ball off from the rest so that Ardshír,
On coming to the ground, accompanied
By young and old, and looking at the boys,
Could from his bosom heave a deep, cold sigh,
Could point his son out to his minister,
And say: "Behold a young Ardshír is yonder !"

The counsellor replied : " O Sháh ! thy heart
Hath testified to thine own son, but wait
Till yon fair children drive the ball anear thee."

Then Sháh Ardshír bade an attendant: "Go,
And drive the ball from them that I may see
Which boy will come forth bravely midst the brave,
As though a lion, and bear off the ball
Before my very eyes, regarding none
Of all this company, for such will be,
Past doubt, my very son in blood and body,
In limbs and race."

The servant did his bidding,

And drove the ball before the cavaliers.
The boys as swift as arrows followed it,
But, when they neared Ardshír, came to a stand,
Albeit unwillingly. Shápúr alone,
That Lion, still came on, seized, and bore off
The ball before his sire, and then, withdrawing,
Restored it to the boys. The Sháh's heart joyed,
As when an old man groweth young again,
The horsemen raised the young prince from the ground,
And passed him on from hand to hand until

The king of kings could clasp him to the breast,
And bless the Judge of all. He kissed Shápúr
On head and face and eyes, and said: " Such wonders
Should not be hidden. I ne'er dreamed of this,   C. 1397
For I presumed him slain just as God greatened
My kingship and increased my monuments
Within the world ! Thou canst not shun His bidding
Though thou shouldst raise thy head above the sun."
    He called for gold and many precious stones
Out of his treasury. They poured them forth
And sifted [1] musk and ambergris withal
Upon Shápúr until his head was hidden
With gold, and none could see his face for jewels.
The Sháh heaped gems too on his minister,
Set him upon a seat inlaid with gold,
And gave him wealth enough to furnish all
His house and halls. The Sháh then bade the daughter
Of Ardawán to go in peace and joy
Back to the palace, pardoned all her fault,
And cleansed his Moon of rust. He had all men
Of parts within the city brought to teach
The boy to write the ancient tongue, to wear
The mien of royal haughtiness, to wheel
His steed in battle, and thus mounted show
His spear-point to the enemy, to quaff,
Give largess, entertain at feasts, array
The host, and all the toil and work of war.
He had a new die struck for all the coinage
Both gold and silver, large and small alike ;
On one side was his own name, on the other
That of his great wazír—one held in honour
As an experienced man and counsellor.
Both names appeared on documents. The Sháh
Gave him the ring, the signet, and the rule,
Bestowed a treasure on the poor that lived

----

[1] Reading with T.

By labour, chose a site where brambles grew,
And made thereof a jocund seat, its name
Jund-i-Shápúr, thus only known to fame.

§ 4

How Ardshír, to find out the Future of his Reign, sent
to Kaid of Hind, and Kaid's Reply

Shápúr grew cypress-tall and, since they feared
The evil eye, was ever with Ardshír,
Attending like wazír and minister.
    The Sháh had not a day's repose from warfare,
Or leisure to disport himself, for when

C. 1398   He had relieved a place of enemies
They rose elsewhere. He said: "I pray the Maker,
Both publicly and privily, that I
May hold earth free from foes and then become
A devotee."
                His glorious minister
Replied: "O Sháh, whose heart is bright, whose words
Are true! dispatch we an ambassador
To Kaid of Hind who is a man of knowledge,
And good at need, can estimate high heaven,
And tell the door of joy, the road to ruin.
He will divine, accounting it no toil,
Nor asking guerdon for his answering,
If thou without a rival wilt possess
The seven climes."
                On hearing this the Sháh
Chose him a high-born youth of ready wit
To go as envoy to the sage of Hind,
With many steeds, with gold, and silk of Chín,
And said to him: "Go to the sage and say:—
'O man of fortune and of truthful speech!

Find from the stars when I shall rest from war,
And win me full possession of the realm,
For if I must be evermore in toil
I will not be so lavish of my treasure.' "
   The envoy came to Kaid with gifts and largess,
And gave the message of the king of kings,
Explaining all. Kaid greeted him, grew grave,
Turned to his arts, brought forth his astrolabe,
Observed the stars, and placed upon his lap
An Indian planisphere to ascertain
High heaven's purpose touching peace, success,
Woe, and mishap, and then informed the envoy:—
" I have discerned the fortunes of Írán,
And of the Sháh. If he will blend with his
The offspring of Mihrak, son of Núshzád,
The Sháh will sit in peace upon his throne,
And need not send his armies anywhither,
His wealth will wax, his travail wane. Depart.
Weigh not these two realms' feud.[1] Írán will prove
Conformable when this hath been achieved,
And he will compass all his heart's desire."
   He gave the envoy gifts, and said : " My sayings
Must not be hidden. If he shall obey,
High heaven will give him cause to prize my
    words."
   The envoy went back to the Sháh and told
What he had heard from noble Kaid, whereat
Ardshír was vexed, his visage grew like gall.
He answered : " God forbid that I should see
Descendants from Mihrak and bring my foe
Out of the street inside my house to war   C. 1399
Against my realm ! Woe for my lavished treasure,

---

[1] We must suppose that the troubles of the Sháh arose from the fact
that two of the sons of Ardawán had taken refuge in Hind which,
either directly or indirectly, was assisting them and their adherents
in Írán. P reads " between these two families," *i.e.* the rival dynasties
of Ardshír and Ardawán.

Mine expeditions sent, and labours borne!
Mihrak hath but one daughter left, and none
Hath seen her. I will bid men search for her
In Rúm, in Hind, in Chín, and in Taráz,
And when I find her I will have her burned,
And make the dust lament for her with tears."
   He sent one skilful in pursuit of foes,
And horsemen also, to Jahram. Now when
The daughter of Mihrak heard this she fled,
And lay concealed within a house ten months.
While she was hidden with a village-chieftain,
Who held her in high honour, she grew up
Like some straight cypress and increased in wisdom,
In Grace, and beauty; not a peer had she;
The realm had not so tall a cypress-tree.

§ 5

The Adventure of Shápúr with the Daughter of Mihrak,
and his taking her to Wife

Within a little while the monarch's fortune
Grew bright. He went to hunt at dawn one day
With wise Shápúr. The horsemen ranged around,
And cleared the plain of game. A spacious seat
Appeared afar with garth, park, hall, and palace.
Shápúr rode on until he reached the village,
And halted at the mansion of the chief.
There was a pleasant garth inside the walls,
A verdant spot, and when the youth went in
He saw a maiden like the moon, who plied
A wheel and bucket at a well. Now when
She saw Shápúr she came and showered blessings:—
"Be happy, smiles and joy be thine, and all
Thy years unscathed! Thy courser is athirst,

No doubt, and all the water in the village
Is brackish, but in this well cold and sweet.
With thy permission I will water him."

Shápúr replied: "What words are these, fair
maid!
I have attendants; they shall draw the water."

The maiden turned her back upon the youth;
She went apart and sat beside a stream.
He bade a servant: "Bring a bowl and draw."

The attendant heard and ran; rope, wheel, and
bucket   C. 1400
Were there, but when the bucket sank and filled
It rose not though he strove with knitted brows,
So heavy was it.   Chidingly Shápúr
Came up, and said to him: "Why, thou half woman!
Did not a woman work rope, wheel, and bucket?
She pumpeth what she will but thou art pumped,
And askest help!"

                        He took the rope himself,
But found the work severe.   Discovering
The bucket's weight he praised that fair-cheeked
maid,
And said: "Good sooth, she is of royal race
To raise a bucket of such weight as this!"

When he had drawn the bucket up the damsel
Came and saluted him most graciously,
And said: "Live happily while time endureth.
May wisdom ever be thy monitor.
The virtue of Shápúr, son of Ardshír,
Could doubtless turn the water in the well
To milk!"

                        He said to that sweet-spoken maid:—
"How know'st thou, moon-face! that I am Shápúr?"

She answered him: "Full often have I heard
This saying from the lips of truthful men:—
'The brave Shápúr is like an elephant

In strength, as bounteous as the river Nile,
In height a cypress, with a frame of brass,
And like Bahman in all.' "[1]

                    He said : " O moon-face!
Tell truly what I ask. Declare thy stock,
Because thy mien is royal."

                    She replied :—
" The daughter of the village-chieftain I,
From whom I get my comeliness and strength."

    " Lies never pass with princes," he rejoined,
" A tiller of the soil would not possess
A moon-faced daughter, fair, all scent and hue."

    " O prince," she said, "when life is guaranteed me,
I will inform thee fully of my birth,
Safe from the anger of the king of kings."

    He said : " Revenge on friends is not a plant
That groweth in our garden, so say on,
And fear not me or our just, noble Sháh."

    "The very truth is that I am," she said,
" The daughter of Mihrak, son of Núshzád.
A pious person brought me as a child,
And gave me to this worthy village-chief;
So now, for fear of the illustrious Sháh,
I draw the water and do other chars."

    Shápúr took up his lodging there and, when
The village-chief was waiting on him, said :—
C. 1401   " Give me, with Heaven as witness, this fair maid."

    The village-chief accorded his desire
With all the rites of those that worship Fire.

---

[1] From whom, according to one of the two genealogies in the
Sháhnáma, the House of Sásán was descended. See p. 199.

§ 6

How Urmuzd was born to Shápúr by the Daughter of Mihrak

It came to pass that soon that straight-stemmed
    Cypress,
Like blossom, came to fruit. Shápúr conveyed her
To his own palace from the chieftain's house,
And cherished her like some ripe quince.[1] Now when
Nine months had passed that Moon-face bare a son,
The image of his sire. Thou wouldst have said :—
" Asfandiyár hath come again or famed
Ardshír, the cavalier."[2] The prince, his sire,
Named him Urmuzd, for he was like a cypress
Midst herbs, and after seven years possessed
No equal in the world. His parents hid him,
And never let him go abroad to play.
   Once when Ardshír went hunting for a week,
As did Shápúr withal, Urmuzd escaped
Unnoticed, weary of his tasks, and ran
Forth to the riding-ground of Sháh Ardshír,
A lasso in one hand and in the other
Two shafts, with other boys with balls and sticks,
Just as the world-lord with his retinue,
And with his shrewd high priest, came from the chase.
When he was nigh the ground one of the youths
Smote strongly and awry so that the ball
Rolled near the Sháh. None followed it, the boys
Stopped short, balked in their game, except Urmuzd
Who, rushing like a blast before the Sháh,
Bare off the ball before his grandsire's face,

---

[1] This sentence is inserted from P.

[2] Probably Sháh Bahman is meant. *Cf.* previous note and Vol. v.
p. 282.

Amid the soldiers' hue and cry, and shouted,
So that the conquering Sháh was all amazement:—
" The sticks, the riding-ground, and pluck are mine,
And mine it is to battle with the brave ! "
    Thus to the archmage said Ardshír: " Inquire
About the lineage of this noble youth."
    The archmage asked. None knew, or would not say.
" Take up the youth and bring him," said the king.
    The archmage went and raised him from the dust,
Then bare him to the Sháh of noble men,
Who said: " Illustrious child ! what is thy stock ? "
    He answered in loud tones: " My name and race

C. 1402   Should not be hidden: thy son's son am I—
Shápúr's—born from the daughter of Mihrak."
    The monarch of the world was in amaze
Thereat, smiled, mused, bade come Shápúr, and asked
Questions past count. Shápúr, that noble man,
Was terrified, his heart was sorrowful,
His cheek was wan. The great Sháh smiled on him,
And said: " Hide not thy child; we need a son,
And whencesoe'er he cometh, it is well,
Since, so they say, he is a prince's child."
    Shápúr replied: " Be blest and with thy looks
Sustain the world ! He cometh from my loins,
And he is named Urmuzd; he shineth like
A tulip midst the grass. I have awhile
Concealed him from the king until the fruit-tree
Should bring forth fruit. The daughter of Mihrak
Bare this illustrious child, who is my child
Beyond all doubt."
                    Then, while his father listened,
He told at large what happened at the well.
    Ardshír rejoiced to hear the tale and went
Back to the palace with his minister,
Embraced that darling child, then sought his throne.
He had a golden ante-throne prepared,

And bade bring torque and golden coronet
Wherewith they decked the young child's head, then
 fetched
Both gold and jewels from the treasury,
And heaped them till the boy's head disappeared,
Whereat his grandsire drew him from the heap,
Bestowed the gold and jewels on the poor,
And still more splendid presents on the sages,
Decked with brocade the Fire-fanes and the hall
Wherein were held Naurúz, and Sada-feast,[1]
Made ready with his lords a banquet-house,
Placed minstrels everywhere, and then addressed
The land's wise chieftains: "Never should one slight
The sayings of a learned astrologer,
For thus said Kaid of Hind: 'Ne'er will thy fortune,
Thy throne, thy realm, thy crown, thy treasure, host,
Thy royal diadem, thy Grace, and state,
Be glad and jocund till the families
Of thee and of Mihrak, son of Núshzád,
Shall be conjoined in blood.' For eight years now
The sky hath blessed our wishes. Ever since
Urmuzd was added to my peace the world
Hath granted what I would, earth's seven climes
All have been ordered, and my heart hath had
Its will of fortune."
     All his underlings
Gave him thenceforth the style of "King of kings."[2]

§ 7

*Of the Wisdom of Ardshír and his Method of adminis-
tering the Realm*

Now hear and learn the wisdom of Ardshír, C. 1403
Who toiled, gave virtue vogue, and everywhere

---

[1] See Vol. i, pp. 74, 123.   [2] *Cf.* p. 254.

Spread love and justice.   As his forces grew
At court he sent his agents to all parts
To say : " Let none of you that hath a son
Allow him to grow up in ignorance,
But teach him horsemanship and how to fight
With mace and bow and shafts of poplar-wood."
    A youth, when trained to strength and grown
        efficient,
Would come up from his province to the court,
The Sháh's famed court, and then the muster-master
Would have him registered and give him quarters.
These young recruits, when war broke out, went forth
Commanded by some paladin, some archmage
Among the officials anxious to excel,
One to each thousand youths.   He went with them
To note their dispositions—cowardly,
Or too infirm for war—and to report
On all by letter to the king of kings,
Who when he had perused it and received
The messenger, would have a robe of honour
Of what was choicest in the treasury
Prepared for those that showed accomplishment;
But non-effectives carried arms no more.
Thus grew his troops so many that they passed
The purview of the stars, and men of counsel
Received promotion at his hands.   A herald
Used to make circuit of the host, proclaiming :—
" Ye men of name and warriors of the Sháh !
Whoe'er hath sought for favour in his sight,
And washed earth with the blood of valiant men,
Shall have from me a royal gift and leave
His fame as his memorial."
                              He ordered
The whole world with his troops, a shepherd he
With soldiers for his flock.
                              He kept a staff

Of experts in his public offices,
Committing naught to those incompetent.
They made a point of style and penmanship,
And when one showed superiority,
And when his principal reported it, C. 1404
The king of kings increased for him his pay.
The second-rate served not the Sháh himself,
But gave assistance to his officers ;
He only kept the scribes that were adepts,
And, when he saw such, he would praise them, saying :—
" A scribe that filleth up the treasury,
And by his talent lesseneth toil, availeth
State, host, and subjects pleading for redress.
The scribes are as the sinews of my soul,
And monarchs in disguise."
                              When governors
Went to their provinces he used to charge them :—
" Hold money vile and sell no man for pelf,
Because this Hostel bideth not with any,
But seek for wisdom and all righteousness ;
Let greed and madness be afar from thee,
And take none of thy kith and kin ; the troops
That I have given thee are friends enough.
Give largess monthly to the poor, but naught
To foes.   If by thy justice thou shalt make
Thy province prosper thou wilt prosper too
And joy in justice, but if any poor
Sleep there in fear thou sellest thine own soul
For gold and silver."
                        All that came to court
On state affairs, or to require redress,
Were met by trusty henchmen of the Sháh,
And asked about the royal governors :—
" Are they just men or covetous ?   Do any
Lie wronged by them ?   What learnéd men are there ?
Are any faint through want ?   Would any be

Of service to the Sháh as being old
And veteran, or devout ?   The king of kings
Saith: ' Let my toils and treasure gladden none
Except the men of wisdom and of lore,
For what is better than one wise and aged ?
I seek experienced men and youths approved,
And patient, for if youths are wise and apt
To learn they fittingly replace the old.' "
    As often as his host went forth to war
He acted prudently and cautiously,
And chose some scribe—a wise, learned, heedful man—
And charged him with a courteous embassage
Lest there be unjust strife.   The envoy used
To visit the Sháh's foe to learn his case,
And list to him if he were wise and held
War's sorrows, toils, and ills calamities.
C. 1405   If so he would have presents from the Sháh,
With grant, with patent, and remembrances;
But if he had a wrathful head, a heart
Revengeful, and blood boiling in his liver,
The Sháh would give the host a donative,
That no one might be malcontent, appoint
Some paladin aspiring, watchful, wise,
And placable, and therewithal a scribe—
A man of precedent and mastery—
To keep watch that the soldiers did no wrong;
Then mounted on an elephant a man,
Whose voice could reach two miles, thus to proclaim :—
" Ye chieftains of the fray, brave, famed, and bold !
No harm must come on poor or rich and noble.
Pay for your provand at each stage and earn
My subjects' thanks, and let God's worshippers
Touch not another's goods.   Whoe'er shall show
The foe his back his outlook will be gloomy,
Because his grave will be at hand, or chains
Will gall his neck and breast, or else his name

Will be struck off the roll, and he himself
Will feed on dust and on dark dust repose."
    Then he would charge the captain of the host:—
" Be neither slack nor rash to attack, keep always
The elephants in front and push out scouts
Four miles. Be instant, when a fight is toward,
To go among the troops, bid them remember
Both who and what they are, why in the field:—
' They are a hundred horsemen to our one,
And yet their hundred to our one are few !
For every one of you, both young and old,
I shall receive a present from Ardshír.'
When cavaliers advance upon both sides
Let not thy warriors, in their eagerness
To fight, press on till they expose the centre,
However large the host. Dispose thy left
Against the foe's right wing that all may have
A chance of fighting and array thy right
Against his left. Let all look to their baggage.
The centre must stand fast, let no one there
Advance a foot; but if the opposing centre
Advance, advance thine own. When thou hast
    triumphed
Forbear to shed the blood of foes in flight,
While, if they ask for quarter, grant it them,
And be not vengeful. When thou seest the foe
Retreat, haste not to quit thine own position,
Or deem thyself secure from ambuscade,   C. 1406
But, once thou art assured, see that thou heed not
Another's words. Bestow the spoil on those
That sought the fray and bravely washed their hearts
Of love of life, and bring withal all captives
Without fail to my court. I will erect them
A city where a thorn-brake stood.[1] As thou
Wouldst live unvexed and scathless turn in naught

---

[1] Reading with P.

From these my counsellings, and in thy triumphs
Incline to God because He is past doubt
Thy guide."
               Whenever there arrived an envoy
From any part, Rúm, Turkistán, or Persia,
The marchlords got to know it, for they held
Such things of moment; lodging was provided,
This was the business of the governors,
With provand, raiment, and no stint of carpets,
Upon the route.   They would inform themselves
As to the envoy's business with the Sháh,
And then a scribe upon a noble beast
Would go to Sháh Ardshír that troops might meet
The envoy.   Then the conquering Sháh would have
His throne made ready and attendants ranked
On either side thereof in cloth of gold,
Would have the envoy summoned to the presence,
Seat him beside the throne, greet him, and learn
His business good or ill, name, and repute,[1]
His views of right and wrong, about his land,
About its customs, king, and armaments,
Conduct him to a palace with the state
That was befitting an ambassador,
And furnish what he needed, then invite him
To feast and revel, seat him by the throne,
Would take him out on royal hunting-days,
Escorted by a countless retinue,
Dismiss him with the forms due to an envoy,
And fashion him a monarch's robe of honour.
   He sent withal archmages to all parts—
Men wise and shrewd and kindly—to build cities,
And lavish wealth thereon, that every man
Resourceless, homeless, and estranged from fortune,
Might have a living and a dwelling-place,
And thus increase the number of his subjects.

             [1] Reading with P.

So his good name is current now as then
Upon the lips and in the thoughts of men,
And one sole monarch [1] in the world we find
That now recalleth lost Ardshír to mind,
And mine 'tis living glory to bestow
Upon him.[2] May his end all goodness know.
   The Shah had many secrets, for he kept
His agents everywhere. Whene'er the rich
Grew poor the Sháh would help him, if informed,
And leave him prosperous with fertile lands,
Home, slaves, and underlings, arranging all
Without the city's ken, and put his children,
If they had talent, in the charge of tutors.
In every quarter of the towns were schools,
With colleges for worshippers of Fire.
He suffered none to want save such as kept
The fact a secret, and his custom was
To go at daybreak to the public ground,
Where all that sought redress could come, and there
Judged subject and friend's son impartially.
His justice made the whole world prosperous,
And all his subjects' hearts rejoiced in him.
   When any king to justice is allied,
In time's despite his footprints will abide.
   Observe the policy of this brave chief,
Who, thou wouldst say, engrossed all excellence.
His agents, wise and watchful officers,
Went through the world. Where any land lay waste,
Or streams ran low, he took the taxes off;
No holding was too mean for his regard.
If any thane was poor, and losing all,
The Sháh supplied both implements and cattle.
And let him not be ousted from his home.
   Now hear, O king! the sayings of this sage
And make the world as bright as in his age;

C. 1407

---

[1] Mahmúd.   [2] Reading with P.

As thou untroubled and unvexed wouldst be,
And pile up wealth not gained injuriously,
Seek that thy subjects may be unvexed too,
And have from all the praises justly due.

   In Rúm and Chín, in Turkistán and Hind,
The world grew as 'twere Rúman silk to him,
Both toll and tax came in continually
From all lands, none opposing him. He summoned
The nobles of Írán and set those worthy
Upon the royal throne, then rose and-made
Oration to them well and graciously:—
" O chieftains of the state, ye that are wise
And prudent! know that swiftly turning heaven
Assaileth not through justice nor embraceth

C. 1408

Through love, but setteth whom it will on high,
And then consigneth him to sorry dust;
His name alone surviveth, all his toils
Go with him to oblivion; one whose aims
Are good may leave a good name, naught besides.
Now as for thee, Urmuzd! thy lot will be
As holy God approveth. Turn and open
Thyself to Him who is the Lord of all,
And multiplieth good. From every ill
Take shelter with the Ruler of the world,
For ill and good are in His power, and He
Will make all hardship easy to thee, give
A bright heart to thee, and victorious fortune.
Judge first by mine experience and perpend
Mine own past good and evil while still fresh.
When I took refuge with the Lord of all
My heart was gladdened by the crown and throne.
I rule the seven climes for so seemed good
To His authority. From Rúm and Hind
I take a tribute, and the world hath grown
Like Rúman silk to me. Thanks be to God,
Who gave me strength, exalted star, and favour

From Sol and Saturn; yet who knoweth how
To praise Him worthily or give Him worship
Proportioned to His work so that He may
Be mindful of my service and set forth
His greatness and omnipotence? And now
What from our sense of justice—our delight—
We purpose we will tell. Although one tenth
From all communities is due to me,
As thane and archimage will testify,
I ask it not, I give it back to you—
The tithe on land and impost on the flocks—
Except the tithe on increase which the agent
Will pay into our treasury.[1] The tithe,
That erst I took, and impost less or more,
I have employed on useful works and kept
A countless host at court. I sought your good,
Your safety, and the abatement of the Faith
Of Áhriman. Clasp, all! your hands to God,
Be diligent and break not His behest,
Who is the Lord and Giver of all things,
The Artist of the sky above, the Helper
Of the oppressed; but glory not o'er others
By reason of His favour, nor thereby
Deceive thy heart, for pride will have a fall.
Where are the men whose crowns erst frayed the
  clouds?
Where those whose quarry was the mighty lion?
They, all of them, are couched on dust and brick,
And he is blest that sowed but seed of good.
List, all of you that are within my realm!
To these my final counsels. Now will I
Point out to you five courses that will profit
Far more than throne and treasury, so list,
Ye young and old! the words of famed Ardshír.

C. 1409

---

[1] " espérant que vos chefs apporteront dans mon trésor ce que vous
aurez de superflu " (Mohl).

The man who knoweth that the Just One is
Will worship holy God and Him alone.
Again, misprize not knowledge, whether thou
Be liege or lord, and, thirdly, be assured
That wise men ne'er forget, and, fourthly, know
That fear of doing wrong availeth more
Than gibbet, bonds, and dungeon.   Fifthly, none
Approveth of a slanderer's words.   To these
I add one counsel more, a counsel better
Than eyes and life and goods: blest is the man
That maketh this world prosper, is the same
In public and in private, and moreover
Soft-spoken, modest, wise, and cordial.
Spend not thy money for the sake of show,
Or waste it foolishly on vanities,
Else there will be no profit, none will praise,
Nor holy men approve, but choose the mean,
Maintain it, and the wise will call thee prudent.
Again, there are five ways of making bright
Thy Faith and conduct, and of furthering
Thy comfort and thy joy, for in their honey
There is no bane to harm thee.   First of all,
Seek not to pass by greed or pains the lot
Assigned to thee by God; the man content
Is rich, for each spring's blooms have borne him fruit.
Next, break the neck of greed, and tell no secret
Before the women.   Thirdly, court not war
And strife, for they bring toil and anguish.   Fourthly,
Seclude thy heart from grief and be not troubled
O'er ills not come, and, fifthly, meddle not
With things irrelevant, for know that they
Are not thy quarry.   Hear ye all! my counsel,
My profitable speech; 'twill be right dear
To all men's hearts, for they will get thereby
Security from loss.   Pause not from learning
If thou wouldst fire thy mind.   If thou hast children

Have them instructed and cut short their play.
Heed, all! my words and pains on your behalf.
Let all the just and shrewd of heart break not
Their mutual intercourse, and compass ye
Heart's peace in four ways good and profitable:
First, fear, respect, and reverence holy God   C. 1410
That He may be thy Helper and thy Guide;
Next, rule thyself and look to thine own skirt,
Take God's commands to heart and tender them
Like thine own body; thirdly, make the right
Plain and ban fraud and falsehood; fourthly, swerve
    not
In thought or action from the Sháh's behest,
But love him like thyself so that thy face
May clear at his command.   Confine thy heart
To loyalty to him, let not thy soul
Swerve from his bidding, love him as thy life,
Perceiving that his justice guardeth thee.
The cares of royalty are with the Sháh,
He seeketh the world's gain and not its loss.
If, knowing that his marchlords and his troops
Afflict his realm, he interveneth not
He is no world-lord, and the crown of kingship
Befitteth him not; he hath blacked out his patent
As king of kings, his Grace is gone.[1]   Know this:
An unjust monarch is a ravening lion
Upon the pasture-land; so is the subject.
That heedeth not with diligence and pains
The Sháh's command; his life will be all grief
And toil, and never will he reach old age
Within this Hostelry.   If thou hast need
Of goodness and of greatness thou wilt win them
Not by thine avarice and arrogance.
May all my subjects' hearts be glad, and may
The world too prosper 'neath my righteous sway."

---

[1] *Cf.* p. 208 and *note.*

§ 8

How Kharrád praised Ardshír

When Sháh Ardshír resumed his seat, an elder,
By name Kharrád, one just in word and thought,
Advanced before the throne, thus saying : " O king !
Be blest while time endureth, ever glad,
And of victorious fortune. May realm, crown,
And throne rejoice in thee. Thou hast attained
To such an eminence that bird and beast
Rank at thy throne, before it and behind.
Exalted over all that wear the crown
Art thou—the greatest man in all the world.
Who can describe thy justice ? Thou art based
On justice and on greatness. More and more
We offer up our praise and thanks to God
That we live in thy days and are thy lieges
In all things, eager to behold thy face,
And yearning for thy gracious words and love.
Mayst thou be safe as we are safe through thee,
And ne'er may we break fealty. Thou hast barred
To us and to our peers the foe's approach
From Hind and Chín, and rapine, war, and tumult
Have passed away ; the shouts of enemies
Reach not our ears. Remain for ever happy,
And let archmages bear the toils of state.
No king is wise as thou, no thought transcendeth
Thy counsel, and thou so hast founded justice
Within Írán that it will glad our sons.
Thy words have grown so potent that thy counsels
Make old men young, and all the nobles here
Joy in thee and thy justice. Thou increasest
The stock of wisdom by thy deeds, the world
Hath been illumed by sight of thee. Thou art
A robe of honour God-bestowed on fortune,

C. 1411

On girdle, crown, and throne. Still may the Sháh
Continue loved and just; the world hath not
A king like thee in mind. The world is safe
By reason of thy might and Grace, and blest
Are they beneath the shadow of thy wings.
For ever be thy seat upon the throne,
The world beneath thy word and will alone."

§ 9

On the Faithlessness of Fortune

Thou, who the marrow of the tale wouldst win!
Divorce thy heart from this old Wayside Inn,
Which hath seen many like to thee and me
But with none resteth; whatsoe'er thou be—
King or attendant—it will outstay thee,
For be thou drudge, or lord of crown and throne,
Thou hast to pack thy baggage and be gone.
The sky will melt thee, though of iron mould,
And favour thee no more when thou art old;
So when the charming Cypress bendeth low,
And when the dark Narcissi overflow,
When cheeks of cercis take a saffron hue,
    And he is grave anon that erst was gay,
Then, since souls slumber not as bodies do,
    Bide not alone, thy mates are on their way.
Be thou a monarch or of subject birth
Thou'lt have no dwelling-place save darksome earth.
Where are the chieftains with their crowns and thrones,
    The cavaliers of fortune ever bright?
Where are the sages and the warlike ones,   C. 1412
    The princes and the leaders in the fight?
On pillows made of bricks and dust they rest,
And he that sowed but seed of good is blest.
A great exemplary is king Ardshír,
So bear in mind my tale when thou shalt hear.

§ 10

How Ardshír charged Shápúr and died

Aged eight and seventy years [1] the watchful world-lord
Grew sick; he knew that death was drawing nigh,
That his green leaf would wither, so he summoned
Shápúr, addressed him counsel past compute,
And said: "Be mindful of my charge, but hold
The words of evil speakers merely wind.
When thou hast heard my sayings practise them,
Discerning haply worth from worthlessness.
I with the scimitar of justice righted
The world and honoured men of noble birth.
That done, the earth waxed but mine own life waned
When I had toiled and sweated much, and treasures
Had multiplied to me. So now I leave
The travail and the pleasure all to thee.
We are in turn exalted and abased,
Such is the process of the circling sky,
Which whiles afflicteth, whiles affecteth, us!
Now fortune is a vicious steed, and scath
Will wreck thee in prosperity, anon
A horse well trained whose neck is arched for thee
In all good will. Know, son! that this false Hostel
Hath terrors even for the happy man.
Be heedful of thine own and wisdom's case
If thou wouldst 'scape ill days. When monarchs honour
The Faith then it and royalty are brothers,
For they are mingled so that thou wouldst say:—
'They wear one cloak.' The Faith endureth not
Without the throne nor can the kingship stand
Without the Faith; two pieces of brocade
Are they all interwoven and set up

[1] *Cf.* p. 254.

Before the wise. The Faith doth need the Sháh,
The Sháh, were Faith to seek, would not be praised.
Each needeth other, and we see the pair
Uniting in beneficence. The man
Of Faith will carry off both worlds when he
Shall prove a lord of counsel and of wisdom.
Whenas the great king watcheth o'er the Faith,   C. 1413
Call it and kingship brothers; when he vexeth
The pious, call him impious. Disallow
In Faith the slanderer of pious kings.
What said the man approved and eloquent?
'The Faith, if thou considerest, is the brain
Of Justice.'[1]
          Three things vex the royal throne:
The first one is the unjust sovereign,
The second, the exalter of the worthless
Above the worthy, and the third is he
That weddeth treasure and is instant still
For more. Be thine aim bounty, Faith, and wisdom,
And let no lie pass current for it darkeneth
A man's face; ne'er will he be great and famous.
See that thou heed not treasure, for dínárs
Involve mankind in toil. If greed of treasure
Possess the great king he will vex his subjects,
For where the thane's wealth is there is the Sháh's
Who, whatsoe'er the toil and pain may be,
Should guard it for him and should bring to fruit
His travail's bough. Strive to put wrath away,
And boldly blink the faults of other men.
If thou art wroth thou wilt repent withal,
So, when they make excuse, seek how to salve them.
Whene'er the Sháh is wroth the good misprize him,
And since he is to blame in seeking ill
He should adorn his heart with good. If once
Thou sufferest fear to come within thy heart

[1] *Cf.* p. 250.

The counsels of thy foes' hearts will prevail.
Be boundless too in bounty; if thou canst,
My son! esteem not wealth. He should be king
The limit of whose bounty is the sky.
Whenever trouble is a monarch's lot
Let him hold counsel with his archimages,
Let him inquire too of the right and wrong
Thereof, and lay the matter up at heart.
" On days when thou art purposing to hunt,
And use the binding hawk, mix not thy pleasures,
As wine and feast with open air and chase ;
Wine maketh heavy as all leaders know.
Abandon such pursuits when foes appear,
Spend money freely, edge the swords, and summon
The troops of all the realm. Defer not thou
The day's work to the morrow and seat not
An evil counsellor beside the throne.

O. 1414
Search not the hearts of common folk for truth,
For from such questing loss will come to thee,
And if they bring ill tidings hearken not,
Nor grieve; they worship neither God nor king,
And clutching at their feet thou hast their heads.
Such are the common people, but mayst thou
Be ever wise. Fear those that compass ill
In secret, for this straiteneth the world.
Tell naught to confidants for they have theirs,
And thou wilt meet thy sayings in the fosse,
Or find them spread abroad, and when thy secrets
Are common talk the sages will lose patience,
Thou wilt be wroth, the sage that calmeth thee
Will call thee light of head   Seek not for faults
In others, that will manifest thine own,
While if thy wisdom be o'er swayed by passion
The sage will count thee not a man at all.
The Sháh and worldlord should be wise that he
May be benevolent to every one.

If any man is rash and insolent,
Prone to accuse and to calumniate,[1]
Let such have no place near to thee although
One of thy counsellors. When thou art Sháh
Lay down revenge and wrath if thou wouldst have
The praises of the pious. He that sitteth
Upon the throne of state should be a wise,
God-fearing man. Be not a chatterer,
Nor make a show of sanctimoniousness
In others' eyes. Hear what men say, lay up
The best, and note what pleaseth thee; weigh well
Thy words to sages, being complaisant
And bright to all; scorn not the poor that beg;
Seat not an adversary on a throne;
Forgive the penitent, requiring not
Revenge for what is passed; be just to all,
And cherish all; the bounteous, patient man
Is blest. What time the foe doth flatter thee
Through fear, array the host, bind on the tymbals,
And go forth to the fight while he is shrinking,
And weak of hand; but if he seeketh peace
And right, and harboureth, as thou perceivest,
No mischief in his heart, take tribute from him,
Seek not revenge, and save his face. Adorn
Thy heart with knowledge; that hath worth; that know
And practise. Thou wilt be beloved if bounteous,
And famed if wise and just. Keep thy sire's charge C. 1415
In mind and leave a like one to thy son.
As I have given my son his heritage,
And injure none thereby, do ye transmit it;
Take not the spirit of my words amiss.
Now when five hundred years have passed away,
Thy dynasty will end, for thy descendants,
And others of thy kin, will turn aside

---

[1] Reading with P.

From this my charge, depart from rede and knowledge
Not heeding the monitions of the wise,
But, faithlessly neglectful of my charge,
Be unjust, harsh, and tyrannous, oppress
Their subjects, scorn the pious, don the robe
Of wickedness, and grow up in the Faith
Of Áhriman.   Then will be loosed what we
Have bound, this Faith that we have fulled be fouled,
This rede and charge of mine will come to naught,
My country seem all desolate.   I pray
The Maker of the world, who knoweth both
The hidden and the manifest, to guard you
From every evil and that all your deeds
May win fair fame.   God's blessing and our own
Shall be upon the man whose warp is wisdom,
Whose woof is justice, who in these regards
Attempteth not to break my charge or striveth
To turn my honey into colocynth.
Two score years and two months have passed since I
Assumed the crown of kingship.   I possess
Six cities, all in pleasurable climes,
And all of them well-watered.   I have named
One Khurra-i-Ardshír;[1] its airs are all
Musk-perfumed and its streams run milk; the second
Is titled Rám Ardshír;[2] thence reached I Párs;
The third Urmuzd Ardshír,[3] whose airs would make
An old man young—the lustre of the province
Of Khúzistán;[4] it hath folk, trade, and water.
Another one is Birka-i-Ardshír,[5]
Well stocked with gardens, pools, and rosaries,
And two are in the district of Baghdád
And the Farát, and rich in cattle, springs,
And grass—foundations both, as thou mayst say,

[1] The Glory of Ardshír.   [2] See p. 202.
[3] *Cf.* p. 302, *note.*   [4] Reading with P and T.
                   [5] The Cistern of Ardshír.

Of Sháh Ardshír.[1]   Bear them in mind when thou
Hear'st aught concerning me.
                          I have prepared
My baggage for the charnel-house.   Bestow
My bier and take my seat.   In this world I
Have borne great toils in public and in private.
Rejoice my soul with justice and be glad,
And conquering, on the throne."
                          He spake, and fortune
Grew dark.   Woe for his head and throne and crown!
   The fashion of this jocund world is thus :   C. 1416
It will not make its secrets known to us.
Blest is the man who greatness ne'er hath known,
And hath no need to vanish from the throne.
Thou strivest, winning wealth in every way,
But man and wealth abide not in one stay ;
Dust in the end is wedded to us all,
Our cheeks must be enshrouded by a pall.
Come bear we all a hand good to fulfil,
And tread not this unstable world for ill.
Oh   well is he that taketh cups of wine
To toast the Sháhs—those men of Faith divine—
For, as his cup of wine is slowly drained,
He droppeth off with ecstasy attained.

§ 11

Thanksgiving to the Maker and Praise of Mahmúd,
the great King

To Him who made it let all praise ascend ;
   The Maker of space, time, and earth is He ;
From Him are the beginning and the end,
   From Him are passion and tranquillity :

----

[1] These may be Bih-Ardshír built to replace Seleucia, destroyed by
Avidius Cassius in A.D. 164, and Karakh-Maishán on the lower Tigris.
They are given in Tabari's list of Ardshír's foundations. NT, p. 19.

He made the starry heavens, earth, and time
   The great and little of the world are His,
From worthless stubble to the throne sublime
   All things bear witness to us that He is.

Call none but Him the Author of the whole,
   Whose ken naught open or concealed can shun,
Who showered blessings on Muhammad's soul,
   And on his comrades also, every one.

They all were holy men and continent;
   None can compute the words which erst they said;
Now by us too let countless words be spent
   In thanking Him by whom the world was made.

Praise we the crown too of the king of kings,
   Whose throne doth cause the moon itself to shine,
World-lord Mahmúd, the source whence largessings
   And bounties spring, and who hath Grace divine.

Brave, bounteous, dowered with Grace, and just is he,
   The age hath grown all joyful 'neath his sway—
The lord of peace, of crown, and treasury,
   The lord of scimitar, of ax, and fray.

Our gracious world-lord, conscious what is meant
   By merit, thanketh God through whom his hold
Is on the crown. Wise, fair, and eloquent
   Is he, in years a youth, in wisdom old.

His Grace compelleth rain from Jupiter,
   We sport beneath the shadow of his wings,
In fight he maketh heaven his echoer,
   He scattereth jewels at his banquetings.

When he is wroth the mountains melt away,
  The welkin quaketh o'er the dust below;
His sires were Sháhs and monarchs ere his day,
  And sun and moon toy with him as they go.

May his renown last ever, may he see
  Till his last day increasing happiness.
I head my story with his eulogy,
  His majesty, his conduct, and address.

Throughout the world I witness his renown;
  Until the end may good attend him still;
His mien hath given lustre to the crown,
  And fortune been his breastplate 'gainst all ill.

Throughout the world all men of Faith divine,
  And all the kings, rejoice in him alone,
Whose glorious fortune maketh heaven to shine,
  For earth but baseth his illustrious throne.

He is a mighty Elephant of bale
  In fight and at the feast a faithful sky,[1]
For there, since his bright projects never fail,
  Each billow of his ocean runneth high.

Earth's monarchs are his quarry in the chace,
  Wild beasts and cattle in his peace abide,
In battle-days the whizzing of his mace
  Dissundereth lion's heart and leopard's hide.

May his head flourish, justice fill his heart,
And with the world his head and crown ne'er part.

[1] A sky that fulfils its promise of rain.

C. 1417

XXIII

SHÁPÚR, SON OF ARDSHÍR

HE REIGNED THIRTY YEARS AND TWO MONTHS

ARGUMENT

Shápúr ascends the throne and addresses the chiefs. He wars with success against. Rúm, appoints Urmuzd his successor, and dies.

NOTE

This reign affords a good illustration of the inaccurate way in which events are recorded even in the most historical of the four dynasties of the Sháhnáma. Shápúr, son of Ardshír (Sapor I., A.D. 241-272), is confused with Shápúr, son of Urmuzd (Sapor II., A.D. 309-379). Important historical events are transferred from the former's reign to the latter's where, to save repetition, they will be dealt with. Again, Shápúr son of Ardshír's two wars with Rome, which historically are parted by a considerable interval of time, are rolled into one. The first war ended in A.D. 244, and the second did not begin till some fourteen or more years later. The latter is the one chiefly commemorated in the Sháhnáma. In the course of it the Roman Emperor Valerian, the Bazánúsh of Firdausí, was defeated and taken prisoner in Mesopotamia owing to the treachery of Macrianus, his Prætorian prefect, and died in captivity. Shápúr then made a raid into Cilicia and Cappadocia—names which appear as Kaidáfa and Pálawína in the poem.[1] Subsequently he withdrew his forces, and during his retreat was handled very roughly by Odenathus, prince of Palmyra, who later on made himself master of Mesopotamia and ruled from the Tigris to the Mediterranean till his assassination in A.D. 267. A trace of Shápúr's mishap seems to survive, but

---

[1] NT, p. 32, and *note*.

the tale is told in connexion with Shápúr, son of Urmuzd. The triumph over Valerian was commemorated in many memorials by his conqueror.[1] The name of the city built for the Roman captives was Gund-i-Shápúr, probably the Shápúr Gird of Firdausí as both cities are described as being in Susiana. It was between Susa and Shúshtar, and its situation is indicated by the ruins of Sháhábád.[2] The great dam in connexion with the river Kárún is still in existence. It is very likely that Shápúr's Roman prisoners helped to make it. It is known as the " Band-i-Kaisar."[3]

§ 1

How Shápúr sat upon the Throne and delivered a Charge to the Chieftains

To tell the kingship of Shápúr be thine,
And hold discourse on festival and wine.
    Whenas Shápúr sat on the throne of justice,
And donned the heart-illuming crown, the sages,
Wise magnates, and archmages, met before him.
He thus harangued the noble gathering—
The great and understanding counsellors :—
"I am the lawful son of Sháh Ardshír,
The utterer and layer up of knowledge.
Heed, all of you ! my bidding and be loyal,
Scan what I say and blame it if 'tis crude.
In mine experience as to good and ill
Two dispensations are conspicuous.
One is the Sháh, the warden of the world,
And guardian of the wealth of high and low.
If he is just and fortunate 'tis clear
That wisdom watcheth over, helpeth, him,
And o'er the dark clouds will exalt his head.
His whole quest is for justice, and for knowledge
That maketh music in his soul. The other
Is whosoever manfully essayeth   C. 1418
To compass wisdom and is wise in knowing

---

[1] See the illustrations in RSM, pp. 82, 91.   [2] NT, 41, *note.*
[3] Cf. *Ency. Brit.*, 11th ed., *s.v.* " Shushter."

That it is God to whom his thanks are due.
Blest is the sage that knoweth God; the wise
Is worthy of the kingship; gold is worthless
In wisdom's stead. The man that is content
Is well to do; the avaricious heart
Is but a house of smoke. The more the greed
The more the care, so strive to shun its fruits.
Incline to peace and things of good report,
And flee the ill-disposed, for little wits
Will grasp at others' goods. I love you more
Than there are stars to glitter in the sky;
The customs of the exalted Sháh Ardshír
Assuredly will I confirm to you,
And take a thirtieth only from the thanes
To pay my soldiers somewhat. I have weal,
An ample treasure, courage, manliness,
And constancy. We covet no man's goods,
For they turn friends to foes. The way is open
For you to us. We love the suppliant.
We will send agents everywhere, search shrewdly
The world's affairs, and ne'er ask other blessings
Than those which men invoke from God on me."

Rose high and low, prepared their tongues to make
A fair reply, called praises down on him,
And scattered emeralds on his crown. The customs
Of Sháh Ardshír revived withal, and then
Both young and old joyed in that regimen.

§ 2

How Shápúr fought with the Rúmáns, how Bazánúsh, their General, was taken Prisoner, and how Cæsar made Peace with Shápúr

Then tidings spread: "The throne of king of kings
Is occupied no more, wise Sháh Ardshír
Hath died and left Shápúr the throne and crown."

The battle-cry went up in all the coasts,
And hubbub from Kaidáfa [1] unto Rúm.
When news reached Sháh Shápúr he made him ready
Troops, flags, and drums, and led toward Pálawína
A flying column with no baggage-train.
An army that bedimmed the sun with dust
Marched from Kaidáfa, and a host withal   C. 1419
From Pálawína 'neath a paladin
Hight Bazánúsh, a noble cavalier
Of ardent soul, a chief and lasso-thrower
Prized by the Cæsars. When from those two hosts
Rose tymbal-din came from the Rúman centre
An eager warrior, from the Íránian
A famous chieftain hight Garshásp the Lion;
What man or lusty elephant could match
That valiant cavalier in battle-tide?
   These two engaged and strewed the stars with dust,
Used all their skill, but neither could prevail.
Then clashed the hosts together mountain-like;
Rose their drum-roll and shoutings. Bold Shápúr
Bestirred him at the centre. At the din
Of trump and Indian bell thou wouldst have said
That heaven shook; the earth rocked, and the air
Was full of dust, the war-spears gleamed like fire,
And all the men of wisdom called on God.
Amid the central host brave Bazánúsh,
All sorrowful of heart, was taken captive,
While of his Rúmans were ten thousand slain
At Pálawína in the ranks of war,
And twice eight hundred taken prisoners;
Those warriors' hearts were full of sore distress.
Then Cæsar sent a well-instructed envoy
To ask Shápúr, the son of Sháh Ardshír:—
"How much blood wilt thou pour out for dínárs?
What wilt thou say to our just Judge and Guide

[1] See p. 294.

When questioned at the Day of Reckoning?
How make excuse to Him who giveth all?
Add not to our distress for I will pay
The wonted tribute, will submit, dispatch
Abundant hostages of mine own kin,
And, if thou wilt withdraw from Pálawína,
Will send thee in addition what thou wilt."

Shápúr remained till Cæsar sent to him
The tribute in ten ox-hides of dínárs
Of Cæsar's coinage with much wealth besides—
A thousand male and female Rúman slaves,
And countless splendid pieces of brocade.

Shápúr abode a week in Pálawína,
Then leaving Rúm he journeyed to Ahwáz,[1]
And there he built a city named Shápúr Gird:
He finished it upon the day of Ard.

C. 1420 It took a year besides much toil and treasure.
He built a city for the prisoners
From Rúm and filled it with inhabitants;
The district is the gate of Khúzistán,[2]
And in the great high-way whereby all pass.

He built himself a city too in Pars,
Great, fair, and wealthy, and the ancient fortress [3]
Of Nishápúr, they say, without forced labour.
He carried Bazánúsh about with him,
And heeded him. Now there was at Shúshtar
A stream so broad that fish could cross it not.
He said to Bazánúsh: "If thou hast skill
Make over this a bridge as 'twere a rope,
For we return to dust but it will bide
Firm through the science of its architect.
'Twill be a thousand cubits long; request
Whate'er thou needest from my treasury.
Employ thou to some purpose in this land

---

[1] Susiana.   [2] Id.
[3] Mohl keeps Kuhandizh (old fort) as a proper name.

The skill of Rúman engineers and, when
The bridge is finished, come and be my guest
For life in mirth and safety, and afar
From evil and the hand of Áhriman."
   Brave Bazánúsh began the work and built
The bridge in three years' space, then left Shúshtar
And set his face to hurry to his home.
Shápúr was just, in counsel well approved,
His star exalted and his throne unmoved.[1]

§ 3

How Shápúr seated Urmuzd upon the Throne and died

When thirty years and two months had gone by
The Grace and glory of the Sháh were spent.
He called Urmuzd. "The freshness of my face,"
He said, "is sere; be vigilant, be world-lord,
And ever rule with justice, but be ware
Of putting trust in sovereignty; peruse
Both day and night the volume of Jamshíd;
Do only what is just and good; be thou
The lowly's shelter and the mighty's Grace;
Toy little with dínárs, be bounteous, just,
And glorious; exclaim not at slight ills   C. 1421
If thou wouldst have good fortune as thy friend,
And keep in mind my counsels, every whit,
As I myself possess them from Ardshír."
   He spake, the colour paled upon his cheek,
The heart of that wise man grew full of anguish.
   What can this Wayside Hostel do for thee?
Wouldst hug renown? Wouldst fill thy treasury?
A narrow coffin will be all thy spoil,
Some worthless one will batten on thy toil,

---

[1] In C, the reign ends here, but we have followed the arrangement
of P, which seems preferable.

Thou wilt be clean forgotten by thy sons,
Thy nearest kinsfolk and companions,
The heritage wherein thou'lt have thy share
Is that of malediction, for where'er
Bezoar is the poison too is there.
Turn then to God and multiply His praise,
Who feedeth thee and guideth all thy ways.

XXIV

URMUZD, SON OF SHÁPÚR

HE REIGNED ONE YEAR AND TWO MONTHS

ARGUMENT

Urmuzd, whose reign proved to be a very brief one, succeeds his father and harangues the nobles. Feeling the approach of death he summons his son Bahrám, appoints him successor, gives him good counsel, and dies.

NOTE

The romantic story of Urmuzd's (Hormisdas I., A.D. 272–273), birth,[1] is all that survives in connexion with him, apart from Firdausí's common form in dealing with the short reigns,[2] in the Sháhnáma. In the Kárnámak he is represented as a great prince, being confused probably with his father. It is likely that he made a reputation for courage and energy in the wars against Rome and as governor in Khurásán. At all events, according to tradition, he earned for himself the title of "the hero." It is told of him that, being falsely accused of disloyalty, he cut off one of his hands and sent it, wrapped in silk, to his father to prove his innocence as no mutilated person could succeed to the throne. His father, deeply distressed, arranged that mutilation should be no bar in that instance.[3]

---

[1] See p. 268 *seq.*   [2] *Id.* p. 249.
[3] NK, 68, and *note;* NT, 43, 45, and *notes;* RM, Pt. I., vol. ii. p. 335.

§ 1

How Urmuzd addressed the Assembly

Now will I make the diadem and throne
  Of Sháh Urmuzd as brilliant as the moon
Upon the day whose name and his are one.[1]
  His reign had but one fault—it ended soon.
Whenas great Sháh Urmuzd had ta'en his seat
The sheep and wolf alike came to his cistern.
He thus addressed the noble men of lore,
And chieftains veteran and experienced :—
" I shall pursue the just and right, for he
That keepeth in his mind his sire's advice
Is blest.   Since God, the Giver of all good,
Hath given good to me, and therewithal
The crown that is upon the head of kings,
I would by kindness win you as my friends,
And share your secrets.   Know that self-willed men
Are hated by the mighty ; led away
By their impatience they have ne'er enough,
For envy is the scimitar of fools,
And fortune ever mocketh them.   Again,
Short will the life and provand be of one
Ashamed to work.   Avoid the common folk
If so thou canst, their hearts are doors of greed.
Pass not in life his portal whom thou findest
Devoid of knowledge; but the men of wisdom,
With prudence and good rede, confirm the throne.
May thy heart live by prudence and good sense ;
Do thou thine utmost to avoid all ill.
Knowledge and wisdom are like earth and water,
And should combine.   What marvel if the heart

---

[1] Urmuzd was the name of the first day of each solar month—a day considered particularly propitious for beginning any undertaking—*e.g.* a journey.

Of any king that putteth from him love
Shall darken? May my subjects all rejoice
And worship God, may He approve of them,
And wisdom aid them inly and without.
The sage, conversing with the devotee
About the Sháh, should weigh his utterance,
Because good speech is never out of date;
Speak but good words thyself and list to none
That speaketh ill; the great king's heart will note
Thy secret, and his ear will hear thy voice,
For ' Walls have ears,' as one that could both speak,
And listen, said."
                    The whole assembly blessed
That Sháh so shrewd of heart and pure of Faith,
And broke up glad in that o'ershadowing Cypress.
    That wise Sháh kept the precepts of Shápúr,
The son of Sháh Ardshír, and all the world
Rejoiced in him. How good are kings when just
And generous! He ruled with modesty
And justice till a while had passed, and then
The place of musk with camphor was o'erspread,
And in the garth the Cercis-bloom lay dead.

C. 1422

§ 2

*How Urmuzd gave up the Throne to Bahrám, charged
him, and died*

Urmuzd, when ware that death could not be shunned,
Wept many a tear of blood. He had a son,
Imperious, whom the wise Sháh called Bahrám.
He had the carpet laid within his hall,
Bade, and Bahrám appeared, to whom he said :—
" Mine own true son exalt in manliness
And knowledge! feebleness hath come upon me,
And made my face self-coloured with my hair.

Bent is the straight-stemmed Cypress, and the rose,
Erst crimson, hath the colour of the quince.
Be world-lord when thy time shall come, be wise,
And do no hurt; turn not from those that cry
For justice; pardon not oppressors' faults;
Refrain thy tongue from falsehood if thou wouldst
Illume thy throne; let wisdom be thy soul
And modesty thy minister; in speech
Be eloquent, and let thy voice be soft;
Be thine ally the Lord of victory,
And may thy quarry be thy subjects' hearts.
Abate strife and make passion alien;
God grant it rule thee not. Refuse thyself
To scandal-mongers, foolish folk, and knaves.

C. 1423 Thou wilt but suffer from the ignorant,
So heed them not. Know that none honoureth
The shameless and the babbler. Let thy lord
Be wisdom, wrath thy slave, and be not hasty
Against the temperate. Be ware lest greed
Encompass thee because it causeth wrath
And fear and need, but practise all forbearance,
And uprightness, and banish from thy heart
Both fraud and falsehood. Shun an evil name,
For that will mar thy fortune. No wise quit
The way of wisdom. Haste will bring repentance,
But tarriance will show the proper course.
Quit not the path of virtue. Patient men
Will keep their temper and will shut their eyes
To what is not to be, yet, since the bold
Take patience in excess for feebleness,
The master of the throne will choose the mean
Of wisdom. Neither haste nor slackness serve;
Let wisdom guide thy soul. See to it, thou!
That no detractors win thine approbation,
And seek no friendship with thine enemy
Although he hail thee king; that tree is green

Its fruit is colocynth, and if thou graspest
His feet thou hast his head. Exalt or base,
Whiche'er thou art, be not illuded. Fortune
Is ill to the malignant; be not so.
The assemblies of the noble scorn a chief
That breaketh covenant. Take hold on wisdom,
For that will grace thy soul, crown, host, and wealth.
Guard word and covenant, and read the motions
Of sun and moon. Affect not wealth and pleasure,
Because this Wayside Inn will cease for thee;
Consult the wise alone and keep the customs
Of former Sháhs; fray foemen by thy hosts,
And look with heed behind thee and before.
He that will flatter worthless men to gain
His ends may by his words destroy thyself;
Let such not age with thee, yet hold one less
Than man that hath no use for praise, for God
Approveth praise and straiteneth slanderers' hearts.
He that can wink at others' faults, and swallow
His wrath with ease, will grow each day in wealth, C. 1424
While hasty men will have full hearts. No sage
Is he that seeketh combat with the sea.
Slight not my sayings, make thy heart a bow,
Thy tongue an arrow, let thy chest be broadened,
And thine arm straight, then shoot at what thou wilt.
Conform thy tongue and heart withal to wisdom,
Then please thyself in talk. The brainless man
Hath all his counsel and his words inept.
When with thy counsellors consult in private,
If thou hast counsel and experience
Thou wilt be day by day more prosperous,
Thy spirit will be shrewder than thy foe's,
Thy heart and brain and counsel more prevailing.
One that is led by passion will not prosper.
By gratifying friends thou wilt increase
Their pleasure and their welfare. Frown on foes,

And make the faces of ill-wishers pale.
Give alms; so is thy treasure best employed.
Shun envy; from it spring hot tears of blood,
And upright men condemn it in a king.
For fourteen months I reigned unwittingly,
Expecting to retain the crown and throne
For years, but now my time hath come, and thou
Must gird thyself to rule."
                          A noble scribe
Wrote out this testament, and the wazír
Laid it before the Sháh, who heaved a sigh,
While his flushed face became like withered leaves.
Now, when those cheeks grew golden, pain and grief
Became the portion of Bahrám who mourned
For forty days and left the lofty throne
Unoccupied, for he was sorrowful.
Thus will it be while heaven shall turn above,
At whiles all anguish and at whiles all love.

'Tis the Urmuzd of Dai, and night; be thine
To rest from speech and put thy hand to wine.

XXV

BAHRÁM SON OF URMUZD

HE REIGNED THREE YEARS, THREE MONTHS, AND THREE DAYS

NOTE

To the reign of Bahrám (Varahran I., A.D. 273–276) properly belongs the end of the career of the great heresiarch, Mání, who, having been banished by Shápúr, son of Ardshír, and recalled by his son Urmuzd, was executed by order of Bahrám. Mání, however, is relegated in the Sháhnáma to the reign of Shápúr, son of Urmuzd (Sapor II.).[1]

Historically Bahrám appears to have been the son of Shápúr, son of Ardshír (Sapor I.), not of Urmuzd, son of Shápúr.[2]

§ 1

How Bahrám succeeded to the Throne, charged the Nobles, and died

The diadem of Sháh Bahrám essay—
A Sháh whose kingship swiftly passed away.[3]
Whenas Bahrám sat on the throne of gold,   C. 1425
In grievous trouble at his sire's decease,
The Íránian chiefs all came to him in tears,
And girt to serve him. They invoked God's blessing
Upon him, saying: "Be while place endureth,
Because the royal throne becometh thee;

---

[1] See p. 358.   [2] NT, p. 49, *note.*
[3] The previous reign ends here in C.

Thou hast the kingship from thine ancestors.
Be thy foes' faces pale, and may thy soul
Cease to deplore the dead."
                              He answered : "Chiefs,
Brave cavaliers, and nobles ! let no thane,
Or other liege, put hand to ill. Behold
How this unresting Dome respecteth neither
The fostered nor the fosterer. Bind fast
The hands of passion and reject its bidding.
Whoever shall abstain from evil-doing,
And smircheth not himself by his ill deeds,
Will live glad days and pass in peace. The Sháh
Should guard the wealth of others, tender dearly
Men of good conduct, and protect the Faith,
Because it is the crown upon his head.
He that is wise in wrath, and acteth not
Injuriously, is blest. In times of stress
His heart is great and glad. Oh ! may the world
Lack not the sage, and sage indeed is he
That trampleth not [1] upon a vanquished foe.
Vindictiveness proceedeth ill from those
That seek renown. Abstain and use it not.
Know that thanes, troops, and kings unoccupied,[2]
Hold no set course ; the idle slumbereth,
And waketh to remorse ; well said, ill done,
Gain thee no praise or jocund Paradise.
Seek fame, do well, and break no good men's hearts.

C. 1426 I am possessed of treasure and dínárs
In plenty, I have majesty and kingship,
And might of hand. Enjoy your own and know
That one who hath not is of those that have
Because my purse is open : none must want."
    Not many days passed by ere that crowned head
Came to the shears. The Sháh possessed a son—
His heart's delight—Bahrám, son of Bahrám,

---

[1] Reading with P.   [2] Reading with P and T.

For whom he sent, set him beneath the throne,
And said: " Green offshoot from my stem ! not long
Have I enjoyed the crown, but be thy time
All glorious. Rejoice, increase, and pass
Thy days and nights in mirth. So walk that thou,
When questioned at the Great Account, hast not
To turn in shame from Him who gave thee all.
By justice and by bounty cause the world
To flourish and thy subjects' hearts to joy,
For whether one be king or archimage
The world abideth not with him for ever."
   Three years, three months, three days passed o'er his
     head,
And then the world-illuming throne was void,
And as Bahrám gave to Bahrám the world
The son gave to the sire the charnel's peace.
   Know, 'tis no outrage of the turning sky;
It holdeth but as wind that passeth by
All that hath breath, and till it cease to roll
Thus will it be; why then afflict thy soul?
Why seek or speak concerning what should be?
Discourse on things like these is not for thee.
E'en though in greed thy soul be grown not sere
Thy resting place is but a narrow bier.
Since death then cometh of such wolfish breed
A mighty bowl of wine will fill my need,
And one of silvern form and cypress-tall,
A charmer sweet of speech and kind withal,
With jasmine scent, bright cheeks, a moon in mien,
Musk-scented, and with looks of sun-like sheen.

XXVI

BAHRÁM, SON OF BAHRÁM

HE REIGNED NINETEEN YEARS

NOTE

The reign of this Bahrám (Varahran II., A.D. 276–293), is in the Sháhnáma as bare of events as that of his predecessor, and Tabarí has next to nothing to say of him. Mas'údí, however, tells us that he began badly till once, when returning from the chase, the Sháh in company with the high priest passed through a hamlet, recently abandoned, amid whose ruins naught was heard but the hooting of the owls. The Sháh asked the high priest if he knew any one that understood their language. The high priest answered that he himself had that gift, and that what the bird said was true. The Sháh inquired what it was, and the high priest replied :—"This owl is a male and wishes to wed. He asked the female owl to accept him as her mate so that their offspring might bless God and perpetuate their name. The female said that she should like it of all things, but that she would accept him only on certain conditions. To begin with he must present her with twenty villages chosen from the chief demesnes that had become vacant under the reigning sovereign." "What was the male's reply?" asked the Sháh. "Your majesty!" answered the high priest, "the owl made this response :—'If the reign of this monarch prove a long one I shall be able to give you a good thousand villages, but what do you propose?' 'From our union' rejoined the female, 'will spring a numerous succession of children, and we shall be able to give each of them a share of these ruins.' 'Nothing can be simpler and easier than what you wish' replied the male, 'and I agree in advance, for I am overstocked with this kind of wealth. Tell me what you want more.'" The Sháh was struck by the high priest's apologue, and ruled thereafter for his people's good.[1]

---

[1] MM, ii. 169 *seq.*

§ 1

*How Bahrám, Son of Bahrám, ascended the Throne, charged
the Nobles, and died*

While mourning Sháh Bahrám for forty days
Bahrám himself did not assume the crown.
The warriors, the men exceeding wise,
All grief, all wailing, and all lamentation,
Came and sat with him in his woe and mourning,
Wan-cheeked with lips of lapis-lazuli,
Until a prudent archmage came and said :—
" Will not the Sháh be seated on the throne ? "
  For one whole se'nnight urgently he strove,
And ceased not till the throne was occupied.[1]
  Now when Bahrám assumed his seat, rejoicing,   C. 1427
And crowned himself as kings are wont, he first
Praised God—the Light of circling time, the Increaser
Of knowledge and of uprightness, the Marrer
Of falsehood and of fraud, the Lord of Saturn
And of revolving heaven, who asketh naught
But love and justice from His slaves—and then
Said thus : " Tried sages and pure archimages !
Hold knowledge great and be not bold with kings.
The man endowed with increase, eloquence,
And leadership by God will strive, if wise,
To compass excellence and cultivate
Humanity, whose attribute is patience,
Because the rash are held contemptible.
Security produceth happiness,
For then distress and toil have turned to wind,
And gathering wealth is like wind too to one
Of noble heart for he is rich already.
Yet get some havings if thou hast them not,

---

[1] The previous reign ends here in C. We follow the arrangement
in P.

For folk despise the indigent. The man
Possessed of nothing hath no influence,
And none respect him. When thou art content
Thou feel'st at ease, but practise greed and thou
Wilt live in fear, so toil not thus to vex
Thy body and thy soul for greed of treasure.
Choose thou the mean if thou wouldst have folk's praise
In matters temporal. If thou contentest
The world with justice thou wilt be made glad
Thyself thereby and rich. Security
And uprightness, and no default in justice,
Are needful. When joy faileth spirit faileth,
And wisdom 'twixt the twain is impotent,
While if greed clutch thy heart thy soul remaineth
Within the gullet of the Crocodile."

When he had reigned for twenty years save one
Life mourned him, that crowned Sháh espoused the
        dust;
A charnel hid him from the jocund world.

C. 1428   Such is the fashion of the turning sky,
Though thou art feeble it hath mastery,
And such the fashion of this world as well;
It hath its secrets but it ne'er will tell !

XXVII

BAHRÁM BAHRÁMIYÁN

HE REIGNED FOUR MONTHS

NOTE

According to Tabarí this Sháh (Varahran III., A.D. 293) reigned four years,[1] but Mas'údí, like Firdausí, says four months.[2] Professor Nöldeke suggests that he reigned for four months only in the capital, but ruled longer in other parts of the kingdom, probably in conflict with Narsí,[3] his uncle, historically, as Bahrám Bahrámiyán appears to have been the son of Urmuzd, son of Shápúr.[4] The true owner of the title of "Kirmánsháh" is Bahrám, son of Shápúr (Varahran IV., A.D. 388-399).

§ 1

How Bahrám Bahrámiyán succeeded to the Throne and died four Months after

Bahrám Bahrámiyán sat on the throne,
And girt himself for justice and for bounty.
They sprinkled emeralds upon his crown,
They called him Kirmánsháh, and thus he said :—
"May God, the just and only God, bestow
Upon us wisdom for our portion, justice,
And counsel. This our Wayside Hostelry
Abideth not with any. Goodness help us,
Lean we and cleave thereto, and make our heart
Our witness by our justice and our bounty,

NT, p. 50.   [2] MM, ii. 174.   [3] NT, p. 416.   [4] *Id.* 436 a.

313

For since the good and evil that we do
Are our memorials sow thou naught but good."
   When he had reigned four months the throne and
    crown
Bewailed him bitterly.   When certified
That death was near—that crocodile which hunteth
Rhinoceros and elephant—he gave
His son the world, and said: "Be thy reign glorious!
Array thyself, drink wine, walk delicately,
Be bountiful; make not thy day with throne
And crown unfortunate." [1]
                    Thus moments speed,
Their breaths uncounted by the man of greed!
O happy fortune! bring red wine to me,
For now the poet's years are sixty-three.

[1] In the glossary to C "inverted."   The word properly has the meaning of "bright," but what is bright is easily reflected, what is reflected is inverted, and inversion well may imply misfortune.

XXVIII

NARSÍ, SON OF BAHRÁM

HE REIGNED NINE YEARS

NOTE

Narsí (Narses, A.D. 293–302) does not appear to have been the son of Bahrám Bahrámiyán but of Shápúr, son of Ardshír Pápakán.[1] Historically his reign was an important one as we learn from sources other than Persian and Arabic. Firdausí, Tabarí, and Mas'údí have little or nothing to record of him, but Mírkhánd states that he abdicated in favour of his son Urmuzd, and, further, that his prowess in the chase won him the title of 'The mighty Hunter.'[2]

§ 1

How Narsi succeeded to the Throne, counselled his Son, and died

Bahrám, when fortune's day no longer shone,
Surrendered to Narsí the crown and throne.
This is the way; there is no end thereto,
The wanton sky hath ever something new!
  Whenas Narsí sat on the ivory seat,   C. 1429
And donned the crown that gladdeneth the heart,
The nobles all approached with offerings,
And mourning in their sorrow for his sire.
The chief blessed them, and said: "My loving lieges,
Adherents both of justice and the Faith!

---

[1] NT, p. 50, *note*.   [2] RM, Pt. I., vol. ii. p. 340.

Know that the Maker so hath ordered all!
That me of all the world He hath endowed
With wisdom and with generosity,
Good counsel, modesty, and gentle speech,
And if my star shall prove beneficent
I will secure prosperity for you.[1]
When any wise man hath become thy friend
Know that he is one skin with thee.[2]   Expect
Great deeds from great men, wisdom from the sage.
True courage hath reflection for its base,
And valiant men are worthy of all praise;
But he that fleeth from the work in hand
Will ne'er find fame and honour on the field.
The indolent are cowardly as well,
For indolence and cowardice agree."
   This man of rede and counsel lived nine years,
And by his sayings profited the world;
But when his day approached, when fortune loured,
And when his casque of steel became like wax,
Urmuzd, bright as a tulip midst the grass,
Ran to the pillow of the noble Sháh,
Whose son he was and splendent as the moon
At night.   The Sháh said: "Gently nurtured youth!
Refrain thy hand with all thy strength from ill.
Soul of Narsí art thou, Bahrám's own fortune,
Crown-worthy and the glory of the throne.
Oh! may the crown ne'er weep, the people's heart
Consume, for thee who hast such stature, Grace,
Limbs, and unmatched achievement in all knowledge.
Rule thou the world by royal precedents
As thou hast learned them from thy pious sire.
At length thine own day too will pass away,
And restless heaven tread thee down; so act then
That when thy God shall question thee thine answer

---

[1] Reading with P.   *Cf.* Vol. i. p. 110.

May make thy bliss secure."

                              This said, he drew
The mantle o'er his head and heaved a sigh.
That day thou wouldst have said that he was not,
And had no throne or seat or diadem.
   Thy lot is naught but toil and misery;
'Tis so—a mystery to every eye!

XXIX

URMUZD, SON OF NARSÍ

HE REIGNED NINE YEARS

NOTE

The reign of this Sháh (Hormisdas II., A.D. 302–309) seems to be regarded as uneventful by all authorities. He left, apparently, three sons, Ázarnarsí, Urmuzd, and one unnamed, in addition to one or more posthumes. After the Sháh's death Ázarnarsí succeeded, but within a year was deposed for cruelty, Urmuzd was imprisoned but escaped long afterwards to the Romans,[1] the unnamed one was blinded, and a posthumous child became Sháh.[2] He proved to be one of the most famous of the dynasty.

§ I

How Urmuzd, Son of Narsí, ascended the Throne and how his Life ended

C. 1430
When great Urmuzd came to the throne wolves' claws
Were hindered of their quarry, he maintained
The world in peace, the work of Áhriman
Was in abeyance. First of all he praised
Almighty God, all-knowing, all-providing :—
"He fashioned night and day and turning heaven,
Sol, Mars, and Saturn. Victory and Grace,
The just heart and the imperial diadem,
Proceed from Him. May justice ever fill
Our heart, and may our subjects' hearts rejoice.

---

[1] *Cf.* p. 325. [2] NT, p. 51, *note.*

318

The hearts of men ignoble win not praise;
If so thou canst consort not thou with such,
And take not counsel with the ill-disposed,
But, if thou seekest it, incline to good.
The pious will not call him bountiful
Whose bounty is designed to gain applause,
While men will hold the thankless flatterer
As naught. The hard man trembleth being friendless.
The wise man taketh not the slack as guide,
And if thou ask the indolent to help thee
Thou art no judge of men and lack'st ambition.
Beware of thinking highly of thyself,
And be not fierce because thou hast a throne.
When one ill-natured groweth poor and vile
He layeth all to fortune and will spend
His years in indolence,[1] bewailing fortune,
Is not possessed of rede and understanding,
And is no ornament to any throne.
The simple deprivation of all wealth
Will ruin him in heart and soul and brain;
He will take pride in want and evil nature,
And hold his head up high in his unwisdom,
His lack of goods, of knowledge, rede, achievement,
Of Faith and of all thankfulness to God.
May both your nights and days be prosperous,
The marrow of your foemen's lives plucked out."
   The chiefs applauded and saluted him
As earth's great king. When heaven had turned nine
      years
Above his head his face that had resembled
Pomegranate-bloom became like yellow roses,
The head that wore the crown was sick to death;
He died without a son beside his couch.
That famed man, who discoursed so pleasantly,   C. 1431
Left in his youth this ancient hostelry;

---

[1] Reading with P.

Such while the heavens endure will be the event,
For they are strong and we are impotent.

The people mourned for him for forty days,
Regardless of the throne, which for a while
Remained unoccupied: the nobles' heads
Were full of care.   Meanwhile an archimage
Surveyed the women's bower of Sháh Urmuzd;
One tulip-cheeked and radiant as the moon,
With lashes like a dagger of Kábul,
And locks like mazy Babylonian script,
All intertwined and knotted on her head,
Was there, and that fair lady was with child;
The world rejoiced in her.   The archimage
Brought her and set her on the lofty throne
Of kings with joy, o'er her they hung the crown,
And on that golden circlet drachms showered down.

XXX

SHÁPÚR, SON OF URMUZD, SURNAMED ZÚ'L AKTÁF

HE REIGNED SEVENTY YEARS

ARGUMENT

Shápúr is born Sháh. In his youth he builds a bridge at Taisafún and punishes the Arabs for their raids during his minority. Later on he goes to Rúm in disguise, is imprisoned, but escapes, defeats the Rúmans, takes Cæsar prisoner, and dictates terms of peace, which include the cession of Nasíbín (Nisibis). The poet then tells of the heresiarch Mání, his doctrine and death. Shápúr appoints his brother Ardshír regent, and dies soon after.

NOTE

The duration of the reign of Shápúr (Sapor II., A.D. 309–379), as given by Firdausí, is correct. He was Sháh all his life, contemporary with ten Roman Emperors, and one of the greatest of Sásánian rulers.

As has been stated already, some of the events attributed in the Sháhnáma to the reign of this Sháh really belong to that of his predecessor, the first of his name.[1]

§ 1. The story of the building of the bridge over the Tigris at Taisafún (Ctesiphon) is told also by Tabarí, who says that the additional bridge was constructed by sunset on the same day as that on which the command for its erection was given![2]

Shápúr's chief places of residence were in Susiana and Mesopotamia, not in Párs as Firdausí states.

§§ 2, 3. Two Shápúrs (Sapor I. and Sapor II.) and much history are confused in this account, in which the taking of Hatra in the early days of the Sásánian dynasty and probably by Shápúr, son

---

[1] See p. 294 and below.

[2] NT, p. 54.

of Ardshír, is bound up artificially by a romantic incident with
the expedition made by Shápúr, son of Urmuzd, into Arabia
to avenge the Arab incursions into Persian territory that had
taken place during his minority. Hatra or Al Hadr was the capital
of a small principality which had become independent during
the later days of Parthian rule. It grew up in the Mesopotamian
desert, some forty miles west of the Tigris, in an oasis formed
by the river Tharthar. Its magnificent ruins stand some forty
miles south of Mosul and some two hundred north of Baghdád
which is itself some twenty miles higher up the Tigris than the
sites of the twin cities of Ctesiphon and Seleucia. The ruins
form a complete circle surrounding a central square. The circle
has a diameter of a little over a mile and is made up as follows.
Outside of all is a broad rampart; within this is a deep moat,
now dry, and within this again an immense stone wall with
towers at intervals. Within the wall are the ruins of what was
once the city. The dwellings of the inhabitants now are represented for the most part by mounds of earth, but in the centre of
the area surrounded by the city wall is a square walled enclosure
with bastions or towers similar to those of the city wall itself.
The four sides of this enclosure front to the four cardinal points,
and each side measures 340 yards in length. This enclosure may
be regarded as the citadel, and within it were the palace and the
temple of both of which the ground-story, consisting of vaulted
halls and other buildings, is still upstanding. The whole of the
remains, walls, bastions, and all, are of coarse limestone beautifully
fitted, every stone also being marked with a letter or number
and often carved to represent human faces, foliage, birds, griffins,
and other monsters.[1] The place, as will have been seen from
the above description, was immensely strong, its inhabitants were
warlike, it was only a little over two hundred miles from Ctesiphon
and Seleucia—attractions that, as experience was to show, were
not beyond the reach of raids from the more distant Palmyra[2]—
and Ardshír Pápakán not unnaturally desired its reduction.
This he, or his son Shápúr, actually achieved. The stronghold
had withstood successfully sieges by the Emperors Trajan and
Severus. It fell at last through treachery. According to the
story the Arabs had made a successful foray in the neighbourhood
of Ctesiphon and Seleucia during the absence of Shápúr. The
leader of this raid was a certain Daizan or, as Firdausí calls him,
Táír, and there may be here some reminiscence of the capture
by Odenathus of some of Shápúr's harem after the war with

---

[1] See JRGS, Vols. ix. 467, xi. 11.   [2] *Cf.* p. 325.

Valerian.[1] At all events the raider was some Arab chief, but in our story was the king of Hatra. Shápúr, informed of what had happened, beleaguered the city. Now Daizan had a daughter, the Málika of Firdausí, and it so happened that in the course of the siege, which lasted four years, she and Shápúr fell in love with one another, and he promised, if she would get him possession of Hatra, to make her his queen. This she accomplished, her father was put to death, and Shápúr married the traitress. Now she had a very delicate skin, and, when she was reposing on silk stuffed with raw silk, complained of discomfort. It was found that a myrtle-leaf was pressing against her! Shápúr asked her on what her father had fed her. She told him on cream, marrow, the honey of virgin bees, and the finest wine. "And yet," he said, "though you have known me only a short time you love me better than your father who gave you such food!"[2] He had her bound by the hair to the tail of a wild horse and dashed to death. By rights this story should come under the reign of Shápúr, son of Ardshír, or of Ardshír himself ; it has been brought, however, into connexion with that of Shápúr, son of Urmuzd, by the romantic addition, found in Dínawarí and Firdausí, that the treacherous daughter—the Málika of the Sháhnáma—was the child of the king of Hatra by the daughter of Narsí—Dukhtnúsh in Dínawarí and Núsha in Firdausí—whom he had made captive in the raid above mentioned. Now Shápúr, son of Urmuzd, was noted far more than his predecessor, Shápúr, son of Ardshír, for his dealings with the Arabs, and is said to have acquired his title of "Zu'l Aktáf" on account of the severity with which he treated them. Zu'l Aktáf has been explained to mean that he dislocated their shoulders, or removed their shoulder-blades, or strung his captives together in couples by boring their shoulders and passing a ring through them. Originally, however, the title may have been one of honour only, "the

---

[1] *Cf.* p. 294.

[2] This ignores the fact that love often ousts affection when the two come into antagonism. Hence the popularity in the past of Gretna Green. The story seems to show that, though the lady was in love with Shápúr, he himself was only pretending. That in the classics of Nisus and Scylla is very similar. Nisus, king of Megara, had a lock of hair on which his existence depended. He had too a daughter named Scylla. Minos, king of Crete, besieged Megara, and Scylla, who had fallen in love with him, cut off from her father's head the fatal lock, and he perished in consequence. Minos, like Shápúr, was not really in love and, like him, had the lady put to death.

broad-shouldered" like Dirázdast "the long-handed."[1] Be this
as it may, the above story was adapted in Íránian legend to
make it applicable to the better known of the two first Shápúrs
and the one whose dealings with the hated Arabs redounded
most to the credit of the empire. It is, as will be seen, softened
somewhat in the adapted version. The half Persian descent of
Málika is meant to account for and excuse her treachery,[2] and
Shápúr's conduct to her is not brutal. A trace of the earlier and
harsher version may survive in the words of Táír,[3] where he says
in effect, anticipating those of Brabantio to Othello :—

> "She has deceived her father and may thee." [4]

But we are not told that Shápúr acted on the hint.

The scene of the story is laid by Firdausí in distant Yaman,
the 'Ínánians, of whom Táír is made the king, being a tribe in
that region.

In one place Firdausí refers to Núsha as the "daughter of
Bahrám."[5] She was the granddaughter.

§§ 4–10. Here we have another historical confusion but on a
larger scale. Sháhs, Emperors, times, and events are confounded and transformed so into terms of romance that it is
not easy to "disentangle from the puzzled skein the threads
of" history.

First, Shápúr, son of Ardshír, is confused with Shápúr, son
of Urmuzd.

Secondly, the Emperor Valerian is mixed up with the Arab
prince Odenathus and with the Emperors Julian and Jovian.
The Bazánúsh of the Sháhnáma, who in the reign of Shápúr, son
of Ardshír, represented Valerian, here represents Jovian, and
Julian, the Yánus of Firdausí, leads, not as Cæsar but as Cæsar's
brother, an expedition against Persia.

Thirdly, a few dates are instructive. Shápúr, son of Ardshír,
reigned A.D. 241–272. Shápúr, son of Urmuzd, reigned A.D.
309–379. The Emperor Valerian was taken prisoner in A.D. 258.
Julian died, and Jovian made his treaty with Persia, in A.D. 363.
Odenathus, prince of Palmyra, was assassinated in A.D. 267.

Fourthly, the historical events here confused are :—

The second war of Shápúr, son of Ardshír, against Rome in

---

[1] See Vol. v. p. 281, and for the above generally NT, p. 33 *seq.* and
notes, p. 53 *seq.* and *notes*.

[2] So too the damsel who rescues Shápúr from his imprisonment by
Cæsar is described as being an Íránian by birth. See pp. 338–9.

[3] p. 334.   [4] Act i. scene 3.   [5] See p. 334.

which the Emperor Valerian was taken prisoner and died, some years later, in captivity.

The ensuing war of Odenathus, prince of Palmyra, against the conqueror of Valerian, in the course of which he captured part of the great king's harem, and marched up to the gates of Ctesiphon.

The expedition of the Emperor Julian against Shápúr, son of Urmuzd, which ended in a disastrous retreat, his own death, and the humiliating treaty made by his successor Jovian.

§ 4. Already we have had instances of kings and chiefs going in disguise to spy out the enemy. So Rustam made his way into the camp of Suhráb,[1] and Sikandar to that of Dárá,[2] to the court of queen Kaidáfa,[3] and to the palace of the Faghfúr.[4] We shall find too Bahrám Gúr, in the next volume, going as his own ambassador to Shangul, king of Hind. The exploits of Odenathus in connexion with Shápúr, son of Ardshír, and the capture of the great king's harem, seem to be adumbrated here in the capture and misfortunes of the second Shápúr at the court of Cæsar. Valerian, whose own capture is here post-dated, is credited with the successes of the Arab chieftain. Shápúr's misfortunes are ante-dated as a foil to his final triumph later on.[5]

The denouncer of Shápúr at the court of Cæsar may be identified perhaps, historically, with the Persian prince Urmuzd (Hormisdas) who was imprisoned by the nobles after the death of his father Urmuzd, son of Narsí, and after a long captivity escaped in A.D. 323 to the Romans, by whom he was held in high honour, and accompanied Julian in his campaign to the East.[6]

We have had an instance already in the case of Garsíwaz of the punishment of being sewn up in fresh raw hide, which contracts and stiffens as it dries, and is very painful if not always fatal. According to some accounts the Khalífa Walíd (A.D. 705–715), under a misapprehension, had his great general Muhammad Kásim put to death in this fashion,[7] but this does not seem to be historically correct.

§ 5. Sympathetic damsels are much in evidence in this portion of the Sháhnáma as aids to embarrassed heroes. One helped Ardshír Pápakán,[8] as did two more according to the Karnámak.[9] Shápúr is aided thus here for the second time.[10]

Such scenes of lowly life as that between Shápúr and the

---

[1] Vol. ii. p. 149.   [2] See p. 38.   [3] *Id.* p. 127.
[4] *Id.* p. 170.   [5] NT, p. 65, and *note.*
[6] NT, p. 51, and *note ;* RSM, pp. 149, 194.   *Cf.* p. 318.
[7] Vol. iv. p. 265 ; EHI, i. p. 209.
[8] p. 217.   [9] p. 201.   [10] For the first time see p. 331.

gardener become more frequent in the latter part of the poem.

§ 7. Here we have, for the second time, the account of the capture of Valerian, post-dated by more than a century. His treatment in captivity is represented as being much more severe in this version on account of his rough usage of the Sháh which, historically, represents the successes gained by Odenathus over Shápúr, son of Ardshír, after the defeat of Valerian. The proposed terms of peace similarly are more stringent. Their parallel is the building of the bridge at Shúshtar.[1]

§ 8. This appears to be an account of Julian's expedition to the East in A.D. 362–3. It will be seen that he is not regarded as an Emperor but as the Emperor's brother. This was necessary owing to the form that the story took in Firdausí's authorities. Cæsar (Valerian) was supposed to be still alive though a captive and was engaged in collecting all the ransom that was possible from Rúm.[2] The throne was not technically vacant, so Yánus could not be Emperor. Later on the troops of Rúm make a new choice altogether and elect Bazánúsh (Jovian). The repetition of the story of Valerian has the effect of dwarfing the more historically placed expedition of Julian, and Julian's status suffers accordingly.

§ 9. Here, after the overthrow of Yánus (Julian) Bazánúsh (Jovian) is elected Emperor in succession, romantically, to Cæsar (Valerian), historically, to Julian. Historically, too, the negotiations for peace were begun a few days after the death of Julian, and during the retreat of the Roman army, not by the newly elected Emperor Jovian but by Shápúr, who took that step to delay the retirement of the Romans till some definite agreement had been arrived at. The result was a great triumph for Persian diplomacy.

§ 10. That we have here a version of the historical treaty of peace between Jovian and Shápúr is clear from the stipulation for the cession of Nasíbín (Nisibis)—one of the most important provisions of the actual treaty. Shápúr had besieged it three times already without success. There was a stipulation that the Roman inhabitants of that and other places ceded should have liberty to withdraw. Tabarí tells us that in the case of Nisibis they were replaced by twelve thousand natives of Istakhr and elsewhere.[3]

Both the accounts of Valerian in the Sháhnáma agree that he ended his days in captivity, and the general consensus of historians is to the same effect. Whether he died a natural death or not is uncertain, but the former seems the more probable.[4]

---

[1] p. 298. [2] p. 357.
[3] NT, p. 63. [4] *Cf. id.* pp. 33, 66, and *notes;* RSM, pp. 86, 87, 125.

Shápúr continued the ancient practice of transporting conquered populations to new homes, settling them in cities that he himself had built, restored, or renamed. The two in Khúzistán mentioned in the text—Khurram Ábád and Kinám-i-Asírán—may be represented by the ruins of Karkh and Shús, now known as Íwán-i-Kerkh, not far from the ruins of Susa. Pírúz Shápúr is better known as Ambar, a city on the Euphrates.[1] It served as the original capital of the 'Abbasid Khalífat but was superseded before long by Baghdád.

§ 11. There was so much in common between the first two Shápúrs—similarity of name, wars with the Arabs and the Romans, religious excitement and consequent persecution, and, in addition to all this, the fact that the six intervening Sháhs had failed to impress their personalities on the popular mind and consequently left hardly any trace of themselves in popular tradition—that it was only natural for events properly belonging elsewhere to gravitate towards the later, longer, and more important reign of the two. We have had several instances of this tendency already, and here we have another in the case of the famous heresiarch, Mání, whose career, historically speaking, ended before the second Shápúr was born. Mání's life seems wholly to have been included within the third century A.D.—a period when new religious ideas were being disseminated broadcast, and old religions were passing through a season of revival. In the Sásánian empire Zoroastrianism, Christianity with its many gnostic offshoots, and Judaism, were striving to assert themselves, and in the midst of the ferment Mání was born A.D. 215-16. He is said to have begun his public career as a religious teacher on Sunday, March 20th A.D. 242—the day apparently of the coronation of Shápúr, son of Ardshír.[2] Shápúr, at first disposed to listen to the new teacher, afterwards banished him, and he remained in exile till he was allowed to return by Shápúr's successor, Urmuzd, who allowed him evangelical freedom and presented him with a place of residence. Urmuzd's reign, however, proved to be a very brief one, and under the next Sháh, his son or brother, Bahrám, Mání is said to have been flayed alive, and his body, stuffed with straw, exposed on one of the gates of Gund-i-Shápúr, which gate consequently became known as "the Mání gate." According to some accounts Mání was recalled by Bahrám and afterwards put to death by him or by his son and successor, but at all events the great gnostic died before the time of Shápúr, son of Urmuzd. Mání's followers of course were persecuted.

---

[1] On Shápúr's cities see NT, p. 57 *seq.* and *notes.*
[2] NT, pp. 47 and *note* 412 *seq.*

Máni's teaching was an eclectic one, and the materials for it were drawn from the various Faiths amid which he grew up or with which he came into contact later on. No doubt in his enthusiasm he hoped to find a formula that would reconcile them all. In the result he was regarded by the orthodox of each as the false friend who is worse than the open enemy, and suffered accordingly. His chief opponents were the priests of the state-religion—Zoroastrianism—just then in the flowing tide of its revival, but the arguments put into the high priest's mouth by Firdausí are more Mohammedan than Zoroastrian. Máni's offence, so far as his doctrine was distinguished from Christianity, lay in his high and pure asceticism, which was antagonistic to the somewhat self-indulgent Faith of Zoroaster. The Zoroastrian was a family man, a flesh-eater, and a wine-drinker. The Manichæan was not permitted to injure any living thing, whether animal or plant, for the sake of obtaining food, and was a celibate, a vegetarian, and a rechabite.

The followers of Máni were famous for the neatness and ornamentation of their sacred books, and this gave rise to the notion that Máni himself had been a painter. There are allusions to him in that capacity in the Sháhnáma.[1]

§ 12. For Ardshír see the next reign.

§ 1

How Shápúr, Son of Urmuzd, was born forty Days after his Father's Death, and how he was crowned

Passed forty days, then like the shining sun
A babe was born of that fair dame. The archmage
Named him Shápúr and gave a feast for joy.
Thou wouldst have said: "The infant is all Grace,
And wisdom is his banner and his shade."
For forty days they revelled, then prepared
The child a royal throne. The nobles came
With golden girdles and hung over it
The crown of gold. That babe of forty days
They set, when fed and swaddled up in silk,
Upon his glorious father's throne beneath

[1] See Vols. ii. p. 19 and *note*, v. 118.

The crown of gold; the chiefs all homaged him,
And showered gems.　An archimage by name
Shahrwí, wise, apt, and potent, came and sat
Upon a golden seat to serve the babe
As minister, and with good rede and justice
Ruled o'er the world.　He led the folk to good,
Collected troops and treasure, and adorned
The palace and the throne, for young Shápúr,
Who grew in stature with the passing years.　　C. 1432
　　Attended by that wise archmage the Sháh
Was sitting on an eve in Taisafún.
When Sol grew wan, and night's dark livery showed,
A din rose at the way o'er the Arwand.
"Greet they?" he asked.
　　　　　　　　"O famed and valiant prince!"
The archmage answered thus the little Sháh,
"The merchants and the workmen are returning
Home from their shops and, as they pass each other,
They fear to jostle, for the bridge is narrow,
So crow like cocks at drum-beat."
　　　　　　　　　　　Said Shápúr:—
"Ye famous sages and my counsellors!
Then let us have two bridges, one to go,
The other to return, so that our subjects,
Both soldiers and civilians, may cross
At ease; our treasury shall bear the costs."
　　The archmages all joyed much that that young Tree
Was showing leaf, and, as the young Sháh bade,
Their chief gave orders for a second bridge.
His mother's heart rejoiced, she gave him tutors,
But by his rapid progress he outstripped them.
At seven years old he went upon the ground
To learn the art of war and play at polo;
At eight he learned the etiquette of courts;
Thou wouldst have said that he was Sháh Bahrám.[1]

[1] Reading with P.　Perhaps Bahrám Gúr is meant.　*Cf.* p. 378 *seq.*

He exercised himself in every grace,
And made Istakhr his royal residence
By his own glorious fathers' precedent,
Men pure, accepted, and preeminent.

§ 2

*How Táïr, the Arab, carried off the Daughter of Narsí and
married her, how Shápúr went to Yaman to fight him,
and how his Daughter fell in Love with Shápúr*

Anon, and when the world-illuming crown
Grew bright, Táïr, the 'Ínánian lion-hearted,
Whose scimitar would bolden heaven, led forth
From Rúm and Párs, from Kurdistán, Bahrain,
And Kádisíya, up to Taisafún

C. 1433   A host surpassing all compute of knowledge.
He gave the country up to pillage.   Who
Could fight or fly him ?   Hearing tell of Núsha,
Who was the Sháh's aunt and a youthful Spring,
He sought her palace, while all Taisafún
Was full of hue and cry.   They bore her off,
And made her prisoner, for he and his
Were coarse and ignorant.   When she had spent
One year of grief and care with him she bore him
A daughter like the moon and like Narsí,
Thou wouldst have said, when he had crown and
    throne.
Her father called her Málika on seeing
That she was fit for queenship.
                          When Shápúr
Was six and twenty, and had grown to be
A valiant, sun-like monarch, he reviewed
His troops upon the plain and chose him out
Twelve thousand warriors and for each a camel
Wind-footed, and a hundred guides withal.
The warriors mounted, leading each his steed.

Then too the Sháh himself and his own meiny
Took seat upon their beasts. He girded up
His royal belt for raiding and pursued
The monarch of the 'Ínánians—Táír,
That over-weening one, that raging Lion—
And slaughtered many of his warriors,
Which when Táír perceived he showed his back.
Then followed hue and cry, and many captives
Were taken while that host fled to a stronghold
Within Yaman; men, women, children wailed.
Shápúr led forth such forces that the ways
Were barred to ant and gnat. He found[1] Táír
With troops within the hold, and turned from him
The means of fight and flight. The siege continued
A month both day and night, the garrison
Ran short of food. One morning full of ardour
Shápúr, the hero, mounted on his steed
With bow in hand, a kingly, black cuirass
Upon his breast and black flag fluttering o'er him.
Now Málika looked from the castle-walls,
And saw that flag and head of chiefs, whose cheeks
Were then like rose-leaves and his hair like musk,
His lips like jujubes and his breath musk-scented.
Both sleep and peace went from her; with her heart
Possessed by love, she sought her nurse, and said:—
" This sun-like Sháh, come hither for revenge,
Is great, my very blood, and him I call
' The world' because he is the world to me.
Now bear a message for me to Shápúr;
He came to fight us, bid him to a feast
With me. Say: 'Thou and I are of one race,   C. 1434
And of the seed of brave Narsí as well.
Moreover I will aid in thy revenge,
For I am of thy kindred—Núsha's daughter.
If thou wilt marry me the hold is thine,

---

[1] Reading with P.

And with the palace thou shalt have its Picture.
Arrange all with my nurse and pledge thy word
Of honour.'"
                    She replied: "As thou commandest
So will I speak and bring thee news of him."
    When night and murk took kingship of the earth
From sea to sea, when it became pitch-hued,
The hills like indigo, the stars like lamps,
And thou hadst said: "Three hundred thousand lights
Have been suspended from the eighth heaven," the nurse
Went quaking, full of fear and fright. Her heart
Was sundered through her terror of Táír.
She reached the camp, approached a trusty man,
And said: "If thou wilt bring me to the Sháh,
Thou shalt receive from me a crown and ring."
    That wise and prudent man conducted her
Toward the valiant monarch from the gate.
She came, with her eyelashes swept the ground,
And told him all. Her words rejoiced the Sháh,
Who smiled. He gave her fifty score dínárs,
A necklace, pair of bracelets, crown, and cloak
Embroidered with brocade of Chín, and answered:—
"Speak much and kindly to the moon-faced maid,
And say to her: 'He sware by sun and moon,
The girdle of Zarduhsht,[1] the throne and crown:—
"Whate'er thou askest of me, though it be
To cantle mine own realm, thine ear shall hear
No angry word from me, nor will I seek
To part from thine embrace."' For I will buy her,
God willing, at the cost of throne and crown,
Of treasure and of host."
                    On hearing this
She hurried from the camp back to the hold,
Informed the silver Cypress what had passed,
And added: "Venus is conjunct with Sol."

                    [1] Cf. Vol. v. p. 16.

She told of Sháh Shápúr, his looks and height,
All she had noted of that Moon so bright.

§ 3

How Táír was bemused by his Daughter and how she came
to Shápúr, who took the Hold and slew Táír

Now Málika, when Sol's crown westward shone,
And on the earth its yellow flower became
Like teak in hue, won from the treasurer
And minister of king Táír the keys
That oped the stores of provand and of wine,
And sent the leaders and the veteran chiefs
Supplies thereof with sweet narcissus-blooms
And fenugreek.   She called to her the server,
Spake much and graciously to him, and said :—
"Thou pourest wine to-night; give it Táír
Neat, and keep all of them with wine in hand
That they may fall asleep and be bemused."
   The server answered her: "Thy slave am I,
And only live because thou willest it."
   Now when the sun was yellow in the west,
And murky night bade it "Avaunt," Táír
Called for a cup of royal wine, and first
They drank "The 'Ínánians."   When one watch had
   passed
Táír slept careless of the din around,
And all withdrew to rest, whereat that Moon
Bade her slaves speak in whispers and undo
With stealth the castle-gate.   Now Sháh Shápúr
Was waiting, angered at the drunken din,
But when the light shone through the gate he cried :—
"Our mate is sleepless fortune !"
                              Then he bade
To lodge that fair maid daintily in camp,

C. 1435

Collected all his forces, chose out men,
Both mounted and afoot, approved in valour
And fitted for the fray, and entering
The hold 'gan slay, and seized the ancient treasures.
The more part of the garrison were drunk,
The rest, but half awake, prepared to fight;
None showed his back through fear. The noble Sháh
Slew many while Táír, who was made captive,
Came naked and, albeit unwillingly,
Apace before him. Hold and goods were both
Shápúr's. One man was rich and only one!
He waited till the dawn and, when Sol showed
Its golden cap, they set a throne of turquoise,
As was the custom, in the hold and held
An audience. When the Sháh had made an end
The Rose of early Spring drew near to him;
She wore a ruby coronet and shone
In cloth of gold of Chín. He seated her
Beside him on the throne and presently
Called for Táír in bonds who, when he came,
Bare-headed, and beheld his daughter crowned,

C. 1436   Knew that the sorcery was hers and she
Had wrought the mischief, and he said: "O Sháh,
And noble man! see how my child hath dealt
With me! Be thou too wary of her love,
And hold all strangers enemies henceforth."

    Shápúr made answer to that miscreant:—
"When thou didst take the daughter of Bahrám
From her seclusion, and insult our race,
Thou didst arouse a sleeping feud."

                      He bade
The deathsman to behead Táír and fling
His body to the flames. The head he trailed
In blood contemptuously and flung away.
He would not let his Arab captives speak,
But had their shoulder-blades removed—an act

Which horrified the world. The Arabs used
To call him Zú'l Aktáf because he wrenched
Their shoulders from the spine. Thence he returned
To Párs where all men came and homaged him.
All that got quarter with their shoulders whole
Refused to him no longer tax and toll.

§ 4

*How Shápúr went disguised as a Merchant to Rúm, how he
was taken by Cæsar, and how Cæsar ravaged the Land
of Írán*

Thus heaven revolved awhile, then changed its favour.
The day came when Shápúr, although possessed
Of crown and treasure, dreaded what might be,
And, when two watches of the night had passed,
Called his astrologers and asked concerning
The imperial throne and weal and woe to come.
The astrologers brought forth their astrolabes,
And cast his prospects of repose and rest,[1]
To see if ill would reach, or Grace divine
Grow greater with, the Sháh. This seen, they said:—
"Great king, world-lord, of ardent heart and pure!
A grievous, painful task confronteth thee,
But what none dareth tell."
                                              Shápúr replied:—
"O learnéd men and seekers of the way!
By what device can this be made to pass
From me, and mine ill star not tread me down?"
    The astrologers made answer: "None, O Sháh!
By courage and by knowledge can escape
The revolution of the restless sky;   C. 1437
We cannot strive with it; what is to be

---

[1] Or "And banished rest and slumber for his sake."

Will happen all, past doubt."
                    The noble Shàh
Rejoined : "God is our refuge from all ill,
For He created circling heaven above,
Created strength and weakness."
                    He spread out
His justice through the realm and for a while
Was glad and free from trouble.   Having rendered
The whole land prosperous he greatly yearned
To visit Rúm and see the state of Cæsar,
His army, treasury, and puissance.
He told his minister, a paladin
Both just and prudent, of his secret purpose,
But hid it from all other folk, and added :—
"Administer the realm with equity,
For that will make you glad."
                    He had prepared
Ten caravans of camels—noble beasts ;
There was a chief to every caravan.
He loaded thirty camels with dínárs,
The rest with jewels and brocade.   He left
The peopled parts and journeyed full of care
Till he arrived in Rúm and saw a suburb
Where dwelt both thanes and citizens.   He entered
The dwelling of a man of means and asked :—
"Can I have lodging here ?"
                    With many greetings
The goodman said : "Receive we not such guests ?"
   Shápúr abode that night, ate, and gave presents,
Receiving back the blessings of the thane.
At morn he packed and went to Cæsar's palace,
Like wind, and coming to the chamberlain
Saluted him and gave him gifts, who asked :—
"Who art thou ?   Say, because thou art a king
In limbs and looks."
                    Shápúr replied : "Not I.

I am a Persian, a religious man,
And with my merchandise have come from Jaz.
I have a caravan of silks and linens,
And came to court in hope to be received
By Cæsar. If among my merchandise
Aught liketh him, or of my gems and arms,
Let him accept such from his slave and place them
Among his treasures. This will please, not grieve, me.
The rest I shall sell boldly in reliance
On his protection, purchase what I need
In Rúm, and bear it to Írán."
                              The elder
Went and told Cæsar, who bade raise the curtain,   C. 1438
And granted audience. When Shápúr approached
The presence he gave praises as was fitting,
While Cæsar, gazing on him, liked him well,
Bade spread the board, and put all strangers forth.
   There was in Rúm a native of Írán,
A man of much experience, but withal
Injurious, oppressive, and accursed,
Who said to Cæsar: "O exalted one!
List to my news in secret: this great merchant,
Who taketh our dínárs for his brocade,
Is, I assert, Shápúr, the king of kings,
In speech, in countenance, in Grace, and bearing."·
   When Cæsar heard he was amazed, looked black,
And set a watch, but kept the matter close,
And·scanned Shápúr as he arose bemused.
The guard came up, and said: "Thou art Shápúr,
Son of Narsí, disguised."
                           They carried him
Off to the women's house and bound his hands;
None 'scapeth from the net of bale by valour.
What booteth to consult astrologers
Since all their calculations naught availed?
   They lit a candle by the drunken man,

And vilely sewed him up in ass's hide.
All said : " The wretch hath gained an ass's skin,
And lost a throne ! "
              There was a dark, strait cell
Whereto they bare, and whereinto they flung,
That luckless one forthwith and locked the door.
Now Cæsar gave the custody of key,
And of that captive wrapped in alien hide,
To his own wife, and told her : " Give him bread
And water lest his soul may pass too soon.
If he survive awhile he will perceive
The worth of throne and crown, and none that is not
Of Cæsar's race will covet Cæsar's throne."
    She locked the cell. Her own home was elsewhere.
She had for treasuress and confidant
A moon-faced girl, Íránian by descent,
Who knew her lineage from sire to sire,
And Cæsar's wife put in her charge the key,
And brave Shápúr fast in the ass's skin,
Whom Cæsar left thus straitened, and that day
Led forth his host. Now when he reached Írán
His army drew the falchion of revenge,

C. 1439   And bore off many captives. Their brave foes
Had none to aid them, and Írán was stripped
Of men and women, children and all havings,
Both great and small. No news came to the host
Of Sháh Shápúr alive or dead. Írán
Fled before Rúm, the land was void of folk,
While countless others had a Christian call,
And flocked before the bishops, one and all.

§ 5

*How the Damsel took Measures to free Shápúr, and how he
fled with her from Rúm*

Time passed, the army of Írán was scattered,
And all the while in Rúm the keepers watched
Shápúr both day and night, howbeit the damsel,
That was Íránian-born, rejoiced not o'er him,
But wept for him, thus clad in ass's hide,
Incessantly; her heart burned for Shápúr.

One day she said: " O goodly man! who art thou ?
Speak and fear not, for in this ass's skin
Thy graceful form hath neither sleep nor rest.
Thou wast a Cypress with the moon full-orbed
Above it, and that moon had musk-black curls,
But now thy cypress-form is like a hoop,
Thine elephantine body like a reed.
My heart is burning, mine eyes weep, for thee
Both day and night. What wouldst thou in thine
     anguish ?
Why tell not me thy secret ? "

                              Said Shápúr :—
" If thou art well disposed to me, my Fair !
I ask thy promise—one confirmed by oath
That thou wilt keep it—not to tell my foes
My secret, but be mindful of mine anguish ;
Then will I tell thee what thou wouldst—the truth."

The damsel sware to him by the All-just,
The cincture of the priest [1]—that stalwart guide—
The life of Christ, the Passion of the Cross,
The master of Írán, and love and fear :—
" I will not tell or benefit thereby."

---

[1] Or of " Shammas," a legendary founder of Fire-worship, in which
case we may suppose that the lady, to make assurance doubly sure,
pledged herself by both religions.

He told all, hiding neither good nor bad,
And said to her : " Now if thou wilt perform
My hest, and pledge thy heart to keep my secret,
Thy head shall be exalted o'er all dames,
The world be at thy feet.   At meal-time thou
Shalt bring warm milk and supple me this hide.
Soak it because it shall become world-famous,
And after my decease the men of wisdom
Will tell the tale for many a year."
                        The damsel
Used her endeavours to obtain hot milk,
But furtively and speaking 'neath her breath.
On coming back with milk she used to set
Upon the fire a bowl thereof, then bear it
In secret to Shápúr, informing none.
In two weeks' time the ass's hide was moistened,
And when with aching body and full heart
Shápúr came forth therefrom he said to her
In confidence : " O pure one, vigilant,
And kindly in thy deeds ! we must advise,
And frame a stratagem to 'scape from Rúm :
May blessing never light on such a land !"
   The damsel said to him : " Tomorrow morn
Our chiefs will set forth to the banquet-place.
There is a feast in Rúm that men and women,
And children will attend.   Whenas the queen
Shall leave the city for the merrymake
Upon the plain, the coast will be all clear,
And I will manage, reckless of mishap;
My wits shall get for thee two steeds, two maces,
And bow and arrows.
                   Hearing this, he praised
That worshipful, foreseeing maid, grew bold,
And in this case took wisdom for his guide.
   Whenas the Fount of Light sank in the west,
And night drew o'er its head the Veil of Pitch,

C. 1440

Shápúr mused much : "What will she do tomorrow ?
When Sol arose in Leo, when day waxed
And slumber waned, the great men of the city
Went to the feast.   That damsel, like a man
Full of resource, began to ply her schemes.
She had the empty palace to herself,
Had lion's heart withal and leopard's claws.
She brought two noble horses from the stalls,
Chose weapons fit for valiant cavaliers
With all that she had need of in dínárs,
In pearls, in rubies, and in every thing.
When all was ready, and the night had come,
The pair resolved to act and started forth
Toward Írán, both full of secret joy,
In quest of safety.   Night and day alike
They hurried onward, neither slept nor ate,
And from the city through the thornbrakes reached
A province civilised.   When steeds and riders
Grew faint with hurrying they sought a place
To halt at, came upon a pleasant village
With gardens, park, and pleasances, and there,
Toil-worn and fleeing from calamity,
Knocked at a gardener's door, who hurried out —
A hospitable man of kindly heart—
And, seeing two with armour, spears, and helms,
Said to the Sháh : "Why is this visitation ?
Whence hast thou sprung at this untimely hour,
Armed for an expedition ? "
                                    Said Shápúr:—
"Good friend ! thou askest much of one astray !
A traveller I, a native of Írán,
And bent on flight.   I am in Cæsar's danger
And in his troops', and never may I see
His head and crown !   If thou wilt be my host
To-night, and play the marchlord's part discreetly,[1]

C. 1441

---

[1] *I.e.* in receiving those who have just crossed the frontier.

Sure am I that one day 'twill profit thee;
The tree that thou shalt plant will bear thee fruit."
      The gardener said : "The house is thine, the gardener
Himself thy guest.   Whate'er I can I will,
Informing none."
                    Then Sháh Shápúr alighted,
He and the damsel, and the gardener's wife
Gat ready food for them as best she could.
When they had eaten bread they turned to wine,
And had a lowly chamber dight.   The gardener
Gave to Shápúr the wine forthwith, and said :—
Drink thou to whom thou wilt."
                              "My host," he answered,
" And gardener eloquent and excellent !
The man that bringeth wine should drink it first,
When first in years and wisdom.   Thou art older
Than I and, since thou furnishest the wine,
Thou shouldst begin."
                    "Great sir !" the gardener said,
" The man of Grace should drink first.   Lead the way
As old in wisdom though more young in years.
I seem to scent a crown upon thy locks ;
Thy visage too is like the sun."
                              Shápúr
Smiled, took the wine, and sighed.   "O pious man !"
He said, "what tidings from Írán hast thou ?"
C. 1442   The gardener said : "O thou of kingly mind !
May foe ne'er harm thee.   May the ills that Cæsar
Hath brought upon the Íránians now befall
Our foemen.   All are scattered in Írán,
And tilth and crop remain not.   Massacre
And pillage have dispersed our mighty folk,
While many have turned Christians and come zoned
Before the bishops, many don priests' caps
That they may have a land and resting-place !"
      The other said : "Where then was Sháh Shápúr,

Who used to shine resplendent as the moon
Upon Urmuzd, that Cæsar thus should dare,
And fortune overcast the Íránians' lustre?"
　　The gardener answered him: "Exalted one!
Be majesty and pleasure ever thine.
No tidings of his whereabouts, alive
Or dead, hath reached the Íránian potentates:
The people of Írán are slaves in Rúm."
　　The gardener, the Sháh's host, wept bitterly,
And added: "Thou shalt stay three days, and then
My house will be the lustre of the world
Because a sage said when the world was young:—
'Unwise is he whose courtesy is scant
To guests; black fortune will ensure him want.'
So tarry, rest, and take a cup of wine,
And when thy heart is merry tell thy name."
　　Shápúr said: "Good! Our host is our Great King,
At present."
　　　　　　　　He abode, ate, and conversed,
That night, and when morn rose above the mountains,
When rose the Golden Banner from the dales,
The master of the garden visited
His guest, and said: "Good day to thee, and may
Thy head be o'er the rain-clouds. This abode
Was not a fitting resting-place for thee,
Nor was the season suited for repose."
　　Shápúr replied: "My friend! I should prefer
This house to crown and throne. And now bring forth
A Zandavasta and thy sacred twigs
That while I mutter I may ask thee questions."[1]
　　He did according to the Sháh's command,
Made the twigs ready and the place of prayer.
Then as he prayed the Sháh said: "Tell me truly
Where the high priest is now."
　　　　　　　　　　　　His host replied:—

---

[1] See Vol. i. p. 80, *s.v. Bài,* and *Barsam.*

"Sweet-tongued and holy man! I can discern
His house from here."

The Sháh said privily:—

"Request some seal-clay of the village-chief."

　　The gardener got it and returned at once.
The world-lord pressed his signet on the clay,
Returned it to the gardener with his thanks,
And said to him: "Give this clay to the high priest,
And mark his words."

That morn the gardener

Went with the impress of the royal signet,
But on arrival found the portal barred,
And armed men stationed round. He clamoured loudly
To be admitted and proceeded straightway
Before the high priest, showed the signature,
And did obeisance. When the high priest looked,
And saw the impress, that wise statist's heart
Began to throb with joy and, weeping greatly
Upon that name, he asked: "What man is this?"

The gardener said: "My lord! the cavalier
Is staying at my house and hath with him
A Moon, slim cypress-like, wise, fair, and graceful."

The high priest said: "Now as to this aspirant,[1]
What is he like in stature and in face?"

The gardener answered: "One that ne'er hath seen
Spring, and a cypress by the water's side,
Would yet at sight of this man's looks and stature
Find music in his heart. His arms are like
A camel's thighs, his chest is like a lion's,
His cheek like blood. Shame reddeneth at his grace,
The crown's decore proceedeth from his face."

[1] Reading with P.

§ 6

How the High Priest and the Captain of the Host, hearing
of Shápúr's Arrival, went to him with the Troops

The wise high priest, while listening to the gardener,
Perceived with his shrewd mind: "This Lion-heart
Can be none other than the Sháh; his mien
Befitteth but the throne!" and seeking out
A wary messenger he sent to tell
The captain of the host: "The Grace of Sháh
Shápúr is manifest. Assemble troops
From every side."
                    The high priest's messenger
Came speeding to the captain of the host,
Who gladdened at the words and then and there
Set both his cheeks upon the ground, and said
To God: "O righteous Judge! I serve Thee only.
Who ever thought that Sháh Shápúr and army
Would see each other more? O one just God,
The Master of the world and Guide to good!
I thank Thee."
                    When night raised its sable flag,   C. 1444
And stars began to twinkle round the moon,
Troops gathered from all quarters, and wherever
Chiefs were they made their way, by ones and twos,
Toward that city and reached joyfully
The hospitable gardener's door. Now when
The troops had gathered, that good man approached
The Sháh who bade that they should be admitted
Although his court was lowly. As they came
They bent their faces to the ground before him.
The Sháh embraced the chieftains and began
To wail his woes, told of his sufferings
Within the ass's skin, of Cæsar's words,

And what that fair Íránian slave had done
For love of him : " I have through her and God
Preserved my life.   May Fortune smile on her.
Grant but a virtuous slave and thou wilt be
The slave of such though king and glorious.
I am the slave of this fond slave whose heart
Is open and who keepeth secrets well.
Wherever I have forces, and my rule
Is recognised, send thither men and give
The tidings.   Scatter scouts upon the roads,
Secure them, and the one to Taisafún
In chief.   The news must not transpire.   If Cæsar
Hear of me that the Grace of king of kings
Appeareth he will come, destroy my host,
And break the Íránians' hearts and backs.   We cannot
Withstand him yet or cope with his lush fortune,
But when the high priest cometh and shall bring
Troops we will bar the road to ants and gnats.
We will be instant then and take new order
To clear our garden quietly of weeds,
To every corner spies shall be dispatched,
And outposts be on guard by day and night.
Thenceforth I give no Rúman liberty
To sleep in peace or lay his armour by."

§ 7

How Shápúr made a Night-attack, and how Cæsar was taken

Shápúr, whose troops were soon six thousand strong,
Sent veteran chiefs to spy out Taisafún,
And notify his high and glorious court
Of Cæsar.   Instantly they went to find
How matters stood, then told the exalted Sháh :—
"No thought hath Cæsar save for wine and chase.
His troops are scattered everywhere to pillage.

C. 1445

There are no guards or sentries day or night,
His troops are like a flock without a shepherd.
He seeth not a foe on any side,
And so it pleaseth him to live at ease."
   Shápúr rejoiced; his troubles turned to wind.
He chose three thousand of the Íránians,
All horsemen mailed on barded chargers, armed
Himself, and marched on Taisafún by night.
He marched by night and turned aside by day.
His route lay over wilderness and mountain
By track or no track, and two leagues and more
Ahead were scouts till Taisafún was nigh.
In the third watch he reached the camp of Cæsar,
Of whom he felt no fear, heard no man's voice,
No sentries' challenge and no tinkling bells.
Tents and pavilions covered all the waste.
Who wotted of that onset? In his tent
Lay Cæsar drunk, his troops were all abroad.
Shápúr, the valiant, gave his royal steed
The rein, on seeing this, led on his powers
Against the camp, and grasped his massive mace.
Rang cloudward clarion, mace, and Indian bell;
Rose battle-cry and tumult everywhere.
Thou wouldst have said: "May be the heaven is rent,
And through the air blood droppeth from the sun!"
Gleamed Káwa's flag, gloomed night, flashed violet
    swords;
Thou wouldst have said: "The air is raining them;
The world is in a mist!" Heaven disappeared
Amid the dust, the stars drew in their skirts,
And brave Shápúr wrecked worthless Cæsar's camp.
They slew twelve thousand Rúman cavaliers
And over, fired the camp, dashed heaven to earth,   C. 1446
And in the end made Cæsar prisoner.
His good stars grew averse. Among the tents
They captured many of his nobles, horsemen

Elect and brave, and put them into bonds.
    Such is the action of the lofty sky
At whiles up-lifting and at whiles low-laying,
At whiles delighting and at whiles affraying!
    The innocent that hath humanity
    Is best; almighty God is his ally.
When it was day, when night withdrew its skirt,
And Sol's flag showed aloft, Shápúr commanded
A scribe to come with writing implements.
They wrote to every province, to each king,
And chief. Shápúr began: "Our heart-felt praise
Be to almighty God who helpeth others
To good but hath no need of others' help.
Since Cæsar hath kept not God's laws, but sown
Naught but the seed of wrong within Írán,
Bonds chafe him sorely, for he had not wisdom
To guide his soul. He hath resigned to us
The crown of kingship and reserveth only
His infamy. His host and court are broken
By God's own might who pointed out the way.
Those Rúmans whom ye capture in your cities
Must have their portion of the scimitar.
Seek ye all justice, do as I command,
And swear allegiance unto me afresh."
    A cameleer came to each quarter quickly,
And brought the letter of the ardent Sháh,
Who left the camp for Taisafún and there
Held session safely with his counsellors,
And, having donned the ancestral crown, gave thanks
To God, the Giver of all good. He bade
A scribe to go inside the prison-house,
And make a list of all the captives' names.
There were a thousand and five score and two
Of Cæsar's kindred and high rank in Rúm.
The world-lord lopped the hands and feet of those
That had been chief in ill, and then commanded

To bring in Cæsar, lord of Rúm.   The guard
Brought him from prison like a man insane.
That tyrant, when he saw Shápúr's crown, wept;
He rubbed his visage red upon the ground,   C. 1447
And swept it with his lashes, grovelling,
And blessing crown and throne.

                    "O thou compact
Of ill," the Sháh said, " Christian and God's foe,
Ascribing unto Him who hath no mate,
No period, and no origin, a son !
Thou art a very knave, a lunatic,
A miscreant, fool, and utterest naught but lies,
Which are an evil, unilluming fire.
Where are thy counsel, modesty, and heart
Inciting thee to good, if thou art Cæsar ?
Why bind me in an ass's hide and so
Fling greatness to the dust ?   I came to feast
In merchant's guise, I came not forth to fight
With drums and troops, but thou didst clothe thy guest
In ass's skin and march against Írán.
Now shalt thou feel the clutch of valiant men,
And seek no more to fight Írán."

                      "O Sháh !"
Said Cæsar, "who can 'scape God's ordinance ?
The royal throne put wisdom far from me,
And made my soul a hireling of the Dív.
Thou wilt be famous, doing good for ill,
Because thy name ne'er will grow old, and thou
Wilt compass all thy longing by thy prowess.
If I have safeguard for my life from thee
Wealth and dínárs are worthless in mine eyes,
Then will I be a slave about thy court,
And seek for nothing but to grace thy throne."
   The Sháh replied: "Vile wretch ! why didst thou
     turn
This country upside down ?   If all the spoil

That thou didst bear to Rúm (ne'er mayst thou look
On that cursed land again!) thou wilt restore
Back from thy house to this exalted folk;
Next, if whate'er was harried in Írán,
And made the lair of lions and of pards,
Thou wilt recover at thine own expense,
And in requital for thine evil deeds;
Next, if for those Íránians whom thou slewest
Thou choosest Rúmans of the royal race,
And givest me ten for every one of ours,
Surrendering their lives as hostages,
And I will take but men of Cæsar's stock
To be with me here in this happy land;
And, next, if for each tree felled in Írán,
(None well-disposed would fell the trees of others)
Thou plant another, reinstate all walls,
And thus abate the anger in our hearts,
Shall I not bind thee as thou bindest me?
Can I forgive thee for the ass's skin?
C. 1448   If thou shalt fail in aught that I have said
My men shall rend thy skin from head to foot."

As soon as he had finished his demands
Shápúr, the world-lord, as the conqueror
Split with his dagger both his prisoner's ears,
And having bored his nostrils put a bit
Therein in memory of the ass's hide,
And loaded both his feet with heavy chains;
The guard moreover bare him back to ward.

They held review and muster, and demanded
The treasury-key. The monarch massed and paid
The host, then, bent on justice and revenge,
Marched from Íran upon the coast of Rúm.
All that were in the desert and that land
They slew and set the houses there on fire,
So that the world was lighted by the blaze.
When news reached Rúm: "Our fertile lands are wasted,

And in a night-attack illustrious Cæsar
Hath been made captive," all the people wept,
And at Shápúr's name were consumed with dread.
" Ungenerous Cæsar wrought this woe," they said.

§ 8

*How Shápúr went to Rúm and fought with Yánus, Cæsar's
Brother*

Though Cæsar's sire was dead, his mother lived;
He had a younger brother too—Yánus—
A generous and potent atheling.
Troops mustered at his gate, his warlike mother
Gave them a donative, and said to him :—
" Avenge thy brother: seest not that a host
Hath come forth from Írán ? "
       He beat the drums,
And carried out the Cross. The Cross was great,
The army fierce. The hosts met face to face;
The warriors had no rest. The ranks were ranged;
A shout went up; Yánus led on the van.
Black dust-clouds rose, and none could see his way
Amid the murk. Upon one flank were mountains,
And on the other, where the troops were massed,
A river ran. The din of battle rose,
Sword, mace, and arrow flashed, while azure-dim
Was air with dust of horsemen, spearheads gleamed,
And banners fluttered while the stars looked down C. 1449
Upon that strife—all wreak and malison.
 The warriors of Rúm all girt their loins,
Like furious lions, for that strife. The air
Was lapis-lazuli, the ground was iron,
Dark dusk rose cloud-ward, and thou wouldst have
  said :—
" The air is all a mist whence diamonds pour."

The Sháh's troops likewise girt their loins for blood-
shed.
Thus blew the blast of battle till the sun
Grew dim.   They slew until earth's surface turned
To iron with the breast-plates of the slain.
Then from the centre Sháh Shápúr advanced
His battle, calling on his left and right,
And on his meiny.   Sháh and chiefs made hot
Their steeds, earth trembled, and the armies reeled.
He charged the Rúman host, and great and small
Were one.   Aware that he could not withstand
The Sháh, Yánus fled with his troops, pursued
By valorous Shápúr, who robbed the air
Of lustre with his dust-clouds.   On all sides
He piled the foe in heaps, smirched earth with brains,
And slew so many of the host of Rúm
That all the plain was heads and feet and trunks.
No host and Cross remained upon the field,
No crucifix and bishop in the holds.
He took such spoil on all sides that the troops
Were in amaze.   He gave it all to them,
Reserving to himself but Cæsar's wealth,
Who had seen travail in amassing it,
And found his travail end not with his treasure !
The host of Rúm, assembling, said of him :—
" Be such chief ours no more !   May Cæsar's name
Cease out of Rúm !   The girdle of the priests,
And their archbishop's crozier are consumed !
So now for us Rúm and Kannúj are one,
Because the call of Christ's Faith is fordone ! "

§ 9

How the Rúmans placed Bazánúsh upon the Throne of Cæsar ;
his Letter to Shápúr and the Answer

There was a man of noble lineage,
And of the famous Cæsars' stock withal,
A man of wisdom, Bazánúsh by name,
Fraught with good counsel both in mind and tongue,
To whom the army said : "Be Cæsar thou,　　　　　C. 1450
This very day the captain of the host ;
The troops will be attentive to thy words :
Illume the crown and renovate the throne."
　　They set for him the throne of ivory
Whereon he sat in all his glory crowned,
While all the Rúmans hailed him as the Cæsar.
He sat and mused on war and battlefield,
And, knowing that to strive in fight against
The exalted Sháh would bring disaster, chose
An envoy shrewd and modest who could speak
Wise words with gentleness—a scribe expert,
Experienced, learned, wise, and well approved—
Set him hard by, dictated subtle words,
And wrote a letter full of benisons
From God almighty on the king of earth :—
" Be thy crown ever bright and all the great
Thy slaves.　Thou know'st that pillaging and bloodshed,
And harrying the innocent, are hateful
To noble men both in Írán and Rúm.
If this feud first began about Íraj
'Twas settled by the might of Minúchihr.
Now Salm is dust, and Túr is swept away,
In vengeance.　If Sikandar and Dárá
Embroil us now that feud is obsolete
In Rúm ; the one good fortune left, the other

Was slain by his two ministers, while Cæsar,
If he be cause, is galled within thy prison
By fetters. Rúm must not be desolate,
For never there hath been a land like Rúm.
Now, if thy purpose is to waste and slay,
The Rúmans cannot either fight or flee.
Their wives and children are thy prisoners,
Or wounded by thy swords and shafts. 'Tis time
To minish wrath and vengeance; wrath and Faith
Ne'er fare together. Be our ransom then
All our possessions, for this feud is wasting
Our lives. Be kind, burn not so many cities.
Such days must cease. The Maker of the world
Will not approve a world-lord set on wrong,
And vengeance. May He bless the Sháh, and may
The Sháh's exalted star encrown the moon."

The scribe laid down his pen when he had written
That royal letter whereunto they set
The seal of Cæsar, and the ambassador
C. 1451 Set forward to the Sháh. The wise man came,
And tendered Cæsar's letter to Shápúr
Of glorious race, who, when they read to him
The letter, showering on him those fair words,
Was gracious, wept, and bent his warrior-brows.
He wrote at once an answer and detailed
All that had happened both for good and ill;
He said: "Who sewed his guest in ass's hide?
Who lighted up the mart of ancient feuds?
If thou art wise arise and come to me,
Thou and thy honest counsellors, for I
Have granted quarter and I will not fight.
The world is never straitened to the wise."

The messenger returned with this reply,
And word for word discharged his embassy.

§ 10

How Bazánúsh went to Shápúr and made a Treaty of Peace

When Bazánúsh saw that reply the heart
In his pure body throbbed with joy.   He bade
A hundred nobles quit fair Rúm with him.
They made up sixty asses' loads of drachms,
Of gems, and full-dress robes, and thirty thousand
Dínárs for largess gàthered from all sides.
　　They went before the Sháh with naked feet
And heads all bare, and, as they poured dínárs,
Bestrewed the gold with gems.   Shápúr received
The Rúmans graciously and seated them
In due degree.   He said to Bazánúsh :—
"From Rúm no lack of curst and unjust men
Hath đome.   Where there were cities in Írán
Now there are thorn-brakes.   I demand redress
For what hath been laid waste and made the lair
Of pard and lion."
　　　　　　　　Bazánúsh replied :—
"Say what thou wilt and since thou gav'st us quarter
Frown not upon us."
　　　　　　　　Said the noble Sháh :—
"If thou wouldst have full pardon for the wrong
Thou must pay tribute in dínárs of Rúm—
Two hundred thousand thrice in every year,
And further give up Nasíbín to me,
If thou wouldst end my vengeance."
　　　　　　　　　　　　Bazánúsh
Replied : "Írán, Arabia, Nasíbín
Are thine, and I agree to this vast tribute,
For we can not withstand thy wrath and vengeance."
　　Shápúr agreed by treaty not to march
On Rúm thenceforth, excepting by permission

In friendly wise, that Rúm might not be injured.
Then he dismissed those magnates graciously
And honourably, on their departure marched,
And thanked his Maker much.   He sought Istakhr—
The world-famed glory of the land of Párs—
Rejoicing.
　　　　　　When the news of these events
Reached Nasíbín the people rushed to arms,
Exclaiming: "We will not let Sháh Shápúr
Take Nasíbín or bring an army hither
Because he is not Christian but observeth
The Zandavasta and the cult of Fire.
He will not hear us when he cometh hither,
And we will not accept the Zandavasta,
And ancient Faith."
　　　　　　　　The populace prevailed,
The Faithful mounted for the war.   When tidings
Reached Sháh Shápúr that Nasíbín rebelled
He was enraged against the Christian Faith,
And set a countless host upon the march.
He said: "Applaud I cannot an evangel
Whose author suffered death among the Jews."

For one whole week they fought; the city's gate
Grew all too narrow for the combatants;
The Íránians slew a multitude of chiefs,
And placed those that survived in heavy bonds.
The citizens wrote to the Sháh for quarter,
Who pardoned them and bade his host withdraw.

He gained renown in all parts of the earth,
He gained supremacy o'er all the world.
Men used to call him "The victorious Sháh,"
And long did he possess the throne and crown.
She who had freed and given him his greatness,
Whom he named Diláfrúz-i-Farrukhpái, [1]
Was dearer to him than all other fair.

　　　　[1] *I.e.* The lucky-footed lustre of the heart.

Moreover on the gardener he bestowed
Great treasure and dismissed him well provided;
But Cæsar stayed in prison and in bond,
In abject, evil case, and lasso-bound,
While all the treasure that he had in Rúm,
And toiled to gather in from every side,
He had conveyed and given to Shápúr.
He lived awhile with sighs upon his lips,
Within his prison-house, and there he died,
And let another have the crown of might.
Then Sháh Shápúr dispatched the corpse to Rúm,
Encrowned with musk upon a bier, and said :—
" This is our end but where we shall find rest
I know not.   One is covetous and foolish,
Another wise and dowered with Grace, but life
Will pass with both.   The good and abstinent   C. 1453
Alone are blest."
                          He mounted on the throne
Of kings and ruled the world awhile.   Thereafter
He settled many folk for good or ill
Within the land of Khúzistán and built
A city for his prisoners : folk at large
Shared not therein.[1]   'Twas called Khurram Ábád,[2]
But who were they who shared that pleasant place ?
The men whose hands Shápúr had stricken off
Had this assigned to them as their abode;
They had it all, and every year a robe
Of honour.   He erected too in Shám
A city which he called Pírúz Shápúr,[3]
And in Ahwáz a third with palaces
And hospitals, Kinám-i-Asírán [4]
They called it; prisoners there had rest and ease.
He reigned until he passed his fiftieth year
Of sovereignty; the age had not his peer.

[1] Reading with P.   [2] Pleasant Abode.
[3] Victorious Shápúr.   [4] The Prisoners' Nest.

§ 11

How Máni, the Painter, came to Shápúr with Pretence of
being a Prophet, and was slain

There came from Chín a man of eloquence,
Whose peer in painting earth will not behold,
By which accomplishment he gained his ends.
He was a man of might by name Máni.
He said : "I prove my mission by my painting,
And am the greatest of evangelists."
    He came from Chín, asked audience of Shápúr,
Soliciting his help in that evangel,
And speaking with such unction that the Sháh,
Filled with misgivings and keen interest,
Convoked the archmages and held talk at large
About Máni : "This suasive man of Chín
Hath plunged me into doubts about his Faith :
Hold converse with him ; ye may be converted."
    They said : "This man—a worshipper of pictures—
Is not the equal of our own high priest ;
Hear what Máni saith and then call for him :
Máni will be dumfoundered in his presence." [1]
    The Sháh bade that Máni should come who spake
At large, discoursing with the archimages,
In presence of the Sháh, of Light and Darkness [2]
Until Máni was checked in full career
By what the high priest said to him concerning
The ancient Faith : "Thou worshipper of pictures !
Why layest thou thy daring hand on God—
The Being that created Heaven above,
Created space and time, with light and darkness,
Therein, and is supreme of principles ?
The nights and days of high, revolving heaven

C. 1454

―――――――――

[1] Reading with P.   [2] Lit. of white and black.

Are both thy source of safety and mishap.
How canst thou take a picture for a proof,
And disregard the counsel of the Faithful,
Who say that holy God is One, and thou
Hast no alternative to serving Him?
If thou wilt give these pictures motion, then
Thou mayst appeal thereto. Thy proof, thou knowest
Is naught, and no one will esteem it valid.
Were Áhriman God's equal, darksome night
Would be like shining day, and both would be
Of equal length throughout the year, and neither
Would in their revolutions wax or wane.
The Maker of the world is compassed not
By thought, for He is higher than thought and space.
Thy words are those of lunatics. Enough!
No one will side with thee."

                    He spake much else,
For he was one of knowledge and of courage.
Mání was all confounded by the words,
His favour changed, the king was wroth with him,
So that his days were straitened, bidding some
To drag him from the court disgraced, and said:—
"This worshipper of pictures is unfit
To live, so since he causeth turmoil here
Flay him from head to foot, and let his skin
Be stuffed with hay, and then, that no one else
May make pretences to like dignity,
Hang up the skin upon the city-gate,
Or on the wall outside the hospital."
  So did they. All the people blessed the Sháh,
And cast dust on the body of the slain.
  The fortune of Shápúr was such that men
Saw in his garth no thorn upon the rose.
He was so just, so wise, and politic,
Brave, bounteous, active, that not anywhere
Was left a foe, or evil e'en a lair.

§ 12

*How Shápúr made his Brother Ardshír Regent till his own
Son should grow up, and how his Days ended*

C. 1455 When he had naught to hope for from high heaven,
For he had passed his three score years and ten,
He called a scribe, the high priest, and Ardshír,
His younger brother, youthful still and crowned
With justice and with wisdom.   Now the Sháh
Had but one son—an infant—named Shápúr,
Not yet matured by fortune, so the king,
In presence of the magnates and the scribes,
Said to Ardshír: " If thou wilt make a pact
With me in all good faith, and pledge thyself
To keep it, that what time my son shall come
To man's estate, and when the breath of greatness
Shall breathe on him, thou wilt resign to him
The treasure and the throne and crown, and be
His loyal minister, I will commit
To thee this crown of kingship and transfer
Withal to thee the treasure and the host."
    Ardshír agreed before the great and wise
To give up to the child when grown to manhood,
And fit for diadem and throne of might,
The kingship and intreat him lovingly.
Whereat Shápúr, in presence of the lords,
Gave the world's crown and signet to Ardshír,
Then said : " Take seriously the world's affairs.
Know, O my brother ! that an unjust king
Regardeth not the interests of the realm,
But yearneth to fill up his treasuries,
Exceeding all his officers in greed.
Blest is the upright king that serveth God
Because in him his subjects' hearts delight ;
He groweth rich by equity and bounty,

He leadeth every one toward the Faith,
He guardeth all his kingdom from the foe,
He lifteth to the clouds his head and crown,
He gathereth wealth by justice and in peace,
Disperseth trouble from the heart by largess,
He passeth o'er the offences of ill-doers,
And ever practiseth humanity.
He that hath sought these virtues will attain
To wisdom and right rede and watchfulness.
Kings must be wise and teach both young and old,
For subjects not instructed in God's way
Will err, and if the king is wroth with such
He violateth justice and the Faith.
Man's heart and brain are joint kings of his body,
The other members are the soldiery.
When, then, the heart and brain have been defiled,
And lost to good advice in their despair,
The life within that body is distraught;
Will troops left chiefless live on happily?
Left in the dark they are dispersed and cast,
A corpse, to dust. So with an unjust king:
The world [1] is turned by him all upside down.
He will be held accursed when he is dead,
And men will know him as ' The impious Sháh.'
Keep both thine eye and body in the Faith,
For eye and body both belong to God.
The king who chooseth any other way
Should wash both heart and hands of this our world.
He scattereth his subjects from his realm,
His lieges from his gate, ignoring all
The sage's words which cleanse thy heart of guile.
The tyrant is accursed: haunt not the portal
Of men intent on greed. Know, O my brother!
That from a king the sage expecteth much—
First, that he be victorious, not turning

C. 1456

---

[1] Reading with P.

From foes in fight; again, that he entreat
His troops with equity and recognise
The greatness of the high-born: whosoever
Is fitted for the kingship will not put
The men of rank into the ranks; [1] next, thirdly,
That he be upright and defeat not justice;
And fourthly, that to those who are his subjects,
And to the old retainers of his court,
He keep not tightly barred his treasury's door,
But from his branches drop a shower of fruit.
The king's gate should be not without a host,
And he should keep his treasure for his troops.
Thou wilt rejoice in treasuries increased
By justice, and thy troops will joy in thee.
Look on thy mail as thy true ornament;
Some night it may bestead thee well.   Trust not
Thy guards too much; direct thine own concerns
As thou wouldst be secure though, whether thou
Shalt prove obscure or thy own age's lustre,
Death past all doubt will come to thee at last."
       The brother, hearing this, wept sore.   Shápúr
Wrote his last wishes out, lived on one year,
Then passed, and left this saying in men's minds:—
"Sow not within the world the seed of greed
Because thy days will pass, and foes enjoy
The product of thy toils.   Whene'er the laws
Both of Urmuzd and of Bahman [2] are kept
This palace will become a happy home."
C. 1457   Bring tulip-tinted wine, O Háshimí! [3]
From jars that never need replenishing.
       Why seek I, who am deaf at sixty-three,
The world's grace and observance ?   Now I sing
(Mark thou) the story of Ardshír, the king.

[1] Reading with P.
[2] *Cf.* Vol. iii. p. 327.
[3] *I.e.* O descendant of Muhammad's great-grandfather (Háshim)!

XXXI

ARDSHÍR, BROTHER OF SHÁPÚR

HE REIGNED TEN YEARS

NOTE

The reign of Shápúr, son of Urmuzd, was preceded, as we have
seen, by those of six Sháhs, none of whom left any mark on
Íránian legend, and it was followed by those of three others no
less insignificant. Some of the six preceding Sháhs had been
men of importance historically, but even this cannot be said of
Ardshír (Artaxerxes II., A.D. 379–383) and his two successors.

Ardshír must have been either an elder brother of Shápúr or
else, like him, a posthumous child. At any rate he must have
been seventy years old or more at the time of his accession.
Shápúr is represented elsewhere in the Sháhnáma as brotherless,[1]
but historically this was not the case.[2]

Ardshír is credited by most authorities with a reign of four
years only. Tabarí says that he was deposed by his subjects.[3]

§ I

How Ardshír sat upon the Throne and gave a Charge to the Officers

Whenas Ardshír sat in the royal seat,
And graced the throne of old Shápúr, he girt
His loins and called the Íránians, seating them
Beneath the golden throne, and thus he said:—
" I would not that the process of high heaven
Should injure any. All the world shall be

---

[1] See p. 319.   [2] See p. 318.   [3] NT, p. 70.

Within my peace if it obey my will;
But if this giddy world prove recusant
We will take order for it.   Now my brother
Left me the world in trust because his son
Is but a child.   Our blessings on his soul,
For he hath purged the earth of wicked men.
Whenas Shápúr, son of Shápúr, shall reach
To man's estate, and knoweth how to prize
The crown and throne, I will resign to him
Them and the host according to my pledge
To Sháh Shápúr.   I only hold the throne
As viceroy and in memory of his sire.
Know this: what we enjoy will pass away;
At death our travail will be turned to wind."
    Through his ten years of rule he took his fill
Of joy and lavished bounty as he would.
He asked from no man tribute, toll, or tax,
But made the crown and throne a charge to none;
Men therefore called him " The Beneficent,"
For all felt safe with him.
                                    Now when Shápúr
Was fit for crown and throne Ardshír resigned
The glorious crown, made good what he had spoken
And, like a man, maintained his pledge unbroken.

XXXII

SHÁPÚR, SON OF SHÁPÚR

HE REIGNED FIVE YEARS AND FOUR MONTHS

NOTE

According to Tabarí, the death of this Sháh (Sapor III., A.D. 383–388) was not due to the accidental fall of a tent-pole; the tent-ropes were cut, and the tent fell and killed him.[1]

§ 1

How Shápúr, Son of Shápúr, sat upon the Throne and gave a Charge to the Officers

Whenas Shápúr sat in his uncle's place   C. 1458
Most joyed but some were sorry in Irán.
He thus harangued the noble men of lore,
And veteran, adviceful archimages :—
" Know that henceforth we favour not the liar,
For lying is not policy and that
Ensureth greatness.   Treat not nidderings
As friends and sow not weeds within the garden.
The man of brains should make a mock of none.
Tongues should be guarded, not imbued with bane,
For he that speaketh much in the assembly
Will minish his repute, but when a sage
Discourseth, hear, for learning ageth not.
The covetous have aching hearts, do thou

---

[1] NT, p. 71.
365

Abstain from greed and make not friends with liars,
Or men of evil rede.   Four qualities
Are needful in a man: first, being modest,
Just, and accomplished; secondly, sincere
And single-hearted; thirdly, moderate
And welcoming whatever fortune bringeth ;
And, fourthly, never speaking foolishly,
But using fools for profit not for sport.
The hearts of noble men obtain both worlds,
But justice pleaseth not the hearts of churls,
Who in this world possess an evil name,
And in the other win not Paradise.
The vain withal hath but a brief career
Because he dissipateth wealth in folly,
While he is lauded that doth choose the mean;
He showereth benedictions on himself.[1]
God aid you, be your fortune ever bright,
And may He help us, for the throne of greatness
Abideth not with any."
                              Thus he said.
The nobles rose and blessed him.

C. 1459   When five years
And four months had passed by, the Sháh one day
Went out to hunt, the world was full of cheetahs,
Of hawks, and hounds, these flying and those coursing.
A tent was pitched to make a resting-place
Where when the Sháh had eaten he reposed ;
He drank three goblets full of royal wine,
And, musing, drowsed.   His comrades all dispersed
While he reclined.   He slept.   Then from the waste
A tempest rose, so great that none recalled
The like, and brought the wood-work of the tent
Down on the Sháh's head !   He that had aspired
To win the world—the valorous Shápúr—
Died and resigned the royal crown to others.

[1] Couplets transposed.

This whirling world is evermore the same,
   And constant only to the knavish one,
Who in his jugglery is void of shame
   To filch from any or to foist upon.
Act, then, enjoy, disport, but fret thee not.
   Why grasp at vengeance, toy with treasury?
Within this gloomy orb accept thy lot,
   Seek honour, and let this world's secret be.
Discovery will make thee writhe with pain;
Then pry not, let its mystery remain.

XXXIII

BAHRÁM, SON OF SHÁPÚR

HE REIGNED FOURTEEN YEARS

NOTE

The Oriental title of this Sháh (Varahran IV., A.D. 388–399) renders it doubtful whether he was the son of the second or third Shápúr, and the authorities differ on the point. He is supposed generally to have reigned eleven years. He was the ruler of Kirmán at the time of his accession, and to him rightly belongs the title of Kirmánsháh which Firdausí gives to Bahrám Bahrámiyán.[1] A seal of his, so describing him ("Varahran Kerman Malka") is extant.[2] Tabarí says that he built a city in Kirmán, perhaps the existent Kirmánsháhán south-east of Yazd,[3] and that he was killed by an arrow shot at him by assassins.[4]

§ I

*How Bahrám sat upon the Throne and gave a Charge
to the Officers*

Wise, prudent Sháh Bahrám mourned for his sire
Some months. When seated on the place of power
He spake thus from the imperial throne: " This know:
The kings that justly gather freely spend.
May holy God be gracious unto us,
And may the foemen's hearts be filled with smoke.
His is all knowledge, and we are His slaves
For weal or woe. He is supremely just;

[1] See p. 313.　[2] See RSM, p. 265.　[3] NT, p. 71, and *note*.　[4] *Id.* p. 72.

His kingdom knoweth neither gain nor loss.
One that is rich in generosity,
Discreet, intelligent, and vigilant,
Should lock not fast his treasures, least of all
If he is lord of throne and diadem,
And if a wealth of words be thine to give,
Be lavish, knowledge faileth not.   Incline
To God in good and ill as thou wilt have
Thy good endure.   If thou acknowledgest   C. 1460
That all thy good and evil are from Him
Thy guerdon will be jocund Paradise;
But if thou choosest this world's vanities
Thou wilt remain unransomed in their clutch.
If God shall cease to keep thee 'neath His hand
Thou wilt abide in endless woe.   I trust
To holy God that, when I lay my head
Within this darksome dust, He may account me
A conquering king, a Lustre of the world.
Is it not better then to lavish justice
Than to get wealth unjustly, for our labours
Endure here but our wealth will be past doubt
Our foe's.   We leave our memory good or bad;
Forbear thine utmost to sow seed of ill."
    When this Sháh's reign had come to twice seven years
The graceful Cypress of the Orchard slept;
The Sháh was sick awhile, his subjects grieved.
He had a daughter, but no son, and likewise
A younger brother unto whom he gave
Perforce the host and treasure, crown and throne,
And royal signet, then, when he had ruled
For twice seven years, this youthful world-lord died.

    Old man, whose years amount to sixty-three!
        Shall wine be still the burden of thy lay?
    Without a warning life may end with thee;
        Think of repentance then, seek wisdom's way.

May God approve this slave.   May he attain
In wisdom riches and in singing gain ;

For mid his song he plucketh at his hair,
  Yea teareth it in his obscure estate.
No wonder, if a work—his manhood's care—
  Completed in old age, he dedicate
To him who hath the sword—the king of kings,
A whole head higher than his underlings.

May his throne's seat serve Luna for a crown,
  The age be wholly subject to his sway,
For his is might and with him is renown.
  Oh ! may the crown rejoice in him, and may
He walk in knowledge and in majesty,
From all his foemen's clutches ever free !

XXXIV

YAZDAGIRD, SON OF SHÁPÚR

HE REIGNED THIRTY YEARS

ARGUMENT

Yazdagird succeeds his brother as Sháh and rules wickedly. His son Bahrám is born and brought up by the Arabs, to whom he returns after a visit to, and imprisonment by, his father. Yazdagird is warned of his death by the astrologers and tries to evade his fate, but is killed by a mysterious horse. The Íránians, resolved that none of his family shall succeed him, elect Khusrau. Bahrám, supported by the Arabs, claims the throne, proves his right to it by ordeal, and becomes Sháh.

NOTE

The authorities are divided on the question whether Yazdagird (Isdigerd I., A.D. 399–420) was a son of Bahrám, the previous Sháh, or of Shápúr. Tabarí takes the former view,[1] Mas'údí the latter,[2] which leaves it still uncertain as to which Shápúr—Shápúr, son of Urmuzd, or Shápúr, son of Shápúr—was intended.

Like Akhnaton of Egypt Yazdagird seems to have been a man of remarkable character. He sought peace and ensued it, he attempted to win over furiously raging fanatics to the principles of religious toleration, failed in the attempt, tried to prevent persecutors from persecuting—an act which in those days was regarded as a kind of persecution in itself—assumed the title of "The Most Peaceful" on his coins, and acted up to it in his political relations with foreign states even when most tempting opportunities for aggrandisement presented themselves, was honoured, at least in legend, by being appointed formally by will the guardian of the son of an Eastern Roman Emperor—an office

---

[1] NT, p. 72.   [2] MM, ii. 190.

which he is said to have accepted and faithfully executed—died a mysterious death, and received from his subjects the titles of " The Sinner " and " The Harsh." The indictment of him in Tabarí is very severe. Among his other enormities it is recorded that if any one dared to address him on behalf of another he said immediately : " How much does he pay you, for whom you ask me, or what have you received already ? " on which Professor Nöldeke observes that he knew his Persians. Apparently he did, and the native chroniclers, drawn for the most part from a class that could not understand or appreciate him, have covered his memory with infamy. Against them may be placed a contemporary testimony from another source :—" The good and merciful king Yazdagird, the Christian, the blest among kings, whose memory may be a blessing and his future life still more beautiful than his former ; every day he did good to the poor and wretched." [1] This perhaps was written after he had begun to punish the Magi for interfering with the Christians, and before Abdaas, bishop of Ctesiphon, had burnt down, and refused to reinstate, the great Fire-temple of that city [2]—acts that forced Yazdagird's hand and compelled him to allow the Magi to retaliate, which they did in drastic fashion.

§§ 2–5. This account agrees closely with that given in Tabarí, [3] but scarcely can be regarded as historical, being, as Professor Nöldeke says of the latter, too poetically finished. [4]

§ 2. Surúsh is the name of the messenger of Urmuzd, but is used here as a rhyme-word. Hushyár, the name of the other astrologer, means " wise." In Tabarí the astrologers advise the Sháh that Bahrám should be brought up in a foreign land. [5]

Nu'mán was prince of Híra during the reign of Yazdagird and was succeeded by his son Munzir. Firdausí reverses the relationship, Munzir being the more prominent historically of the two. The poet makes him monarch of Yaman. [6]

§ 6. It is highly probable that such a youth as Bahrám did not get on well with his father, and he may have been sent to Híra for a while in semi-disgrace.

The name of the Roman ambassador that pleaded for him—Tainúsh—is a form of Theodosius, the reigning Eastern Roman Emperor at the time—Yazdagird's ward according to the legend. [7]

§ 7. We have here one of the legends localized in Firdausí's own neighbourhood, Sav being the spring of Tús—the poet's birth-place. Similar instances of such localization have occurred

---

[1] NT, p. 74, and *notes*.   [2] RSM, p. 275.   [3] NT, p. 85 *seq.*   [4] *Id.*, *note.*
[5] *Id.* p. 86.   [6] *Id.*, *note*, and *cf.* p. 387.   [7] See p. 371.

already.[1] Tabarí, however, says that Yazdagird's death is supposed to have taken place in Gurgán (Hyrcania or Mázandarán), and omits the details about the presage of the astrologers and the expedition to the spring of Sav. According to Tabarí the horse was sent in answer to the prayers of Yazdagird's oppressed subjects. Professor Nöldeke thinks that conspirators took advantage of the absence of the Sháh in distant Hyrcania to murder him and then, to cover themselves, spread abroad a fiction to account for his end, and that the various stories of the death of this Sháh may be referred to a common origin—the version of the Bástán-náma made by Ibn Mukaffa.[2]

§§ 8-13. This account agrees closely with that of Tabarí.[3] Historically it would appear that Yazdagird, at the time of his death, had another son living—Shápúr—whom he had made king of Armenia some years previously. Shápúr, hearing that his father was in ill-health, returned to court and after Yazdagird's death attempted to seize the throne, but there was another candidate for it whom the nobles preferred, and Shápúr was assassinated. On some of Yazdagird's coins a second name appears, which may be read either as Ardshír or Bahrám.[4] There seems no doubt that Yazdagird had made himself so unpopular with the Persian nobility and clergy that they were anxious that no son of his should succeed him. Bahrám, moreover, was considered probably to be too much under Arab influence as Tabarí expressly states.

§ 10. As soon as Jawánwí sees Bahrám he is conscious that he is in the presence of the rightful Sháh, on whom the divine Grace of kingship already had descended.[5]

§ 12. The selection of a successor to Yazdagird by a process of elimination is not in Tabarí.

We had instances of the mutilation of prisoners in the reign of Shápúr, son of Urmuzd.[6] It is said too that Alexander the Great, on approaching Persepolis, was met by a band of about 4000 Greek captives whom the Persians had maltreated grievously.[7]

§ 13. Bahrám is said to have been twenty years old at the time of his accession.[8] It was followed by a great persecution of the Christians and war with Rome. He had to put himself right with the Magi and also to find employment for his turbulent chiefs wearied of the political self-restraint of Yazdagird, The Most Peaceful.

---

[1] Vols. i. pp. 235, 296; iii. 14; iv. 295; v. 202.

[2] See p. 16, and NT, 77, and *note*.   [3] *Id.* 91 *seq.*   [4] RSM, 277 *seq.*

[5] *Cf.* too pp. 221, 251, 406.   [6] See pp. 323, 334, 348, 357.

[7] HQC, v. 5.   [8] NT, p. 98.

§ 1

How Yazdagird sat upon the Throne and gave a Charge to the Officers

When Yazdagird became the world's great king
He gathered all the soldiers of the realm,
Assumed the crown which once his brother wore,
At whose sad death he joyed, and thus harangued

C. 1461   The notables: "All ye disposed to justice!
Make first your benisons to God, your hearts
All jubilant and laughing through our justice.
I will let not the wicked live who strive
To compass evil. He that cometh to us
For justice shall have rest from fraud and falsehood,
I will increase his state and banish greed
And vengeance from the heart. We will consult
None but the great men and the archimages,
Wise and shrewd-hearted; but the vicious man,
Intoxicate with power, tyrannizing
The helpless, and elated with conceit
Of his own wealth, will we withstand and quell,
But multiply our favours to the poor.
The neck of him that heedeth not our wrath,
And fareth insolently in our eyes,
Is longing for an Indian sword, his body
To pillow in the dust. Scan well our bidding,
And, thus endeavouring, make your breast-plate
    wisdom."

    Thereat the men of mace and scimitar
All shook like willow-trees.

               Now when his power
Waxed strong his love waned as his greatness grew;
He scorned the sages and grew negligent
Of royal usages. The governors,

The paladins, the notables, and all
The learned and noble sages, were as wind
To him; his dark soul had grown tyrannous;
Both love and justice ceased within his heart;
He answered no petitions; he misprized
All men alike and paused not on their faults.
All that were at his gate as ministers—
The Lustre of his fortune and his crown—
Agreed to speak not of the land to him,
And all men writhed with fear and died of fright
Because of him. When envoys came, or subjects
That clamoured for redress, a minister,
When notified, would learn their business,
And then with warm and kindly words dismiss
The envoys shamefastly, and say: "The Sháh
Will not transact affairs; ye cannot see him.
I have acquainted him with all your case,
But in his judgments right hath little place!"

§ 2

*How Bahrám Gúr, Son of Yazdagird, was born and sent
to be brought up by Munzir, the Arab*

When of his reign seven years had passed, and all
The archmages were in travail and dismay,
In Farwardín, when the eighth year began,
And showed the world the sun which they adored,
Upon Urmuzd's day there was born a child
With good stars and earth-brightening presages.
His sire forthwith gave him the name Bahrám,
Rejoicing in that little one. At court
There were astrologers, for it is well
To hearken to their words. One was a noble
With Grace and sense, an Indian chieftain named
Surúsh, another hight Hushyár, a Persian,

C. 1462

Who by his arts could curb the sky itself.
These prudent seekers of the Way appeared
Before the Sháh at his command. They used
Their astrolabes to take the stars and sought
To read the future with their Rúman tablets.
The stars ordained : " The child will be a king,
Lord of the seven climes, glad-hearted, holy."
      They went before the Sháh forthwith and took
Their astrolabes and tablets. Thus they said :—
" We have collected knowledge of all kinds,
And learned that heaven will love this goodly child.
The seven climes will be his realm, and he
Will be a mighty Sháh and worshipful."
      As soon as they had left the court, the chiefs,
And ministers, the holy archimages,
Sat and consulted o'er some shift whereby
The babe might favour not his sire but be
A righteous sovereign, "for if he hath
His father's temper he will wreck the realm,
The archimages and the paladins
Will not rejoice, and he will be not glad,
And bright of soul."
                        Then all the archimages
Approached the Sháh with open, loyal hearts,
And said : " This sprightly babe is far beyond
Reproach and calumny. Now all the world
Is under thy command ; the toil and service
Of every clime are thine. Look for some place
Where knowledge is, and its possessors make
C. 1463   Their land rejoice, and choose among the great
Some statist who is lauded in that land,
And let this virtuous prince learn worth from him,
So that the world may joy in his behests."
      The Sháh, on hearing this, assembled all
The envoys of his realm and sent them forth
To Rúm, to Hind, to Chín, and other lands

Inhabited. A chief, too, went among
The Arabs to discern if they would prove
A gain or loss. To every quarter fared
A crier seeking one to educate
Bahrám, some man of eloquence and learning,
Accomplishment and knowledge; so there came
From every clime an archmage wise, advised,
And fortunate, and, as they reached the court,
Each sought for that appointment from the Sháh,
Who, after welcoming them graciously,
Assigned to each a lodging in the city.
Thus on a night Nu'mán came with Munzir,
And likewise many famous Arab spearmen.
　　When all these chiefs had gathered thus in Párs
They came to Yazdagird, the king, and said :—
" We are thy slaves to hear and answer thee.
Who of these nobles is so fortunate
As to embrace the world-lord's precious child,
To be his teacher, and to cause the light
To shine upon the darkness of his heart ?
We out of Rúm and Hindústán and Párs,
Geometricians and astrologers,
Philosophers and men exceeding wise,
Men of affairs and rhetoricians,
Are all of us the dust upon thy feet,
And all thy guides to knowledge. See thou then
Which one among us is approved by thee,
And which of us will profit thee the most."
　　Then spake Munzir on this wise : " We are slaves
Who only live in this world for the Sháh.
He knoweth all the worth of us, for he
Is as the shepherd, we are as the flock.
Bold, riders we, adept in horsemanship,
More than a match for sages. We possess
No readers of the stars in figures versed,
But we have minds devoted to the realm,

And in this matter we are strong, O Sháh!
Moreover we are slaves before thy son,
And sing the praises of his majesty."
　　When Yazdagird had heard he summoned up
His spirits and his wisdom, and, perceiving
From such an outset what would be the outcome,
Consigned Bahrám, the precious, to Munzir,
For whom, for so the Sháh bade, they prepared
A robe of honour and exalted sky-ward

C. 1464 His head.　They robed his person and then called
The charger of the monarch of Yaman.
Then plain-ward from the hall of Yazdagird
Went camels, horses, litters, slaves, and nurses,
Past count, and stretched from palace to bázár.
The road through the bázárs were draped with hangings,
And all was decked from city-gate to court.
　　Now when Munzir approached Yaman the men
And women all went out to welcome him.
Or ever he reached home he 'gan to seek
For many women of illustrious birth,
And made his choice among the landed folk
Of Persian race, among the Arabians,
Among the wealthy, great, and eminent,
And chose four ladies—two of Arab stock
And two of royal Persian—whose high strain
Was manifest in their accomplishment,
To serve as nurses.[1]　Thus they tended him
Four years.　When he had had his fill of suckling,
And grew apace, they weaned him, which was hard
To do, and reared him delicately.　At seven
What said he to Munzir in princely fashion?
"Great chief! make me not out a babe unweaned!
Entrust me unto tutors that are learned,
My time is being wasted; scorn me not."
　　Munzir replied: "Not yet, O prince! hast thou

---

[1] Reading with P.

A need for knowledge. When that time shall come,
And thou hast grown solicitous to learn,
I will not leave thee playing in the house:
But playing is the thing to make thee grow."
 Bahrám rejoined: "Make me not out to be
An idle child for, though my years are few,
And though my neck and chest are not yet those
Of warriors, I have wisdom. As for thee,
Thou hast small wisdom though thou hast the years.
I am not as thou deemest. Know'st thou not
That one in quest of opportunities
Will start with matters that concern him most?
To seek twice is to sacrifice one's prospects.
What is ill-timed is fruitless. Of man's body
The head is chief, and thou shouldst have me taught
What the great king should know. The first thing needful
Is knowledge since it is the head of right,
And blest is he that from the first ensueth
His próper end."
      Munzir scanned him with wonder,
Invoking God beneath his breath, and sent
Upon a dromedary to Shúrsán
A chief forthwith who found three archimages,
Accomplished men and well reputed there.
One was to teach the young prince penmanship,   C. 1465
And lighten the dark places in his heart;
The second to instruct him in the use
Of hawk and cheetah for his recreation,
As well as polo, archery, swordmanship
Against the foeman, how to rein his steed,
And to exalt himself among the brave;
The third to inculcate the arts of kingship,
The style and business of administration,
And everything that he should bear in mind.[1]

---

[1] "As well as . . . . . in mind," following the readings and
arrangement of P.

When these archmages came before Munzir
They held much talk with him, and in their charge
He placed the prince, because Munzir himself
Was both a scholar and a warrior.
Bahrám, that seed of kings, grew so adept
That he was competent to play the man,
And when he heard of new accomplishments
He longed to learn them. When he was eighteen
The valiant warrior was like the sun;
He needed not archmages to instruct him
In erudition, how to play at polo,
In manage of the cheetah and the hawk,
To wheel a steed upon the battlefield,
And charge. Thus said he to Munzir: "O man
Of honest rede! send these professors home."
    Thereat Munzir bestowed great gifts upon them,
And they returned rejoicing. Then the prince
Said to Munzir: "Call for the spearmen's steeds,
And bid the cavaliers to wheel before me,
To couch their lances, and then name the price
Of what I fancy; I will better it."
    Munzir said: "O accomplished atheling!
The keeper of my steeds is thine to bid,
The master of the horse is all thine own;
Why should I toil and trouble for such things
If thou art forced to purchase Arab steeds?"
    Bahrám replied: "O famous one! may all
Thy years be satisfied with good. I want
A steed that I may spur adown the height,
And never draw the bridle in alarm,
Then, having rendered him so sure of foot,
Cause him to vie with winds upon the course,
Because one should not press a beast untried."
    Munzir then bade Nu'mán: "Go thou and choose
A drove of our own valiant herdsmen's horses;
Go round the desert of the spearmen, see

What chargers thou canst get."

He hurried forth,
Chose, and produced a hundred warriors' mounts.
Bahrám, on seeing them, went on the plain,
And wheeled about upon them for a while,
But every steed, albeit fleet as wind,
Possessed no wings when ridden by Bahrám.
At length he chose a chestnut broad of breast,
With feet like wind, and, of another brand,
A bay. Thou wouldst have said : "A crocodile
Hath come forth from the deep !" His shoes flashed
        fire,
And from his ruddy breast fell drops of blood.
Munzir paid for the two what they were worth
(The wood of Kúfa was their native place)
And bold Bahrám accepted the two steeds,
Bright as Ázargashasp, and guarded them,
Like some fresh apple, lest a blast should harm.
    One day the young prince spake thus to Munzir :—
" O man of understanding, bright of mind !
Thou hast no pretext for thus keeping me,
Not sparing me a moment from thy sight.
There is a secret impulse in the hearts
Of all that thou beholdest. As grief paleth,
So pleasure greateneth, a man. In short
Some fair-faced damsel will increase my joy,
For woman is the solace of our pains.
In woman doth a young man find repose,
Be he a monarch or a paladin ;
She is his guide to Faith and to all good.
Command to have some damsels brought to me,
Some five or six, like suns and full of charm.
Perchance, when I have chosen one or two,
My thoughts will fix on justice and the Faith.
It may be too that I shall have a child
To ease my heart, the world-lord will approve me,

C. 1466

And I shall have the praise of every one."
    On hearing such words from the youth, Munzir
The agéd, blessed him and then bade a man [1]
To make all haste to the slave-dealer's shop
Upon that quest, who brought out forty damsels
Of Rúm, all fit to please and soothe the heart,
As tall in stature as a cypress-tree,
All objects of desire, of charm, and grace.
Bahrám chose two, among those rosy-cheeked,
With rosy skins and bones of ivory.
One of these Stars could play upon the lute,
The other with her cheeks all tulip-like
Was as Canopus of Yaman, in height
A cypress, and with tresses lasso-wise.
Munzir paid for them when they were approved.
With cheeks bright as the gem of Badakhshán [2]
Bahrám gave thanks with smiles upon his face,
And spent his days at polo and the chace.

§ 3
How Bahrám went to the Chase with a Damsel and how
he displayed his Accomplishment

C. 1467   It happened that one day without attendance
Bahrám went with the lutist to the chase.
Ázáda was the Rúman damsel's name;
Her cheeks were coral-hued.   Bahrám had mounted
A dromedary with the noble [3] Cypress,
Who had her lute in hand.   She was his charmer,
His love; her name was ever on his lips.
For such occasions he required a camel,
And set thereon a housing of brocade,
While from it hung four stirrups.   Thus he pricked

---

[1] Reading with P.   [2] The ruby.
[3] Ázáda, to pun on the girl's name.

O'er hill and dale. Two stirrups were of silver,
Two were of gold, and all were set with jewels,
And furthermore he had beneath his quiver
A stone-bow; that brave youth was all-accomplished.
He came upon a pair of deer and laughing
Said to Ázáda: "O my Moon! when I
Have strung my bow and in my thumb-stall notched
The string, which shall I shoot? The doe is young,
Her mate is old."

     She said: "O lion-man!
Men do not fight with deer. Make with thine arrows
The female male, the agéd buck a doe,
Then urge the dromedary to its speed,
And, as the deer are fleeing from thy shafts,
Aim with thy cross-bow at one creature's ear
That it may lay its ear upon its neck,
And when the beast shall raise its foot to scratch
The ear that hath been tickled though not hurt,
Pin with one arrow head and ear and foot
Together if thou wouldest have me call thee
'The Lustre of the world.'"

     Bahrám Gúr[1] set
The string upon his bow and caused commotion
Upon that quiet plain. Within his quiver
He had a double-headed shaft for use
While hunting on the waste and, when the deer
Sped off, he shot the buck's two horns away
Much to the girl's amaze. Forthwith the sportsman
Shot two shafts at the doe which struck her head
Just where the horns should be and furnished her
Therewith. Her breast grew red with blood. He rode
Toward her mate again, set in his stone-bow
A bolt, hit the buck's ear, and was well pleased,   C. 1468
For he had aimed thereat. The creature scratched

---

[1] The first occurrence of his full title—"Onager Bahrám"—as we
might say "Buffalo Bill."

Its ear.   Forthwith within his bow of Chách
He set an arrow and pinned head and ear
And foot together ; but Ázáda's heart
Was vexed about the deer, and when the prince
Said : " When I hunt I bring them down by thousands
Thus," she replied : " Thou art an Áhriman,
Else how canst thou shoot thus ? " [1]

Bahrám stretched out,
Flung her from saddle headlong to the ground,
And made his dromedary trample her,
Besmearing hands and breast and lute with blood.
He said to her : " O thou lute-playing fool !
Why shouldst thou seek for my discomfiture ?
If I had drawn mine arms apart in vain
My race had been dishonoured by the shot."
When he had trampled her beneath his camel
He never more took damsels to the chase.[2]
Next se'nnight with a noble troop he went
Forth to the hunting-ground with hawk and cheetah,
And near a mountain saw a lion that tore
An onager's flanks.   Impetuously he strung
His bow and notched therein a shaft three-feathered,
Then pinned both preyer's back and heart of prey
That underneath the blood-stained lion lay !

§ 4

*How Bahrám showed his Accomplishment in the Chase
before Munzir*

Another week Nu'mán went with Munzir
To be Bahrám's companion in the chase,

---

[1] Reading with T.

[2] Bahrám's feelings, though the outcome of them is more tragic, are
somewhat like those of De Lorge in Browning's poem " The Glove,"
and Ázáda, when she sought to shame Bahrám by setting him what
she intended to be an impossible task, had not the excuse that the
English poet ingeniously puts into the mouth of the French lady.

And took withal some Arab men of name
As judges of his failure or success.
Munzir desired Bahrám Gúr to display
His horsemanship and strength before these men.
Anon a flock of ostriches appeared,
Each running like a dromedary loose.
On seeing them Bahrám Gúr rushed like wind.
He handled smilingly his bow and stuck
Four poplar arrows in his belt. He laid
The arrows in his bow successively
To slay those birds, and pierced in sportsman's fashion
Their plumes. No arrow by a needle's breadth
. Was lower than another, none more high,
And, when the nobles went to see the outcome,
They found the horseman's shots true to a hair,
Whereat Munzir called blessings down on him,
As did the other spear-armed warriors.
Munzir said: " O my king ! I joy o'er thee   C. 1469
As roses joy o'er springtide. May thy Moon
Ne'er wane, thy girdlestead be weakened never."
    Munzir, returning to his palace, held
Bahrám Gúr high as Saturn. Many a painter
He sought for in Yaman, and all the best
Assembled at his court. He bade them limn
On silk a picture of Bahrám Gúr shooting.
They drew with ink thereon a cavalier
To represent him, thews and all, as seated
On his tall camel, shooting wondrously;
The stone-bow, lion, deer, and onager;
His breast expanded, all his markmanship,
And strength; the ostriches, the wilderness,
And impact of the arrow. Then Munzir
Dispatched a cavalier to bear the picture
To Yazdagird, and all the host assembled .
At that communication. In amaze
The chiefs all called down praises on Bahrám.

Thenceforth, whenever he did anything
Of note, they sent it pictured to the king.

§ 5

How Bahrám came with Nu'mán to Yazdagird

The Sháh was eager to behold Bahrám—
Bahrám? Nay rather an imperious Sun!
That Lion said thus to Munzir: "Albeit
I could abide however long with thee
My father's wish inciteth me to go,
And, since I shall be safe, mine own heart urgeth."
  Munzir prepared whatever was required—
Gifts from Yaman, exceeding all compute,
As Arab steeds with golden furniture,
And other things of noted costliness,
Striped cloth, and falchions, of Yaman, and what
The mines afforded in 'Adan. Nu'mán,
Who was in favour at the Persian court,
Went with Bahrám, conversing of the Sháhs,
Until they reached Istakhr. When tidings came
About the Sháh's son and Nu'mán the Arab,
The archimages and shrewd-hearted sages
Went from the court to meet them. When the Sháh
Saw from afar Bahrám, his Grace, his limbs,
And girth, he stood amazed at seeing him
So tall, well trained, and fair to look upon,
Received him well and lodged him near at hand.
C. 1470 He chose Nu'mán a dwelling in the city,
And for the prince a palace as was meet,
Supplying him with handmaids and with slaves
Befitting his degree. The son attended
His sire by night and day, and had not time
To rub his head. Nu'mán abode a month,
And then requested licence to depart.

The monarch summoned him by night, then set him
Upon the throne, and said: "Munzir hath seen
Much toil in fostering high-born Bahrám,
And I must make him a return therefor,
For your esteem is as Urmuzd to me.
I laud the weighty counsels of Munzir,
For he inclineth, as I see, to wisdom;
Still, while thou tarriest at our court, I trow
That he is looking for thee on the road."
    Then of dínárs out of the treasury
They gave him fifty thousand with king's raiment,
And from the stalls ten steeds that bore a name,
With gold and silver trappings, gave withal
Slaves, carpetings, perfumes, and coloured stuffs,
And goods of all kinds.   These Mihrán produced
Out of the world-lord's treasures and bestowed them
All on Nu'mán, son of Munzir.   He opened
The door of largess gladly to bestow
Upon Nu'mán's companions fitting gifts.
The Sháh then wrote a letter to Munzir,
A letter that was worthy of the state,
With thanks for his entreatment of the prince,
Whose love the monarch of Yaman had gained:—
  I will endeavour to repay thy deeds;
Mine own head is exalt by such a son."
    Bahrám Gúr wrote: "My lot here is not happy.
It was not what I hoped for from the Sháh
That he should look upon his subject thus.
I am not here as either son or servant,
Or, like a younger brother, light of heart."[1]
  He told Nu'mán, what had been hidden from him,
The evil ways and customs of the world-lord.
    Nu'mán, when he had left the royal court,
Came to renowned Munzir and gave to him
The world's king's letter which, when he had kissed,

[1] Or " Or as a liege glad-hearted at a court."

He laid upon his head, joyed at those gifts,
And multiplied his praises.   Afterward
The envoy spake in private to Munzir
At large about Bahrám Gúr.   When the scribe
Had read the other letter out to him
His visage grew like gall.   He wrote forthwith
An answer full of good advice: " Famed prince!
See that thou turn not from thy father's way.

C. 1471   Approve both good and evil from the Shá,
Be wise and serve.   When princes are submiss
Ills pass.   Men's heads have need to compass wisdom.
'Tis all the doing of the circling sky,
And we are impotent.   It hath a heart
All love, a heart all hate, a face all frowns.
The Master of the world hath framed it so,
And we must be disposed as He disposeth.
Henceforth I will dispatch to thee dínárs,
And royal gems, according to thy needs.
Let not thy heart be troubled, for thy trouble
Importeth more to me than heaped up treasure.
Lo! now by way of offering I send
Five hundred score dínárs and lo! withal
The handmaid that was erst thy confidant,
And thine own heart's delight behind thy curtains,
To brighten thy dark soul.   When thou hast spent
All these dínárs lean not upon the king,
For I will send to thee still many more,
And things of all descriptions from this realm ;
But do thy service, utter words of praise,
And serve with an increasing instancy,
For e'en in thought thou canst not separate
Ill temper and the monarch of the world."
    He sent off ten Arabian cavaliers—
Men who were loyal, shrewd, and eloquent.
They came to prince Bahrám with sacks of coin,
And with his loyal slave-girl.   Wise Bahrám

Rejoiced thereat, his sorrows turned to wind,
And thenceforth, as Munzir advised was right,
He failed not in attendance day and night.

§ 6

How Yazdagird put Bahrám in Bonds, how he escaped by the good Offices of Tainúsh, and how he returned to Munzir

It chanced that in the banquet-hall one day
Bahrám was in attendance on the Sháh;
That night came on and he was wearied out
By standing long and could not keep awake.
His father, seeing that his eyes were closed,
Cried violently in an angry voice,
And bade an executioner : " Arrest him.
Henceforth he shall not look on crown and girdle.
Ward him within this house and then return.
He graceth not this place of fame and fight."
   Within the palace, with a broken heart,
That year he looked not on his father's face
Save on Naurúz and at the Sada feast   C. 1472
When he drew near among the other nobles.
   It happened that Tainúsh, the Rúman, came
As envoy to the Sháh with purses, slaves,
And with the tribute sent from Rúm by Cæsar.
The king of kings received him graciously,
And lodged him worthily.   Bahrám dispatched
This message to him: "Shrewd and potent man !
No grievance hath the Sháh against his subject,
Yet guiltless I am banished from him thus !
Ask him to grant me pardon for thy sake,
That so my withered fortunes may revive,
And send me to my fosterers:[1] Munzir

---

[1] Reading with P.

Was more to me than mother and than father."

Tainúsh gave ear, accomplished his desire,
And made Bahrám's afflicted heart rejoice.
He was released from his degrading bonds,
Bestowed much largess on the mendicants,
And gat him ready to depart in haste.
He called his followers and, when the night
Was dark, led forth the company like wind,
Exclaiming to his friends: "Thanks be to God
For our escape and safety from distress."

When he came near the monarch of Yaman,
Men, women, children, went to welcome him;
So did Nu'mán, so did Munzir, so did
Their honest spearmen. As Munzir drew nigh
Bahrám the day was darkened with the dust
Of troops, both chiefs dismounted, and Bahrám
Detailed his sufferings whereat Munzir
Wept much, and said: "What is the Sháh's star then
For ne'er he walketh in the way of wisdom?
I fear that he will suffer for his deeds."

Bahrám said: "Never may the Sháh himself
Grow conscious even of his own ill star!"

Munzir received him then and there as guest,
And heaped new benefits upon the old.
Bahrám Gúr's whole employ was banqueting,
Disporting on the riding ground, gift-giving,
And combating. Thenceforth the grief and joy
Of Yazdagird were to his son but breezes
Upon the day of Ard.[1] Time passed. Bahrám
Was glad in hall and glorious on the waste.

Now Yazdagird, concerned about the realm,
Assembled archimages from all quarters,
And bade the readers of the stars discover
How he would die and darkness whelm his head,
And, when this happened, where his royal cheeks

---

[1] One of the lucky days.

Would wither. They replied: "Let not the Sháh
Take thought of death, but when the royal fortune
Shall founder he will seek the spring of Sav,
Take thither with him troops with trump and drum, -
And set out joyfully to visit Tús.
That is the place wherein the Sháh will die.
Of such a day as that his ear hath heard not,
And pondering such knowledge is not good;
It is a secret veiled by God Himself."
    The Sháh, on hearing this, swore by Kharrád,
And by Barzin, and by the yellow sun :—
"I will not, whether I be glad or wroth,
Behold the spring of Sav."
                                Three month rolled by,
And then the Sháh's blood caused the age concern.
One day his nostrils bled, and leeches came
From every quarter to advise thereon;
They made a shift the bleeding to restrain
One week with drugs, then it began again.

§ 7

How Yazdagird, by the Advice of an Archmage, went to the
Spring of Sav and was killed by a Water-horse

An archmage said to him: "Thou hast, O king!
Departed from the ways of Providence.
Thou said'st: ' I will escape the hand of death!'
But where is death not alway in full leaf?
The course for thee is this : by way of Shahd
Go in a litter to the spring of Sav,
There make thy prayer before all-holy God,
Go in abasement round that burning soil,
And say thus: 'I, a feeble slave, whose oath
Hath set a snare before his soul, have come
Now to inquire how long I have to live,

O righteous Judge!'"
                The Sháh approved thereof
As helpful to his anguish, had brought forth
Three hundred litters, and, thus borne, proceeded
Toward the river Shahd both night and day
Post haste, his nostrils bleeding still at whiles.
As soon as he had reached the spring of Sav
He left his litter, gazed upon the stream,
·Poured somewhat of the water on his head,
And called on God, the Giver of all good.
Anon the bleeding ceased.   He ate and rested
Among his counsellors, grew proud, and said:—
"This was the course!   Why need I tarry longer?"
   Now when the Sháh in his conceit imagined
That he had wrought the cure upon himself,
A white steed issued from the stream, with buttocks
Round like an onager's, and short of leg.
It pranced and seemed as 'twere an angry lion;
'Twas stately, black of belly, raven-eyed;
It had a trailing tail, a crest, and mane,
Black hoofs, and foamed; it was a lion-slayer.
Thus to his chiefs said Yazdagird: "Let troops
Encircle it."
              The herdsman with the help
Of ten rough-riders hemmed it in and took
A saddle and a lengthy coiled up lasso.
How could the Sháh wot of the World-lord's purpose
In bringing him that dragon of a steed?
It foiled alike the herdsman and the troops,
Whereat the monarch was exceeding wroth,
And taking up the saddle and the reins
Drew near the horse exultingly which proved
So docile that it did not stir a foot.
The monarch took the bridle from the herdsman,
And gently put the saddle on the mount.
He girthed it.   That fleet Crocodile stood stirless.

C. 1474

He went to put the crupper on.   That charger,
Flint-hooféd, neighed and kicked him on the head !
His head and crown descended to the dust.
    The dust received him and the dust begot.
From yon seven heavens on high what wouldst thou
        ask ?
    Their revolution thou escapest not ;
To pay them worship is a fruitless task.
Incline to God—the Master of the sky,
Of sun, and moon—to Him for refuge fly.
    The water-horse, when Yazdagird was slain,
Returned like flying dust to that blue spring,
And vanished 'neath the surface !   None e'er looked
On such another marvel.   Like a drum-roll
Rose from the host a shout : " O Sháh ! thy fate
Led thee to Tús."
                          The chieftains rent their clothes,
And flung dust on their heads.   The archimages
Then oped the head and body of the Sháh,
Embalmed them both with musk and camphor, wrapped
The dry corpse in brocade, draped therewithal
His shining breast, and set upon his head
A crown of musk.   Then on a bier of gold,
And on a teaken litter, he departed
Unthroned and crownless back again to Párs.
    Thus is it with this Wayside Hostelry !
Will peace, though thou ensue it, come to thee ?
Though meek thyself, the world is unrestrained ;
So having eaten let the cup be drained.
Religion is a better thing than sin
For one that hath the power to walk therein.

§ 8

How the Íránians took Counsel and placed Khusrau
upon the Throne

C. 1475 Now when the monarch of the world was buried,
And from Írán the chieftains came in tears—
Archmages, governors, and paladins,
With prudent ministers, men shrewd of heart—
All met in Párs and gathered round his charnel,
As Gustaham, who rode down elephants,
And slaughtered them, Káran the warrior,
Son of Gashasp, Mílád, Árash the marchlord,
Parwíz the horseman of Gurzbán, and others.
Withal too those in hiding in Írán—
The great men and the leaders of the world,
Whom Yazdagird was wonted to abase—
Assembled in the city, and Gashasp,
The scribe—a man of eloquence—thus spake :—
" Ye nobles young and old ! since God created
The world none hath beheld a king like this,
Who knew but how to slaughter and contemn,
To cause distress and travail, and withhold
His counsel and his treasure from his subjects,
Respecting none and setting all at odds.
No man hath seen a fouler Sháh or heard
Of one among the paladins of yore.
We want no more of this race on the throne,
And cry against his very dust to God.
Illustrious Bahrám is his own son,
His very kin in purpose, heart, and brain.
His talk is all Munzir.   We will not have
A tyrant on the throne."
       Then all that were
Chiefs in Írán swore mighty oaths and said :—

"We will not have another of this race
As king of kings with crown and throne of might."
　　That done, they rose and sought another Sháh.
When tidings of the death of Yazdagird
Spread 'mongst the chiefs—the monarch of the Aláns,
The paladin of Párs, Bíward, Shikbán,
The warrior of the world, Bihzád who had
Barzín to sire and was of Rustam's race,
And Sám the hero sprung from Kai Kubád—
All said : " The sovereignty is mine from earth
To Pisces," and the whole world was fulfilled
With tumult, for the head that wore the crown
Had vanished from the throne.　Then in Írán
Chief, paladin, and archmage, all that were
Of ardent soul, met to debate in Párs :—
"Who is there worthy of the throne of kings ?　　C. 1476
Consider who can enter on the work.
We see not any one, approved by God,
To wear the golden girdle on the throne,
And to allay the troubles of the time :
A kingless world is but a pasturage."
　　There was an ancient man, by name Khusrau,
Of generous instincts, masterful, and ardent.
Moreover he was born of noble race,
And one among the wealthy of the land.[1]
The nobles gave to him the crown and state,
And troops from all sides gathered at his gate.

§ 9

*How Bahrám Gúr heard of the Death of his Father
and invaded Írán*

Thereafter to Bahrám Gúr tidings came :—
"Heaven hath apportioned to thy sire the grave ;

----

[1] Reading with P and T.

Thy father, eminent midst kings, is dead,
And ta'en with him the name of sovereignty;
They have enthroned another and acclaimed him
As monarch by the title of Khusrau.
The warriors have bound themselves by oaths:—
' We will not have a monarch of the race
Because Bahrám, the son, is like the sire,
And, skin and marrow, of his father's seed.' "
    Báhrám Gúr, when he heard it, tore his cheeks,
So troubled was he at his father's death,
And for two se'nnights went up from Yaman
Wails from child, man, and woman.   When Bahrám
Had sorrowed for a month he graced the throne.
Nu'mán drew near together with Munzir,
And Arabs of Yaman both great and small,
All shedding tears of sorrow with their Sháh,
While anguish wrought on them the effects of fire.
Then setting loose their tongues they counselled thus:—
" O virtuous and most exalted prince !
We came to this world to be turned to dust,
Came not in quest of any remedy.
All mother-born will die, and to God's justice
We must resign our hearts."
                              Bahrám Gúr said
Thus to Munzir : " Already is the water
" Grown brackish in our stream !   What time my race
Shall lose its royal title it will lose
Its Grace divine, men will send up in dust
The desert of the horsemen and convert
The country of the Arabs to a ditch.
Consider well, assist me, and deplore
My father's death."
                              Munzir gave ear and answered
Right manfully : " This is my chance and this
My hunt-day on the waste.   Sit on the throne,
Observe, and wear through all thy years the crown,

C. 1477

And bracelet."
     All the chiefs approved the course
Suggested by Nu'mán and by Munzir:
They left the presence and prepared for war.
Munzir gave orders to Nu'mán and said :—
"Go gather our brave Lions in a host—
Two thousand of Shíbán, ten of Kibtís,[1]
All dight for battle. I will show the Íránians
Who is the Sháh with treasure, crown, and troops!"
 Nu'mán assembled him a mighty power
Of swordsmen and of spearmen, bade them raid,
And trample down the realm. To Taisafún
All the salt desert route shook with their hoofs,
The women and the children were made captive,
There was no helper, and the world was full
Of fire and harrying since the imperial throne
Was impotent. News came to Rúm and Chín,
To Turkistán, to Hind, and to Makrán :—
"The Íránian throne is void, and none is fit
To rule," and all made ready, in despite
Of justice, to invade the land. They all
Stretched out their hands toward the Íránian throne,
And rose to claim the empire for their own.

§ 10

How the Íránians heard of Bahrám's Pillaging
and wrote to Munzir, and how he replied

The Íránians heard and sought a remedy.
Distracted by their woes they met, and said :—
"These Rúmans, Indians, and desert-horsemen
Have passed all bounds! We must adopt some means
To rid our hearts and souls of this distress."
 They chose a noble envoy shrewd and fluent,

---

[1] *I.e.* Copts.

A warrior hight Jawánwí, a scribe,
A man of high degree and eloquence,
To go to parley with Munzir and say:—
" O noble lord! the world doth need thy name.

C. 1478 Thou watchest o'er Írán and o'er Túrán,
And thou art everywhere the warriors' stay.
What time this throne grew void of Sháh and crown,
And when the marches of our land with blood
Were like the plumage of the francolin,
We said that thou wouldst rule our coasts, for they
Were worthy of thee.   Now thou raidest us,'
And sheddest blood with rapine and contention
On every side !   Thou used'st not to be
An evildoer and wast wont to fear
Reproach and malison.   Consider now
If this doth please thee and doth benefit
Thee with thy hoary head.   There is a Judge
Besides thyself, One higher than all thought.
The envoy will narrate what he hath seen,
Or heard from persons in authority."

　　Wise Jawánwí went from the chieftain's presence,
He journeyed toward the desert of the spearmen,
Spake with Munzir, and gave him the dispatch.
The Arab chief made no reply thereto,
But said to him: " Wise seeker of the way !
Repeat the matter to the king of kings,
Repeat what thou hast said to Sháh Bahrám,
And, when thou seekest for an answer, he
Will point thee out the way."

　　　　　　　　　　He sent a chief
With Jawánwí who reached the monarch's gate.
That man of knowledge, when he saw Bahrám,
Invoked God's blessing on the Sháh whose breast,
Whose stature, and whose limbs astonished him,
Shrewd-hearted though he was: " Thou wouldest say
That wine distilleth from his face, the scent

Of musk exhaleth from his hair!"

> That man

Of eloquence grew void of Grace and sense,
And utterly forgot his embassage!
Bahrám Gúr, noting his amaze, and how
The spectacle bedimmed his eyes and heart,
Much greeted him, showed him all courtesy,
And set him graciously upon the throne.
Now when the envoy seemed at ease the Sháh
Asked: "Wherefore hast thou toiled thus from Írán?
Hereafter thou shalt have the fruit of toil,
And well filled treasury, from us."

> He sent

A sage to take him to Munzir and say :—
"Write thou an answer and indite fair words.
See if the envoy hath a verbal message,
And, if so, hear it and reply at large."
  Came Jawánwí and spake, at whose wise speech
Munzir's cheek flushed; he heard that shrewd one out,
Prepared to make his answer to the letter,
And said to Jawánwí: "O full of wisdom!
All that do ill will smart therefor.   Now I
Have heard thy message and the nobles' greeting.   C. 1479
Say thus: 'Who was the first to cause the ill?
Who needs must seek this senseless feud? Bahrám Gúr,
The king of kings, with stature, Grace, and host,
Is with us here, and they who draw the snake
Out of its hole will trail their skirts in blood.
Albeit, were I to advise, no harm
Would come upon the Íránians.'"

> Jawánwí

Had seen and hearkened to the king of kings,
Had questioned him to see if he was fit
For throne and greatness, fortune and success,
And, as he listened to Munzir, conceived
A brilliant notion, and replied; "Great sir,

Who needest not the wits of other men!
If wisdom failed the Íránians, many a chief
Among them hath been slain through that defect.
Now I, old as I am, still seek for fame,
And I will speak if thou wilt hear.   Our land
We gladly yield to thee and brave Bahrám,
The king of kings.   With hawk and cheetah make
A royal progress in Írán to hear
What folk will say: no harm will come of it.
Speak too whate'er is right.   The sage will best
The fool.   Forgo all mischievous intent,
And shrink not at reproach and calumny."
   Munzir, on hearing, gave him gifts and sent
Him home from that fair country, well content.

§ 11

*How Bahrám Gúr arrived at Jahram with the Host of
Munzir, and how the Íránians went out to him*

Munzir, Bahrám Gúr, and the counsellors
All met in privy conclave and resolved
To march upon Írán.   Munzir made choice
Of thirty thousand warlike Arab spearmen,
Gave ample pay, and filled the chieftains' heads
With vapouring.[1]   As tidings reached Írán
Of these things Jawánwí himself returned,
And all the potentates, in deep concern,
Betook them to the Fire-fane of Barzín,
And prayed to God to change their strife to joy
And feasting.

C. 1480   When Munzir had led his troops
Across the unwatered waste, and reached Jahram,
Great Sháh-Bahrám Gúr pitched his camp-enclosure.
His troops surrounded it, and to Munzir

------

[1] Reading with P and T.

He spake thus: "From the country of Yaman
Thou hast come to Jahram, my counsellor!
Which shall it be, when host confronteth host,
A fight or parley?"

      Said Munzir: "Invite
The chiefs and, on their coming, spread the board,
And speak with them. When any are provoked
So be not thou, and we shall learn whom they
Are fain to hail as monarch of the world.
That known, we will take order and avoid
Strife if soft means suffice. If they seek war,
Turn, and display the bearing of a pard,
Then will I make this desert of Jahram
As 'twere a sea,[1] and turn the shining sun
To Pleiades. I wot when folk behold
Thy stature, mien, and lovingkindliness,
Thy wisdom, counsel, and initiative,
Thy gravity, thy knowledge, and thy patience,
That they will want none else to have the crown,
The throne, the fortune, and the pageantry;
But if they err, and wish to take away
The throne from thee, then will I with these horsemen,
And our sharp swords, bring Doomsday on the world;
Then shalt thou see me frown, and may my soul
And body be thy ransom. When they mark
My countless troops, the order that I take,
Our deeds of blood, that God is our ally,
And that the realm is thine inheritance
By right established through a long descent,
They will acclaim as Sháh none save thyself
As fit for crown and to adorn the throne."

  The Sháh heard smiling; his heart throbbed with
    joy.
Now when the sun rose o'er the mountain-tops
The mighty men and nobles of Írán

     [1] *"de sang"* (Mohl).

Made ready to go forth to meet Bahrám Gúr
The sages were convoked, an ivory throne
Was set up for the prince, and he assumed
The glorious crown, and ordered all his court
According to the use of king of kings,
Because he was the monarch of the world.
On one hand sat Munzir and on the other
Nu'mán with sword in hand, while all about
The tent-enclosure there were warriors,
But none that was not on the Arab side.
Then those Íránians that were loyalists
Came to the antechamber of the Sháh,

C. 1481 Who had the curtain lifted and the names
Of those that entered called out at the door.
They came before the presence of Bahrám Gúr,
The Sháh, beheld a splendid crown and throne,
And shouted, saying: "Mayst thou live for ever;
Far from thee ever be the evil eye."
     The king of kings received them graciously,
And ranked them every one in his degree.

§ 12

*How Bahrám Gúr harangued the Íránians as to his Fitness to
rule, how they rejected him but promised him the Kingship
if he would take the Crown from between the Lions* [1]

Bahrám said : " Princes, old, experienced chiefs !
The kingship is mine own by long descent.
Why this to-do of yours ? "
                                   "Expect us not,"
The Íránians shouted, "to endure more loss !
Not one of us will have thee as the Sháh.
Thou hast an army, but the land is ours.
Thy race hath caused us anguish, toil, and woe;
By night and day we writhe and heave cold sighs."

     [1] This heading combines those of two sections in C.

Bahrám thus answered : " Yea, 'tis true, for passion
Is king of every heart.   If ye reject
Me, why thus seat another in my room
Without consulting me ? "

      An archmage said :—
" None, whether he be prince by birth or subject,
May shun the path of justice.   Join with us,
And choose a Sháh that every one will bless."
 They spent three days upon the task of choosing
A monarch from Írán, and then wrote down
A hundred nobles' names—fit Lustres all
For crown and throne and belt.   Bahrám Gúr's name
Was one of them because he charmed the realm.
They cautiously and anxiously reduced
The hundred names to fifty, and of these
Bahrám's name stood the first, who, if he sought
His sire's place, sought but justice.   Of the fifty
They wrote down thirty, and they were the choicest,
Most famous, and most potent of Írán.
Bahrám amongst the thirty led again
Because he was a prince—the destined Sháh.
The wise archmages brought the thirty down
To four, of whom Bahrám was leader still.
When the decisive moment was at hand
The Íránian ancients said : " We will not have
Bahrám who is too headstrong and self-willed,
Though brave."

     An outcry rose among the chiefs,
The hearts of all were darkened, and Munzir
Addressed the Íránians thus : " I fain would know,
For good or ill, why ye are full of pain,   σ 1482
And stricken in your souls, about the Sháh
In his untimé-worn youth ?   In excellence
No king on earth can match him, and in looks
No moon in heaven.   His poplar shafts pierce anvils,
While with his strength he can uproot a mountain.

Though still a youth he is a sage in counsel,
Well skilled, with bright heart and retentive mind."
  The chiefs, by way of answering him, sought out
Full many a stricken Persian, and assembled
Out of Írán upon that plain all those
That Yazdagird had maimed. One still survived
Lopped hand and foot but still intact of trunk ;
Another had lost ears and hands and tongue,
And seemed a lifeless body, while another
Had lost both shoulders, and Nu'mán was all
Astound at those maimed forms. The eyes of one
Had been dug out with nails, and when Munzir
Beheld that sight his anger rose. Bahrám
Was sorely grieved, invoked his father's dust,
And cried: "O hapless one! why didst thou close
The eyes of thine own joy and burn thy soul
In fire?"
        Munzir the aspiring said to him :—
"We cannot blink such evil. Thou hast heard
What they have had to say, now answer them,
For kings should not be at a loss."
                              Bahrám
Then spake on this wise : "Chiefs and veterans!
Ye all said sooth, and this is even worse!
Well may I blame my sire since I myself
Have had a sample, for he darkened all
My fine resolves : his palace was my prison.
When God had mercy, and Tainúsh released me
Out of the clutches of my sire, his hook
Had pierced me to the soul, for which cause I
Took shelter with Munzir, because I never
Saw kindness from the Sháh. May none possess
His temper, for the man is lost that lacketh
Humanity. Now I, thanks be to God,
Have wisdom, my soul eateth of its fruits,
And to this present I have prayed to Him

To be my guide to good that I might purge
My heart and spirit of such crimes as those
Wrought by the Sháh on these men.   I will live
To gratify my subjects' hearts, exist
To worship God according to the Way.
I am the shepherd and my subjects form
My flock.   Let all of us seek peace and justice.
Then I have character, discretion, counsel,
And virtue, which no unjust king possesseth,
Because he needs must be unjust and froward,
And we should weep for one that is unjust.
With me are greatness, kingship, and discretion,   C. 1483
Benevolence and wisdom.   From Shápúr,
Son of Bahrám, back to Ardshír my sires,
Both old and young, were Sháhs, and are my guides
To wisdom and the Faith, while through my mother
I am the grandson of king Samírán,[1]
And every way have wisdom for my comrade.
I am possessed of virtue, wisdom, might,
With courage, strength of hand, and horsemanship.
I know none other fit to call a man
In feast, in battle, or in anything.
I have a secret treasury well filled,
And men of name leal to their sovereign.
My justice shall make populous the world,
And all my subjects shall abide in joy.[2]
Moreover I will make a pact with you,
And pledge my tongue to God.   Let us bring forth
The imperial throne of ivory, and set
The bright crown over it, then let us bring
Two savage lións of the wood and, placing
The crown between them, chain them on each side.
Then let the would be Sháh advance and take
The famed crown from the throne of ivory,

---

[1] "de la reine Schémiran" (Mohl).   Possibly Semiramis is meant.
[2] The § ends here in C.

Place it upon his head and sit between
The lions as the Sháh, the crown above him,
And under him the throne, for we will have
None else, provided he be just and holy.
If ye reject what I have said then choose,
Ye all! some noble, and Munzir and I,
For Arab chieftains know not how to flee,
With mace and trenchant scimitar will send
The dust up from your king of kings, and strew
Your heads upon the moon. Now for your answer,
And speak advisedly in this contention."

He spake, then rose and went inside his tent.
All marvelled at his words. The chiefs, archmages,
And all the people of Írán that heard
The wise Sháh's words, exclaimed: "This is the Grace
Of God, not craftiness or lack of wit!
He speaketh naught but what is just, and justice
Well may rejoice our hearts. For his proposal
About the savage lions with the throne,

C. 1484 And royal crown, between them: if they rend him
The Judge will not require his blood of us;
'Tis his own plan, and if he perisheth
We are content, while if he shall achieve
The crown he will have distanced Farídún
In Grace, and we will have no other king.
In brief we give acceptance to his words."

That night passed by; at dawn the Sháh came forth,
And sat upon the throne. He sent and summoned
The Íránians, and discoursed of yesterday
At large. The archimages cried: "O Sháh,
More knowing than the wise! how wilt thou rule
When thou hast eminence and mastery?
How wilt thou deal concerning right and justice,
So that both fraud and falsehood may abate?"

He answered thus those sages, warriors,
And chiefs: "I will be better than my words,

Will make injustice and informing cease,
And not appoint unworthy governors,
Will rule the world by counsel and by justice,
And, having pacified it, will rejoice
At what my justice hath achieved, will give
Some of my hoarded wealth withal to those
In want, admonish those that are in fault,
And bind them if they err the second time,
Will pay the army promptly and rejoice
The sages' hearts, make tax-collectors just,
And turn their souls from darkness and chicane.
If any one shall die, not having kindred,
And leave excessive wealth, I will bestow it
On mendicants, not add it to my treasures,
Or be enamoured of this Wayside Inn.
I will hold counsel with the experienced,
And take such order as will frustrate greed.
I will consult my ministers whenever
I purpose some new scheme, and not dismiss
The assembly when a man is asking me
For justice, but will give to such their due,
Will utter righteous judgment, and requite
The ill with ill as well becometh rulers.
My witness is all-holy God, and wisdom
Is master of my tongue."
           Then the high priest
And sages—well approved and veteran chiefs—
Exclaimed : "We are thy slaves and bow our heads
To thy command and will."
           Then Sháh Bahrám
Said thus : "Ye men of wisdom and our guides !
If in a year I make my soul and wisdom
Belie my promises I will renounce
Crown, throne, and heritage, and sit thenceforth
Among the luckless."
           Hearing this the sages,

C. 1485

The magnates, and archmages shrewd of heart,
Repented of past words and, being in fault,
Desired to make all well again, exclaiming,
One to another: "Who is worthier
To be the Sháh than he in manliness,
Speech, counsel, birth? None purer hath been born
Within the world! God fashioned him of justice.
May mischief ne'er befall him. We shall have
All good from him, and turn us to the Faith,
And justice. If now we shall speak perversely,
And send our wits to sleep, he with such stature,
Such neck, and arms, is peerless in the world,
While at his back there is the Arab host,
Because in weal and woe Munzir will help him,
And if he win the throne that is his own
Who in the world is better than Bahrám?
What cause hereafter would he have to fear
The Íránians, for what are we but a pinch
Of dust to him?"

        They said: "O prosperous one!
Our minds approve thee for our Sháh. None knew
Thy virtues, purity of person, wisdom,
And counsel, and we all of us have paid
Our homage to Khusrau, son of Pashín,[1]
As Sháh, we all are under oath to serve him,
And stand within his danger, so to speak.
Hereafter if he ruleth in Írán
Our borders will be desolate with war.
One party taketh pleasure in Bahrám,
Another is in favour of Khusrau.
Thine own plan is the right one, and the world
Thereafter will be under thy command:
Ordeal by the lions will suffice,
And thenceforth none will seek the sovereignty."

  Bahrám gave his assent; 'twas his proposal.

---

[1] Reading with P and T.

At the accession of a lawful Sháh
The high priest with three sages used to go
To him, enthrone him, and felicitate
The throne, then bring the crown of gold—the source
Of glory, right, and Grace—and, crowning him,
Would press both cheeks upon his breast in joy.
The Sháh then would bestow on suppliants
All gifts presented to him.   So they put
The crown and throne in charge of the high priest,   C. 1486
And from the city fortunate Bahrám
Departed to the waste.⁻ Brave Gustaham
Had two fierce lions which he gave in chains
To the high priest.   They dragged the savage beasts
Along, the draggers seeming mad with fright,
And to the footings of the ivory throne
Chained them, and set the crown within a nook
Upon it.   All the world—spectator there
Of crown and throne—watched how the prince would
    fare.

§ 13

How Bahrám and Khusrau went to the Waste, and how Bahrám
slew the Lions and took his Seat upon the Throne

Bahrám Gúr and Khusrau went on the waste,
And with full hearts approached the lions.   Khusrau,
On seeing the fierce beasts with the crown between
    them,
Said to the archimages : " He that seeketh
The sovereignty should be the first to try.
Moreover he is young and I am old—
Too feeble to resist fierce lions' claws—
So let him use his youth and vigour first."
    Bahrám made answer, saying : " Good, 'tis well.
We will not blink fair words."
                                        With that he took

An ox-head mace while the world wondered at him.
An archmage said : " O wise and holy king !
Who biddeth thee fight lions ? Canst thou have
More than the sovereignty ? So in its quest
Give not thy life and person to destruction
Thus wantonly. Herein no blame attacheth
To us, 'tis thine own act, the world is thine."
  Bahrám said : " O explorer of the Faith !
Thou and the other folk are not to blame.
I am the man to fight these savage lions ;
'Tis my delight to battle with the brave."
  The archmage answered : "Refuge then with God,
And, if thou needs must go, first purge thy heart
Of sin."
          He did according to that word,
Repented, purged his heart, bathed in a stream,
And sought upon the plain a place of prayer.
Then as he prayed before all-holy God,
And laid his cheeks upon the dusky ground,
He said : " Almighty ! let Thy servants triumph.
If I—Thy servant—justly seek to cleanse
The world of evil give my soul assurance
In this strife, let me overcome the lions."
C. 1487   Thence came the wise Sháh and at once set forth
Upon his way, armed with the ox-head mace.
Now when the valiant lions saw him coming,
One on the instant snapped its chain and charged
The exalted king. That hero smote its head,
And dimmed its eyes, then going to the other
Smote its head whence the blood ran down its breast,
Then took his seat upon the ivory throne,
Placed on his head the heart-delighting crown,
And put his trust in God who is our Refuge,
The Guider of the lost. Khusrau drew near,
Did homage, and thus said : " Exalted Sháh !
Blest be thy sitting on the throne, and may

The heroes of the world be slaves before thee.
Thou art the Sháh, we are thy slaves and further
Thy good in everything."
                              The mighty men
Showered jewels over him, invoking blessings
Upon his crown. A universal shout
Ascended from the world. That jubilance
Was on Surúsh's day in month Ázar
Whereon Bahrám assumed the sovereignty,
And won fruition of the crown and Grace.

A cloud hath risen and the moon's obscured;
From that dark cloud a shower of Milk is poured;
No river, plain, or upland can I spy,
The raven's plumes are lost against the sky;
In one unceasing stream egg-apples [1] fall:
What is high heaven's purpose in it all?
No fire-wood, salted meat, or barley-grain
Are left me, naught till harvest come again!
Amid this gloom, this day of tax and fear,
When earth with snow is like an ivory sphere,
All mine affairs in overthrow will end
Unless my hand is grasped by some good friend.[2]

Now will I tell to thee so strange a tale
That in the wonder wonder's self will fail.

[1] The fruit of the egg-plant (*Solanum esculentum*), of which there are
two varieties—a white and a purple.
[2] Reading with P.

INDEX

This Index and the Table of Contents at the beginning of the volume are complementary. References to the latter are in Roman numerals.

A

'ABBÁSID, 327
Abbreviations, list of, 5
Abdaas, bishop, 372
Abraham, the patriarch, 65
Abú'l Kásim, Firdausí, 20, 207
Abú'l Muzaffar. *See* Nasr.
Abú Mansúr, 16
Accession of a Sháh, ceremony at, 409
Achæmenids, 194, 197, 198
    dynasty of, 194
Adan, seaport and territory in southern Arabia, 386
Ægean sea, 204
Afrásiyáb, ruler of Túrán, 15, 79, 177, 240 and *note*
Africa, 30
Ahdnámak (Andarznámak), Pahlaví treatise, 257
Áhriman, the Evil Principle, 106, 112, 206, 240, 281, 290, 299, 318, 384
    Faith of, 281, 290
Ahwáz (Khúzistán, Susiana), 35, 199, 298, 357
Akesines (Chináb), Indian river, 31, 64
Aknaton, Pharaoh, 371
    a lover of peace like Yazdagird, son of Shápúr, 371
Aláns (Alani), the, people, 395
    monarch of, 395
Alár, place, 205

Alexander I., king of Epirus, 12 ; his Italian expedition, 12
Alexander the Great (Iskandar, Sikandar, *q.v.*), 11 *seq.*, 15 *seq.*, 29 *seq.*; 61 *seq.*, 72, 74 *seq.*, 84, 193, 194, 197, 204, 252, 253, 373
    accompanied by experts to the East, 11
    origin and growth of the romance of, 12 *seq.*
    Syriac Christian Legend of. *See* Syriac.
    referred to by Muhammad in the Kurán, 15, 77
    how he became a Persian national hero, 15
    paternity of, 16, 18
    founds cities, 13, 18
    why so named, 19
    tutored by Aristotle, 29
    and Roxana (Rúshanak), 30, 32
    historic and romantic accounts of the first years of his reign, 30
    his flight from Darius' banquet, 30
    his pursuit of Darius, 31
    his historical treatment of the murderers of Darius, 32
    his romantic treatment of the murderers of Darius, 33
    marries Darius' daughter, 33

Alexander the Great, and the Fakírs, 61
and Calanus, 61
and Porus, historical account of, 63
his device of the iron steeds, 64
his stature, 64
his visit to the camp of Porus, 64
and Cleophis, 65
his visit to the Oasis of Ammon, 65
and Candace (Kaidáfa), 65 *seq.*
assumes the name of Antigonus (Naitkún), 66
Life of, Plutarch's, 67
his visit to the Brahmans, 67
his letter to Aristotle, 68
mistakes the Indus for the Nile, 68
his return march productive of marvels, 69
his admiral (Nearchus), 69
and the Amazons, 12, 72
    legend of, 72
his expedition to the Gloom and the Fount of Life, legend of, in the Pseudo-Callisthenes, 74 *seq.*
legend of his cook (Andreas), 76
    version of, in the Kurán, 77
his barrier in the Caucasus, 78
    legend of, in the Kurán, 78
his correspondence with Aristotle about the succession, 81
his Will, 81
    provisions of, 81
death of, 82
dispute over his place of interment, 82
his corpse taken to Memphis, 82

Alexander the Great, interred at Alexandria, 82
tomb of, 82
    Mas'údí on, 82
    S. Chrysostom on, 82
diagram to illustrate the Persian Romance of, 84
wars on the death of, 197
Alexander, son of Alexander the Great and Cleophis (?), 65
Alexandria (Iskandaríya), city, 13, 15, 17, 83, referred to, 83
the Pseudo-Callisthenes originates at, 13
Alexander buried at, 82
his tomb at, 82
    Mas'údí on, 82
    S. Chrysostom on, 82
Al Hadr. *See* Hatra.
Al Iskandarús. *See* Halai.
Al Khidr (Khisr, *q.v.*), the Green Prophet, 78 and *note*
origin of, 78
Al Mansúr, Khalífa, 254
Amazons, the, 12, 71 *seq.*
    their disputed visit to Alexander, 12, 72
    origin of, 71.
    described, 153 *seq.*
    Sikandar's correspondence with, and visit to, 153 *seq.*
Ambar (Pírúz Shápúr), city on the Euphrates, 327
Ambassadors, instances of kings and chiefs going in person as ambassadors or spies, 325
Amen-Ra, Egyptian god, 16
personated by Nectanebus, 16
Ammon, Oasis of, 30, 65
Alexander's visit to, 30, 65
Amorium. *See* 'Ammúriya.
'Ammúriya (Ancyra, Angora), stronghold, 23 and *note*, 89
Failakús marches from, to encounter Dáráb, 23
Anábdéh, 32

Ancyra. *See* 'Ammúriya.

Andalús (Spain), vi, 66, 121, 122, 138

queen of, 121 *seq.*

Andarznámak (Ahdnámak), Pahlaví treatise, 257

Andreanticus, sea, 77

Andreas, Alexander the Great's cook, 76 *seq.*

legend of, 76

in Kurán, 77

Angora. *See* 'Ammúriya.

Antigonus (Naitkún), name assumed by Alexander, 66

Antiochus, Macedonian general, 76

Antipater, regent in Macedonia, 82

intrigued against by Olympias, 82

Apollo and the Python, 203

Apologue, 310

Apothegms, 50, 303, 343

Apries, 16

Arab, Arabs, the, x, xi, 17, 21, 22, 66, 171, 209, 254, 321 *seq.*, 377, 385, 396, 398, 402, 406

their wars with the Íránians, 17, 21

Dáráb demands tribute from, 22

cymbal, 244

their incursions into Persian territory, 322

steeds, 380

Arabia, 70, 72, 206, 322, 355

Shápúr son of Urmuzd's expedition to, 322

Arabian, Arabians, the, 378, 388. Faith, 95

Arabian Nights, The, 71, 78, 250

quoted, 73

Arabic language, 147, 205

versions of Pahlaví texts, 255 *seq.*

Arachosia, 32

Arar tree, 19

Arash, son of Kai Kubád. *See* Kai Árash.

Árash, Ashkánian king, 197, 210

Árash, Íránian warrior, 394

Arastális (Aristotle, *q.v.*), vii, 35; counsels Sikandar, 35, 179

his sentences over the coffin of Sikandar, 185

Ard, day, 298, 390 and *note*

Ardawán (Bahrám, Artabanus), the last Ashkánian (Parthian) king, viii, 3, 197 *seq.*, 201 *seq.*, 205, 214 *seq.*, 254 *seq.*, 259 *seq.*

= Bahrám, 197, 209 (?), 210

his status in Persian tradition, 201

daughter of, 202

marries Ardshír Pápakán, 202, 229

incited by her brother Bahman to poison Ardshír Pápakán, 259

condemned to death, 260

saved by Ardshír Pápakán's minister, 260

gives birth to Shápúr, 261

restored to favour, 265

writes to Pápak, 214

summons Ardshír Pápakán to court, 214

receives gifts from Ardshír Pápakán, 215

highly esteems Ardshír Pápakán, 215

his sons, 215, 255, 267 *note*

their fate, 228, 229 and *note*, 259

disgraces Ardshír Pápakán, 216

his slave-girl intrigues with Ardshír Pápakán, 217 *seq.*

his eldest son made ruler of Párs, 218 and *note*

consults the astrologers, 218

his vain pursuit of Ardshír Pápakán, 221 *seq.*

Ardawán, returns to Rai, 223
    writes to his son about Ard-
      shír Pápakán, 223
    Ardshír Pápakán marches
      against, 227
    prepares to encounter Ard-
      shír Pápakán, 227
    defeated, captured by Khar-
      rád, and slain by Ardshír
      Pápakán, 228
    buried by Tabák, 229
    his palace at Rai spared (?)
      by Ardshír Pápakán, 229
      and *note*
    his secretary slain by Shápúr,
      256
    = Mihrak = Mithrak = Mádik
      (?), 256
Ardshír (Bahman, *q.v.*), Sháh, 213,
    271 and *note*
Ardshír, brother of Shápúr (Ar-
    taxerxes II.), Sháh, x, 3,
    328, 360 *seq.*
    Shápúr arranges for the suc-
      cession with, 260 *seq.*
    his title, 364
    resigns the crown, 364
Ardshír Khurra, city and district,
    199, 205, 206, 229 and *note*,
    231, 241, 245, 290 and *note*
    Ardshír Pápakán builds a
      Fire-temple in, 230
        makes irrigation-works
        in, 230
    meaning of, 290 *note*
Ardshír Pápakán, Sháh (Artax-
    erxes I.), viii, ix, 3, 61, 81,
    193, 196, 198 *seq.*, 209 *note*,
    213 *seq.*, 238 *seq.*, 250 *seq.*,
    294 *seq.*, 303, 307, 315, 322,
    325, 405
    his rise compared with that
      of Cyrus the Great, 194
    legend of Cyrus the Great,
      transferred to, 195
    his war with the Kurds (in
      Kárnámak), 196
    minister of, story of, 196

Ardshír Pápakán, Sháh, Tabari's
    account of, 198
    marries the daughter of Ar-
      dawán, 202, 229, 259
    his various defeats referred
      to, 202
    birth of, 213
    summoned to court by Arda-
      wán, 214
    equipped by Pápak, 214
    presents gifts to Ardawán,
      215
    in favour with Ardawán, 215
    his prowess in the chase, 215
    disgraced, 216
    writes to Pápak, 216
    advised by Pápak, 216
    intrigues with Gulnár, Arda-
      wán's slave-girl, 217 *seq.*
    hears from Gulnár of the pre-
      sage of the astrologers, 219
    flees with Gulnár to Párs,
      220 *seq.*
    followed by the divine Grace
      in the form of a mountain-
      sheep, 221 *seq.*
    adherents flock to, 223
    addresses his supporters, 224
    founds a city, 202, 224
    receives promises of help, 224
    joined by Tabák, 225
    and Tabák defeat Bahman,
      son of Ardawán, 226
    marches from Párs against
      Ardawán, 227
    defeats and slays Ardawán,
      228
    gives the spoil to the troops,
      229
    spares (?) Ardawán's palace
      at Rai, 229 and *note*
    counselled by Tabák to marry
      Ardawán's daughter, 229
    returns to Párs, 229
    builds Khurra-i-Ardshír, 229
      and *note*
    his irrigation-works at Khur-
      ra-i-Ardshír, 230

Ardshír Pápakán, his war with the Kurds, 230 *seq.*
and Haftwád, 236 *seq.*
message sent by arrow to, 238
worsted by Haftwád and entertained and counselled by two youths, 239 *seq.*
slays Mihrak, 241
marches to attack the Worm, 241
gives instructions to Shahrgír, 241
his stratagem against the Worm, 242
slays the Worm and its attendants, 244
summons Shahrgír, 244 and *note*
takes Haftwád's stronghold, 244
defeats and slays Haftwád and Sháhwí, 245
carries off the spoil, 245
builds a Fire-temple, 245
rewards the two youths, 245
his invasion of Kirmán, 205, 245
goes to Taisafún, 245
his principles of government, 250, 273 *seq.*, 286 *seq.*
his reign, 254 *seq.*
length of, 254
Tarbarí on, 254
and the daughter of Ardawán, stories of, 255
coins of, 256, 257, 265
crowns Shápúr, 257
his cities, 257
his prophecy, 257
enthroned at Baghdád, 258
his title of King of kings, 193, 199, 254, 258, 273
his inaugural address, 258
Bahman's plot with his sister to poison, 259
discovers plot against him, 260
consults his minister, 260

Ardshír Pápakán, condemns the daughter of Ardawán to death, 260
his minister saves her, mutilates himself, and makes record of the fact, 261
his son Shápúr born, 261
hears about Shápúr from his minister, 262
recognises and acknowledges Shápúr, 264
restores the daughter of Ardawán to favour, 265
rewards his minister, 265
makes a new coinage in honour of his minister, 265
builds Jund-i-Shápúr, 266
harassed by wars, consults Kaid, 266
wroth at Kaid's advice, 267
seeks in vain for the daughter of Mihrak, 268
referred to, 270
discovers Urmuzd, 271
counsels Urmuzd, 280
calls and counsels Shápúr, 286 *seq.*
on Church and State, 286
on the· duration of his dynasty, 289
death of, 291
Ariobarzanes, the murderer of Darius Codomanus, 32
Ariobarzanes, satrap, 32 and *note*
Aristobulus, Greek writer, 12
Aristotle (Arastálís, *q.v.*), 29, 81
Alexander's tutor, 29
letter to, 68
correspondence with, about the succession, 81, 83
on the silkworm, 204
Armenia, 202, 203
Armenian version of the Pseudo-Callisthenes, 14
Arrian, historian, 12, 31, 64, 68, 82
his *Anabasis*, 12
his *Indica*, 12
Caspian Gates of, the, 32

Arrian, on the stature of Porus, 64
Ichthyophagi, 69 *seq.*
Alexander and the
Amazons, 72
the death of Alexander,
82
Arsaces, 197
Arsacid, Arsacids, the, 198, 203,
205, 255
their imperial system, 198
some of, escape from Ardshír
Pápakán to Armenia, 203
Arsalás, 32
Arses, 29
Artabanus (Ardawán, *q.v.*), 201
Artaxerxes Ochus, 18 *note*, 29
conquers Nectanebus II., 18
note, 29
murdered, 29
Artaxerxes I. *See* Ardshír
Pápakán.
Artaxerxes II. (Ardshír, brother
of Shápúr), 363
Arwand (Tigris), 329
Asfandiyár (Spento-data, Span-
dat), son of Gushtásp, 15, 49,
55, 200, 213, 224, 242, 251, 271
Ashk, Ashkánian king, 197, 210
meaning of, 197
Ashkánian, Ashkánians, the, race
and dynasty, viii, 193,
194, 196, 197, 209
duration of their rule, 193
times, Firdausí's lack of
materials for, 193
surviving traditions of,
transferred to other
dynasties, 194
importance of, 194
genealogy of, 197
Asia Minor, 30
Central, 73
Astawadh. *See* Haftwád.
Astyages, 194
Atbara, river, 65
Atkinson, James, 250
on the Sháhnáma, 250
Atropatene, kingdom, 198

Attock, 62
Avasta. *See* Zandavasta.
Avidius Cassius, Roman general,
291 *note*
Ázáda, Rúman slave-girl, 382
goes hunting with Bahrám
Gúr, 382
tries to shame Bahrám Gúr
in his markmanship 383
slain by Bahrám Gúr, 384
and *note*
Ázar, month, 411
Ázarbáiján, 198, 203
Ázargashasp, the spirit of the
lightning, 381
= Gushasp, 212 and *note*
Ázarnarsí, son of Urmuzd, son of
Narsí, 318

B

BÁBAK. *See* Pápak.
Bábil (Babylon, *q.v.*), vii
Babylon (Bábil), 17, 31, 81, 83,
176, 178, 180, 181, 183
Sikandar marches towards,
176, 178
prodigious birth at, 81, 180
Sikandar sickens at, 181
dies at, 81, 183
Babylonian, 254
script, 320
Bactria, 32, 198
Badakhshán, region in northern
Afghánistán, 382
gem of, 382 and *note*
Bæton, Greek writer, 12
Baghdád, city, viii, 254, 290, 322,
327
Ardshír Pápakán enthroned
at, 258
Bágíz, 32
Bagoas, 29
Bahman (Vohu Manau), amesha-
spenta, 362 and *note*
Bahman (Ardshír), son of Asfan-
diyár, Sháh, 20 *note*, 34 and
note, 49, 200, 213, 270 and
note

Bahman, son of Ardawán, viii, 202, 218 and *note*, 225, 227, 260
made ruler of Párs, 218
referred to, 222
bidden by Ardawán to seek out Ardshír Pápakán, 223
defeated by Ardshír and Tabák, 226
escapes to Hind after the defeat of Ardawán, 228
urges his sister to poison Ardawán, 259
Bahrain, island in the Persian Gulf, 330
Bahrám, 197, 209
= Ardawán, 197, 209 (?), 210
Bahrám, son of Urmuzd, Sháh (Varahran I.), ix, 3, 303, 306
reign of, 307 *seq.*, 327
Bahrám, son of Bahrám, Sháh (Varahran II.), ix, 3, 308
reign of, 310 *seq.*
story told of, 310
Bahrám Bahrámiyán, Sháh, (Varahran III.), ix, 3, 315, 316, 324, 334, 368, 405 (?)
reign of, 313
his inaugural address, 313
resigns the throne to his son, 314
Bahrám, son of Shápúr, Sháh (Varahran IV.), xi, 3, 313, 368, 371
ruler of Kirmán, 368
his title, 368
his seal, 368
Tabarí's account of, 368
his daughter, 369
resigns the throne to his brother, 369
dies, 369
Bahrám Chubína, 250
Bahrám Gúr, Sháh (Varahran V.), xi, 3, 250, 325, 329 and *note*, 372, 373, 394 *seq.*
his stay at Hira, 372
his age at accession, 373

Bahrám Gúr, his persecution of the Christians, 373
his war with Rome, 373
birth of, 375
the magnates advise Yazdagird to choose a governor for, 376
put in Munzir's charge, 378
goes with Munzir to Yaman 378
his nurses, 378
his education, 378 *seq.*
has his tutors dismissed, 380
makes choice of steeds, 380
slave-girls, 381
goes to the chase with a slave-girl, 382
his marksmanship, 383 *seq.*
slays his slave-girl, 384 and *note*
goes hunting with Nu'mán and Munzir, 384
picture of, hunting, sent to Yazdagird, 385
returns with Nu'mán to Yazdagird, 386
complains of Yazdagird to Munzir, 387
receives advice and his slave-girl from Munzir, 388
falls into disgrace at court, 389
asks Tainúsh to intercede for him, 389
released and returns to Munzir, 390
welcomed by Munzir, 390
hears of his father's death and of the election of Khusrau, 395, 396
claims the kingship and is supported by Munzir, 396 *seq.*
his interview with Jawánwí, 398
negotiates with the Iránians, 401 *seq.*

Bahrám Gúr, the Íránians produce examples of Yazdagird's cruelty to, 404
addresses the Íránians, 404
proposes to decide the question of the kingship by ordeal, 405
promises to rule justly, 406
agrees to be the first to face the ordeal, 409
Baidá (Bardí), hill fort, 198 and note, 199
Baitú'l Harám (the Kaaba), 119, 121
Balásh, king of Kirmán, 205
Balúchistán (Balochistan, Gedrosia, Makrán), country, 12, 70
Banák, Íránian chief, 202
Bandáwa, Sindian chief, 175
defeated by Sikandar, 175
Band-i-Kaisar, 295
Barbar, country, 114
Bardí. See Baidá.
Barrier, Alexander's (Sikandar's), in the Caucasus, 78, 249
legend of, 78
site of, 79
described, 164
Barsaentes, satrap, 32
executed, 32
Barsine (Stateira), daughter of Darius Codomanus, 33
marries Alexander the Great, 33
Barzin, Íránian chief, 395
Barzin, sacred Fire, 391, 400
the Íránians worship at, 400
Bástán-náma, 16, 17, 84, 373
Bazánúsh (Valerian), ix, x, 294, 297
his defeat and capture by Shápúr, son of Ardshir, 294, 295
his single combat with Garshásp, 297
builds bridge at Shúshtar, 298

Bazánúsh (Jovian), x, 324, 326, 353 seq.
elected emperor, 353
sues for peace, 353
accepts Shápúr's terms, 355
Bázrangí, dynasty of Tribal Kings, 198
Beas (Hyphasis), Indian river, 64
Berber, race, 73
Bessus, satrap, 32
executed, 32
Bhután, Indian kingdom, 81
Biháfrídh, 200
Bih-Ardshír, city, 254, 291 note
Bihzád, Íránian chief, 395
Birds, green, 160
Sikandar holds converse with, vii, 160
Birka-i-Ardshír, city, 290 and note
Bíward, Íránian chief, 395
Bízhan, Íránian hero, 194
Bízhan, Ashkánian king, 197, 210
Black Stone, the, 65
Blest, Country of, 74, 76
Bombyx Mori. See Silk.
Book of Indication and Revision, Mas'údí's, 252
quoted, 252
Bowl, the full, symbolism of, 63
Brabantio, 324
Brahmans (Gymnosophistæ), the, vii, 61, 64, 67, 143 seq.
Palladius on, 61
Sikandar's interview with, 67, 143 seq.
country of, 143, 147
hear of Sikandar's coming and write to him, 143
described, 144
reply to Sikandar's questions, 144 seq.
Sikandar quits, 147
Brides of the Treasure, 250
Browning, Robert, his poem of "The Glove," 384
Bucephala, city, 18
Bucephalus, horse of Alexander the Great, 18, 31

Bucephalus, birth of, 18, 26
  death of, 18, 64
  a mare, 18 (Ethiopic version)
  city built by Alexander in
    memory of, 18
  offered by Darius to Porus, 31
Buddhist saints, story of two, 63
Budge, Dr. E. A. Wallis, 14, 17 *note*
  his editions of the Syriac and
    Ethiopic versions of the
    Pseudo - Callisthenes, 14,
    17 *note*
Budini, race, 73
Burjak and Burjátúr. *See* Youths,
  the two.
Bust, fortress and district in
  Sístán, 175

C

CÆSAR, ix, x, 24, 26, 49, 112 *seq.*,
  122, 124, 126, 297, 298, 324
  seq., 336 *seq.*, 341 *seq.*, 345
  seq., 389
  = Failakús, 24, 26, 27
  = Sikandar, 40, 42, 49, 113,
    114, 118, 121, 122, 124, 128,
    129, 142, 158, 161, 170, 174,
    178, 183
  = Valerian (Bazánúsh, *q.v.*),
    ix, x, 326
  = Jovian (Bazánúsh, *q.v.*), x,
    353, 354
  pays tribute to Shápúr, son
    of Ardshír, 298
  Shápúr in disguise visits, 336
  entertains Shápúr, 337
  discovers who Shápúr is, 337
  arrests Shápúr, 337
  has Shápúr sewn up in an
    ass's skin and imprisoned,
    338
  charges his wife with the
    custody of Shápúr, 338
  invades and rávages Írán, 338
  Shápúr prepares to attack, 346
  overthrown by Shápúr at
    Taisafún, 346 *seq.*

Cæsar, his treatment by Shápúr,
    349, 357
  mother of, 351
Calanus (Sphinés), Indian ascetic,
    61
  Onesicritus and, 61
  Alexander the Great and, 61
  death of, 61
  derivation of, 61
  identical with the sage sent
    by Kaid to Sikandar, 62.
    See Four Wonders, the.
Callisthenes, Greek historian, 12,
    74
  the Romance of Alexander
    fathered on, 13
Callitris quadrivalvis, the Arar
    tree, 19
Cambyses, son of Cyrus the Great,
    16
Candace (Kandake, Kaidáfa, *q.v.*),
    dynastic title of the queens
    of Ethiopia, 13, 65, 72
  and Alexander, 65 *seq.*
Canopus, star, 382
Cappadocia (Pálawína), 294
Captain of the host, x
Captives, mutilation of, 323, 334,
    348, 357
  settlement of, 327, 357
Carthaginians, the, 30
  Alexander's legendary visit
    to, 30
Casaubon, Isaac, 13
Caspian Gates, 31, 32
Cassander, son of Antipater, 82
Caucasus, the, 15, 79
  Alexander's barrier in, 78
  legend of, in the Kurán, 78
  site of, 79
Chách (Táshkand), city in Túrán,
    197
  thane of, 197, 210
  referred to, 229 and *note*
  bow of, 384
Chaghwán, place, 174, 175
  Sikandar arrives at, 174
  quits, 175

Chahram (Jahram), city in Párs, 44
Dárá goes to, 44
Charbar, place on the coast of Balúchistán (Makrán), 70
Chares of Mytilene, Greek writer, 61
Charogos. *See* Tainúsh.
Chess, 201
its introduction into Persia, 201
Chín, country (often = Túrán), vii, 80, 179, 182, 186, 268, 280, 284, 358, 376, 397
Khán of, 35
ambassadors from, come to Dárá, 35
pen of, 57, 99
Sikandar's expedition to, 80
silk of, 85, 266
ornaments of, 102, 139
lord of = Sikandar, 113
= Faghfúr, 171
implements of, 122
robes of, 128
fringe of, 138
stuffs of, 143, 215
sea of, 149
Sikandar goes to, 169
rarities of, 171, 173
paper of, 172
coasts of, 173
brocade of, 173, 182, 184, 332
gold cloth of, 182, 334
China, 204
silk industry of, 204
Chináb (Akesines), Indian river, 31, 64
Chinese language, 147
Chosroes, king of Armenia, 202
Christ, 133, 339
Faith of, 133, 352
Christian, 342, 356
rites of marriage, 104
Faith, 356
Christianity, 138
Cilicia (Kaidáfa), 294
City of Women (Harúm), vii

Cleophis, Indian queen, 65
and Alexander the Great, 65
Climes, the seven, 179, 262, 266, 273, 280, 376
Colchians, the, 72
Contents, Table of, v
Cos, island, 204
silk industry of, 204
Country of the Blest, 74, 76
Crete, island, 323 *note*
Cross, the, 351, 352
the religion of, 138
Passion of, 339
Ctesias, historian, 13, 68
legend of Cyrus in, 195
Gutschmid on, 195
Ctesiphon (Taisafún, *q.v.*), 321, 322, 325, 372
Cup of Kaid, the. *See* Four Wonders, the.
described, 94, 100
principle of, explained, 109
Cybele, goddess, 71
= Hittite Ma, 71
Cyrus the Great, 194
his rise compared to that of Ardshír Pápakán, 194
legend of, transferred to Ardshír Pápakán, 195

D

DAI, month, 306
Daizan (Táír, *q.v.*), Arab chief, 322, 323
legend of, 322
daughter of, legend of, 323
Dakíkí, poet, 196
Damascus, Nicolaus of, 195
Damáwand, mountain, 202
Dandamis. *See* Mandanes.
Dárá, son of Dáráb, Sháh (Darius Codomanus, *q.v.*), v, 17, 27, 29, 33 *seq.*, 83 *seq.*, 112, 113, 123, 124, 132, 137, 170, 172, 188, 325, 353
legendary son of Dáráb, 17, 27

Dárá, appointed by Dáráb to succeed him, 27
historical account of, 29
movements of, after his final defeat by Alexander (Sikandar), 31
Sikandar's correspondence with the wife and daughter of, 33
accession of, 34
his letter to the kings, 34
pays his troops, 35
ambassadors come to, 35
demands tribute from Sikandar, 36
marches against Sikandar, 37
Sikandar's visit to the camp of, 38
invites Sikandar to a banquet, 40
his ambassador recognises Sikandar, 40
sends horsemen in pursuit of Sikandar, 41
defeated by Sikandar, 43
collects another army, 43
again defeated, 44
goes to Chahram, 44
goes to Istakhr, 44
takes counsel with his chiefs, 45
collects a new host, 46
marches from Istakhr, 46
is defeated, 46
withdraws to Kirmán, 46
bewails himself, 47
his letter to Sikandar, 49
his letter to Fúr, 50
marches against Sikandar, 51
abandoned by his troops and flees, 51
murdered by his ministers, 52
his murderers arrested by Sikandar, 53
his dying interview with Sikandar, 53
vengeance promised him by Sikandar, 53

Dárá, tells his last wishes to Sikandar, 54
bestows Rúshanak upon Sikandar, 55, 86
dies, 55
his burial, 56
his son Sásán, 211
his kindred support Ardshír Pápakán, 223
Dáráb, Sháh, v, 11, 16, 20 *seq.*, 34 and *note*, 49, 83, 84, 86 -132, 137, 172, 188
father of Sikandar in Persian legend, 16
legendary father of Dárá, 17
harangues the chiefs, 20
ambassadors come to, 21
employs Rúman artificers, 21
wars with the Arabs, 21
defeats and demands tribute from them, 22
wars with Rúm, 22
defeats Failakús, 23
grants terms of peace to Failakús, 24
marries the daughter of Failakús, 25
returns to Párs, 25
becomes disaffected towards his wife (Náhíd), 25
marries again, 27
Dárá is born to him, 27
fails in health, 27
appoints Dárá to succeed him, 27
dies, 28
Dáráb, Dárábgird, city, v, 17, 198, 199
Dariel, Pass of, 79
Darius Codomanus (Dárá, *q.v.*), 16, 17, 29, 30
defeated at Issus, 30
Alexander escapes from the banquet of, 30
defeated at Gaugamela, 31
asks that his family may be restored to him, 31
writes to Porus, 31

Darius Codomanus, the historical account of the death of, 31
his daughter marries Alexander, 33
his corpse sent to Párs, 33
the punishment of his assassins, 33
Darkness, Land of. *See* Gloom, the.
Darmesteter, Professor, 203
on the story of the Worm, 203
Haftwád, 206
Daughter of Kaid. *See* Four Wonders, the.
described, 94, 100, 102, 104
married to Sikandar, 104
Dhoulkarnain, *See* Zu-'l-karnain.
Diagram to illustrate the Persian Romance of Alexander, 84
Dihkán, 95 and *note*
Faith of 95
Diláfrúz-i-Farrukhpái, Íránian slave-girl, 3, 338 *seq.*
referred to, x
slave to Cæsar's wife, 338
has compassion on Shápúr, 339
discovers who Shápúr is, 339
frees Shápúr from the ass's skin, 340
escapes with Shápúr from Rúm, 340 *seq.*
entertained by a gardener, 342
praised by Shápúr, 346
named and honoured by Shápúr, 356
Dílam, city in Gílán, 227
Dílamán, region, 202 and *note*
Dilárái, wife of Dárá and mother of Rúshanak, v, 87 *seq.*
visited by Náhíd, 89
Dínawarí, historian, 16, 64, 80, 81, 256, 323
Dínkard, Pahlaví text, 252
Diognetus, Greek writer, 12
Dionysus, temple of, visited by Sikandar, 71

Dirázdast, title, 324 and *note*
Dív (Daéva), demon, 135, 146, 150, 241
= Ahrímán, 349
Dragon, vii, 71, 132, 146
Sikandar's adventure with 71, 151
= Fúr, 113
= Ardawán, 222
Drangiana (Makrán, Balúchistán), 32
Dreams, Kaid's, 91 *seq.*
Dukhtnúsh. *See* Núsha.

E

EGYPT (Misr), 12, 13, 16, 17, 72, 81, 82
the Pseudo-Callisthenes written in, 13
invaded by Alexander the Great, 30
Egyptians, the, 16
falsification of history by, 16
Ekbatana (Hamadán), 31, 32
Elam, kingdom, 194, 198
Elephants, 115
Fúr's, 115
Sikandar's device to overcome, 115
Elymais, kingdom, 198
Enótokoitai, the, 80
Epirus, country, 12
Alexander I. of, 12
his expedition to Italy 12
Ethiopia, 18 *note*, 72
flight of Nectanebus to, 18 *note*
a western and an eastern, 68
= India, 68
Ethiopians, Ethiops, 43, 71, 80
= Indians, 13, 68
western and eastern, 68, 71
Ethiopic version of the Pseudo Callisthenes, 17 and *note* 18, 30, 33, 66, 67, 71, 74, 82, 83

Eumenes, Greek ephemerist, 12
Euphrates, river, 31, 327
Euxine sea, 72

F

FAGHFÚR, the, dynastic title of
the princes of Chín and
Máchín, vii, 35, 80, 113
169 *seq.*, 325
ambassadors from, come to
Dárá, 35
Sikandar visits, as his own
ambassador, 170
gives audience to Sikandar,
170
entertains Sikandar, 171
answers Sikandar, 172
his gifts to Sikandar, 173
sends envoy with Sikandar,
173
Failakús, Philip II. of Macedon,
the father of Alexander
the Great, v, 22 *seq.*, 57,
102, 112, 125, 130, 131, 151,
182
wars with Dáráb, 22
allied with the king of Rús,
22
marches from 'Ammúriya to
encounter Dáráb, 23
is defeated and returns to
'Ammúriya, 23
sues for peace, 23
agrees to send tribute, and
give his daughter in mar-
riage to Dáráb, 24, 25
adopts Sikandar as his heir,
27
Faith, Faiths, the four, 92, 95
of Christ, Christian, 133, 352,
356
of Áhriman, 281, 290
Fakírs, the, 61
Alexander and, 61
Onesicritus and, 61
Farát (Euphrates), 37, 42, 43, 290
Farídún, Sháh, 73, 172, 209, 406

Farwardín, month, 375
Faryán, king, father-in-law of
Kaidrúsh, vi, 66, 67, 124
seq., 171, 172
his city taken by Sikandar,
124
slain, 125
his daughter and son-in-law
taken prisoners, 125
brought before Naitkún,
126
sentenced to death, 126
pardoned, 126
Firdausí, vii, 16, 17, 31 *seq.*, 62,
64 *seq.*, 72, 78, 80 *seq.*, 197,
198, 200, 202, 250, 254, 255,
294, 295, 313, 315, 321 *seq.*,
326, 328, 368, 372
his derivation of Iskandar
(Sikandar), 19
his praises of Mahmúd, 20,
207, 279, 292, 370
his account of Alexander's
battles with Darius, 31
invents names for Darius'
murderers, 32
introduction to the story
of Kaid, 62
his veiled attacks on Mahmúd, 62, 92 *seq.*, and *note*
his lack of subject-matter for
Ashkánian times, 193
and the Cyrus legends, 195
Kárnámak, 196, 200 *seq.*,
255 *seq.*
on Mahmúd's remission of
the land-tax, 196
his treatment of the short
reigns, 249, 301
his fondness for wine, 291,
295, 306, 309, 314, 362,
369
gives his age as sixty-three,
314, 369
refers to his work, 370
reverses the historical relationship of Nu'mán and
Munzir, 372

Fire, Fires, sacred, 21
Fírúzábád. *See* Gúr.
Fish, the salt, legend of, 76 *seq.*
-eaters, *See* Ichthyophagi.
Folin, 73 and *note*
Fortifications, vitrified, 79
Fount of Life, the, 74, 158 *seq.*
   Sikandar's expedition to, 74
    seq., 158 *seq.*
     account of, in the Pseudo-
     Callisthenes, 74 *seq.*
   Sikandar hears of, 158
   prepares to visit, 158
   goes in search of, 159
   fails to find, 160
Four Wonders, the, of Kaid, vi,
   94, 97 and *note*, 99 *seq.*
Faiths, the, 91, 95
Frúbá, sacred Fire, 201, 255
Fúr (Porus, *q.v.*), dynasty and
   Indian king, vi, 31, 50, 51,
   62, 64, 110 *seq.*, 123, 132,
   135, 137, 170, 172, 175
   Dárá's letter to, 50
   Sikandar's war with, 67,
   112 *seq.*
   routed by Sikandar's iron
   steeds, 116
   his single combat with
   Sikandar, 117
   slain, 117
   his troops submit to Sikandar, 118

G

GABRIEL, angel, 138 *note*
Gaiúmart, Sháh, 208
Ganges, river, 64
Garden of the Hesperides, 74
Gardener, a, 341
   entertains Shápúr, son of
   Urmuzd, 341 *seq.*
   sent by Shápúr to the high
   priest, 344
   describes Shápúr, 344
   rewarded by Shápúr, 357

Garshásp, Íránian chief, 297
   his single combat with
   Bazánúsh, 297
Gashasp, Íránian warrior, 394
   addresses the nobles on the
   succession to the throne, 394
Garsíwaz, brother of Afrásiyáb, 325
Gaugamela, 31, 32 *note*
   battle of, 31
Gaumata, the false Smerdis, 207
Gaza, city, 30
   siege of, 30
Gedrosia (Makrán, Balúchistán),
   69
Gemini, constellation, 155
Genealogies, fictitious, 199
   of Pápak in Tabarí, 200
    Mas'údí, 200
Genealogical table, 3
Germany, 73
Ghee, 105
Gíl (Gílán), region, 227
Girduni Sirdarra, pass, 32
Girih, 199
Gív, Íránian hero, 194
Gloom, the (Land of Darkness),
   vii, 73, 74, 79
   conception of, 73
   Sikandar's expedition to, 74
   seq.
    account of, in the Pseudo-
    Callisthenes, 74 *seq.*
   Sikandar hears of, 158
   enters, 159 *seq.*
   the jewels of, 162
   emerges from, 162
Glory. *See* Grace.
Glove, The, Browning's poem of,
   referred to, 384 *note*
Gog and Magog (Yájúj and
   Májúj, *q.v.*), 78
   legend of, in Kurán, 78
Gordyene, kingdom, 198
Grace, or Glory, the divine, 27,
   47, 51, 85 and *passim.*
   follows Ardshír Pápakán in
   the form of a mountain-
   sheep, 221 *seq.*

Granicus, river, 30
  battle of the, 30, 31
Greece, 30
Greek, Greeks, the, 68, 82
  their conception of India, 68
  captives, mutilation of, by the
    Persians, 373
Green Prophet, the. *See* Al Khidr.
  Sea, the, 174 *note*
Gretna Green, 323 *note*
Gúdarz, Íránian hero, 194
Gúdarz, Ashkánian king, 197, 210
Gulár, place, 206
Gulnár, slave-girl of Ardawán,
    217 and *note*
  her intrigue with Ardshír
    Pápakán, 217 *seq.*
  reports the presage of the
    astrologers to Ardshír Pá-
    pakán, 219
  flees with Ardshír Pápakán
    to Párs, 220
Gund-i-Shápúr (Shápúr Gird ?),
    city, 295, 327
  Mání-gate of, 327
Gúr (Zúr, Fírúzábád), city, 199,
    205, 229 *note*, 230, 245
Gurgán, region, 373
Gurzbán, a city between Balkh
    and Harát (?), 394
Gushasp, sacred Fire, 201
Gúsh-bistár, 80, 177 and *note*
  his interview with Sikandar,
    177
Gushtásp, Sháh, 20, 49, 55, 200,
    213, 251, 252, 258
Gustaham, Íránian warrior, 394
  his lions slain by Bahrám
    Gúr, 409
Gutschmid, Alfred von, 195
  on the Cyrus legend in
    Ctesias, 195
Gúzihr, Tribal King, 198, 199

H

Habash (Ethiopia), vii, 149
  people of, encountered by
    Sikandar, 149

Haftánbúkht. *See* Haftwád.
Haftwád (Haftánbúkht, Asta-
    wadh), Tribal King, viii,
    199, 205 *seq.*, 232 *seq.*
  account of, in Tabarí, 205
  daughter of, 205, 206, 233,
    234-
  becomes guardian of the
    Worm, 236
  Nöldeke and Darmesteter on,
    206
  son of, 206, 236
  helps his father against
    Ardshír Pápakán, 236
  story of, 232 *seq.*
  his seven sons, 233, 235
  his rise to power, 235
  builds, and migrates to, a
    stronghold, 235
  and Ardshír Pápakán, 236
    seq.
  slain by Ardshír, 245
Halai (Olympias (?), Náhíd),
    daughter, in legend, of
    Philip II. of Macedon, 19
  reason for her repudiation by
    Dáráb and her naming her
    son Iskandar (Sikandar),
    19
Halai-Sandarús. *See* Halai.
Hamadán (Ekbatana), 31
Hamza, Arabic historian, 257
Harám, 65, 120 and *note*, 121
  Baitu'l, 119, 121
Harúm, the City of Women, vii,
    73, 153 *seq.*
  visited by Sikandar, 153 *seq.*
  Sikandar's correspondence
    with the ruler of, 153 *seq.*
Háshimí, 362 and *note*
Háshish, 32
Hatra (Al Hadr), city, 321 *seq.*
  account of, 322
  besieged, 322
  fall of, legend of, 322
  king of, 323
Hecatæus, 13
Helenopolis, 61

Herodotus, 13, 16, 68, 72, 73
  legend of Cyrus in, 195
Hesperides, Garden of the, 74
High priest, x, 343 *seq.*
  hears of Shápúr's return, 344
  informs the captain of the
    host, 345
Himálaya, 74, 81
Hind, Hindústán, vi, viii, 21, 51,
    80, 81, 91, 98 and *passim*
  ambassadors from, come to
    Dáráb, 21
  ambassadors from, come to
    Dárá, 35
  ruler of=Fúr, 51
  Sikandar invades, 98
  silk of, 99
  king of=Kaid, 103
  Sikandar becomes king of,
    118
  people of, help the Sindians
    against Sikandar, 175
Hira, city, 372
Hisham bin Muhammad, 30
Hittite, Hittites, 71
  empire of, 71
Hiuen Tsiang, Chinese traveller,
    63
  quoted, 63, 73
Hoibaras, 195
Holy Ghost, the, 138 and *note*
Homer, 13, 72
  quoted, 68, 73
Hormisdas I. (Urmuzd, son of
    Shápúr), 301
Hormisdas (Urmuzd), son of Ur-
    muzd, son of Narsí, 318,
    325
Humái, Sháh, mother of Dáráb,
    20, 22, 199
Huns, the, 15
Hurmuz, Ashkánian king, 197
Hurmuz (Ormus), 204
Hurmuzdagán, 193, 199
  battle of, 193, 199, 202, 256
Hushyár, astrologer, 372, 375
  takes Bahrám Gúr's horo-
    scope, 375

Hydaspes (Jhílam), Indian river,
    18, 31, 62, 63
Hydraotes (Ravi), Indian river, 64
Hyperboreans, the, 74
  Elysium of, 74
Hyphasis (Beas), Indian river, 64
Hyrcania (Mázandarán), 373

I

IBN Mukaffa, 17, 373
Ibráhím, Abraham, the patriarch,
    119, 120
  house of=the Kaaba, 119
Ichthyophagi, the, 69 *seq.*, 81
  Sikandar and, 69, 147
  Arrian on, 69
  modern accounts of, 70
  their city described, 177
  go to meet, and are visited
    by, Sikandar, 178
  hand over the treasures of
    Kai Khusrau to Sikandar,
    178
Imaus, mountain, 12
'Ínánian, 'Ínánians, the, Arab
    tribe, 324, 330, 331, 333
India, 17, 61, 64, 81, 83, 204
  Palladius on, 61
  Ancient, M'Crindle's, quoted,
    68
  =Ethiopia, 68
Indian, Indians, the, 81, 375, 397
  =Ethiopians, 13, 68
  sages, 61, 83, 91 *seq.*, 143 *seq.*,
    266
  bells, 175
  bane, 259
Indies, Greek conception of two,
    13
  duplicate races in, 68
Indra, Indian god, 203
  and Vritra, 203
Indus, river, 62, 67, 70
  mistaken for the Nile, 68
Iollas, Alexander's cup-bearer, 82
Íraj, the youngest son of Farídún,
    353

Írán, v, x, 16, 17, 21, 38, 39, and
  passim
  monarch of = Dárúb, 21, 26
  and Sháhnáma compared, 193
  invaded by Munzir and
    Nu'mán, 397
Íránian, Íranians, the, xi, 17, 43
  seq., 51, 112, 114, 179 and
  passim
  their wars with the Arabs, 17
  Sikandar's proclamation to,
    44
  bewail themselves, 48
  counsel Dárá to come to
    terms with Sikandar, 48
  ask quarter of Sikandar, 51
  hail him as their king, 56
  after Yazdagird's death meet
    for counsel in Párs, 394
  send Jawánwí to Munzir, 397
  offer prayer at the Fire-fane
    of Barzín, 400
  the loyal, support Bahrám
    Gúr, 402
  their procedure to elect a
    Sháh, 403
  decide to reject Bahrám Gúr,
    403
  remonstrated with by Munzir.
    403
  their object-lesson to Munzir,
    404
  accept Bahrám Gúr's pro-
    posal for settling the ques-
    tion of the kingship by
    ordeal, 406
Iron steeds, Sikandar's, vi, 115
Isdigerd I. (Yazdagird, son of
  Shápúr), Sásánian king,
    371
Ishmael (Ismá'íl), 65; 120, 121
Iskandar. *See* Sikandar.
Iskandar, herb, 26
Iskandaríya (Alexandria), vii, 185
  Sikandar buried at, 185
Island, the = Meroe, 65
Islands, Male and Female, 72
  origin of legend of, 72

Ismá'íl. *See* Ishmael.
Ispahán, 57, 86, 87, 199, 201, 202,
    210
Israfíl, archangel, 78
  Sikandar's interview with,
    vii, 83, 161
Issus, 30
  battle of, 30, 31
  Darius' family taken at, 31
Istakhr (Persepolis), 37, 57, 59,
    198, 199, 202, 211, 223, 225,
    231, 326, 356, 386
  Dárá marches from, to en-
    counter Sikandar, 37, 46
  returns to, 44
  Sikandar crowned Sháh at, 59
  taken by Ardshír Pápakán,
    227
  Ardshír Pápakán marches
    from, against the Kurds,
    230
      returns victorious to, 232
Italy, Alexander of Epirus' ex-
  pedition to, 12
  Alexander the Great's le-
    gendary expedition to, 12,
    30
Íwán-i-Kerkh, 327

J

JACOB of Sarúg, Syriac poet, 15,
    84
  Syriac Christian Legend of
    Alexander versified by, 15,
    74, 78, 84
  his death, 15
Jádústán, 109 and *note*
Jahram (Charam), city in Párs,
  viii, xi, 119, 202, 225, 237,
    241, 268, 400, 401
  desert of, 401
Jalálpúr, Indian city, 18
Jamshíd, Sháh, 45 and *note*, 172,
    209
Jánúsiyár, minister of Dárá, 52,
    88
  murders Dárá, 52

Jánúsiyár, tells Sikandar of
    Dárá's murder,. 52
    arrested by Sikandar, 53
    executed, 56, 88
Jawánwí, Íránian magnate, 373,
    398
    goes as ambassador to Mun-
      zir, 398
    his interview with Munzir,
      398 *seq.*
    recognises the divine Grace
      in Bahrám Gúr, 398
    suggests a course of action to
      Munzir, 400
    returns to Írán, 400
Jaz, Mesopotamia, 337
Jerusalem, 81
Jew, Jews, the, 95, 356
    Faith of, 95
Jhílam (Hydaspes), Indian river,
    18, 31, 63
Johari Das, Bábu, quoted, 81
Joktan, 65
    =Kahtán, 65
Joshua, 77
Jovian, Emperor, 324 *seq.*
    confused with Valerian, 324
Judaism, 327
Judda, the port of Mecca, vi, 121
    Sikandar arrives at, 121
Julian (Yánús), Emperor, 324, 325
    confused with Valerian, 324
    not an emperor in the Sháh-
      náma, 324, 326
    his expedition against Persia,
      324 *seq.*
Julius Valerius, early Latin trans-
    lator of the Pseudo-Callis-
    thenes, 14, 61, 66 *seq.*, 71,
    74, 78, 79, 81
Jund-i-Shápúr, city, 256
    =Rás-Shápúr, 256
    Ardshír Pápakán builds, 266
Jupiter, planet, 138, 172, 292
Justinian, Emperor, 204
    the silkworm introduced into
      the West during his reign,
      204

K

KAABA, the, vi, 65
    Sikandar's expedition to, 67,
      83, 119
Kabtún, king of Misr and the
    progenitor of the Copts, 121
    welcomes Sikandar, 121
    praises Kaidáfa to Sikandar,
      122
Kábul, Kábulistán, 207
    dagger of, 320
Kádisí, Kádisíya, place, 119, 330
Kahtán, Arab chief, 65, 120
    =Joktan, 65
Kaian, Kaiánian, race and dyn-
    asty, v, 9 *seq.*, 17, 34, 48, 55,
    57, 59, 81, 112, 125, 141,
    179, 180, 194, 199, 200, 202,
    210, 223, 237 *note*
Kai Árash, 197, 210, 228
Kaid, Indian king, vi, viii, 61, 62,
    83, 91 *seq.*, 112, 256
    identical with Mandanes
      (Dandamis), 62
    Sikandar and the sage of, 62,
      104 *seq.*
    consults Mihrán about his
      dreams, 92 *seq.*
    his Four Wonders, 94, 97 and
      note, 99 *seq.*
    his dreams interpreted by
      Mihrán, 94 *seq.*
    daughter of, 100
      described, 100
      reference in Sikandar's
        will to, 182
    cup of, described, 100
    leech of, 101
    sage of, 101
    sends his Four Wonders and
      other gifts to Sikandar, 103
    reappearance of, 256
    his prophecy, 256, 257, 267
    consulted by Ardshír Pápa-
      kán, 266
    his advice to Ardshír Pápa-
      kán, 267, 273

Kaidáfa (Cilicia), 294, 297

Kaidáfa (Kandake, Candace, *q.v.*),
vi, 83, 121 *seq.*, 325
obtains Sikandar's portrait,
122
praised by Kabtún to Si-
kandar, 122
receives a letter from Sikandar, 123
answers Sikandar's letter,
123
welcomes Kaidrúsh on his
return from captivity, 127
receives Naitkún (Sikandar)
graciously, 128
her state described, 128, 130,
133
gives audiences to Naitkún
(Sikandar), 128 *seq.*
recognises Sikandar, 129 *seq.*
hears Sikandar's embassage,
129
her covenants with Sikandar,
132, 138
warns Sikandar against
Tainúsh, 133
chides Tainúsh, 135
takes counsel with Sikandar
about Tainúsh, 135
approves of Sikandar's
scheme, 137
takes counsel with her
nobles, 139
her gifts to Sikandar, 140
Sikandar's final message to,
143

Kaidrúsh (Kandaros, Candáules),
son of Kaidáfa (Candace),
66, 134, 135
wife of, 66
and his wife taken by Si-
kandar, 125
brought before Naitkún,
126
sentenced to death, 126
pardoned, 126
gratitude of, 127
returns to Kaidáfa, 127

Kaidrúsh, presents Naitkún (Sikandar) to Kaidáfa, 127

Kaihan. *See* Kaid.

Kai Khusrau, Sháh, 79, 177
the treasures of, found by
Sikandar, 178
Cyrus legend of, 195

Kai Kubád, Sháh, 197, 210

Kai Manush, 200

Kait. *See* Kaid.

Kai Ugí, 200

Kalé (Nereis), daughter of Alexander in the Pseudo-Cal-
listhenes, 77
and the cook Andreas, legend
of, 77

Kand. *See* Kaid.

Kandake (Candace, *q.v.*, Kaidáfa,
q.v.), 66

Kandaros. *See* Kaidrúsh.

Kandaules. *See* Kaidrúsh.

Kanír. *See* Tainúsh.

Kannúj, city in Hindústán, 64,
110, 207, 352
Sikandar reaches, 110

Karakh-Maishán, 199, 291 *note*

Káran, Íránian hero, 194

Káran, Íránian chief, 394

Karkh = Khurram Ábád (?), 327

Kárnámak-i-Ardshír-i-Pápakán,
Pahlaví text, 14 *note*, 61,
198, 200 *seq.*, 205 *seq.*, 255
seq., 301, 325
account of, 195
resembles Yátkár-i-Zaríran,
195, 196
purport of, 196
portion of Sháhnáma corresponding to, 196
compared with, 200
seq., 205 *seq.*, 255 *seq.*

Kárnámak, and Firdausí, 196
polo episode in, 196

Karnaprávaramás, 80

Kárún, river, 199 *note*
dam on, 295

Kashmír, 31
king of, 31

Katíb, Arab chief, 21, 65, 120
Káwa, flag of, 347
Kázirún, 199
Kerátór. See Tainúsh.
Khán, the, 35
    of Chín, 35
    ambassadors from, come
        to Dárá, 35
Kharazm (Khiva), 72
Kharazmians, the, 72
Kharrád, Íránian warrior, ix, 228,
    284
    takes Ardawán prisoner, 228
Kharrád, sacred Fire, 212 and
    note, 226, 391
Khír, district, 198
Khisr (Al Khidr, q.v.), chief and
    prophet, 159
    goes with Sikandar to the
        Gloom, 159
    parts company with Sikan-
        dar, 160
    finds the Fount of Life, 160
Khurásán, 242, 301
Khurm, 82, 184
    meaning of, 82
    oracle of, consulted, 184
Khurra-i-Ardshír. See Ardshír
    Khurra.
Khurram Ábád (Karkh ?), city,
    327, 357 and note
Khusrau, Sháh. See Kai Khus-
    rau.
Khusrau, Íránian noble, xi, 395,
    408
    referred to, 406
    elected Sháh in succession
        to Yazdagird, 395
    proposes that Bahrám Gúr
        should begin at the ordeal,
        409
    does homage to Bahrám Gúr,
        410
Khuzá', Arab tribe, 65, 120
    their rule ended by Sikan-
        dar, 120
Khúzistán (Susiana), 290 and
    note, 298, 327, 357

Kibtís, 397 and note
Kinám-i-Asírán (Shús ?), 327, 357
    and note
King of kings, title of, 193, 197
    meaning of, in Achæmenian
    _ and Parthian times, 198
    assumed by Ardshír Pápa-
        kán, 193, 199, 254, 258, 273
Kings, Tribal, q.v.
Kirmán, region in southern Írán,
    v, 31, 46, 47, 57, 59, 199,
    202, 205, 245, 252
    Dárá retires to, 46
    etymology of, 204, 236
    Ardshír Pápakán's invasion
        of, 205, 245
Kirmánsháh, title, 313, 368
Kirmánsháhán, place, 368
Ktesias. See Ctesias.
Kubád, Sháh. See Kai Kubád.
Kubád, Sháh, father of Núshír-
    wán, 3, 208
Kúfa, city, 381
    wood of, 381
Kujárán, city and province, 205,
    206, 232
    Haftwád migrates from, to
        stronghold, 235
Kuraish, Arab tribe, 65
Kurán, the, 15, 65, 84
    references to Alexander in,
    15, 78, 84
    legend of Moses and the salt
        fish in, 77
    Gog and Magog in, 78
Kurdistán, 330
Kurd, Kurds, the, viii, 193, 203,
    .230 seq., 257
    Ardshír Pápakán's war with,
        in Kárnámak, 196, 206, 256
        in Sháhnáma, 230 seq.
Kurdzád, daughter of Mihrak, q.v.
Kuria Muria Islands, 72

L

LAUS, Ptolemy, son of. See
    Ptolemy.

Land of Darkness. *See* Gloom, the.

Land-tax, Mahmúd's remission of, 196, 208

Latin version, early, of Pseudo-Callisthenes. *See* Julius Valerius.

Leech of Kaid. *See* Four Wonders, the.

Legend, Syriac Christian, of Alexander. *See* Syriac.

Leo, constellation, 172, 180

Libra, constellation, 97

Life, Fount of, *q.v.*
    Water of, vii
    of Alexander, Plutarch's, 67

Luhrásp, Sháh, 55, 200

M

MA, Hittite goddess, 71
    = Cybele, 71
    priestesses of = Amazons, 71

Macan, Turner, 250
    his edition of the Sháhnáma, 60

M'Crindle, 68
    his *Ancient India* quoted, 68, 80

Macedonia, 81, 82

Macedonian invasion of the East, 68, 69

Macrianus, Prætorian prefect, 294
    his treachery to Valerian, 294

Madá, Medes, the, 194

Mádik, king of the Kurds, 203
    meaning of, 203, 256

Magi, the, 372, 373

Magog (Májúj). *See* Gog.

Mahábhárata, Indian epic, 31, 80

Máhiyár, minister of Dárá, 52, 88
    referred to, v
    murders Dárá, 52
    tells Sikandar of the murder, 52
    arrested by Sikandar, 53
    executed, 56, 88

Mahmúd, Sultán, viii, ix, 20, 193
    praise of, 20, 207, 279, 292, 370
    Firdausí's veiled attacks on, 62, 92 *seq.* and *note*
    his remission of the land-tax, 196, 208

Maishán, 199

Májúj (Magog). *See* Yájúj.

Makrán (Gedrosia, Balúchistán), 69, 182, 202, 397
    Alexander's return by, productive of marvels, 69
    etymology of, 69

Málika, daughter of Táír, 3, 323, 324, 330
    referred to, x
    legend of, 323, 330 *seq.*
    offers to betray her father's stronghold to Shápúr, 331
    makes the garrison drunk, 333
    opens the gate to Shápúr, 333
    goes to Shápúr's camp, 333

Manda, the, nomad tribes, 194

Mandanes - (Dandamis, Kait, Kaihan, Kand, Kaid), 61
    and Onesicritus, 61
    identical with Kaid, 62

Máni, heresiarch, x, 307, 327, 358
    account of, 327
    -gate, 327, 359
    his teaching, 328
    his disputation with the high priest, 358
    executed, 359

Marco Polo, 74

Mars, planet, 212, 318

Mas'údí, historian, 62, 63, 82, 193, 257, 313, 315
    his genealogies of Pápak, 200
    his "Book of Indication and Revision," 252
    his apologue of the owls, 310
    on the parentage of Yazdagird, son of Shápúr, 371

Maundeville, Sir John, 13, 72

Mazaga, Indian city, 65
  taken by Alexander, 65
Mázandarán (Hyrcania), 373
Mecca, 64, 120
  Sikandar's visit to, 64, 119
  seq.
  account of, 64
Mede, Medes (Madá), the, 194,
  203
Media, 31, 201, 203
  Magna, 201, 203, 256
Median, 194, 195
  empire, 194
Mediterranean, the, 294
Megara, city, 323 *note*
Megasthenes, 68
Memphis, city, 82
  Alexander's body taken to,
  82
Mercury, planet, 171, 224
Meroe, island and city of, 13, 65
Mesopotamia, Mesopotamian, 30,
  294, 321
  desert, 322
Mihr. *See* Mihr Barzín.
Mihr, month, 24, 33, 55
Mihrak, Tribal King, viii, ix, 3,
  199, 237, 238, 257, 267,
  268, 270, 272, 273
  = Mithrak, 206
  slain by Ardshír Pápakán,
  241
  his daughter, viii, ix, 3, 241,
  256, 257, 268 *seq.*, 272
  escapes, 241, 256, 268
  referred to in Kaid's prophecy, 267
  discovered by Shápúr,
  268 *seq.*
  informs Shápúr of her
  birth, 270
  marries Shápúr, 270
  birth of her son Ur-
  muzd, 271
  = Mithrak = Mádik = Ar-
  dawán (?), 256
  his importance in legend, 257,
  267

Mihrán, Indian sage, vi, 91, 97
  consulted by Kaid about his
  dreams, 92 *seq.*
  interprets Kaid's dreams, 94
  seq.
Mihrán, treasurer to Yazdagird,
  387
Mihr Barzín, sacred Fire, 201,
  212 and *note*
Mihrgán, feast, 230 and *note*, 245
Mihrmas, 200
Mílád, Íránian warrior, 394
Mílád (Taxila), Indian city, 62,
  98, 102, 109, 110
  Sikandar approaches, 98
Minos, 323 *note*
Minúchihr, Sháh, 200, 353
Mírkhánd, historian, 62, 315
Miskál, measure of weight, 24
  and *note*
Misr (Egypt), vi, 37, 114, 115,
  122, 181
  invaded by Sikandar, 37, 121
  king of, defeated by Sikandar, 37
  welcomes Sikandar, 121
  sea of, 120
  Sikandar stays for a year in,
  121
Mithrak, 206
  = Mihrak, 206
  = Mihrak = Mádik = Ardawán (?), 256
Mohl, Jules, 60
  his edition of the Sháhnáma,
  60
  on the story of the Worm,
  203
Mong, Indian city, 18
Moses, prophet, 77, 95
  and the salt fish, legend of,
  77
  Faith of, 95
Mosul, city, 322
Muhammad, the Prophet, 15, 65,
  190, 292
  his reference to Alexander in
  the Kurán, 15, 77

Muhammad Kásim, Arab general, 325
Muhammadans, the, 78
Mukaffa. *See* Ibn Mukaffa.
Mutilation, instances of, 261, 323, 334, 348, 357, 404
Munzir, prince of Hira, xi, 372, 377 *seq.*, 384 *seq.*, 394, 406, 408
  visits Yazdagird, 377
  monarch of Yaman, 378
  returns to Yaman with Bahrám, 378
  chooses nurses for Bahrám, 378
  dismisses Bahrám's tutors, 380
  provides Bahrám Gúr with steeds, 380
  provides Bahrám Gúr with slave-girls, 381
  goes to the chase with Bahrám Gúr, 384
  sends a picture of Bahrám Gúr shooting to Yazdagird, 385
  sends Bahrám Gúr with Nu'mán to Yazdagird, 386
  receives a letter from Yazdagird, 387
  counsels and sends Bahrám Gúr a slave-girl and presents, 388
  welcomes Bahrám Gúr on return, 390
  supports Bahrám Gúr's claim to the throne, 396 *seq.*
  invades Írán, 397
  his interview with Jawánwí, 398 *seq.*
  refers Jawánwí to Bahrám Gúr, 398
  advises Bahrám Gúr to negotiate with the Íránians, 401, 404
Mytilene, Chares of, 61

N

NABARZANES, Persian general, 32
  pardoned by Alexander, 32
Náhíd (Halai (?), Olympias), daughter of Failakús, v, 24 *seq.* and *note*, 89
  marries Dáráb, 25
  troubled by offensive breath, 26
  cured, but repudiated by Dáráb, 26
  returns to Failakús and gives birth to Sikandar, 26
  visits Dilárái and Rúshanak, 89
  referred to, 187
Náhíd, the planet Venus, 214
Naitkún (Antigonus), minister of Sikandar, 66
  his name assumed by Sikandar, 66, 125 *seq.*
  personates Sikandar, 125 *seq.*
  Kaidrúsh and his wife brought before, 126
    sentenced to death by, 126
    pardoned by, 126
  =Sikandar, 131, 133, 134, 141
Napata, city, 65
Naphtha, vi, 115, 116, 165
  Sikandar's iron steeds filled with, 115
  Fúr's elephants and troops routed by the use of, 116
  used to vitrify Sikandar's barrier, 165
Narmpái, the, fabulous tribe, vii, 71 and *note*
  Sikandar and, 150
Narses (Narsí, son of Bahrám), Sásánian king, 315
Narsí, Ashkánian king, 197, 210
Narsí, son of Bahrám, Sháh (Narses), ix, 3, 313, 316, 325, 330, 331, 337
  his reign, 315 *seq.*

Narsí, his title, 315
his inaugural address, 315
daughter of. *See* Núsha.
Nasíbín (Nisibis, *q.v.*), 326, 355
cession of, 355
inhabitants of, refuse to submit to Shápúr, 356
taken by Shápúr, 356
Nasr, Amír, brother of Mahmúd, 196, 207
praise of, 207
Nasr, Arab chief, 65, 120, 121
appeals to Sikandar for help, 120
made ruler at Mecca, 121
Naurúz, 33, 55, 273, 389
Nearchus, admiral of Alexander the Great, 12, 61, 70
his account of the Ichthyophagi quoted by Arrian, 69, 70
Nectanebus II., king of Egypt, 16, 18
personates Amen-Ra and becomes the legendary father of Alexander the Great, 16
story of, 18 and *note*
Negroes, the, 73
described, 73, 157
cause frost and snow to harm Sikandar, 156, 157
Nekht-neb-f. *See* Nectanebus.
Nereis. *See* Kalé.
Nicæa, Indian city, 18
Nicolaus of Damascus, 195
Nile, 42, 65, 169, 171, 269
the Blue, 65
mistaken for Indus, 68
Nímrúz,[1] 175
Sikandar marches to, 175
Niris, lake, 17
referred to, 21
Nishápúr, city, 298
Nisibis (Nasíbín, *q.v.*), 254
peace of, 254
cession of, 326

Nisus and Scylla, story of, 323 *note*
Nitetis, 16
Nöldeke, Professor, 14 and *note,* 198 *note,* 199 and *note,* 253, 313, 372
his treatise on the Alexander Romance, &c., 14 and *note* on the story of the Worm, 203, 205, 206
Haftwád, 206
Northmen, the, 19
found Russian empire, 19
Note on Pronunciation, 8
Nubia, 65
Nu'mán, prince of Hira, xi, 372, 396, 404
visits Yazdagird, 377
goes to the chase with Bahrám Gúr, 384
goes to the Persian court with Bahrám Gúr, 386
returns to Yaman with letters and presents, 387
welcomes Bahrám Gúr on his revisiting Yaman, 390
invades Írán, 397
Núsha (Dukhtnúsh), daughter of Narsí, x, 3, 323, 324, 331
carried off by the Arabs, 323, 330
Núshírwán, Sháh, 3, 201, 208
quoted, 208, 209 and *note*
Núshzád, father of Mihrak, 237, 241, 267, 270, 273

O

Oasis of Ammon, 65
Alexander's visit to, 65
Odenathus, Arab chief, 294, 322, 324 *seq.*
and Shápúr, son of Ardshír, 294, 325
confused with Valerian, 324 *seq.*

Odorico, Minorite Friar and traveller, 13

Olympias (Halai (?), Náhíd), wife of Philip of Macedon and mother of Alexander the Great, 16, 82
her legendary connexion with Nectanebus, 16, 18
her legendary choice of a name for her son, 19
her intrigues, 82

Omphis, Indian king, 62

Onesicritus, pilot of Alexander the Great, 12, 61, 67
an untrustworthy writer, 12
the Fakírs and, 61
Calanus and, 61
Mandanes and, 61

Ormus (Hurmuz), city on the Persian Gulf, 204

Osroene, kingdom, 198

Othello, play of, quoted, 324

Owls, Mas'údí's apologue of the, 310

Oxyartes, father of Roxana (Rúshanak), wife of Alexander the Great, 32

P

PAHLAVÁN, Pahlaváns, 194

Pahlaví, version of the Pseudo-Callisthenes, 14, 16, 84
writing and reading, confusion in, 14, 62, 205, 206
language, 194
text, 195, 196, 257

Pálawína (Cappadocia), 294, 297, 298

Palestine, 30

Palladius, bishop, 61, 62
his treatise on the Brahmans, 61
interpolated into the Pseudo - Callisthenes, 61

Palmyra, 294, 322, 324

Palus Mæotis, 73

Pápak, Tribal King, viii, 3, 194, 195, 198 *seq.*, 211 *note* and *seq.*, 227, 252, 254, 256
and Sásán, 212
daughter of, 213
marries Sásán, 213
Ardawán's letter to, 214
equips Ardshír Pápákan for court, 214
dies, 218
his kindred support Ardshír Pápákan, 223 *seq.*

Pápakán, Ardshír. *See* Ardshír Pápakán.

Paradise Lost referred to, 71

Paris, MSS. of the Pseudo-Callisthenes in National Library at, 14

Párs, country, 17, 25, 32 *note*, 37, 45, 115, 119, 194 and *passim*
the corpse of Darius sent to, 33
Ardshír Pápakán flees to, 220
marches from, against Ardawán, 227
returns to, 229
the Íránians, after Yazdagird's death, meet to consult in, 394

Part Kings. *See* Tribal Kings.

Parthian, Parthians, the, 194, 203, 256, 322
dynasty, 194, 201
uses the title of King of kings, 197
Great king, 198

Parwíz, Íránian chief, 394

Pashín, Íránian noble, 408

Patashwárgar, region, 202 and *note*

Pauravas, Indian race and dynasty, 31

Persepolis (Istakhr), 31, 32 *note*, 373

Persia, 61, 201, 278
introduction of chess into, 201

Persian, Persians, the, 30, 44, 45, 81, 82, 143, 148, 157. 170, 201 and *passim*
language, 147, 205
dispute with the Rúmans over Sikandar's burial, 184
empire, 197
monks introduce the silkworm into Europe, 204
sea or gulf, 204, 205
mutilation of captives, 323, 334, 348, 357, 404
Persis (Párs), 195
Pharasmanes, king, 72
Philip II. of Macedon (Failakús), the father of Alexander the Great, 16, 18, 19, 29
and Nectanebus, story of, 18
names his son Alexander, 19
Philon, Macedonian noble, 76
Phrygians, the, 71
Píruz Shápúr (Ambar), city, 327, 357
Pisces, constellation, 395
Pishdádian, dynasty, 194
Planets, the seven, 206
Pleiads, Pleiades, 169, 401
Plutarch, historian, 67
Polo, 196, 329, 379, 382
episode in Kárnámak and Sháhnáma, 196, 257, 263, 271
Porus (Fúr, *q.v.*), Indian king, 17, 62 *seq.* 66, 67, 76, 80, 83
son of, 18, 63
Darius' letter to, 31
origin of name of, 31
kingdom of, 31
and Alexander, historical account of, 63
in the Pseudo - Callisthenes, 64, 67
his stature, 64
nephew of, 80
Pronunciation, Note on, 8

Pseudo-Callisthenes, the, Greek Romance of Alexander the Great, 13 *seq.*, 30 *seq.*, 62 *seq.*, 71, 72, 74 *seq.*, account, and versions of, 13 *seq.*, 17
vogue of, 17
treatise of Palladius interpolated in, 61
Alexander and Porus in, 64
historic elements in, 83
Egyptian, 83
Persian, 83
Arabic, 83
diagram to illustrate, 84
Ptolemy, son of Lagus, one of Alexander's generals, king of Egypt and historian, 12, 13, 66
Python, Apollo and the, 203

Q

QUINTUS Curtius, historian, 65
on the Amazons, 72

R

RACES, duplicate in West and East, 68
fair-haired, 73
Rai, city and district near Tihrán, 32, 201, 202, 219, 229
Ardawán's capital, 201
Rákshasas, 13
Rám, Fire-temple, 202, 226
Rám Ardshír, city, 202, 290 and *note*
Rámbihisht, wife of Sásán, 198
Rám-Hurmuz, plain of, 199
Rámishn-i-Ardshír, district, 202
Rás-Shápúr, city, 255
  = Gund-i-Shápúr, 256
Ratl, weight, 156 and *note*
Ravi (Hydraotes), Indian river, 64
Rawalpindi, 62
Rawlinson, Professor, 253
Reeds (bamboos), 71

Reeds, gigantic, seen by Sikandar, 148
used in house-building, 71, 148
Rív-Ardshír, city, 202
referred to, 224
Roman, Romans, the, 30, 254, 318, 325, 326
Alexander's legendary visit to, 30
empire, Eastern, 253
emperors, 321, 371, 372
Romance of Alexander the Great, the, 11 *seq.*, 88
its incorporation in the Sháh-náma, 16
vogue of, 17
sources of marvels in, 12, 69
diagram to illustrate, 84
Rome, 194, 197, 203, 301, 324
Shápúr son of Ardshír's wars with, 294, 297
Bahrám Gúr's war with, 373
Roxana (Rúshanak, *q.v.*), 30, 33
and Alexander, 30
account of, 32
Rúdyáb, father of Pápak (in Sháhnáma), 200, 212
Rúm, the Eastern Roman Em-pire, v, x, 21 *seq.*, 35 *seq.*, 40, 41, 45, 51, 53, 81, 94, 104, 113 *seq.*, and *passim*
ambassadors from, come to Dáráb, 21
Dáráb wars with, 22
prince of, 22
chiefs of, 23, 153
withdraw on Dáráb's approach, 23
tribute of, to Dáráb, 24
ambassadors from, come to Dárá, 35
brocade of, 56, 89
reed (pen) of, 85
stuffs of, 143
philosophers of, 115, 154
cavaliers of, 167
Sháh of = Sikandar, 170

Rúm, king of = Sikandar, 172
Sikandar's policy to safe-guard, 178
Arastálís' advice to Sikandar concerning, 179
invaded by Shápúr, 350
slave-girls of, chosen by Bahrám Gúr, 382
Rúman, Rúmans, the, ix, x, 19, 21, 44, 45, 101 *seq.*, 113, 114, 127, 142, 148, 168, 170, 179 *seq.*, and *passim*
king of = Philip of Macedon, 19
carry out works in Írán, 21
= Sikandar, 50, 52, 154
the Íránians ask quarter of, 51
tongue, 160
dispute with the Persians as to Sikandar's burial, 184
sages, 185
their sentences over the coffin of Sikandar, 185 *seq.*
silk, 280
defeated by Shápúr, son of Ardshír, 297
engineers build bridge at Shúshtar, 299
astrologic tablets, 376
slave-girls, 382
Rús (Russia), 19, 22
king of, 22
Rúshanak (Roxana, *q.v.*), daugh-ter of Dárá (in Sháhnáma) and wife of Sikandar, v, vi, 86 *seq.*, 181, 188
account of, 32
derivation of, 33
bestowed by Dárá on Si-kandar, 55
son of, 81, 181
visited by Náhíd, 89
married to Sikandar, 90
reference in Sikandar's Will to, 181
Russia (Rús), 19

Russian, Russians, the, 19
  empire, 19
    foundation of, 19
Rustam, son of Zál, Íránian hero,
  194, 325, 395
  a Personification of the
    Sacæ, 194

S

SACÆ, Scythians, the, 194
  Rustam a Personification of,
    194
Sada, feast of, 33, 55, 230 and
  note, 245, 273, 389
Sage, sages, vi, vii, 101, 103
  Indian, 62
    naked (Brahmans, *q.v.*,
      Gymnosophistæ)
    of Kaid. *See* Calanus *and*
      Four Wonders, the.
    Sikandar and, 62, 104
      seq.
    described, 94, 101
    explains the principle of
      the Cup, 109
Sakláb, Slavonia, 179
Salm, eldest son of Farídún, 353
Salt fish, the legend of, 76 *seq.*
Sám, Íránian hero, 395
Samírán, 405 and *note*
Sandar, Sandarús, the Arar tree,
  19
Sapor I. (Shápúr, son of Ardshír),
  Sásánian king, 294, 321
Sapor II. (Shápúr, son of Urmuzd),
  Sásánian king, 294, 321
Sapor III. (Shápúr, son of Shápúr),
  365
Sarúg, Jacob of, Syriac poet.
  See Jacob.
Sarv, king of Yaman, 73
Sásán, name of Dárá's son and
  several of his descendants,
  200, 211, 224, 255
  descendants of, help Ardshír
    Pápakán, 224
  House of, 251, 270 and *note*

Sásán, father of Ardshír Pápakán,
  viii, 3, 193, 198, 200, 201,
  211 *seq.*, 240
  legend of, 211 *seq.*
  marries daughter of Pápak,
    213
Sásánian, Sásánians, the, viii, 81,
  209, 225, 249 *seq.*, 253, 257,
  321, 327
  genealogical table of, 3, 253
  Tabarí's history of, 14 *note*
  Dynasty, viii, 61, 199, 249 *seq.*
    Tabarí on the rise of the,
      198
  characterised, 249 *seq.*
  Zoroastrianism under, 251
  Mas'údí on Church and
    State under, 251
  duration of, 257
  Empire, 193, 327
  fictitious genealogies of, 199,
    211, 256
  view of Sikandar, 15, 224 and
    note, 240 and *note*
Saturn, planet, 97, 115, 176, 281,
  318, 385
Sav, spring of, xi, 372, 373, 391,
  392
  legend of, 372, 391 *seq.*
Sawurg, Indian king, vi, 64, 118
Sayce, Professor, on the Amazons,
  71
Scandinavians, 19, 73
  found the Russian empire, 19
Scotland, 79
  vitrified forts in, 79
Scylla, Nisus and, story of, 323
  note
Seleucia, city, 254, 291 *note*, 322
Semiramis, queen, 66, 405 *note*
Seven climes, the. *See* Climes.
  Persian nobles, the, legend
    of, 207
    transferred to Ardshír
      Pápakán (?), 207
  planets, 206
Severus, Emperor, 322
  his siege of Hatra, 322

Sháh, accession of, ceremony at, 409
Sháhábád, city, 295
Shahd, river, 391, 392
Sháhnáma, 3 and *note*, 11, 19, 30, 31, 66 *seq.*, 72, 79, 82 *seq.*, 194 *seq.*, 200 *seq.*, 205 *seq.*, 249 *seq.*, 253, 256, 270 *note*, 294, 301, 307, 310, 325, 326
Greek subject-matter in, 11
derivation of *Sikandar* given in, 19
historic period of, 29
and Írán, analogy between, 193
portion of, corresponding to Kárnámak, 196
prose, 196
and Kárnámak compared, 200 *seq.*, 255 *seq.*
Shahrgír, chief in Sikandar's host, 125, 126
takes Kaidáfa's son and daughter-in-law prisoners, 125
Shahrgír, captain of the host to Ardshír Pápakán, 241
Ardshír's instructions to, 241
goes to Ardshír's help, 244 and *note*
Shahrwí, archimage, 329
minister during Shápúr son of Urmuzd's minority, 329
Sháhwí, eldest son of Haftwád, 237
referred to, 206
helps his father against Ardshír Pápakán, 236
executed, 245
Shám (Syria), 357
Shangul, Indian king, 325
Shápúr, Ashkánian king, 197, 210
Shápúr, son of Pápak, 199
Shápúr, son of Ardshír Pápakán, Sháh (Sapor I.), viii, ix, 3, 196, 256, 262 *seq.*, 268 *seq.*, 303, 307, 313, 315, 321 *seq.*

Shápúr, stories of, in Kárnámak, 196, 255
in Tabarí, 255, 257
crowned in his father's lifetime, 257
secret birth of, 261
origin of name, 262 and *note*
recognised and acknowledged by Ardshír Pápakán, 264
discovers the daughter of Mihrak, 268 *seq.*
summoned and counselled by Ardshír Pápakán, 286 *seq.*
confused with Shápúr, son of Urmuzd, 294, 321, 324, 327
his reign, 294 *seq.*
its historical inaccuracies, 294
his wars with Rome, 294, 297
and Odenathus, 294
defeats the Rúmans, 297
receives tribute from Cæsar, 298
builds cities, 298
bids Bazánúsh build a bridge at Shúshtar, 298
summons and counsels Urmuzd, 299
Shápúr, son of Urmuzd, Sháh (Sapor II.), x, 3, 294, 295, 307, 321 *seq.*, 371, 373, 405 (?)
referred to, 318
reign of, 321 *seq.*
his bridge at Taisafún, 321, 329
his places of residence, 321, 330
confused with Shápúr, son of Ardshír, 294, 321, 324, 327
his triumphant treaty with the Rúmans, 326, 355
his cities, 327, 357
birth of, 328
crowned as an infant, 328
his education, 329

Shápúr, son of Urmuzd, Málika offers to betray her father's stronghold to, 331

opens the gate to, 333

sends Málika to his camp, 333

his treatment of his Arab captives, 323, 334

receives the title of Zú'l Aktáf, *q.v.*, 335

returns to Párs and receives tribute, 335

consults the astrologers, 335

visits Cæsar in disguise, 336

entertained by Cæsar, 337

denounced by a Persian resident at Cæsar's court, 337

arrested, 337

sewed up in an ass's skin and imprisoned, 338

pitied by an Íránian slave-girl, 339

freed from ass's skin by slave-girl, 340

entertained by a gardener, 341 *seq.*

sends the gardener to the high priest, 344

described by the high priest, 344

praises the slave-girl, 346

prepares to attack Cæsar, 346

sends spies to Taisafún, 346

sends tidings of his victory over Cæsar to the provinces, 348

his treatment of Cæsar, 349

invades Rúm, 350

defeats Yánus, 352

bids Bazánúsh come to him, 354

dictates terms of peace, 355

returns to Istakhr, 356

takes Nasíbín, 356

names and honours the slave-girl, 356

rewards the gardener, 357

Shápúr, keeps Cæsar captive, 357

sends Cæsar's corpse to Rúm, 357

arranges a disputation between Mání and the high priest, 358

has Mání executed, 359

arranges for the succession with his brother Ardshír, 360 *seq.*

dies, 362

Shápúr, son of Shápúr, Sháh (Sapor III.), x, 3, 251, 360, 364 *seq.*, 371

Ardshír, son of Urmuzd, resigns the throne to, 364

Tabarí on the death of, 365

death of, 366

Shápúr, son of Yazdagird, king of Armenia, 373

Shápúr Gird (Gund-i-Shápúr?), city, 295, 298

Shawwál, the tenth Muhammadan month, 208

Shem, patriarch, 65

Shíbán, 397

Shikbán, Íránian warrior, 395

Shíráz, city, 198 *note*, 210

Shu'íb, Arab chief, v, 21

attacks Dáráb, 21

defeated and slain, 22

Shúrsán = Súristán (Babylonia), 379

Shús = Kinám-i-Asírán (?), 327

Shúshtar, city, 199, 295 and *note*, 299

dam and bridge at, 298, 326

Sicily, 30

Alexander's legendary visit to, 30

Sikandar (Iskandar, Alexander the Great, *q.v.*), v *seq.* 11, 13, 16, 18, 19, 26, 27, 29, 30, 33, 35 *seq.*, 193, 210, 240 and *note*, 325, 353

derivation of, in Tabarí, 19

in Sháhnáma, 19, 26

birth of, 18, 26

Sikandar, adopted as his heir by
Failakús, 27
counselled by Arastálís, 35
refuses tribute to Dárá, 36
prepares for war with Dárá,
37
invades, and defeats king of,
Misr, 30, 37
invades Írán, 37
his visit to the camp of Dárá,
38
invited to banquet with Dárá,
40
takes the golden cups of
Dárá, 40
recognised, 40
escapes, 41
defeats Dárá, 43, 44, 46
issues proclamation to the
Íránians, 44, 47
gives the spoil to his troops,
44, 47
marches from 'Irák against
Dárá, 46
enters Istakhr, 46
answers Dárá's letter, 50
marches from Istakhr, 51
hears of Dárá's murder, 52
arrests Dárá's murderers, 53
finds Dárá still living 53
promises to avenge Dárá, 53
promises to carry out Dárá's
last wishes, 54
Dárá bestows Rúshanak
upon, 55, 86
laments for, and buries Dárá,
55, 56
executes Dárá's murderers, 56
hailed as ruler by the Íránians, 56
sends envoys to Ispahán and
to the family of Dárá, and
letters to the provinces, to
announce his accession, 57
crowned Sháh at Istakhr, 59
reign of, 60 *seq.*
diagram to illustrate Persian
Romance of, 84

Sikandar, his inaugural address,
85
his correspondence with the
wife and daughter of Dárá
33, 86 *seq.*
marries Rúshanak, 90
invades Hind, 98
and Kaid, 61, 98
approaches Mílád, 98
inquires about the Four
Wonders of Kaid, 100
the Four Wonders and other
gifts sent by Kaid to, 103
marries daughter of Kaid, 104
and the sage of Kaid, 62,
104 *seq.*
the principle of the cup explained to, 109
conceals his treasures, 110
and *note*
advances to Kannúj, 110
his troops protest, 113
remonstrates with his troops,
113
his troops ask pardon, 114
his war with Fúr (Porus), 67,
110 *seq.*
hears of Fúr's elephants, 115
his device to overcome,
115
challenges Fúr to single
combat, 116
slays Fúr, 117
Fúr's troops submit to, 118
becomes king of Hind, 118
bestows Hind on Sawurg, 118
his visit to Mecca and the
Kaaba, 64, 67, 119 *seq.*
ends the rule of the Khuzá'
in Arabia, 120
sets up Nasr instead of the
Khuzá', 120
goes to Judda, 121
marches to Misr, 121
welcomed by king of, 121
stays for a year in, 121
and Kaidáfa (Candace), 65,
121 *seq.*

Sikandar, his portrait obtained by Kaidáfa, 122

Kaidáfa praised · by Kabtún to, 122

writes to Kaidáfa, 123

Kaidáfa's answer to, 123

assumes the name of Naitkún (Antigonus), 66, 125 *seq.*

pleads (as Naitkún) for Kaidrúsh and his wife, 126

goes (as Naitkún) to Kaidáfa, 127

graciously received by Kaidáfa, 128

has audiences of Kaidáfa, 128 *seq.*

recognised by Kaidáfa, 129 *seq.*

delivers his message, as envoy, to Kaidáfa, 129, 134

his covenant with Kaidáfa, 132, 138

warned by Kaidáfa against Tainúsh, 133

insulted by Tainúsh, 134

counsels Kaidáfa about Tainúsh, 135

makes covenant with Tainúsh, 136

Kaidáfa's gifts to, 140

returns with Tainúsh, 141

welcomed by his troops, 141

reveals himself to Tainúsh, 142

entertains at a banquet, gives gifts to, and dismisses Tainúsh, 143

his final message to Kaidáfa, 143

the Brahmans hear of the coming of, and write to, 143

his interview with the Brahmans, 67, 144 *seq.*

quits the Brahmans, 147

meets the Fish-eaters (Ichthyophagi, *q.v.*), 69 *seq.*, 147, 177

Sikandar, his adventure with a whale, 71, 147

sees gigantic reeds (bamboos), 71, 148

attacked by snakes, scorpions, and boars, 148

the people of Habash, 149

the Narmpái, 160

his adventure with a dragon, 71, 151

visits the temple of Dionysus, 71, 152, 166

warned of his death, 152, 161, 166

marches toward Harúm, the City of Women, (Amazons, *q.v.*), 153 *seq.*

encounters snow and frost, 156

great heat, 157

the negroes, 157

reaches and inspects Harúm, 157

marches westward and finds a fair-haired race, 73, 158

hears of the Gloom, *q.v.*, and of the Fount of Life, *q.v.*, and prepares to visit them, 158

sets forth with Khisr as guide, 159

and Khisr part company, 160

fails to find the Fount of Life, 160

his interview with birds, 160

Isráfíl, 78, 161

emerges from the Gloom, 162

marches eastward, 163

hears of Yájuj and Májúj, 163

barrier of, 78, 164, 249

and the Male and Female Tree, 79, 167 *seq.*

reaches "The World's End," 168

receives gifts, 169

his expedition to Chín, 80, 169 *seq.*

goes as his own ambassador to the Faghfúr, 170

Sikandar, describes himself, 171
Faghfúr's gifts to, 173
departs with Faghfúr's envoy, 173
his identity discovered by the envoy, 173
dismisses the envoy with gifts and a message to Faghfúr, 174
arrives at Chaghwán, 174
marches to Sind, 175
defeats Bandáwa, chief of the Sindians, 175
marches to Nímrúz, 175
receives gifts from the king of Yaman, 175
meets Gúsh-bistar, 177
carries off the treasures of Kai Khusrau, 178
his policy for safeguarding Rúm after his decease, 81, 178, 197
adopts the advice of Arastálís, 180
arrives at Bábil, 180
prodigious birth at, 81, 180
consults the astrologers on, 180
warned of his end, 180
sickens, 181
his Will, 81, 181
grief of the troops for, 183, 184
dies, 183
dispute as to where he should be buried, 184
his body taken to Iskandaríya, 185
sentences of sages over, 82, 83, 185
his cities, 83, 189
the Sásánian view of, 15 and note
Silk, account of, 204
its introduction into the West, 204

Silk-worm. *See* Silk.
Sind, region and river (Indus), 113
king of, 113
chiefs of, 123
warriors of, 132, 137
Sikandar marches to, 175
Sindbad, the sailor, 71
lands on a whale, 71
Sindians, the, vii, 175
defeated by Sikandar, 175
Sístán,[1] 32, 198
Smerdis, the false, 207
Spain (Andalús), 66
Speaking tree, the, vii, 79, 167 *seq.*
Sphinés. *See* Calanus.
Stateira. *See* Barsine.
Steeds, iron, Sikandar's, vi, 115
filled with naphtha, 115
Fúr's elephants and troops routed by, 116
Stone, the Black, 65
Strabo, geographer, 68, 81
Súfís, 59 and *note*
Sughdiana (Sughd), 72
Suhráb, son of Rustam, 325
Surúsh, angel, 199 *note*, 372
day, 411
Surúsh, astrologer, 372, 375
takes Bahrám Gúr's horoscope, 375
Susa, city, 31, 33, 295, 327
Alexander marries the daughter of Darius at, 33
Susiana (Khúzistán), 295, 321
Swat, river, 65
Syria, 30
Syriac, version of the Pseudo-Callisthenes, 14, 16, 18, 30, 31 *seq.*, 61, 63, 65, 66, 68, 71, 72, 74, 78 *seq.*
Christian Legend of Alexander, 14, 15, 74, 78, 84
quoted, 15
metrical version of, 15, 78, 84

---

[1] See Vol. i. p. 396 *note.*

T

Tabák, Íránian chief, viii, 202, 225
  suspected by Ardshír Pápakán, 225
  justifies himself, 226
  and Ardshír Pápakán defeat Bahman, 226
  buries Ardawán, 229
  advises Ardshír Pápakán to marry the daughter of Ardawán, 229
Tabarí, historian, 14 *note*, 16, 19, 30, 198, 200, 291 *note*, 310, 313, 315, 321, 326
  his history of the Sásánians, 14 *note*
  places Alexander's battles with Darius in Mesopotamia, 30
  on Yájúj and Májúj, 78
  his account of the rise of the Sásánian dynasty, 198
  his account of Ardshír Pápakán, 198, 203
  genealogies of Pápak in, 200
  on the story of the Worm, 205, 206
  his account of Haftwád, 205, 206
  on the length of Ardshír Pápakán's reign, 254
  on Ardawán's daughter, 255
  on Shápúr, son of Ardshír Pápakán, 255, 257
  on the death of Shápúr, son of Shápúr, 365
  on Bahrám, son of Shápúr, 368
  on Yazdagird, son of Shápúr, 371 *seq.*
Table of Contents, v
  genealogical, 3
Tacitus, historian, 73
Tainúsh (Charogos, Kerátór, Kanír), son of Kaidáfa, vi, 66, 67, 134 *seq.*

Tainúsh, Kaidáfa warns Sikandar against, 133
  Fúr's son-in-law, 133
  insults Sikandar, 134
  Kaidáfa chides, 135
  Kaidáfa and Sikandar consult about, 135
  makes a covenant with Sikandar, 136
  accompanies Sikandar on his return, 141
  Sikandar discovers himself to, 142
  asks grace of Sikandar, 142
  pardoned by Sikandar, 142
  entertained at a banquet, presented with gifts, and dismissed, by Sikandar, 143
Tainúsh (Theodosius), xi, 372, 389, 404
  goes to Yazdagird as ambassador, 389
  asked by Bahrám Gúr to intercede with Yazdagird for him, 389
  obtains Bahrám Gúr's release, 390, 404
Táir (Daizan, *q.v.*), Arab chief, x, 3, 322, 324, 330 *seq.*
Taisafún (Ctesiphon, *q.v.*), 245, 321, 330, 346 *seq.*, 397
  Ardshír Pápakán goes to, 245
  Shápúr's bridge at, 321, 329
  sacked by Táir, 330
  Shápúr sends spies to, 346
  Cæsar defeated and taken prisoner by Shápúr at, 347
Takht-i-Bústán, 257
  Sásánian inscription at, 257
Taráz, city in Turkistán and district in Badakhshán, 268
Taurus, constellation, 151
Taxila (Mílád), Indian city, 62, 63
Tharthar, river, 322
Theodosius (Tainúsh), Roman Emperor, 372

Thermodon, river, 72
Tigris, river, 294, 322
  small, the, 199 and *note*
  lower, 291 *note*
  bridge over, 321
Tíri, eunuch of Gúzihr, 198
Tírúdih, village, 198
  birthplace of Ardshír Pápa-
    kán, 198
Trajan, Emperor, 322
  his siege of Hatra, 322
Tree, the speaking, vii, 79, 167
  seq.
  description of, 167 *seq.*
  Sikandar visits, 167 *seq.*
  warns Sikandar of his death,
    168, 169
Tribal, or Part, Kings, the, viii,
  180, 197, 198, 201, 203, 204,
  210, 225, 252, 253
  origin of, 179, 181, 210
  character of their rule, 197,
    198
  number of, 198
  Ardawán the chief of, 201
  Firdausí on, 210
Túr, second son of Farídún, 353
Túrán, 43, 182, 398
Turkistán, 179, 278, 280, 397
Turkman language, 147
Tús, city, 372, 391, 393
  local legend of, 372, 391 *seq.*
Tyre, city, 30
  siege of, 30

U

UROSCOPY, 101, 107, 108
Urmuzd, the Good Principle, 55,
  362, 372, 387
  day, 302 and *note*, 306, 375
Urmuzd, Ashkánian king, 197,
  210
Urmuzd, son of Shápúr, Sháh
  (Hormisdas I.), ix, 3, 257,
  273, 280, 313, 327
  his discovery by Ardshír
    Pápakán, 257, 271.

Urmuzd, birth of, 271
  counselled by Ardshír Pápa-
    kán, 280
  Shápúr, 299
  reign of, 301 *seq.*
  his title, 301
  story about, 301
Urmuzd, son of Narsí, Sháh (Hor-
    misdas II.), ix, x, 3, 294, 295,
  307, 315, 316, 325
  reign of, 318 *seq.*
  his sons, 318
  his inaugural address, 318
  a pregnant wife of, enthroned,
    320
Urmuzd (Hormisdas), son of
  Narsí, Persian prince, 318,
  325
  referred to (?), 337
Urmuzd Ardshír, city, 290 and
  note
Uné, 77
Utterakuri, the, 74

V

VALERIAN (Bazánúsh), Emperor,
  294, 295, 323 *seq.*
  his defeat and capture by
    Shápúr, son of Ardshír, 294,
    295
    memorials of, 295
  confused with Odenathus,
    Julian, and Jovian, 324 *seq.*
  his death in captivity, 326
Varahran I. (Bahrám, son of Urmuzd), Sásánian king, 307
Varahran II. (Bahrám, son of Bahrám), Sásánian king, 310
Varahran III. (Bahrám Bahrámiyán), Sásánian king, 313
Varahran IV. (Bahrám, son of
  Shápúr), Sásánian king, 313,
  368
Venus, planet, 98, 102, 171, 190,
  212, 224, 332
Vitrified fortifications, 79, 165
Vologeses, king of Kirmán, 205

Vritra and Indra, 203
Vullers-Landauer edition of the
    Sháhnáma, 60

W

WÁLID, Khalífa, 325
Water-horse, xi, 373, 392
    referred to, 373
    legend of Yazdagird and the,
    392
Western sea, the, vii, 158
Whale, 71, 147
    mistaken for island, 71, 147
    Sikandar's adventure with a,
    71, 147
Wheeler, James Talboys, quoted,
    81
Will of Alexander, 81
    provisions of, 81, 181
Women, city of, vii. See Harúm.
Wonders, the Four, of Kaid, vi,
    94, 97, 99 seq.
Worm, the, viii, 193, 206, 238 seq.
    story of, 196, 203 seq., 232 seq.
    Mohl, Darmesteter, and
        Nöldeke on, 203 seq.
    cult of, 235
    Ardshír Pápakán's stratagem
        against, 242
    servants of, 242 seq.

X

XERXES, 30
    effigy of, falls, 30

Y

YÁJÚJ and MÁJÚJ (Gog and Ma-
    gog), vii, 78, 79, 163 seq., 211
    note
    legend of, in the Kurán, 78
    Tabarí on, 78
    described, 163
Ya'kúbí, historian, 61
Yaman, country, vii, x, 73, 120,
    121, 175, 324, 331, 385, 386,
    396, 401
    onyx of, 128
    striped stuff of, 175

Yaman, monarch of, 175
    gives gifts to Si-
        kandar, 175
    = Munzir, 378, 387,
        390
    Bahrám Gúr goes to, 378, 390
    Canopus of, 382
Yánus (Julian), brother of Cæsar,
    x, 324, 326
    leads a host against Shápúr,
        351
    defeated, 352
Yátkár-i-Zarírán, Pahlaví text,195
    resembles Kárnámak, 195, 196
Yazd, city, 368
Yazdagird, Sháh (Isdigerd I.), xi,
    3, 371 seq.
    referred to, 369
    reign of, 371 seq.
    his parentage uncertain, 371
    a lover of peace like Aknaton
        of Egypt, 371
    his titles, 371, 372
    Tabarí on, 372, 373
    death of, 373
        Nöldeke on, 373
    coins of, 373
    his evil administration, 374,
        404
    makes search for a governor
        for his son Bahrám Gúr,
        376 seq.
    Nu'mán and Munzir visit, 377
    puts Bahrám Gúr in Munzir's
        charge, 378
    receives from Munzir a picture
        of Bahrám Gúr shooting, 385
    Bahrám Gúr returns to, 386
    gives presents to, and sends a
        letter by, Nu'mán to Mun-
        zir, 387
    disgraces Bahrám Gúr, 389
    sends Bahrám Gúr back to
        Munzir, 390
    consults the astrologers, 390
    his death foretold, 391
    attacked by bleeding of the
        nose, 391

Yazdagird, his death, 393
    his corpse embalmed and
        taken to Párs, 393
Youths, the two, that bid Ard-
    shír Pápakán not to tarry
    in his flight, 201, 222
        entertain and counsel
            Ardshír Pápakán in
            the matter of the
            Worm, 207, 239 *seq.*
        help Ardshír Pápakán to
            slay the Worm, 242, 244
Yúnán, 95 and *note*
    Faith of, 95

Z

ZÁBULISTÁN,[1] 207
Zahhák, Sháh, 15, 45, 172, 209,
    240 and *note*
Zál, son of Sám and father of
    Rustam, 79
Zandavasta (Avasta), 17, 55, 226,
    252, 343, 356
Zarár, 200
Zarduhsht (Zarathushtra, Zoro-
    aster), 55, 252, 328, 332

Zarduhsht, religion of, under the
    Sásánian empire, 251
    girdle of, 332
Zarnúsh, city, 35
Zeus, Babylonian, 82
    oracle of, consulted, 82
Zijának, daughter of Ardawán,
    viii, 255
    story of, in Kárnámak, 255
        Tabarí, 255
        Sháhnáma, 259 *seq.*
Zoroaster. *See* Zarduhsht.
Zoroastrian, Zoroastrianism, 15,
    196, 206, 251, 252, 327,
    328
    under the Sásánian empire,
        251
    millennia of, 252
Zú'l Aktáf, title of Shápúr, son of
    Urmuzd, x, 323
    meaning of, 323
Zú'l-karnain (Sikandar, Alex-
    ander the Great), 15, 84
    legend of, in Kurán, 78, 84
    barrier of, 78
    site of, 79
Zúr. *See* Gúr.

---

[1] See Vol. i. p. 396 *note.*

END OF VOL. VI.

For Product Safety Concerns and Information please contact our EU
representative GPSR@taylorandfrancis.com
Taylor & Francis Verlag GmbH, Kaufingerstraße 24, 80331 München, Germany

www.ingramcontent.com/pod-product-compliance
Lightning Source LLC
Chambersburg PA
CBHW060127280326
41932CB00012B/1450